A+ Certification For Dummies, 3rd Edition

Cheat Sheet

Default system resource assignments

IRQ	Typical Assignment	I/O Address
1	Keyboard	060h
3	COM2/COM4	2F8h/2E8h
4	COM1/COM3	3F8h/3E8h
5	LPT2, Sound card	278h/220h
6	Floppy disk controller	3F0h
7	LPT1	378h
10	NIC	300h
12	PS/2 mouse	064h
14	Primary IDE controller	1F0h
15	Secondary IDE controller	376h

RAID disk drive types

RAID 0: Striped disk array without fault tolerance.

RAID 3: Parallel transfer with parity.

RAID 5: Data striping with parity.

Preparing a hard disk

SCANDISK	Check for media problems
FDISK	Partition the disk
FORMAT	Prepare the disk and load system files

Bus architectures

Architecture	Bus Width
Industry Standard Architecture (ISA)	16-bit
Intelligent Drive Electronics (IDE)	32-bit
Peripheral Component Interconnect (PCI) bus	32- or 64-bit

Laser printing phases

D1238869

Cleaning, transferri...

Phrase ... remember laser printing phases

California Cows Won't Dance The Fandango

On test day . . .

At the testing workstation before the test begins, write down

- ✔ IRQs
- ✔ I/O addresses
- ✔ Laser printing phases
- ✔ System startup files

DOS/Windows 3.x/9x memory management

Conventional memory	The first 640K of system memory
Upper memory area	The upper 384K of the (expanded memory) first megabyte of memory, above conventional memory
High memory area	The first 64K (less 16 bytes) of the second megabyte of memory
Extended memory	Any memory above the high-memory area

Item 4187-0.

For more information about Wiley Publishing, call 1-800-762-2974.

For Dummies: Bestselling Book Series for Beginners

A+ Certification For Dummies, 3rd Edition

Cheat Sheet

DOS/Windows file systems

Operating Systems	File System
DOS	File Allocation Table (FAT) or FAT16
Windows 3.x	FAT16
Windows 9x	FAT16, VFAT, and FAT32
Windows NT/2000	FAT32 and NT File System (NTFS)

POST error codes

Code	Hardware Group
1xx	Motherboard
2xx	Main memory
3xx	Keyboard
6xx	Floppy disk controller
14xx	Printer
17xx	Hard disk controller

Acronyms

CMOS: Complementary metal oxide semiconductor

ESD: Electrostatic discharge

GPF: General protection fault

HCL: Hardware compatibility list

PCMCIA: Personal Computer Memory Card International Association

RAID: Redundant array of independent disks

SCSI: Small computer system interface

UART: Universal asynchronous receiver-transmitter

ZIF: Zero insertion force

Windows 9x files

- **Executable files:** BAT, EXE, and COM
- **Initialization files:** INI
- **System files:** SYS
- **Multiboot entries:** MSDOS.SYS
- **CD extension:** MSCDEX.EXE
- **Command prompt processor:** COMMAND.COM
- **Virtual device drivers:** VXD and 386
- **Program extension files:** DLL
- **Device drivers:** DRV

Windows 2000 files

- **Boot loader:** NTLDR
- **Multiboot entries:** BOOT.INI
- **Hardware configuration:** NTDETECT.COM
- **Windows 2000 kernel:** NTOSKRNL.EXE

Windows 9x startup files

1. BIOS POST
2. Plug and Play (PnP) devices
2. IO.SYS
3. MSDOS.SYS
4. The Registry (SYSTEM.DAT)
5. CONFIG.SYS and AUTOEXEC.BAT
6. WIN.COM
7. Device drivers in Registry and SYSTEM.INI and VMM32.VXD
8. Windows 9x core components: Kernel, GDI, and User
9. Startup files

A+ Certification

FOR

DUMMIES®

3RD EDITION

A+ Certification

FOR

DUMMIES®

3RD EDITION

by Ron Gilster

WILEY

Wiley Publishing, Inc.

A+ Certification For Dummies®, 3rd Edition

Published by
Wiley Publishing, Inc.
111 River Street
Hoboken, NJ 07030-5774
www.wiley.com

Copyright © 2004 by Wiley Publishing, Inc., Indianapolis, Indiana

Published by Wiley Publishing, Inc., Indianapolis, Indiana

Published simultaneously in Canada

No part of this publication may be reproduced, stored in a retrieval system or transmitted in any form or by any means, electronic, mechanical, photocopying, recording, scanning or otherwise, except as permitted under Sections 107 or 108 of the 1976 United States Copyright Act, without either the prior written permission of the Publisher, or authorization through payment of the appropriate per-copy fee to the Copyright Clearance Center, 222 Rosewood Drive, Danvers, MA 01923, (978) 750-8400, fax (978) 646-8700. Requests to the Publisher for permission should be addressed to the Legal Department, Wiley Publishing, Inc., 10475 Crosspoint Blvd., Indianapolis, IN 46256, (317) 572-3447, fax (317) 572-4447, e-mail: permcoordinator@wiley.com.

Trademarks: Wiley, the Wiley Publishing logo, For Dummies, the Dummies Man logo, A Reference for the Rest of Us!, The Dummies Way, Dummies Daily, The Fun and Easy Way, Dummies.com, and related trade dress are trademarks or registered trademarks of John Wiley & Sons, Inc. and/or its affiliates. All other trademarks are the property of their respective owners. Wiley Publishing, Inc., is not associated with any product or vendor mentioned in this book.

> **LIMIT OF LIABILITY/DISCLAIMER OF WARRANTY: WHILE THE PUBLISHER AND AUTHOR HAVE USED THEIR BEST EFFORTS IN PREPARING THIS BOOK, THEY MAKE NO REPRESENTATIONS OR WARRANTIES WITH RESPECT TO THE ACCURACY OR COMPLETENESS OF THE CONTENTS OF THIS BOOK AND SPECIFICALLY DISCLAIM ANY IMPLIED WARRANTIES OF MERCHANTABILITY OR FITNESS FOR A PARTICULAR PURPOSE. NO WARRANTY MAY BE CREATED OR EXTENDED BY SALES REPRESENTATIVES OR WRITTEN SALES MATERIALS. THE ADVICE AND STRATEGIES CONTAINED HEREIN MAY NOT BE SUITABLE FOR YOUR SITUATION. YOU SHOULD CONSULT WITH A PROFESSIONAL WHERE APPROPRIATE. NEITHER THE PUBLISHER NOR AUTHOR SHALL BE LIABLE FOR ANY LOSS OF PROFIT OR ANY OTHER COMMERCIAL DAMAGES, INCLUDING BUT NOT LIMITED TO SPECIAL, INCIDENTAL, CONSEQUENTIAL, OR OTHER DAMAGES.**

For general information on our other products and services or to obtain technical support, please contact our Customer Care Department within the U.S. at 800-762-2974, outside the U.S. at 317-572-3993, or fax 317-572-4002.

Wiley also publishes its books in a variety of electronic formats. Some content that appears in print may not be available in electronic books.

Library of Congress Control Number: 2003105687

ISBN: 0-7645-4187-0

Manufactured in the United States of America

10   9   8   7   6   5   4   3   2   1

3B/QW/RQ/QT/IN

WILEY is a trademark of Wiley Publishing, Inc.

About the Author

Ron Gilster (A+, Network+, i-Net+, Server+, CCSE, CCNA, MBA, and AAGG) has been operating, programming, and repairing computers for more than 30 years. Ron has extensive experience training, teaching, and consulting in computer-related areas, including working on mainframes, minicomputers, and virtually every type of personal computer and operating system that exists. In addition to a wide range of positions that have included College Instructor, Customer Service Manager, Data Processing Manager, Management Information Systems Director, and Vice President of Operations in major corporations and small businesses, Ron has been a management consultant with an international auditing firm and has operated his own computer systems consulting firm.

Ron has authored a number of certification books, including *Network+ Certification For Dummies*, *i-Net+ Certification For Dummies*, *Server+ Certification For Dummies*, *CCNA For Dummies*, *Cisco Networking For Dummies*, *MCSA All-in-One Reference For Dummies,* and *PC Repair Bench Book* (all for Wiley Publishing), as well as several books on computer and information literacy, applications programming, and other computer hardware topics. Ron also acted as the series editor for Wiley Publishing's *End to End* series and *Network+ Certification Bible.*

Dedication

To Connie, Carly, Markus, Kirstie, and Jessica.

Author's Acknowledgments

I would like to thank the virtual "cast of thousands" at Wiley who helped to get this book published, especially Melody Layne, Carol Sheehan, Pat O'Brien, John Edwards, Jean Rogers, Dan DiNicolo, Laura Moss, Laura Carpenter VanWinkle, and Amanda Foxworth, all of whom were on my side all the way.

Publisher's Acknowledgments

We're proud of this book; please send us your comments through our online registration form located at `www.dummies.com/register/`.

Some of the people who helped bring this book to market include the following:

Acquisitions, Editorial, and Media Development

Project Editor: Pat O'Brien

Acquisitions Editor: Melody Layne

Copy Editors: John Edwards, Jean Rogers

Technical Editor: Dan DiNicolo

Editorial Manager: Kevin Kirschner

Media Development Manager: Laura VanWinkle

Media Development Supervisor: Richard Graves

Editorial Assistant: Amanda Foxworth

Cartoons: Rich Tennant (`www.the5thwave.com`)

Production

Project Coordinator: Ryan Steffen

Layout and Graphics: Carrie Foster, Joyce Haughey, Michael Kruzil, Heather Ryan, Jacque Schneider, Julie Trippetti

Proofreaders: Laura Albert, David Faust, John Greenough, Dwight Ramsey, Charles Spencer, TECHBOOKS Production Services

Indexer: TECHBOOKS Production Services

Publishing and Editorial for Technology Dummies

Richard Swadley, Vice President and Executive Group Publisher

Andy Cummings, Vice President and Publisher

Mary C. Corder, Editorial Director

Publishing for Consumer Dummies

Diane Graves Steele, Vice President and Publisher

Joyce Pepple, Acquisitions Director

Composition Services

Gerry Fahey, Vice President of Production Services

Debbie Stailey, Director of Composition Services

Contents at a Glance

Table of Contents

Introduction

*I*f you have bought or are considering buying this book, you probably fit one of the following categories:

- ✔ You know how valuable A+ Certification is to a professional personal computer (PC) technician's career and advancement.
- ✔ You're wondering just what A+ Certification is all about.
- ✔ You think that reading this book may be a fun, entertaining way to learn about computer hardware maintenance and repair.
- ✔ You love all ...*For Dummies* books and wait impatiently for each new one to come out.
- ✔ You're a big fan of mine and can't wait to read all of my new books.

Well, if you fit any of the first four scenarios, this is the book for you! However, I'm not certified in the appropriate medical areas to help you if you are in the last category!

If you're already aware of the A+ Certified Computer Technician program and are just looking for an excellent study aid, you can skip the next few sections of this introduction because your search is over. However, if you don't have the foggiest idea of what A+ Certification is, how it can benefit you, or how to prepare for it, read on!

Why Use This Book?

With over 20 years and layer upon layer of microcomputer hardware and software technology to study, even the most knowledgeable technician needs help getting ready for the A+ exams. This book is intended to shorten your preparation time for the A+ exams.

This book is a no-nonsense reference and study guide for the A+ Core Hardware exam (test #220-301) and the OS (Operating Systems) Technologies exam (test #220-302). It focuses on the areas likely to be on the exam, plus it provides background information to help you understand some of the more complex concepts and technologies.

The concepts, processes, and applications included on the exams are presented in step-by-step lists, tables, and figures without long explanations in this book. The focus is on preparing you for the A+ exams, not on showing off my obviously extensive and impressive knowledge of computer technology (nor on my modesty, I might add). This book will not provide you with an in-depth background on PC hardware and software. It will, however, prepare you to take the A+ Core Hardware and OS Technologies exams.

In developing this book, I made two assumptions:

- ✔ You have knowledge of electronics, computers, software, networking, troubleshooting procedures, and customer relations, and need a study guide for the exams.
- ✔ You have limited knowledge of electronics, computer hardware, and the processes used to repair, maintain, and upgrade PCs and could use a little refresher on the basics along with a review and study guide for the exams.

If my assumptions in either case suit your needs, then this book is for you.

How This Book Is Organized

This book is divided into two "mini-books": one on the Core Hardware exam and one on the OS Technologies exam. Depending on whether or not you plan to take the two exams during the same sitting or not, you should study for them separately. Although there is a certain amount of overlap between the two exams (especially in the networking area), the emphasis of each exam is totally different.

Throughout, this book is organized so you can study a specific area without wading through stuff you may already know. I recommend that you skim the whole book at least once, noting the points raised at the icons. Each part and chapter of the book is independent, and can be studied in any order, which should be helpful for your last-minute cram before the exam. The following sections tell you what I include between the covers of this book.

Book 1: The A+ Core Hardware Exam

Part 1: Laying Down, Some Fundamentals

Book I begins with an overview of what to study for the A+ exam and other general information about taking the exam. It also presents background information on the concepts of electricity, electronics, and numbering systems. And finally, it covers the tools used in computer maintenance with an emphasis on electrostatic discharge protection and prevention.

Part II: Inside the Box

Part II takes you down into the wonderful, incredible world of the motherboard and other electronic field-replaceable modules (FRMs) found inside the case. This part is chock-full of information about the motherboard, memory, bus structures, power supply, disk drives, and other components found inside the case. Also covered in this part are the processes used to install, remove, troubleshoot, optimize, and upgrade these components.

Part III: Outside the Box

You need to know about interfacing input, output, printers, and serial, parallel, USB, and FireWire connections, plus networking and data communications for the A+ Core Hardware exam.

Part IV: Remembering Why It's Called Hardware

Part IV has everything you need to know about the tools and best practices to use for repairing, maintaining, and configuring PC hardware. Read about disassembling and reassembling the PC, performing preventive maintenance, and the processes used to troubleshoot problems on the PC.

Practice Exam

The Hardware Practice Exam on the CD is ready for you to print and evaluate your preparation. If you miss a question, it points you back to the book to improve your knowledge.

Book II: The A+ Operating Systems Technologies Exam

Part I: Operating Systems

This part of Book 2 provides information on the operating systems included on the A+ Operating Systems (OS) Technologies exam: Windows 95, 98, and Me, Windows NT Workstation, Windows 2000 Professional, and Windows XP Professional and Home editions.

Part II: Connecting to a Network

As networking becomes more common in both businesses and homes, the configuration, installation, and troubleshooting of OS networking features becomes more important, and the amount of coverage on networking on the A+ OS exam reflects this.

This part of the book covers both the technologies involved with configuring a workstation to a local area network (LAN) and those involved with connecting to a network remotely. This includes network topologies, the OSI model, TCP/IP protocols, and dialup networking.

Practice Exam

When you think you are ready, print the OS Practice Exam from the CD. If you miss a question, it points you back to the book to improve your knowledge.

Appendix: About the CD

This section gives you information about what's on the CD-ROM in the back of this book and how to use it.

Studying Chapters

A+ Certification For Dummies, 3rd Edition offers a self-paced method of preparing for the exam. You don't have to guess what to study; every chapter that covers exam objectives guides you with preview questions, detailed coverage, and review questions. This step-by-step structure identifies what you need to study, gives you all the facts, and rechecks what you know. The structure is as follows:

- **First page:** Each chapter starts with a preview of what's to come, including exam objectives and study subjects. Not sure that you know all about the objectives and the subjects in a chapter? Keep going.

- **Quick Assessment questions:** At the beginning of each chapter is a brief self-assessment test that helps you gauge your knowledge of the topics that chapter covers. Take this test to determine which areas you already understand as well as to determine which areas you need to focus on.

- **Labs:** Labs are included throughout the book to step you through some of the processes you need to know for the exam, such as installation or configuration of a particular component.

- **Getting Ready for Work:** This feature is included in many chapters of this book. It provides ideas for some hands-on projects that should help you prepare not only for the A+ exams, but also for the workplace.

- **Prep Tests:** The Prep Tests at the end of each chapter gauge your understanding of the chapter's content. These Prep Test questions are structured in the same manner as those you may see on your exam, so try your hand at these sample questions.

Icons Used in This Book

 Time Shaver icons point out tips that can help you manage and save time while studying for or taking the exam.

 Instant Answer icons highlight tips to help you recognize correct and incorrect exam answers and point out information that is likely to be on the test.

 Shocking Information icons point out ESD and other electrical dangers that you should be aware of for the test and on the job.

 Warning icons flag problems and limitations of the technologies included on the exam and things to avoid when working with certain technologies.

 Remember icons point out important background information and advantages of the technology that may appear on the exam.

 Tip icons flag information that can come in extra-handy during the testing process. You may want to take notes on these tidbits!

Feedback

I'd like to hear from you. If an area of the test isn't covered as well as it should be, or if I provide more coverage than you think is warranted about a particular topic, please let me know. Your feedback is solicited and welcome. E-mail me at feedback@rongilster.com.

Book 1

A+ Hardware
Technology Exam

Part I

Laying Down Some Fundamentals

The 5th Wave By Rich Tennant

"Look at that craftsmanship. Notice the patina. It's already three years old. In the computer industry, that makes it a genuine antique."

In this part . . .

Not everything about the world of PC service technicians is on the A+ exams. There are some things you
are just expected to know; for example, basic electronics,
electricity, and number systems. CompTIA, the A+ exam
organization, has assumed that you know this stuff or you
wouldn't be working (or wishing to be working) as a PC
service technician and getting ready to take the A+ exams.

Before you begin preparing for the test, use this part of
the book to get an overview about the two A+ exams and
to review some of the basic and underlying knowledge
you'll need for the exams.

Chapter 1

The 2003 A+ Certification Exams

A+ certification assures employers and computer owners that a PC repair technician has the requisite knowledge to build, upgrade, troubleshoot, and repair personal computer (PC) systems. The A+ exams measure the ability and knowledge a PC technician should have after six months of on-the-job, hands-on training. Certified PC technicians are always in great demand, so passing the A+ certification exams is well worth the time that you spend preparing for the exams. A+ certification is a lifetime certification, meaning that you never have to take the test again (at least as of this writing).

If you are A+ certified from either the 1996, 1998, or 2001 exam versions, you don't have to take the 2003 exams. Unless you *really* want to.

Who Is CompTIA?

Computing Technology Industry Association (CompTIA) is a membership trade organization that was formed in 1982 to promote standards of excellence in computer technology. Its goals are to develop ethical, professional, and business standards and provide educational opportunities to the industry. Its members include more than 13,000 computer resellers, VARs (value-added resellers), distributors, manufacturers, and training companies in 89 countries around the world (but mostly in the United States and Canada). These companies range from multinational corporations to local computer repair shops and individual entrepreneurs. Visit CompTIA's Web site at www.comptia.org/about for more information.

Why Get A+ Certification?

Why cram for a pair of tests and sweat bullets over taking them to get a piece of paper that says, "I know computer repair stuff"? Well, I can think of a number of good reasons. The first is that more than 500,000 A+ Certified Technicians worldwide may be competing for the same job you want.

What Do the A+ Exams Cover?

The exams are based on an industry-wide analysis of what a PC repair service technician with six months of on-the-job experience should know to be considered competent. The results of this analysis have been validated in a worldwide survey of thousands of A+ certified professionals.

The two A+ certification exams are the Core Hardware exam (Exam 220-301) on microprocessors, displays, storage media and devices, printers, modems, buses, and other hardware components of a PC; and the OS Technologies exam (Exam 220-302). Neither exam has more than 90 questions. Each test measures your knowledge over several technical domains.

Each test domain focuses on a specific area of technical service procedures, tools, and skills. Some domains are emphasized more than others, so the number of questions from any particular domain varies. Tables 1-1 and 1-2 list the domains, the percentage of coverage of each domain on the total test, and the approximate number of test questions for each domain.

Table 1-1	A+ Core Hardware Exam Domains	
Domain	**Percentage of Test**	**Number of Questions**
Installation, Configuration, and Upgrading	35%	9–12
Diagnosing and Troubleshooting	21%	5–7
Preventive Maintenance	5%	1–2
Motherboard/Processors/Memory	11%	3–4
Printers	9%	2–3
Basic Networking	19%	5–7

Table 1-2	A+ OS Technologies Exam Domains	
Domain	*Percentage of Test*	*Number of Questions*
OS Fundamentals	28%	7–10
Installation, Configuration, and Upgrading	31%	7–11
Diagnosing and Troubleshooting	25%	6–8
Networks	16%	4–6

For more information about the A+ exams, visit CompTIA's FAQ (Frequently Asked Questions) Web site at www.comptia.org/ certification/a/faqs.asp.

Who Can Get Certified?

A+ certification is open to anyone who registers for the exams, pays the exam fees, and passes the exams. You don't need to have the six months of work experience, be a working PC repair technician, work for a particular company, or have any specialized training to qualify for A+ certification. Just pass the exams, and you're certified.

How to Get Certified

The A+ exams are scored on a *scaled* method, meaning that some questions and answers are worth more than others. The total possible points on each exam is 900. To pass the Core Hardware exam, you must get a score of at least 683; to pass the OS Technologies exam, you must get a score of at least 614. (You get 100 points for just filling out your name.)

You have 90 minutes to complete each of the two exams. You can take the two exams on the same day or schedule them on different days; it's up to you.

You must pass *both* A+ exams before the next update. However, if you've passed either 2001 exam version, you can take the remaining exam in either the 2001 or 2003 versions to get your certification.

Where to Go

You can find a testing center and register for the exams online on these Web sites:

- ✔ **Prometric:** www.2test.com
- ✔ **VUE:** www.vue.com

How Much Does It Cost?

The cost of CompTIA's exams range from $89 USD to $225 USD, depending on your country and whether or not you or your company are CompTIA members. Corporate CompTIA members are given substantial discounts on certification exam vouchers, among other benefits.

Watch for training or study material vendors that offer discounted exam vouchers.

You can find discounted vouchers for slightly more than the member rate if you shop around.

Studying for the Exams

This book and the resources listed, named, or cited throughout its contents are your sure-fire best first steps to getting there.

Chapter 2

Basic Electronics and Number Systems

Exam Objectives

▶ Identifying the concepts, terminology, and properties of electronics and electricity in the PC

▶ Identifying ESD (electrostatic discharge) and ESD protection devices

▶ Reading and converting binary, decimal, and hexadecimal number systems

The fundamentals of computer troubleshooting, repair, and maintenance require understanding of electricity, electronics, and number systems. You need a basic knowledge of electricity and electronic principles to even begin preparing yourself for the A+ Certification exams. Although specific electronics or electricity questions aren't on the test, many questions assume a basic understanding of electricity concepts and terminology and the function of a few electronic components. Even if you know enough about electricity to repair a PC without destroying either the equipment or yourself, you may need a refresher on the names, definitions, concepts, and applications of electricity and electronics. This chapter presents the groundwork with a very brief review of electricity and basic electronics.

Binary and hexadecimal number systems are used in the PC for addressing and data display. You may be asked to convert a binary number or two on the exam, and you can count on binary and hexadecimal references in several questions. That's why this chapter reviews the binary and hexadecimal number systems. I also include a couple of labs to help you review the process of converting hexadecimal and binary numbers to and from decimal values.

Quick Assessment

Identifying the concepts, terminology, and properties of electronics and electricity in PCs

1 _____ measures the electrical pressure in a circuit.

2 _____ measures an electrical current's strength.

3 A semiconductor that can store one of two toggled values is a(n) _____.

4 Households use _____ current electricity.

5 PCs use _____ current electricity.

6 A(n) _____ is a device that can measure more than one property of electricity.

Identifying ESD and ESD protection devices

7 ESD stands for _____.

Reading and converting binary, decimal, and hexadecimal number systems

8 The _____ number system uses only the numbers 1 and 0.

9 The _____ number system uses the numbers 0–9 and the letters A–F.

Answers

1 *Voltage*. Review "Counting electrons."

2 *Amps*. See "Counting electrons."

3 *Transistor*. Check out "Reading binary numbers."

4 *Alternating*. Review "Switching from AC to DC."

5 *Direct*. Direct yourself to "Switching from AC to DC."

6 *Multimeter*. Check out "Measuring the current."

7 *Electrostatic discharge*. Read "Don't Give Me Any Static."

8 *Binary*. Review "Reading binary numbers."

9 *Hexadecimal*. See "Working with hexadecimal numbers."

Understanding Electricity

Everything inside or attached to the PC system unit runs on electricity. Electricity is both the lifeblood and the mysterious evil of the personal computer. It's a flowing entity, measured in amps, ohms, and volts. Approach it with respect, if not outright fear.

Nothing helps you understand a complex technical topic better than a real-life analogy that you can relate to. I tried hard to create a new and original analogy to help you understand electrical properties and measurements and to dazzle you with my cleverness. Unfortunately, I have failed. One analogy that I thought had a lot of potential involved Twinkies and beer, but it fell flat. So I am forced to use the same old *water-in-the-hose* analogy that you have probably seen and heard a thousand times. If you have heard it before, skip the next few paragraphs. If it's new to you, read on.

Electricity flowing through a circuit is much like water running through a hose. When you open a water faucet, the *pressure* in the water line forces the water to flow at some gallons-per-minute rate into the hose. *Friction* reduces the force and rate of the water before it exits the hose. When electricity flows into a wire from a source such as a battery, some of its pressure is lost to *resistance* in the wire.

Table 2-1 puts this analogy into a little better perspective. The electrical measures are listed with a description and an example of how they're applied on the PC.

Counting electrons

The forces of electricity inside the computer can be measured, and each type of measurement tells you something different about the computer. I include the electrical measurements in Table 2-1 to provide you with an introduction to these units of measurement. Chapter 9 provides more information on the power used in the PC and how it is measured.

Table 2-1	Common Electrical Measurements	
Measurement	*Description*	*Application*
Amps	Measures a current's strength or rate of flow	The amount of current needed to operate a device; for example, a hard disk drive needs 2.0 amps to start up, but only 0.35 amps for typical operation.

Measurement	Description	Application
Ohms	Measures a conductor's resistance to electricity	Resistance of less than 20 ohms means that current can flow through a computer system.
Volts	Measures the electrical pressure in a circuit	A PC power supply generates 4 levels of voltage: +5 volts (V), –5V, +12V, and –12V.
Watts	Measures the electrical power in a circuit range	A PC power supply is rated in a range of 200 to 600 watts.
Continuity	Indicates the existence of a complete circuit	A pin in a DIN connector registers 5V on a digital voltage meter (DVM or multimeter) when grounded to another pin.

Measuring the current

The primary measurements of electricity are volts and amps. Volts measure pressure, and amps measure current. Current isn't needed for voltage. When a water faucet is off, water pressure still exists. There is just no current. Likewise, when an electrical circuit is open, voltage (pressure) is still in the line although no current is flowing. If you touch the wire and close the circuit, the current begins to flow, and you can feel all of its pressure as a *shock*.

Several devices can read the power and fury of an electrical current. Ammeters, ohmmeters, and voltmeters measure specific properties; a multi-meter or DVM combines these instruments into one tool.

Switching from AC to DC

Current is the flow of electrons in a wire. Electricity has two current types:

✔ **AC (alternating current):** AC is what you get from the outlets in your house or office.

In alternating current, the current changes directions about 60 times per second. The voltage changing rapidly from a positive charge to a negative charge causes the current to also switch the direction of its flow in the wire. AC power exists because it has advantages for the power company and your household electrical appliances; these advantages have little value on a low-voltage system like a PC.

✔ **DC (direct current):** DC is the type used inside the computer.

When the flow of the electricity is in one direction only, it is direct current. What happens in direct current is that negatively charged particles seek out and flow toward positively charged particles, creating a direct electrical current flow. DC power maintains a constant level and flows in only one direction — always, predictably, and measurably, from a negative charge to a positive charge.

The PC uses DC power. The PC's power supply converts power from the AC wall outlet into DC power for the computer. Peripheral devices, such as printers, external modems, and storage drives (including CD-ROM and Zip drives), use an AC power converter to convert AC power into DC power.

Okay, so the computer runs on direct current electricity. What does this fact have to do with the A+ exam?

3.3V, –5V, +5V, –12V, and +12V represent 3.3 volts, minus 5 volts, plus 5 volts, minus 12 volts, and plus 12 volts are DC power levels produced by the power supply.

Don't Give Me Any Static

The term *static* has several meanings in computer technology. To the computer technician, static means both *static electricity* (electrostatic charge) and its evil twin — *electrostatic discharge*, also called *electrical static discharge;* ESD, as it is infamously called, is the evil demon that lies in wait for the unsuspecting service technician who fails to don the sacred wrist strap before kneeling at the PC altar.

Throughout this book, you see repeated warnings, cautions, and preventive actions for ESD. Focus on preventing ESD damage.

Always wear a grounded wrist strap that's connected to either a grounding mat or the PC chassis when you work on any part of the computer (except the monitor). Chapter 12 explains why you don't wear your strap when working on a monitor.

Static electricity is what makes your hair stand on end when you rub a balloon against your head. Of course, this assumes that you have hair — and that you'd rub a balloon against your head. Static electricity also occurs when you walk across a carpet. Static electricity is not by itself a problem; the danger is in the discharge of the static electricity. You know, when you reach for the doorknob and — zap! — a blue spark as big as a towrope jumps from your finger to the metal. Although this may seem harmless (other than the pain), the potential for damage to a PC exists in that seemingly harmless spark. Lightning is ESD in its most dreaded form.

A mere 30 volts will damage electronic components. A human feels ESD at around 3,000 volts; ESD is a greater threat to the PC than anything else the PC service technician might do accidentally. An electrostatic discharge you can't feel can harm an electronic component.

Looking at the dark side of ESD

Most PCs are designed for some ESD protection as long as their cases are intact and closed properly. Cases are chemically treated or have copper fittings designed to channel electrostatic discharge away from the sensitive components inside.

The danger from ESD damage begins when the case is opened and the fragile components on the motherboard are exposed. When a human with a static electrical charge touches anything inside the case, the charge can travel along the wires interconnecting the various electronic components. One of the wires may lead inside a component, and when the charge gets close enough to a metal part with an opposing charge, the internal wires and elements of components can explode or weld together.

Take a look at some ESD facts:

- Most of the computer's electronic components use three to five volts of electricity.
- An ESD shock of 30 volts can destroy a computer circuit.
- An ESD shock you can *feel,* such as on a doorknob, has around 3,000 volts.
- An ESD shock you can *see* carries about 20,000 volts.

The real problem with ESD damage is that not all of it is obvious. If an entire component is destroyed, you know it, and you replace the piece. When a component has been damaged but continues to work, though, days, weeks, or even months may pass before the component fails completely. More frustrating is intermittent partial failures that can't be isolated.

Eliminating static electricity

You can avoid static electricity. Good environmental preventive measures that help to eliminate, or reduce, static electricity are as follows:

✔ When working inside the PC, always wear an ESD grounding strap on your wrist or ankle that is connected to either the chassis of the PC or to a grounding mat.

✔ Treat carpeting inexpensively with antistatic chemicals to reduce static buildup. Aerosol cans of these chemicals are available in most computer or carpet stores. If your employer doesn't provide antistatic carpet treatment, ask for it.

✔ Store all electrical components in antistatic bags when not in use.

✔ Install a grounded pad under the PC. Before you touch the computer, touch the pad to discharge any built-up static electricity.

✔ If all else fails, install humidifiers to place moisture in the air. Keep the humidity above 50 percent. Dry air can cause static electricity.

When working on the monitor, *never* wear a grounding strap. The monitor has a very large capacitor in it and a grounding strap invites all of its stored charge to run through your body — not always a pleasant experience.

Polishing Up on Number Systems

A+ exam questions reference hexadecimal addresses for such PC components as IRQs and COM ports. The ability to read and understand binary and hexadecimal values helps you understand some questions.

For example, a test question may ask you for the address of where BIOS is commonly located in memory. The answer choices listed are hexadecimal values such as A0000 to AFFFF, B0000 to BFFFF, C0000 to CFFFF, and F0000 to FFFFF. Your ability to discern which of the numbers represents the range closest to the 1MB boundary for the upper memory area is your key to the answer.

Your ability to work with binary and hexadecimal numbers can also help you with questions related to troubleshooting and debugging situations.

Reading binary numbers

The binary number system is the foundation upon which all logic and data processing in the PC is built. In its simplest form, the *binary number system* consists of only two digital values: *1* and *0*. Because a transistor is a semiconductor that can store only one of two toggled values, the binary number scheme and the electronics of the PC are made for each other.

Binary values are the result of the number 2 being raised to various powers. This is true for all number systems. The decimal number system is based on values of the number 10 raised to increasing powers. For example, 2^2 is 8, and 2^{10} is 1,024. An 8-bit byte can store the value 255 (which is the limit on virtually everything in the PC).

An exam question may ask you to convert a binary number such as 00000101 to a *decimal value* — you know, ordinary numbers. The key is to remember that each position represents a power of 2, starting with 0 on the right end up through 7 at the left end. For example, the binary number 00001010 contains

$0 * 2^0 = 0$ (any number to the zero power is worth 1)

$1 * 2^1 = 2$ (any number to the one power is the number)

$0 * 2^2 = 0$ (two times two)

$1 * 2^3 = 8$ (two times two times two)

Totaling 10 (the remaining positions are all zero)

So, 00001010 in binary is the same as 10 in decimal. Just count the positions, starting from the right with zero, and then calculate the powers of two for each position with a one. You add up the decimal values of each position to get the resulting decimal number, which in this case was 2 + 8 to get 10.

Addressing in binary

The computer stores all data as a binary value, so the size of the computer's bus (8, 16, 32, or 64 bits) controls the highest address that can be transferred or stored (and accessed) and the largest value that can be transferred or stored at any address. A 16-bit address bus can store an address or value of 2^{15}, or 32,768 — my lucky number! A 32-bit word length handles 2^{31}, or 2,147,483,648, and 64 bits stores a really big number with lots of commas.

The largest number that can be stored in a certain number of bits is calculated by raising two to a power represented by the number of bits minus one.

Working with hexadecimal numbers

The word *hexadecimal* means *six and ten,* and that's just what this number system is about. While binary includes only *zero* and *one,* hex (as it's known to its friends), includes the decimal numerals 0 to 9 (the *ten*) and replaces the decimal values of 10 to 15 with the symbols A, B, C, D, E, and F (the *six*).

Expect to be asked for the hexadecimal addresses of at least one IRQ, LPT, or COM port on the test. (See Chapter 5 for more information on these and other system resources.) For example, 2F8 is the default address of IRQ3 and COM2. The decimal equivalent of this number is unimportant, but the ability to convert hexadecimal numbers is a good basic skill for PC repair technicians, because you often need to convert a range of addresses to decimal to determine the size of a memory, storage, or address range.

The DOS DEBUG program gives memory locations in hexadecimal with a hexadecimal offset to indicate its size. You need to be able to convert this number to know how big an area is being referenced.

Concentrate on the *hexadecimal addresses* of the IRQs, COM, and LPT ports, not the *decimal* equivalents of these hexadecimal values.

Converting hexadecimal numbers

Converting any nondecimal number system to decimal requires two things:

- ✔ **The *radix* (base value) of the number system**

  The radix of a number is the value that 10 represents in that number's number system. The radix of decimal is 10, the radix of binary is 2, and the radix of hexadecimal is 16.

- ✔ **The numeric value of each position**

  In binary numbers, each position represents a different power of two; the same holds true in any number system (including hexadecimal, where each position represents a different power of 16).

Getting Ready for Work

Here are a couple of number system conversion labs you can use to master the conversion of decimal to binary and hexadecimal to decimal.

Converting decimal to binary

The steps in Lab 2-1 convert the numbers in your street address to a binary number. (If your house number is larger than 65536, use a smaller number.)

Lab 2-1 Converting Decimal to Binary

1. **Figure out the largest power of two values that can be subtracted from the number.**

   For a house number of 63529, the largest binary value that can be subtracted is 32,768, or 2^{15}. Probably, a very scientific way exists to determine this number; I use trial and error to find the largest power of 2 that can be subtracted from the starting number. For example, 2^{16} is 65,536 and that was too big; 2^1 is the same as 2 and that's just too small; so if I try 2^{15}, I find that it is just right, and a 1 can be placed in position 16 of the binary number (remember the first power of two is a zero — so 2^{15} values go in the 16th position. Got it?). So far, I have 1000000000000000 for the binary number. This represents the following:

2^{15}	2^{14}	2^{13}	. . .	2^2	2^1	2^0
1	0	0	. . .	0	0	0

2. **Subtract 32768 (2^{15}) from your original number.**

   The difference in this example is 30761. Repeating the process used in Step 1, the highest value that can now be subtracted from 30761 is 2^{14} or 16384. The binary number is now 1100000000000000.

   Continuing this process through each remaining value of the original decimal number and for each digit in the binary number, the final binary number for this example is 1111100000101001.

Being able to convert decimal numbers to binary is a good skill for a PC repair technician. You don't have to demonstrate this skill on the A+ test.

Converting hexadecimal to decimal

What is the decimal equivalent of the hexadecimal number A012F? Use the process in Lab 2-2 to convert it.

Lab 2-2 Converting Hexadecimal to Decimal

1. **Because each position represents a power of 16, the A in A012F represents the positional value of 16^4 (as was the case in Lab 2-1, powers of the radix increase from 0 starting with the rightmost position). The A has the decimal equivalent of 10. So, this position is worth 10 * 16^4, or 655,360 (trust me on this).**

2. **The next position of value is a 1 in the position of 16^2, which is worth 256. The 0 in the 16^3 position has no value.**

3. The next position has a value of 2 * 16^1, or 32.

4. The last position has the value of F (15) * 16^0, or 15. Any number to the zero power is worth 1, so this is the same as 15* 1.

5. Add up the values: 655360 + 256 + 32 + 15. The sum is 655,663 — the decimal equivalent of A012Fh hexadecimal.

Hexadecimal numbers are usually written with a small *h* at their end to indicate that a number is being expressed in hexadecimal form.

Hexadecimal numbers are far easier to convert with a calculator, but knowing how to convert them can be handy when taking an A+ exam.

Prep Test

1 The decimal equivalent of 00000110 is

A ○ 8
B ○ 5
C ○ 110
D ○ 6

2 The number A06F is most likely from which numbering system?

A ○ Decimal
B ○ Binary
C ○ Hexadecimal
D ○ Octal

3 Electrical current is measured in

A ○ Amps
B ○ Ohms
C ○ Volts
D ○ Watts

4 What is the most common threat to PC hardware when being serviced by a technician?

A ○ ESD
B ○ Accidental breakage of a component
C ○ Improper tools damaging a component
D ○ Placing components on the wrong type of surface to work

5 Electrical resistance is measured in

A ○ Amps
B ○ Ohms
C ○ Volts
D ○ Watts

6 You should ground yourself with an ESD wrist strap when working on which of the following? (Choose all that apply.)

A ❑ Memory board

B ❑ Motherboard

C ❑ Hard drive

D ❑ System board

7 The microcomputer operates on _____ current electricity.

A ○ Alternating

B ○ Direct

C ○ Switchable

D ○ Directional

8 The decimal equivalent of A00h is

A ○ 44

B ○ 32,768

C ○ 2,560

D ○ 65,536

9 Computer components can be damaged by an ESD charge of

A ○ 2,000V

B ○ 30V

C ○ 30,000V

D ○ 3 to 5V

10 What does ESD refer to?

A ○ Electronically safe device

B ○ Electrical static discharge

C ○ Electric surge protector

D ○ None of the above

Answers

1 **D.** The binary number 00000110 is the same as adding 2^2 (4) and 2^1 (2) to get 6. *Take a look at "Reading binary numbers."*

2 **C.** A binary number consists of only 1s and 0s. An octal number has no digits higher than a 7; and this is obviously not a decimal number. Any number that has the characters A through F and 0 through 9 is a hexadecimal number. *Check out "Working with hexadecimal numbers."*

3 **A.** The strength of an electrical current is measured with an ammeter in amps. *Review "Counting electrons."*

4 **A.** ESD damage is far more common than any other damage inflicted by the repairperson or user. *Look at "Don't Give Me Any Static."*

5 **B.** Electrical resistance, or the amount of resistance in a conductor to the flow of electricity, is measured with an ohmmeter in ohms. *See "Counting electrons."*

6 **A, B, C,** and **D.** Wear an ESD grounding strap when working all of these FRMs (field replaceable modules). The only part of the computer you don't want to be grounded to is the Cathode Ray Tube (CRT) — see Chapter 12 for more information. *Check out "Don't Give Me Any Static."*

7 **B.** Household appliances operate on alternating current, but the computer operates on direct current. The power supply converts AC to DC. *Take a look at "Switching from AC to DC."*

8 **C.** A00h is the same as 10 * 256 (16^2), or 2,560. *Review "Converting hexadecimal numbers."*

9 **B.** It doesn't take very much of an ESD charge to zap the internal components of a computer. *Check out "Looking at the dark side of ESD."*

10 **B.** ESD is the abbreviation for either electrical static discharge or electrostatic discharge; both terms are used interchangeably. *Zap over to "Don't Give Me Any Static."*

Part II
Inside the Box

The 5th Wave   By Rich Tennant

"I hear some of the engineers from the mainframe dept. project managed the baking of this year's fruitcake."

In this part . . .

Much of a PC service technician's world exists inside the PC case in the world of the motherboard, processor, memory, BIOS, bus structures, the power supply, disk drives and other hot, temperamental gadgets, widgets, and doodads.

Nearly half of the Core Hardware exam and about one-third of the OS Technologies exam relate to the components found inside the case. So, this part of the book should be a first stop in your preparation for the test.

Chapter 3

The Motherboard

Exam Objectives

▶ Defining the function and purpose of the motherboard

▶ Identifying motherboard form factors

▶ Explaining the function of a chipset

▶ Describing the operation of cache memory

▶ Upgrading the motherboard

*T*he A+ exam tests your knowledge of the motherboard's central role. The motherboard is by far the most important electronic circuit in the computer. It acts as the gatekeeper to the CPU (Central Processing Unit), meaning that all outside devices wishing to interact with the CPU must pass through the motherboard. It is all-powerful! It is all-knowing! Ignore the man behind the curtain!

Questions about the motherboard, its bus structures, CMOS, BIOS, chipsets, and the compatibility of the system components on the motherboard are at least 30 percent of the Core Hardware exam. Another 30 percent relate to CPUs, memory, installation, and troubleshooting.

You need to know about data and address buses, processor capabilities and compatibilities, the contents of the CMOS and how they are updated, and the role of the system ROM and BIOS in booting the system.

I can hear you asking, "Is that all?!" It's only natural that an exam with "Core" in its name tests you on the core components and issues of the PC. In the PC, nothing is more "core" than the motherboard, processor, and memory. Because so much of the A+ Core Hardware exam deals with these areas, I chose to spread out the review on motherboards, processors, BIOS and CMOS, bus structures, and memory systems over a few chapters. This arrangement should help prevent a brain boil-over while you're studying.

Quick Assessment

Defining the
function
and purpose
of the
motherboard

1   A main printed circuit board that houses many of the essential parts of
a PC is more commonly called the _____.

Identifying
motherboard
form factors

2   A _____ defines the size, shape, and mounting of a motherboard.

3   The three most common motherboard form factors are _____, _____,
and _____.

4   The most popular motherboard form factor is the _____.

Explaining
the function
of the
chipset

5   The motherboard feature that includes I/O and bus structure controllers
is the _____.

Describing
the operation
of cache
memory

6   _____ is fast memory that is used as a data buffer between the CPU
and RAM.

7   _____ is usually located outside the CPU.

8   The _____ sets the limit for amount of memory a PC can cache.

9   Three major considerations for upgrading the motherboard are _____,
_____, and _____.

10   An important factor in choosing a replacement motherboard is the
_____ of the CPU.

Answers

1 *Motherboard* (or *systemboard* or *mainboard*). See "By any other name, it's still mother."

2 *Form Factor*. Review "Motherboard Sizes, Shapes, and Styles."

3 *AT, Baby AT,* and *ATX*. Take a look at "Motherboard form factors."

4 *ATX*. Check out "The ATX form factor."

5 *Chipset*. Peruse "Stacking Up the Chipsets."

6 *Cache memory*. See "Caching In on a Good Thing."

7 *L2 (Level 2) or external cache memory*. Review "Caching levels inside and outside the CPU."

8 *Chipset*. Check out "Counting your cache."

9 *CPU, form factor,* and *documentation*. Take a look at "Upgrading the Motherboard."

10 *Mounting*, or *slot*, or *socket*. See "Upgrading the Motherboard."

Understanding the Motherboard

This section prepares you to meet the exam objective of identifying popular motherboards and their components, architecture, and compatibilities. I can't overemphasize the importance of this material for the exam. It has its own domain in the exam blueprint, and it is reflected throughout the exam.

Every essential component directly or indirectly involved with making the PC function is either *on, attached,* or *connected to* the motherboard. For all intents and purposes, the motherboard *is* the computer. A computer without a motherboard is simply an empty metal box that just sits there.

The primary components of the PC attach or plug into the motherboard, which creates the functionality of the PC. The major components included on or connected to the motherboard include the CPU, memory, expansion cards, disk drives, keyboard, mouse, and monitor. You know — all of the really important parts of the PC.

By any other name, it's still mother

The motherboard is often referred to as a *systemboard* (at one time there was a distinction between the two). A systemboard integrated video, audio, graphics, and other device support into the board's architecture; a motherboard didn't. IBM has always called its motherboard a systemboard. Apple Computer calls its motherboard a *logic board,* while a few others refer to theirs as a *planar board.* These terms are still around today; for the most part, they are interchangeable because most motherboards are now systemboards and vice versa. I favor the term motherboard, but I may call it a systemboard for variety.

A PC motherboard is a large printed circuit board that's home to many of the essential parts of the computer, including the microprocessor, chipset, cache, memory sockets, expansion bus, parallel and serial ports, mouse and keyboard connectors, and IDE, EIDE, or SCSI controllers. The motherboard binds the PC's operational components together. Even devices (such as printers, hard drives, and CD-ROMs) are either connected to or controlled by the devices or controllers on the motherboard.

A wide variety of shapes, sizes, and types of motherboards are available. Regardless of a PC's age and its form factor (see "Motherboard form factors," later in the chapter), at least one manufacturer probably produces a motherboard to fit it. Manufacturers attempt to set their motherboards apart from the others and increase their value by incorporating more or fewer controllers, expansion buses, processor sockets, external connectors, and memory slots. For consumers, a wide range of motherboards with a deep list of features is available to fit into an even wider range of PCs. However, if you don't do your homework before buying a new motherboard, this wide range of selection can be bad news, and you can end up with lower-quality components than you want.

Motherboards and systemboards are manufactured under a number of competing standards. Each was designed to solve a particular design, engineering, or marketing problem. Motherboards come in every size — from tiny to huge. Some styles even divide the motherboard into several interconnecting pieces.

For the A+ Core Hardware exam, you need to know a lot about the various components that populate any motherboard, as shown on Figure 3-1. However, you need to know about only a few specific motherboard form factors and what differentiates them.

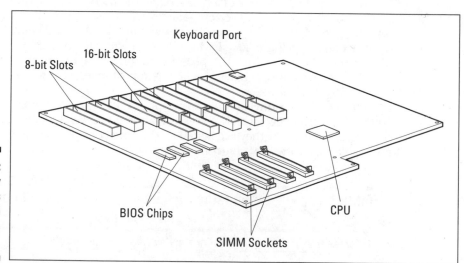

Figure 3-1: The primary components of a typical mother- board.

Motherboard form factors

The shape, packaging, and to a certain extent, the function of a motherboard are defined by its *form factor*. Many different form factors are available — some are generally accepted in the industry and others are open to interpretation by manufacturers. However, the exam blueprint for the A+ Core Hardware exam lists only the three most commonly used motherboard form factors:

✔ **AT:** This motherboard is patterned after the original IBM PC AT motherboard.

✔ **Baby AT:** This motherboard is a smaller version of the AT form factor motherboard.

✔ **ATX:** Similar in size to the Baby AT, the ATX adds features. This is the most often used form in today's PCs. The ATX motherboard allows for easier installation of full-length expansion cards and cables and is easier to cool.

More information on each of these form factors is included later in the chapter in the section "Motherboard Sizes, Shapes, and Styles."

The components on the motherboard

The motherboard consists of layers of components added to the basic circuit board, similar to the layers of a pizza. Using the pizza analogy, think of the motherboard as the crust; the components, which add its functionality, are the toppings. For the A+ Core Hardware exam, you need to know what makes up the crust and each ingredient. In this chapter, I cover the details of the motherboard and the chipset; the other major components of the motherboard have their own chapters (which is a clue of the importance of these topics).

In addition to the motherboard, processor, and CMOS, you need to know the components listed in Table 3-1. These components are usually found inside the system unit. After they are installed, they are considered a part of the motherboard's sphere of control.

Table 3-1	Motherboard Components You Must Know for the A+ Exam
Component	*Where You Can Find It in This Book*
BIOS and CMOS	Chapter 4 — "BIOS"
Bus architectures	Chapter 5 — "Bus Structures"
Cache memory	See "Caching In on a Good Thing" later in this chapter
Microprocessors	Chapter 6 — "Microprocessors"
Memory	Chapter 7 — "Memory Systems"

Component	Where You Can Find It in This Book
Storage devices	Chapter 8 — "Storing Data"
Power supply	Chapter 9 — "Powering and Cooling the PC"
I/O ports	Chapter 10 — "Input/Output Ports"

Riding the Bus

Part of understanding the operation of the motherboard is understanding its bus structure. Most of the motherboard exam questions are about bus architectures. This section provides you with a brief overview of the bus structures on the motherboard. For a more in-depth coverage of the various bus structures of a PC, check out Chapter 5.

The CPU moves data values and signals around the computer on a network of fine wires that interconnect it to all the other components on the motherboard. This network is called the *bus*.

✔ The lines that move data within the computer form the *internal bus*.

   Think of the internal bus as being a hallway in a large building, such as a huge hospital (the ones with the colored lines on the floor) or the Pentagon.

✔ The lines that communicate with peripherals and other devices attached to the motherboard form the *external bus*.

   The external buses are like hallways that lead directly to outside doors.

You can find four primary types of bus structures on most motherboards:

✔ **Address:** The components on the motherboard pass memory addresses to one another over the address bus.

✔ **Control:** Used by the CPU to send out signals to coordinate and manage the activities of the motherboard components.

✔ **Data:** Because the primary job of the computer is to process data, logically the data must be transferred between peripherals, memory, and the CPU. Obviously, the data bus can be a very busy hallway.

✔ **Power:** The power bus is the river of life for the motherboard's components, providing each with the electrical power it needs to operate.

The number of wires in a bus controls the number of bits that can be transferred over the bus. For example, a 32-bit bus must have 32 wires.

Motherboard Sizes, Shapes, and Styles

Although the blueprint of the A+ Core Hardware exam lists only the AT, Baby AT, and ATX form factors, don't be surprised by references on the exam to other form factors. For that reason, you should review the form factors listed in Table 3-2 to familiarize yourself with the various form factors that have been produced.

Table 3-2	Motherboard Form Factors		
Form Factor	*Width (in inches)*	*Length (in inches)*	*Design Type*
IBM PC	8.5	13	Motherboard
IBM PC XT	8.5	13	Motherboard
AT	12	11–13	Motherboard
Baby AT	8.5	10–13	Motherboard
LPX	9	11–13	Backplane
Micro-AT	8.5	8.5	Motherboard
ATX	12	9.6	Motherboard
Mini-ATX	11.2	8.2	Motherboard
Mini-LPX	8–9	10–11	Backplane
Micro-ATX	9.6	9.6	Motherboard
NLX	8–9	10–13.6	Backplane
Flex-ATX	9	7.5	Motherboard

Essentially, a *form factor* defines a motherboard's size, shape, and how it is mounted to the case. However, form factors now include

✔ The size, shape, and function of the system case

✔ The type, placement, and size of the power supply

 ↙ The system's power requirements

 ↙ The location and type of external connectors

 ↙ The case's airflow and cooling systems

Remember that the motherboard, power supply, and system case can each have a form factor. In a single PC, they usually have the same form factor; some power supplies and cases can handle several motherboard form factors.

The AT form factor

After the early success of its PC and PC XT models, IBM introduced its 16-bit PC AT (which allegedly stood for "Advanced Technology"), which added enough additional circuitry to increase the size of its motherboard (and case). The size, shape, and mounting placements of the AT's case were the standard that clone manufacturers used for their XT-upgrade motherboards. The popularity of the PC AT and its form factor established it as the first real motherboard form factor standard. The AT form factor motherboard, shown in Figure 3-2, is nearly square at 12 inches x 11–13 inches.

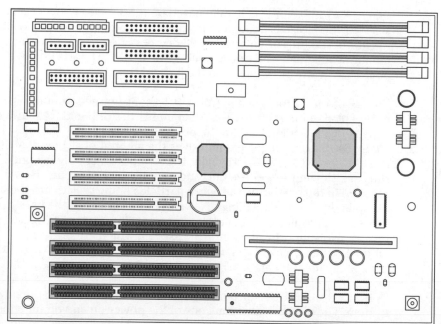

Figure 3-2:
An AT
form factor
mother-
board.

The Baby AT form factor

Following the success of the IBM PC AT, clone manufacturers began releasing their own 16-bit PCs. Higher integration technology reduced the space required by support chipsets and circuitry, which allowed the motherboard to be reduced as much as 3.5 inches in width and 2 inches in height. This new style board became known as the Baby AT, as shown in Figure 3-3. Because the Baby AT fit the AT form factor mountings, it quickly surpassed the AT as the form factor of choice. Most of the computer cases manufactured between 1984 and 1996 were Baby AT form factors.

The ATX form factor

The ATX form factor is the default form factor of the A+ Core Hardware exam. It's the one you'll see most often on the job.

Expect questions that require an understanding of the motherboard, its design, and its components; don't expect many questions directly about the design and features of any of the motherboard form factors.

The ATX form factor is generally based on the smaller Baby AT motherboard size. However, size is about all they have in common. The ATX form rotates the motherboard's orientation by 90 degrees and incorporates a new set of mounting locations and power connections. The I/O ports on an ATX motherboard are in a two-row block on the back of the PC.

The ATX form factor resulted from the lessons learned from the Baby AT and other small motherboards. The ATX mounts the CPU and RAM away from its expansion slots and closer to the power supply's cooling fan, as shown in Figure 3-4. This arrangement improves the amount of airflow available to cool the CPU and RAM chips. Originally, the ATX power supply fan pulled air into the case, flowing it over the CPU and out of the case's vents. However, this resulted in dust and other airborne particles being pulled into the case, such as chalk dust and metal filings. Newer ATX designs vent the case by pulling hot air away from the CPU and RAM and passing it out of the case. The ATX design also supports an additional case fan, which are recommended for PCs with 3-D video accelerators, multiple hard drives, and other high-heat-producing adapter cards.

The ATX design also incorporates a number of features into the power system. The motherboard can control the power on and off functions of the power supply, a feature called *soft switching*. The ATX form provides *split voltage* (a range of voltages, usually 12v, 5v, and 3.3v) to the motherboard, which eliminates the need for a voltage regulator included on earlier form factor motherboards.

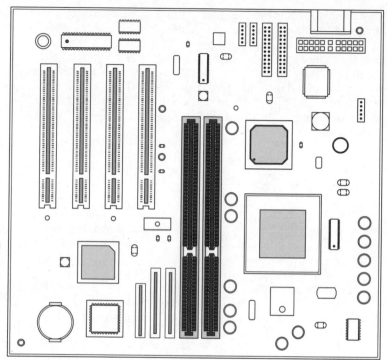

Figure 3-3:
A Baby
AT form
factor
mother-
board.

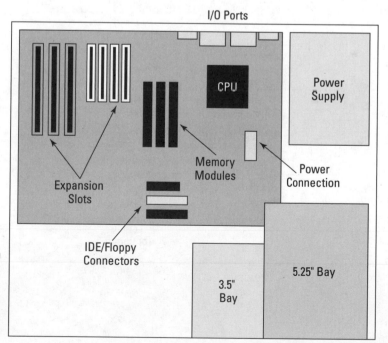

I/O Ports

CPU

Power
Supply

Memory
Modules

Power
Connection

Expansion
Slots

IDE/Floppy
Connectors

3.5"
Bay

5.25" Bay

Figure 3-4:
The
standard
ATX layout.

The ATX form factor locates the I/O ports in a two-row block on the rear of the board, as shown in Figure 3-5. The top row includes a PS/2-type keyboard or mouse connector, a parallel port, and a blank slot that can be used for a second parallel port. The bottom row includes a second PS/2-type keyboard or mouse connector, two serial ports, and a series of blank ports that might be used for sound or video card connectors. The defined size of the connector area on an ATX motherboard is small (6.25 inches x 1.75 inches), which helps eliminate the clutter of cables found near the rear panel of a Baby AT motherboard.

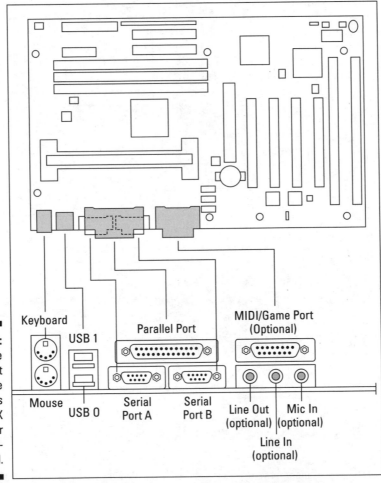

Figure 3-5:
The
placement
of the
I/O ports
on an ATX
form factor
mother-
board.

Keyboard

USB 1

Parallel Port

MIDI/Game Port
(Optional)

Mouse

USB 0

Serial
Port A

Serial
Port B

Line Out
(optional)

Mic In
(optional)

Line In
(optional)

Expect references to the ATX and the Baby AT form factors on the Core Hardware exam. In most instances, the reference will be to attaching devices, such as expansion cards and power supplies.

Stacking Up the Chipsets

The bus structures and interfaces supported by the motherboard and CPU are controlled by functions included on the chipset. The *chipset* is a group of chips that together help the processor and other peripheral devices plugged into the motherboard communicate with each other. The chipset controls the bits (data, instructions, and control signals) that flow between the CPU and system memory over the motherboard's buses. The chipset also manages data transfers between the CPU, memory, and peripheral devices. It also supports the expansion bus and any power management features of the system. However, the chipset contains only enough instructions to issue control commands to device drivers, which actually control the peripheral device.

Chipsets are integrated into the motherboard and usually cannot be upgraded without changing the entire motherboard. A PC's chipset is matched to the motherboard and the CPU as a set. Usually, a given chipset is matched to a single processor type; however, some chipsets support more than one processor. Along this line, you often see the chipset referred to by the CPU's mounting on the motherboard, for example, Socket 7 chipsets, Socket 370 chipsets, or Slot A chipsets.

At one time, a chipset consisted of several smaller single-purpose controller chips. Each separate controller, which could be one or more chips, managed a single function, such as controlling the cache memory, handling interrupts, or managing the data bus. Today's chipset combines this set of controller functions into one or two larger, multifunction chips. VLSI (very large-scale integration) has allowed these many chips to be combined into one or two chips.

Chipsets, especially two-chip chipsets, are divided into a North Bridge (the larger chip) and a South Bridge (the smaller chip). The North Bridge provides support and control for main memory, cache memory, and the PCI bus controllers. The South Bridge provides control for peripheral devices and those controllers that are not essential to the PC's basic functions, such as the serial port controller.

The chipsets are not the only controller sets on the motherboard. The most prominent controller sets are the keyboard controller and a superset of input/output device controllers called the Super I/O controller. The Super I/O chip combines controllers that are common to all systems. Controller chips are also found on many high-end devices and adapter cards.

Caching In on a Good Thing

Expect questions on the A+ Core Hardware exam about cache memory, which is a motherboard component. Understand why it exists, what it is, its limitations, and how and when it is used.

A mystery of the PC is that nearly all of its components, including the processor, the memory, the motherboard data buses, and the hard drive, operate at different speeds and data transfer rates. Because they are the products of competition, these cannot be well coordinated. No single company makes all of the components that go into a PC (although Intel certainly is trying).

Two motherboard components that must overcome their differences and work together are the CPU (processor) and primary memory (RAM). RAM works in nanoseconds (billionths of seconds) and is seemingly faster than the CPU, which works in megahertz (millionths of seconds). However, when the CPU requests data from the RAM, it takes a fair amount of time to locate the data and then transfer it over the data bus to the CPU. However fast the RAM may be, the CPU must wait while all of this is happening; this is bad! One of the underlying design goals of the PC is to prevent the CPU from being idle as much as possible. This is where cache memory comes in.

Thanks for the cache memories

Cache memory is an extremely fast memory type that acts as a buffer between RAM and the CPU. It holds frequently requested data and instructions so that they are immediately available to the CPU when needed.

Cache memory and the caching process hold data and instructions from a slower resource or process so that they are ready when needed by a faster device or process.

A *cache* is a buffer that mitigates the speed differences between devices. Today's PCs often include cache memory between the RAM and the CPU and between the hard drive and RAM. Caching is used in two ways on the PC:

- ✔ **Cache memory:** This is a relatively small and very fast memory storage located between the PC's primary memory (RAM) and its processor (CPU); it holds data and instructions retrieved from RAM to provide faster access to the CPU.

- ✔ **Disk cache:** This cache buffer accelerates the transfer of data and programs from the hard drive into RAM. Disk cache, which is either in RAM or additional memory on the disk controller, holds large blocks of frequently accessed data.

Cache memory is usually a small amount of Static Random Access Memory (SRAM). SRAM is made up of transistors that don't need to be frequently refreshed like DRAM, which is made up of capacitors. (But you already knew that.)

SRAM is very fast, with access speeds of 2ns (nanoseconds) or faster. This is much faster than DRAM, which has access speeds around 50ns. Because of its speed, SRAM cache memory can transfer data to the CPU at a much faster rate than it would take to transfer the same data from main memory. Another contributing factor to the speed of the cache is its proximity to the CPU, which eliminates most of the latency (delay) involved with transfers from RAM.

SRAM isn't used for primary memory in a PC for practical and economic reasons. SRAM can cost six times more than DRAM and requires a lot more space on the motherboard to store the same amount of data as DRAM.

Caching in operation

The CPU interacts with RAM through a series of *wait states,* during which the CPU pauses for a few cycles to allow time for the data it has requested to be located and transferred from RAM to its registers. If the data is not already in RAM (which means it must be fetched from the hard drive), additional CPU wait states are required. Cache memory attempts to eliminate CPU wait states by eliminating any CPU idleness.

Caching involves more than a little gambling. The operations of cache memory are based on the *principle of locality of reference,* which assumes that the next data to be requested is very likely located immediately following the last data requested. Caching copies the data just beyond the last data requested into cache memory (if it will be the data that CPU will ask for next). As iffy as this may sound, PC caching systems are surprisingly successful about 90 to 95 percent of the time.

Without cache memory, all requests for data and instructions by the CPU would be served from RAM. Only the data requested would be supplied with no anticipation of what the CPU would be asking for next. This is similar to having to go all the way to the supermarket for a single can of your favorite drink every time you want a cold one. Without caching, the CPU would get bogged down in memory requests, just as you would spend all of your time running to the store every time you got thirsty.

Adding cache memory is a lot like buying an ice chest — it saves you time because it gives you a place to store your beverages, so you won't have to go to the store as often. Because caching anticipates the CPU's next request, the whole system speeds up. With a hit ratio of 90 to 95 percent, caching saves many CPU cycles, just like the ice chest saves you trips.

Caching levels inside and outside the CPU

Cache memory is located in two general locations: inside the processor (internal cache) and on the motherboard (external cache):

- ✔ **Internal cache:** Also known as *primary cache,* internal cache is located inside the CPU chip, also called *on the die.*

- ✔ **External cache:** Also called *secondary cache,* external cache is located on the motherboard outside the CPU. This is the cache referred to on PC specifications.

Cache is also commonly referred to by its level or proximity to the CPU. Cache is designated in two levels:

- ✔ **Level 1 (L1) cache:** Level 1 cache is often used interchangeably with internal cache and rightly so. L1 cache is placed internally on the processor chip and is, of course, the cache memory closest to the CPU.

- ✔ **Level 2 (L2) cache:** L2 cache is normally placed on the motherboard close to the CPU; but because it is not inside the CPU, it is designated as the second level of cache. Although L2 cache is commonly considered the same as external cache, L2 cache can also be included on the CPU, just a little behind L1 cache.

Level 1 is not higher in ranking than Level 2 cache. The levels of cache work together, and data are located on either level, depending on the rules and policies of the caching system. Level 1 cache cannot be increased without changing the CPU. On the other hand, L2 cache can be upgraded on most motherboards. L2 cache modules plug into special cache module mounts or cache memory expansion sockets on the motherboard.

Counting your cache

When it comes to cache memory, more is better. However, there are limits and exceptions to how much cache a system and its chipset will support. Adding more cache to a PC usually increases its overall speed, but it may also decrease its performance. Should you add too much cache, simply keeping the cache filled from RAM can eat up the CPU cycles you were hoping to save.

If one ice chest provides enough drink cache to eliminate some trips to the store, it makes sense that two chests will save twice as many trips. There is some logic to this, but your savings depend on your ability to carry two chests' worth of drinks on each trip. If you can't carry enough to fill both ice chests on a single trip, you will need to make a second trip; that seriously eats into your time savings. Adding too much L2 cache to some PCs can affect the system's performance in this same way. The first 256K of L2 cache should improve the performance of a PC, but an additional 256K of L2 actually may *reduce* its performance.

Most Pentium class PCs include enough cache memory to cache (buffer) 64K of RAM, which is the standard sizing for L2 cache on most newer systems. The PC's chipset sets the limit of how much RAM it can cache, and an upper limit of 64K is common. What this means is that regardless of how much RAM you add to the PC, no more than 64K will be cached; this can affect the PC's performance. Before upgrading cache memory, read the documentation of the motherboard and chipset.

Upgrading the Motherboard

If your PC isn't as fast or as powerful as you'd like, you can either get a new PC or upgrade its motherboard and/or its components. Depending on the upgrade you want, upgrading the motherboard or the components on the motherboard usually costs less than a brand new PC. However, buying a new PC is not a part of the A+ exams; upgrading the motherboard *is* part of the exam.

There are three major considerations when looking to upgrade a motherboard: the *CPU,* the *form factor,* and *documentation.* Other considerations should fall into place if you get these three right.

Consider these criteria when evaluating the upgrade of a PC:

- ✔ **CPU:** The CPU that can be used to upgrade the PC depends on the motherboard, its form factor, and its chipset. The CPU can be upgraded on nearly all Pentium motherboards. However, the CPU socket on the motherboard controls which CPU can be used to upgrade the system. Some upgrades aren't practical. For example, trying to replace a Pentium 75 MHz processor with a Pentium III Xeon also involves replacing the motherboard, chipset, and probably the power supply. However, stepping up to the next level of processor can be relatively effortless, provided the new processor is within the motherboard's specification. Some processors, such as the Pentium Pro and Pentium II processors, have unique motherboard configurations and aren't usually compatible with other Pentium-based motherboards.

- ✔ **Sockets and slots:** Replacement motherboards usually have at least one ZIF (zero insertion force) socket. The most common socket style on newer computers is the Socket 7 mounting. Processors with SEC (Single-Edge Connector) packaging require either a Slot 1 or Slot 2 connection. You must consider the mounting of the CPU when considering an upgrade.

- ✔ **Bus speed:** The bus speeds supported by a motherboard and chipset must be matched to the processor. In addition to the processor, most motherboard components, especially the cache memory, are matched to the motherboard's speed.

- ✔ **Cache memory:** Virtually all Pentium motherboards have between 256K and 512K of Level 2 cache memory on the board; and some, such as the Pentium Pro and higher processors, include L2 cache on the CPU chip. Additional L2 cache can be added to the motherboard, but it must be matched to the motherboard's bus speed.

- ✔ **Memory modules:** Depending on the vintage of your PC, it may use DIP (dual inline packaging), SIMM (single inline memory module), or DIMM (dual inline memory module) for its memory. Before you start cramming memory modules into open slots, verify

   - The total amount of memory the motherboard supports

   - The memory technology the processor and chipset support

   Chapter 7 covers memory modules and technologies.

- ✔ **Expansion bus:** Before you run out and buy a new motherboard, it is important to consider the expansion cards and adapters installed on the current motherboard. Unless the new motherboard will replace some of the cards with built-in connectors, the current expansion cards will need compatible slots on the new motherboard.

- ✔ **BIOS:** When choosing a new motherboard, pick one with a BIOS that features flash ROM, Plug and Play (PnP), ATA and Fast ATA, and the newer power management standards, such as APM (Advanced Power Management) or SMM (System Management Mode).

- ✔ **Chipset:** The chipset is matched to the processor and the motherboard. Usually, this is a part of the motherboard and cannot be replaced.

- ✔ **Form factor:** If you aren't changing the PC's case, you are limited to the form factor of the case or those that will fit into it. An ATX case will take some of the later form factors, but check with the case manufacturer on this. If the PC is older, the case may be (no pun intended) that the form factor is Baby AT.

- ✔ **Power supply:** The power supply shares the form factor with the case and motherboard. Usually, the power supply is included with a new PC case (but not always).

- ✔ **Built-in controllers and interfaces:** Depending on your preferences, you may want more or fewer built-in controllers and plugs on the motherboard. Consider the connections and adapter cards on the current motherboard in making this choice.

- ✔ **Documentation:** To paraphrase the current cliché, the motherboard with the most documentation wins. (Documentation on the Internet counts.)

Make sure that none of the expansion slots, when occupied, block access to a memory socket, the ROM BIOS, password-clear jumper, or CMOS battery. This may save you some hassle during later maintenance or repair.

Prep Test

1 Which of the following is not a common name for the primary printed circuit board in a PC?

A ○ Mainboard

B ○ Motherboard

C ○ Planar board

D ○ Systemboard

2 Which of the following are common motherboard form factors? (Choose three.)

A ❑ Mother AT

B ❑ AT

C ❑ ATX

D ❑ Baby AT

3 Which of the following motherboard form factors is nearly square?

A ○ Mother AT

B ○ AT

C ○ ATX

D ○ Baby AT

4 Which of the following FRMs does not get its size and shape specified in a form factor standard?

A ○ Power supply

B ○ System case

C ○ Memory

D ○ Motherboard

5 The feature used to resolve the speed differences of the CPU and RAM is

A ○ Disk cache

B ○ Main memory

C ○ Cache memory

D ○ Data bus

6 Which computer component contains the circuitry necessary for all components or devices to communicate with each other?

A ○ Motherboard

B ○ Adapter board

C ○ Hard drive

D ○ Expansion bus

7 Which statement best describes the purpose of the motherboard?

A ○ Supplies DC power to the peripheral devices

B ○ Interconnects the primary components of the PC

C ○ Executes all instructions of the PC

D ○ Stores and processes the data of the PC

8 The principle of locality reference says that

A ○ The next data to be requested is the one before last

B ○ The hard drive should not be next to the CPU

C ○ The next data to be requested is the last one

D ○ The next data to be requested is located immediately following the last one

9 Level 1 cache is located where?

A ○ On the motherboard

B ○ On an adapter card

C ○ On the CPU

D ○ On the ROM BIOS

10 Cache memory is what type of memory?

A ○ DRAM

B ○ SRAM

C ○ Virtual memory

D ○ There is no standard memory type used for cache

Answers

1 **C.** Okay, so this is a trick question. Planar board is an older term that was once used for passive backplane boards. Don't expect to see planar on the exam. *See "By any other name, it's still mother."*

2 **B, C, D.** Now, don't go thinking that all the questions on the A+ exams are this easy. Mother AT is obviously not a form factor, but it's all easy and obvious when you know the material. *Review "Motherboard form factors."*

3 **B.** The AT motherboard is 12 inches wide x 11–13 inches tall. *Look it up in "AT form factor."*

4 **C.** Typically the form factor includes the size and shape and fit of the case, power supply, and motherboard. *See "Motherboard Sizes, Shapes, and Styles."*

5 **C.** Cache memory holds the data that the CPU is likely to use next, which speeds up the transfer to the CPU, hopefully eliminating CPU wait states. *Review "Caching In on a Good Thing."*

6 **A.** The bus structures are located on the motherboard/systemboard. *Check out "Understanding the Motherboard."*

7 **B.** The motherboard is the platform that interconnects all of the primary components of the PC. *Take a look at "Understanding the Motherboard."*

8 **D.** The caching system uses the principle that the next data is likely the data located immediately after the last one requested. *See "Caching in operation."*

9 **C.** Level 1, also known as internal, cache is located on the CPU, which is also called on the die. *Look over "Caching levels inside and outside the CPU."*

10 **B.** Cache memory is usually a small amount of SRAM. *Review "Thanks for the cache memories."*

Chapter 4

BIOS

Exam Objectives

▶ Reviewing BIOS basic terms, concepts, and actions

▶ Listing the actions of the boot process

▶ Defining the purpose and usage of the CMOS

▶ Upgrading the system BIOS

▶ Troubleshooting boot and BIOS problems

*B*efore computers got their first operating systems, programmers had to write their own input and output routines to get input in and output out. They had to include a routine in each program to read the input and create the output. During the computer's evolution, a smart programmer figured out that, because every program needs to get input and produce output, creating standardized versions of these functions and including them as a part of the system's software might be an excellent idea. This concept has advanced to the point where the computer even has specialized instructions that tell it which peripheral devices are attached and whether they're operating properly so that the PC can look for the appropriate input and output device drivers it needs. These instructions form the PC's Basic Input/Output System (as it's more commonly known, the *BIOS*).

In the Core Hardware exam's objectives, the system BIOS and associated topics are listed in four of the six test domains. The BIOS, boot process, CMOS, and other system startup and input/output topics and activities are important to the PC repair professional, both on the A+ exams and on the job. The BIOS holds the key to the system's efficient operations; it can be the best diagnostics tool in your toolkit — not to mention that it starts up the PC every time you power it up.

If you are in the habit of ignoring the process that brings the PC to its operating state each time you start it, you may want to pay attention to this valuable and critical process, because you need to know and understand it for the A+ exam.

Quick Assessment

Reviewing BIOS basic terms, concepts, and actions

1 BIOS refers to _____.

2 The address of the first instruction of the BIOS is called the _____.

Listing the actions of the boot process

3 The type of startup performed when a PC is off is a(n) _____.

4 The type of startup performed when a PC is on is a(n) _____.

5 The process that is used to test and verify the PC's hardware during startup is called the _____.

Defining the purpose and usage of the CMOS

6 CMOS refers to _____.

7 The PC's system configuration is stored in the _____ memory.

8 Removing the _____ will reset the user and supervisor passwords.

Upgrading the system BIOS

9 Upgrading the ROM BIOS under software control is called _____.

Trouble-shooting boot and BIOS problems

10 Errors that occur before the monitor is available are signaled with a(n) _____.

Answers

1 *Basic Input/Output System.* See "Getting to Know the BIOS."

2 *Jump address.* Review "Booting Up the System."

3 *Cold boot.* Check out "Starting cold and running warm."

4 *Warm boot.* Take a look at "Starting cold and running warm."

5 *POST (Power On Self-Test).* See "Running the POST process."

6 *Complementary Metal Oxide Semiconductor.* Review "Verifying the hardware."

7 *CMOS memory.* Look over "Setting the BIOS configuration."

8 *CMOS battery.* Check out "Security and passwords."

9 *Flashing.* Take a look at "Updating the BIOS."

10 *Beep code.* See "Running the POST process."

Getting to Know the BIOS

The *BIOS (Basic Input/Output System)* is a collection of software utilities and programs that can be invoked by the operating system or application software to perform many hardware-related tasks. Although many operating systems now contain their own device-oriented programs to improve performance, the BIOS contains a program for almost every activity associated with accessing hardware, including programs for starting the system, testing the hardware, reading and writing to and from storage devices, and moving data between devices.

The BIOS is the PC's opening act. It ensures that the hardware is alive, well, and ready for the operating system, and then gets the operating system running. If you're like most PC users, you probably give the system BIOS of your PC very little notice each time it does its magic when you power it up. That is, until there's a problem, and then you'd probably like to shoot the messenger.

The BIOS performs three vital functions for the computer:

- ✔ Boot the PC.
- ✔ Verify the configuration data that tells it the internal and peripheral devices that are supposed to be connected to the PC.
- ✔ Provide the interface between the hardware (the attached devices) and the software (such as the operating system, device drivers, and application software).

Booting the PC

The instructions that start up the PC and load the operating system into memory and keep it running are part of the group of instructions that are collectively referred to as the *system BIOS*. The process of starting up the computer and loading the operating system is commonly called *booting the computer,* or simply the *boot sequence.* When the computer boots, the BIOS is in charge.

Booting and *boot* are derivatives of the phrase "pulling oneself up by one's own bootstraps," or being able to self-start.

When the PC is powered on, the BIOS supplies the PC with its first set of instructions. The instructions supplied by the BIOS are what the PC executes during its power on or boot up sequences until it is able to fetch and execute instructions on its own.

Verifying the hardware

The configuration of a PC is stored in a special type of nonvolatile memory, called *Complementary Metal-Oxide Semiconductor,* or *CMOS* (pronounced "sea-moss"), which requires little power to hold onto its contents. CMOS is the technology used in nearly all memory and processor chips today. However, in early PCs, it was used only to store the PC's configuration data. So, although it's used throughout the PC's circuits, CMOS is synonymous with the storage of the PC's configuration data.

CMOS runs on about 1 millionth of an amp of electrical current. This efficiency allows it to store configuration data for a long time (maybe years), powered only from either low-voltage dry cell or lithium batteries. On newer PCs, the CMOS battery is located on the motherboard; however, in many older systems, it may actually be a pair of AA batteries mounted in a plastic battery pack that is attached to the sidewall of the system case.

When the system starts the boot sequence, the BIOS starts a *Power-On Self-Test,* or *POST,* program that verifies the data in the CMOS to the physical devices it can detect on the system. More on this later in the chapter in the "Running the POST process" section.

Getting input in and output out

After the PC is running, its peripheral devices communicate with the system through their device drivers. The system BIOS allows your old PC AT software to run on your Pentium III PC. The BIOS interacts with the hardware to carry out the actions demanded of it. After the PC is booted, the BIOS becomes part of a four-layer software operating environment that allows software to run on many PC platforms without too much trouble.

The application layer (for example, a word processing application) interacts with the operating system, such as Windows, to process its inputs and outputs. The operating system, which can't possibly be created to be exactly compatible with every configuration of PC, interacts with the BIOS, which in turn interacts with the PC's hardware. The BIOS allows the operating system and the application to be created for a general class of hardware, because it's specifically created to work with certain types and configurations of hardware. The layers use a standard interface, supplied by the BIOS, to interact with the layer below (or above) it.

BIOS Chipology

An essential part of studying the BIOS is studying the chips (as in integrated circuits made from silicon "chips") on which it is stored and delivered to the PC. You don't need to become an electronics engineer to take the A+ Core Hardware exam, but it sure wouldn't hurt to know these common chip terms:

- ✔ **Read Only Memory (ROM):** Although not solely a BIOS chip, ROM chips are permanently loaded with instructions during the manufacturing processes. The instructions written to a ROM chip, which cannot be changed under any circumstance, are called *firmware*. No longer a common vehicle for the system BIOS, on earlier PCs, the BIOS was stored on a ROM chip (see Figure 4-1).

- ✔ **Programmable Read Only Memory (PROM):** A PROM is essentially a blank ROM chip that can be programmed with data or instructions. A PROM burner (also called a *PROM programmer*), a special device used to write to the PROM, enables you to store any data you want. The PROM burner induces high voltage (12 volts compared to the 5 volts used for normal PROM operations) to load the data to the chip. The higher voltage burns a memory location to turn its preexisting binary 1 into a 0, if needed. This process is irreversible, so what you burn is what you get (WYBIWYG). After you burn that zero into the PROM, there's no going back. For that reason, you may hear PROM memory referred to as One Time Programmable Memory.

- ✔ **Erasable Programmable Read Only Memory (EPROM):** An *EPROM* (pronounced "e-prom," which isn't a dance attended over the Internet) is a variation of the original PROM with the added feature of data that can be erased so that the chip can be reprogrammed. Unlike the PROM, you can reuse the EPROM instead of discarding it when its contents are no longer valid. The EPROM has a small quartz crystal window on the top of the chip through which ultraviolet (UV) rays can access the chip's circuitry. The UV light causes a chemical reaction that erases the EPROM by turning the 0's back into 1's again. To prevent accidental erasure of the EPROM chip, a label tape is normally placed over the quartz crystal window. Figure 4-2 shows an EPROM chip. The downside of an EPROM is that it must be removed from the system to be reprogrammed, which is not always possible.

- ✔ **Electronically Erasable Programmable Read Only Memory (EEPROM):** An EEPROM (pronounced "e-e-prom") is the common BIOS chip on newer systems. An EEPROM chip can be reprogrammed like the EPROM; unlike the EPROM, it doesn't need to be removed from the motherboard. An EEPROM can be updated through specialized software that is usually downloaded from the BIOS or chip manufacturer's Web site. This process is known as *flashing,* which is why this chip is also commonly called *flash ROM.* Because they're easy to upgrade, EEPROM chips are also used in many other things, such as cars, modems, cameras, and telephones.

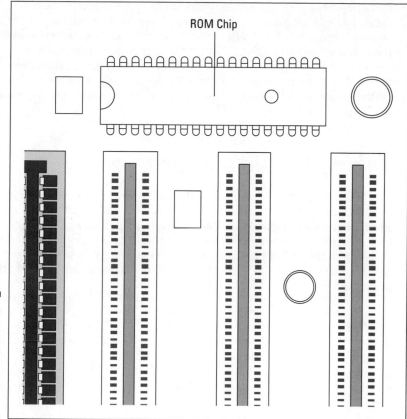

ROM Chip

Figure 4-1:
A ROM
BIOS chip
mounted
on a PC
mother-
board.

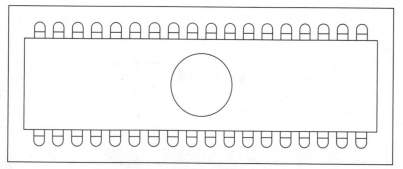

Figure 4-2:
An EPROM
chip.

Starting up the BIOS

When you power up your PC, the processor is eager to go, but its memory is
empty and the processor has nothing to do. So there must be a mechanism on
the system to provide the first instructions to be executed into RAM. Because

this chapter is about the BIOS, you shouldn't be surprised that the BIOS contains that mechanism. Getting the processor its first instructions is a fairly simple arrangement. Each time the PC starts up, the processor must execute the same set of instructions to start the ball rolling. Because the processor can't execute any instructions to find these instructions, they must be available in the same place every time. This first set of instructions (that loads the BIOS into memory) is hard-wired to a fixed, standard location, called the *jump address,* on the BIOS ROM chip.

Taking the high memory road

The BIOS program is loaded to the last 64K (upper 64K) of the first megabyte of RAM (memory addresses F000h to FFFFh), also known as *high memory area,* as shown in Figure 4-3. Processor and BIOS manufacturers established this location as a standard so that the processor always knows the exact location of the BIOS in memory. The processor gets its first instructions from this location and begins executing the BIOS program, which starts the boot sequence.

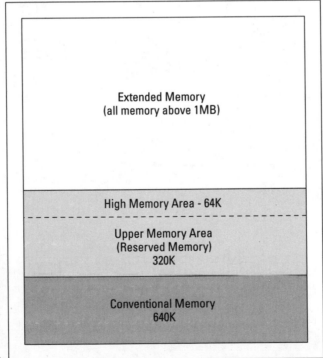

Figure 4-3:
The standard DOS memory allocation.

Extended Memory
(all memory above 1MB)

High Memory Area - 64K

Upper Memory Area
(Reserved Memory)
320K

Conventional Memory
640K

Several BIOS programs exist in a PC. Besides the main BIOS program, there are also BIOS programs to control many of the peripheral devices. For example, most video cards have their own BIOS programs that provide additional instructions used for controlling the video display. Hard drives and many SCSI adapters also have their own BIOS programs.

Booting Up the System

What the BIOS actually does during its boot sequence varies slightly from manufacturer to manufacturer; these basic steps are performed during the boot sequence:

1. When the PC is powered on, the internal power supply initializes.

   The power supply doesn't immediately provide power to the rest of the computer. First, it determines whether it can supply the proper voltages that the PC's components require. The power supply sends out a POWER GOOD signal when it determines that it can supply reliable power to the rest of the PC. When the chipset receives this signal, it issues a SYSTEM RESET signal to the processor.

2. When the processor receives the SYSTEM RESET signal, it accesses the jump address for the start of the BIOS boot program at its hard-wired preset address and loads it into RAM.

   The *jump address* contains the actual address of the BIOS boot program on the ROM BIOS chip. The jump address is usually located at address FFFF0 (hexadecimal) or 1,048,560 (decimal), which is the upper end of the first megabyte of system memory.

3. With the primary part of the BIOS now loaded to RAM, the POST process begins.

   If any fatal errors happen during the POST process (problems that prevent the PC from operating normally), the appropriate error beep codes sound or perhaps an error message displays, and the boot process stops. At this point in the boot process, only the system speaker (because it's technically part of the motherboard) can notify the user of errors.

4. If all is well, the boot sequence continues, and the system BIOS loads the device BIOS of the video adapter (if there is one) and loads it to memory.

   As your PC boots, the video adapter's information displays on the monitor.

5. Any other device-specific BIOS routines, such as those for the hard drives or SCSI devices, are loaded.

   Information, usually including the manufacturer and the BIOS version, displays. The BIOS begins a series of tests on the system, including a run-up count of the amount of memory detected on the system. Because the display is now available, any errors found in this process are displayed on the monitor as an error message instead of a beep code played through the system speaker.

6. The system determines whether the devices listed in the CMOS configuration data are present and functioning, including tests for device speeds and access modes.

7. The serial and parallel ports are assigned their identities (such as COM1, COM2, and LPT1), and a message is displayed for each device found, configured, and tested.

   If the BIOS program supports Plug and Play (PnP), any PnP devices detected are configured. Although it usually goes by much too fast to read, the BIOS displays a message for each device it finds and configures.

8. The configuration is confirmed.

   The BIOS displays a summary screen that details the computer as the BIOS sees it. This summary screen signals that the system is verified and ready for use.

9. The CMOS data contains the sequence in which storage devices are to be checked by the BIOS to locate the operating system. Typically, the first hard drive is listed first, but the BIOS can be set to have the BIOS check the floppy disk, a CD-ROM, or another hard drive first with the order in which the other devices are checked also specified. Depending on the CMOS data, the following actions occur:

   • If the boot device is the hard drive, the BIOS looks for the master boot record.

   • If the boot device is a floppy disk or a CD-ROM, the BIOS looks at the first sector of the disk for the operating system's boot program.

   • If the boot program is not found on the first device listed, the next device indicated is searched, and then the third, and so on until the boot program is found.

   • If no boot device is found, the boot sequences stop and an error message ("No boot device available") is displayed.

Starting cold and running warm

One of the first A+ Core Hardware exam objectives is to identify the basic terms, concepts, and functions of a PC's boot processes. This includes the actions and the sequence of the actions that either start the computer from a power-off status (cold boot) or restart a PC that's already running (warm boot).

Cold boot

A *cold boot* starts when the PC's power is switched on.

A cold boot is the whole BIOS enchilada. It causes the BIOS to guide the PC's boot sequence through a series of steps that verify the computer's integrity. The exact steps vary slightly, depending on just about everything about or in your PC (manufacturer, BIOS, and hardware configuration).

Expect one or two questions on the cold boot process and the sequence of its actions in the "Installation, Configuration, and Upgrading" Core Hardware exam domain. You may also see two or three boot sequence or POST questions in the "Diagnosing and Troubleshooting" domain.

Warm boot

A *warm boot* is performed whenever the PC is restarted or reset with the power already on.

A warm boot does not run the POST and reestablishes the operating system and drivers on the PC.

One of the most common ways to start the warm boot is by using the official keystrokes of the PC repair technicians' secret club — Ctrl+Alt+Delete — but then you already knew that. However, on newer operating systems, especially Windows 2000 and Windows XP systems, Ctrl+Alt+Delete doesn't restart the PC. Instead, this key combination displays a control panel from which you can restart the PC, if you wish.

Running the POST process

Questions on the boot sequence usually ask about the POST process. The POST is a hardware diagnostic routine built into the BIOS that checks the PC's hardware to make sure that everything that's supposed to be there is present, and that everything is working properly. The POST process ensures that the system is ready to begin the boot sequence.

- ✔ If the POST process detects errors, it generates a signal to indicate where in the process the error occurred and which device had the error. Not all POST errors are fatal; the POST process generally continues past nonfatal problems.

- ✔ If a fatal error is detected, (such as "no memory is found") the POST process signals its error code and halts the boot process immediately.

✔ If the POST detects an error before the device drivers for the monitor are loaded, then it must signal an error as sounds (actually beeps) through the PC's system speaker.

The meaning of a beep code depends on the manufacturer of the BIOS. Each BIOS maker has its own set of beep codes, which can also vary from one version to the next — similar to having a different Morse code scheme for every ham radio. Well, maybe not really *that* bad!

Almost all BIOS programs sound a single beep before displaying the BIOS startup screen. If the boot sequence continues, the beep doesn't indicate a problem. BIOS beep codes can be used to troubleshoot hardware failures occurring in the POST procedure.

Decoding POST messages

After the POST and boot sequence have advanced to the point at which they have use of the video to display messages, they can display a numerical error message to indicate a failure that occurred during the POST or boot sequence. For example, a POST message code in the 300 series indicates that a keyboard error was detected during the POST.

For the exam, know the major groups of numerical error codes such as those listed in Table 4-1, which lists the major groups of the POST hardware diagnostics messages commonly used on PC systems. Each BIOS system uses many of the listed codes, but no BIOS uses all of these codes. I include only those codes that you may encounter on the test. Many more exist, especially in the IBM system world. One of the problems of these error codes is that the list continues to grow without much being deleted.

Table 4-1	POST Hardware Diagnostic Message Groups
Code	**Description**
1xx	Motherboard errors
2xx	Main memory errors
3xx	Keyboard errors
5xx	Color graphics adapter errors
6xx	Floppy disk controller errors
14xx	Printer errors
17xx	Hard drive controller errors
86xx	Mouse error

Floppy disk controller POST error messages are in the 600 range and keyboard errors cause POST errors in the 300 range.

Other boot errors can look like POST errors when they are more often caused by a new or recent addition to the system. For example, after a new hard drive is installed, the system may boot to a blank screen if the new slave hard drive is not properly configured in the CMOS settings as a slave. A new hard drive that has not been partitioned or formatted will likely cause a no operating system error.

Other devices can also cause boot time errors:

✔ An improperly installed motherboard may indicate other device problems.

✔ Newly installed RAM can cause parity and other fatal memory errors to appear at POST time if the RAM either is the wrong speed or uses a different data width.

BIOS startup screen

Immediately after the BIOS loads the video and other device-specific BIOS programs, it displays its startup screen. Although this display varies by manufacturer, it generally contains the following information:

✔ **Version:** The BIOS manufacturer and the BIOS program's version number and version date.

✔ **Startup program keys:** The keyboard key or keys used to access the BIOS setup program. Usually, these are the Delete (Del) key or a Function (F1 or F2) keys; there could also be a key combination (such as Ctrl+Esc).

✔ **Logos:** A logo from at least one of the following: the BIOS manufacturer, the PC manufacturer, or the motherboard manufacturer.

✔ **Energy Star:** If the BIOS supports the Energy Star standard (also known as the Green standard), an Energy Star logo is displayed. Virtually all newer computers display this logo, but only those pre-Pentiums with an upgraded BIOS display it.

✔ **Serial number:** The BIOS program's serial number appears either at the end of the display or at the bottom of the screen. The serial number of the BIOS is specific to the combination of the motherboard, chipset, and program version.

For more information on system BIOS than you ever thought you'd need, visit Wim Bervoets' excellent BIOS Web site (www.wimsbios.com).

System configuration summary

After the BIOS completes its work (but before it starts loading the operating system into memory), it displays a summary of the system configuration. What's displayed depends on the manufacturer and version of the BIOS. Usually, the following information is displayed:

- ✔ **Processor:** The type of microprocessor, such as Pentium or Pentium Pro.

- ✔ **Coprocessor:** If a math coprocessor or floating point unit (FPU) is installed on the system, it is indicated as "Installed." Virtually every processor since the 386DX (with the exception of SX models of the 386 and 486 processors) has an integrated FPU and is indicated as "Integrated."

- ✔ **Clock speed:** Measures the clock speed of the processor in MHz. This information may be displayed on the same line as the processor type.

- ✔ **Floppy disk drives:** Indicates whether the system has any disk drives, the size, and capacity of each floppy disk.

- ✔ **Hard drive, CD-ROM, and DVD drives:** If the system includes ATA disk drives or ATAPI optical or tape drives, the BIOS displays the drive types detected, including the primary master and slave drives and any secondary slaves and masters found (including the manufacturer, capacity, and access modes of each drive).

- ✔ **Memory size:** Indicates the amount of memory in base, extended, and cache memory. The base memory (conventional memory) size is always 640K. Displays the amount of extended memory on the system minus the amount set aside for the BIOS. The BIOS doesn't report the amount of memory reserved for the high-memory area that contains the BIOS itself. The cache size is displayed separately.

- ✔ **Memory type:** The type and configuration of the physical memory is displayed, including the number of memory banks or modules installed and the memory technology in use. For example, the display may indicate "EDO DRAM at Bank 1" or "FP: 0 was detected."

- ✔ **Video type:** Unless your computer is more than 10 years old, the display type is usually "VGA/EGA," which really doesn't tell you anything except that the video adapter was detected.

- ✔ **Serial ports:** The system resource addresses (usually 3F8h and 2F8h) of any serial or COM ports detected.

- ✔ **Parallel ports:** The system resource address (usually 378h) of the parallel port is displayed.

- ✔ **Plug and Play (PnP) devices:** If any PnP adapter cards are detected by the BIOS, a description of each may be displayed.

Setting the BIOS configuration

Usually a PC is shipped from the factory with all the peripheral devices it will ever have already installed and its system configuration already complete and stored in CMOS. If a PC needs upgrading or new peripherals installed, you can view and alter the configuration as necessary. The BIOS setup and configuration data is accessed through a startup program. This program, called the _setup,_ is available for only a very short time during the system boot sequence and you can access it by pressing a specific key or combination of keys.

Always create a backup of the BIOS settings each time the BIOS configuration changes and for every new PC added to the network. To make a backup of the BIOS settings, simply write them down on paper and keep it in a safe place.

Setup program

To gain access to the BIOS setup program, press a key designated by the BIOS, which is displayed during the initial boot process. Figure 4-4 shows the information displayed during the boot sequence. Notice that it shows that the F1 function key accesses the setup program. Table 4-2 lists the keystrokes used to access the setup program for most of the popular BIOS programs.

Figure 4-4: A sample BIOS startup screen.

```
PhoenixBIOS 4.0 Release 6.0
Copyright 1985-1998 Phoenix Technologies Ltd.  All Rights Reserved
Copyright 1996-1998 Intel Corporation.
404CL0X0.15A.0006.P02


Intel® Celeron(tm) processor 333 Mhz
128MB System RAM

Legacy Keyboard . . . Detected
Legacy Mouse . . . . . . Detected

Fixed Disk 0: QUANTUM FIREBALL EX10.2A-(PM)
ATAPI CD-ROM: MATSHITA CR-588-(SM)
ATAPI Removable Drive: IOMEGA ZIP 100-(SS) ATAPI

Press <F1> to enter SETUP
```

Table 4-2	BIOS Setup Program Access Keys
BIOS	**Keys**
AMI	Del (Delete)
Award	Del or Ctrl+Alt+Esc
Compaq	F10
Dell	Del, F2, or Fn+F1
Gateway 2000	F1
Hewlett Packard	F1
IBM Aptiva	F1
Phoenix BIOS	F1 or F2

The setup program manages the hardware configuration stored in CMOS memory. The settings included in the configuration, although somewhat standardized, vary with the BIOS. Pressing the startup program access key starts the program used to display and modify the system setup data. The setup program menus are the first things displayed.

Standard configuration menu

On nearly all newer PCs, the configuration data is managed and maintained on two levels:

- ✔ **The standard configuration:** Includes the system clock and basic data on the hard drives, floppy drive, and video adapter.

- ✔ **The advanced setup:** The standard configuration menu may also list the processor type, memory type and speed, and the amount and type of memory.

Here's a list of the basic standard settings and parameters you normally find on the standard configuration menu:

- ✔ **System date:** Sets the MM/DD/YY date for the system. On Windows 98 and 2000, this BIOS setting can be adjusted from the built-in Date/Time Properties feature.

- ✔ **System time:** Displays the time in the 24-hour clock format (11:00 PM displays as 23:00). Like the system date, this setting can be adjusted from the Date/Time Properties feature of Windows.

✓ **IDE primary and secondary masters:** The parameters of the hard drives configured as the primary master or secondary master (if any) are configured in these entries. On most BIOS systems, the default setting is commonly "Auto," for autodetection.

✓ **IDE primary and secondary slaves:** The parameters of the hard drives configured as the primary slave or secondary slave, if any, are configured in these entries. On most BIOS systems, the default setting is commonly "Auto," for autodetection.

✓ **Floppy disk drives A and B:** Listed separately, because there is commonly no B floppy drive installed, the type of disk drive in the system is indicated in this entry. The default for the A drive is usually the 1.44MB drive and "Not Installed" for the B drive. The choices are usually

- **1.44MB:** The normal everyday 3½-inch floppy disk drive.

- **1.2MB:** Although rarely used anymore, the normal 5¼-inch floppy disk drive.

- **2.88MB:** The high-density 3½-inch floppy disk drive, called the Big Floppy. Rare, but in some of the latest systems.

- **720K:** The low-density 3½-inch floppy disk drive.

- **360K:** The dinosaur of floppy disk drives, the low-density 5¼-inch disk drive.

- **None or Not Installed:** No floppy drive is installed in the A or B positions.

✓ **Video display:** This setting defines the display standard in use and is usually VGA/EGA, indicating that the PC is using a VGA or SVGA card.

✓ **Halt on:** Some BIOS programs enable you to set which errors you want the BIOS to stop (halt) during the POST and boot sequence. The choices range from all errors (a good choice), to no errors (a bad choice), and many "All but the . . ." settings (it depends) that prevent errors on certain devices from stopping the boot.

The truly cautious and wise PC repair technician creates a complete backup of the PC's hard drive before messing with the PC's BIOS or its setup configuration, especially the advanced settings.

Advanced setup menu

The settings in the advanced features or advanced setup menu are specific to the motherboard, processor, and chipset. Usually, access to these settings is a menu choice listed on the startup program's menu page.

You should know the kinds of things that are included under the advanced settings, but don't spend much time memorizing them. Just understand the basic differences between the standard configuration and the advanced settings. To really lock this in, boot your own PC and access the startup program and the CMOS configuration data. Review the standard and the advanced settings and make a mental note of the types of settings included in each.

Plug and Play options

The startup program should also include special menus for PnP. If a PnP menu is available, a general PnP option may be listed in the advanced features. You can set this option on or off to match the operating system.

You can't simply count on the operating system to handle PnP devices. Some operating systems (such as Windows NT) don't directly support PnP, which means that the BIOS must deal with any PnP device configurations.

Extended System Configuration Data (ESCD)

If the BIOS supports PnP, the startup program stores *Extended System Configuration Data (ESCD)* in CMOS.

- ✔ ESCD defines the system resource assignments of PnP devices.
- ✔ ESCD serves as a communications link between the BIOS and the operating system for the PnP devices.

Other startup menus

Depending on the BIOS, you may find other menus listed on the setup program's menu page. These menus usually focus on one particular aspect of the system's configuration. Some of the menus you may find are

- ✔ **Power management:** Contains options used to control the system when it is automatically powered down through power conservation settings.
- ✔ **Integrated peripherals:** Defines the configuration of the devices that are integrated into the motherboard, such as serial and parallel ports, audio, and USB ports.

Security and passwords

The ability to set the user and supervisor password for the BIOS and the CMOS data is included on a separate menu or in the advanced features menu on older systems.

If the user password is set, the computer isn't allowed to boot until the proper password is entered. The supervisor password protects the BIOS program's settings and the system configuration. Without the supervisor password, a user can't access the BIOS settings, but the system will boot. If you choose to set either of these passwords, you put yourself in the situation of really needing to remember them, but there are second chances.

If you forget the user password and remember the supervisor password, you can enter the BIOS setup data and clear or change the user password. If you forget both passwords, you're stuck. Your only recourse is to open the computer and use the password-clear jumper (see Figure 4-5) located on the motherboard near the CMOS chip and its battery. You can also clear the CMOS settings, including all advanced settings that you may have changed and the passwords, by removing the CMOS battery, which is shown in Figure 4-6. That's one reason that you want to keep a backup copy of the system setup written down and kept in a safe place.

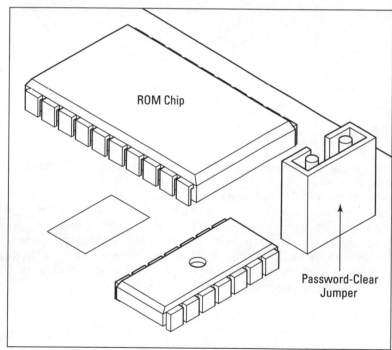

Figure 4-5:
The
Password-
Clear
jumper
on a PC
mother-
board.

ROM Chip

Password-Clear
Jumper

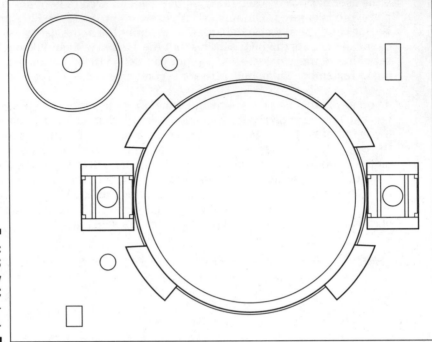

Figure 4-6:
The CMOS
battery
on a PC
mother-
board.

Updating the BIOS

Upgrading the BIOS on most older PCs (those with the BIOS loaded on a ROM chip), required you to physically remove the BIOS ROM chip and replace it with the new ROM chip containing the new BIOS version — something that was not always easy or possible to do. This really cramped your style if you wanted to upgrade the processor or chipset, which usually requires a BIOS upgrade. This process could introduce a wide range of problems into the PC, including ESD, bent pins on the chips, and damage to the motherboard from clumsy fingers. For many people, it was easier to simply upgrade to a new PC and avoid the anxiety and potential problems.

For the Core Hardware exam, you should know

✔ When a system BIOS should be updated

✔ How the update is done

✔ Problems to expect if the BIOS upgrade process is interrupted

✔ How the BIOS is recovered

For the A+ exam, you should be aware of both approaches to upgrading the BIOS, but focus on *flashing*. Fortunately, the EEPROM has replaced the PROM and is the BIOS ROM of choice. This is fortunate because the EEPROM can be updated in place on the board through flashing. Flashing allows you to upgrade the contents of the EEPROM under the control of a software utility program. (Some motherboards require the BIOS ROM to be physically replaced to upgrade it, but they are rare.) Virtually all new systems include flash BIOS.

The BIOS manufacturers that produce flash BIOS provide software utilities to control the flashing process. The flash utility is easily obtained from the manufacturer's Web site or by mail. Depending on the manufacturer, the flash utility contains routines to verify the BIOS version to the motherboard and chipset and to prevent the BIOS from receiving the wrong version. The flash software runs on a PC after it has booted. Be sure you follow the manufacturer's instructions to the letter.

Flashing dangers

Flashing, for all its benefits, carries a few risks:

✔ When you begin flashing a BIOS ROM, you absolutely must complete the process. Remember that the flash process is replacing the contents of the EEPROM. If the flashing process is interrupted — for example, somebody trips over the power cord, a power failure occurs, the flash software has a bug, or the PC is accidentally knocked off the table — depending on where you are in the flashing process, the probability of having a corrupted BIOS chip is high.

✔ Flashing the wrong BIOS version is another way to corrupt the BIOS ROM. Flashing can be unforgiving and many flash utilities will load whatever BIOS version you give it without question. The software provided to flash your BIOS may not include security features to prevent this from happening. The flashing utilities from the larger BIOS companies (such as Award, Phoenix, and AMI) include features that check the version of the flash file against the model of motherboard and let you know of any mismatch. A corrupted BIOS leaves you in a real Catch-22 situation. To flash your BIOS ROM, you must boot the PC, and you can't boot the PC with a corrupted BIOS.

In spite of the dangers, the whole process of flashing the BIOS usually takes only a few seconds and the risks are low. But you should take no chances:

✔ Avoid flashing your BIOS in an electrical storm.

✔ Be sure your computer is protected against power surges or brownouts by an uninterruptible power supply (UPS).

✔ Check twice that you are flashing your BIOS with the current version.

Preventing accidental flashing

After you flash your BIOS, you still may have the flash utility on your PC and that means there is a chance of accidental flashing. If this happens and you replace the BIOS with the same complete version, there should be no harm. However, if the accidental flashing operation is interrupted, or your current BIOS is replaced by an older or incompatible version either inadvertently or maliciously, the effect is the same as no BIOS at all — a PC that won't boot.

Most motherboards that support flash BIOS include a jumper block that can be set to disallow flash updates. To flash the BIOS ROM, the flashing security jumper has to be in the correct position. If you plan to flash your BIOS, open the system case and check the position of this jumper. After you flash the BIOS, reset this jumper and you're prevented from accidentally flashing it again. Another good reason to use the flashing security jumper is to prevent access from computer viruses that attempt to change the flash BIOS code.

The BIOS savior

The boot block is a 4K emergency boot program included with the BIOS. The flashing recovery mode allows you to recover from an incorrect or corrupted BIOS. The boot block will restore the BIOS from a special floppy disk or CD-ROM, available from the BIOS manufacturer. If the motherboard supports it, this feature may need to be enabled through a jumper.

Getting Ready for Work

Lab 4-1, which details the process used to flash a PC's BIOS, provides an opportunity to sharpen your BIOS knowledge and working skills. This lab is intended to provide you with essential knowledge for the workplace, but it can't hurt your chances for passing the A+ Core Technologies Exam.

This doesn't involve trench coats and dark alleys, but it involves changing the contents of your PC's EEPROM or flash ROM. Before you start this lab, you should try to have a copy of the documentation for the PC's motherboard, processor, and chipset, and you should absolutely have a written copy of all of the configuration settings in the PC's BIOS setup files. And it can't hurt to take a full backup of the PC's hard drives too.

Lab 4-1   Flashing Your BIOS

1. **Using the serial number and model number of the motherboard, locate on the manufacturer's Website the Web page that allows you to download the latest revisions to your PC's BIOS.**

2. Following the instructions on the manufacturer's Website, download the flashing software and update file to your PC.

3. If you don't already have one, either create a bootable disk (or CD), or visit www.bootdisk.com for a boot disk for your operating system. A Windows 98 boot disk should work.

4. Copy the .bin file (which should be something like bios.bin) from the BIOS update and the flashing utility (something like AWDFLASH.EXE) to the boot disk.

5. Reboot the PC to the boot disk and at the A:\ prompt, enter the name of the flashing utility and enter the name of the BIOS update file when requested. Be sure not to interrupt this process at all.

   In fact, hold your breath and stand perfectly still until the message appears that the BIOS update has completed. Okay, so you don't need to be that careful, but be careful all the same.

6. Remove the floppy disk and reboot your PC. Check the BIOS settings against the written backup you created to ensure that any advanced settings are carried forward.

Prep Test

1 **What does the acronym BIOS stand for?**

A ○ Binary Input Output System

B ○ Basic Independent Operating System

C ○ Basic Input Output System

D ○ It has no specific meaning.

2 **Starting the PC when it's powered off causes which type of boot cycle to be performed?**

A ○ cold boot

B ○ warm boot

C ○ dead boot

D ○ restart

3 **The hardware configuration and chipset features of a PC are stored in which type of memory?**

A ○ ECC

B ○ DRAM

C ○ CMOS

D ○ EDO

4 **Which of the following ROM types can be reprogrammed under software control?**

A ○ ROM

B ○ PROM

C ○ EPROM

D ○ EEPROM

5 **Using a software utility to upgrade the BIOS is called**

A ○ flashing

B ○ strobing

C ○ burning

D ○ upgrading

6 The BIOS is loaded into which area of system memory?

A ○ Conventional

B ○ Upper memory block

C ○ Extended memory

D ○ High memory area

7 What event signals the end of the boot sequence?

A ○ POWER GOOD signal

B ○ The operating system is running

C ○ A single beep code

D ○ The POST process ends

8 POST error messages in the 3xx series indicate an error with which component?

A ○ Motherboard

B ○ Keyboard

C ○ Floppy disk controller

D ○ Hard drive controller

9 What is the purpose of the boot block?

A ○ Prevent the system from rebooting during flashing

B ○ Reboot the system when the power supply is dead

C ○ Restore the BIOS if it becomes corrupted

D ○ Restore the supervisor and user passwords

10 Which of the following actions is not performed during the boot sequence?

A ○ A backup copy is made of the CMOS configuration data

B ○ POST process

C ○ Serial and parallel ports are assigned their port identities

D ○ The configuration summary screen is displayed

Answers

1 **C.** The BIOS is the basic input/output interface between the operating system and the hardware. *See "Getting to Know the BIOS."*

2 **A.** The "cold" refers to fact that the system is not powered on or warm. *Review "Starting cold and running warm."*

3 **C.** The CMOS memory holds all of the BIOS related hardware and advanced feature settings. *Check out "Setting the BIOS configuration."*

4 **D.** Electronically Erasable Programmable Read-Only Memory (EEPROM) can be reprogrammed using special software utilities. *Take a look at "BIOS Chipology."*

5 **A.** Flashing is the process used to upgrade a BIOS by replacing the contents of the BIOS ROM with a newer version. *Peruse "Updating the BIOS."*

6 **D.** The last 64K of the first megabyte of memory is reserved for the BIOS program. *Look over "Taking the high memory road."*

7 **B.** The last step of the boot sequence is to load the operating system and turn control over to it. The BIOS remains in RAM to handle interactions with the hardware. *See "Booting Up the System."*

8 **B.** The 300 series indicates a boot error with the keyboard. The specific error depends on the BIOS manufacturer and how they have assigned the error codes. *Review "Decoding POST messages."*

9 **C.** On those systems equipped to do so, the boot block provides a safety net that allows the BIOS to be restored from a floppy disk or a CD-ROM. *Check out "The BIOS savior."*

10 **A.** A backup copy of the CMOS is not made; you should make a copy on paper every time you make any changes to the BIOS configuration settings. *Take a look at "Booting Up the System."*

Chapter 5

Bus Structures

● ●

Exam Objectives

▶ Identifying PC motherboard expansion buses

▶ Explaining the function of Plug and Play (PnP)

▶ Defining the PC Card (PCMCIA) interface

▶ Configuring IRQs, DMAs, I/O addresses, and logical devices

● ●

*I*nterfacing with the system is one area of the A+ exams that's detail oriented and precise. In many exam domains, a general knowledge of basic concepts is usually sufficient; that's not true for the topics in this chapter.

As a PC repair technician, much of your job is adding new or replacing old hardware, which involves installing new adapter cards and cabling in customer PCs. These tasks require a thorough understanding of each motherboard's associated bus structures, IRQs, DMA functions, and input/output addressing. A solid understanding of how these technologies function gives you the confidence to plug a new high-priced video card into the appropriate expansion slot and set it up correctly with the operating system. Installing, configuring, and cabling new peripherals and adapter cards are the most techie parts of being a PC technician.

This is a chapter to read carefully, especially if you don't often do this type of work. Although its specific domain will have only around ten questions, as much as 40 percent of both A+ tests may have questions relating to this chapter's topics. I condense many facts and concepts into this chapter to help you prepare for the questions that probably trip most of the people who fail the exams.

Quick Assessment

Identifying PC mother-board expansion buses

1   The two general types of bus structures on every motherboard are _____ and _____.

2   The system bus provides four different system necessities: _____, _____, _____, and _____.

3   The ISA architecture provides a(n) _____-bit bus.

4   _____ was the first 32-bit architecture.

Explaining the function of Plug and Play

5   _____ is a configuration standard that allows the BIOS and operating system to automatically configure expansion boards and device adapters.

Defining the PC Card (PCMCIA) interface

6   The Type II PC Card is primarily used to add _____ or _____ to portable computers.

Configuring IRQs, DMAs, I/O addresses, and logical devices

7   _____ are the resources used to interface, communicate, and control individual device adapters and controllers.

8   A(n) _____ channel allows a device to bypass the processor to access memory directly.

9   A(n) _____ is a signal from a device to the processor that a service or special action is needed.

10   The default IRQ for COM1 is _____.

11   The default I/O address for LPT1 is _____.

Answers

1 *Internal, external.* See "Bus Structure Basics."

2 *Power, control signals, addresses,* and *data.* Review "Understanding the internal bus."

3 *16.* Study "Plugging into the expansion bus."

4 *MCA (Micro-Channel Architecture).* Review "Plugging into the expansion bus."

5 *Plug and Play.* Review "Fun with Plug and Play."

6 *Modems* or *NICs (network interface cards).* Take a look at "Upgrading notebooks and portables."

7 *System resources.* See "Working with System Resources."

8 *DMA (direct memory access).* Review "Accessing memory directly with DMA."

9 *Interrupt.* Study "Requesting an interrupt, or how to get IRQed."

10 *IRQ 4.* Take a look at "Using input/output (I/O) addresses."

11 *378h.* See "Using input/output (I/O) addresses."

Bus Structure Basics

Although a question on the Core Hardware exam may involve the definition of a bus, most of this first section is background information for the real techie stuff that follows. The bottom of any PC motherboard is an interconnecting maze of pathways that transport data, addresses, and instructions around the system. Each of these pathways is a *bus,* which is a group of tiny, very thin wires that carry signals from one part of the motherboard to another.

Two general types of bus structures are on every motherboard:

- **Internal bus:** Interconnects main memory, the CPU, and all other components on the motherboard
- **External (expansion) bus:** Connects the outside world of peripherals to the motherboard

When I compare a bus to a multilane highway, I'm referring to the size (meaning its width or capacity) of the bus. The width of a bus determines the amount of data and how large an address it can transmit. The width of a bus is stated in bits. Just like a 4-lane highway has a capacity for 4 vehicles at a time, a 16-bit bus is capable of transmitting 16 bits of data at a time, and a 32-bit bus can transmit 32 bits of data. Obviously, the wider a bus is in bits, the more data it can carry.

The speed at which data moves on a bus is controlled by its clock speed, which is measured in megahertz (MHz). If the speed limit on the highway is faster, more cars and trucks per hour can move over it. Likewise, higher bus speeds can transmit more data per second. Think of it this way: If a bus (a passenger bus) must carry 300 people from point A to point B, but has a carrying capacity of only 66 people at a time, it must make several trips. The faster the bus makes its outbound and inbound trips, the sooner all the people get to beautiful downtown point B. Another solution would be to get a bigger bus. A faster bus (the computer kind) can transfer more data faster, which makes the operating system and applications run faster. For the exam, you must understand the compatibilities, capabilities, and limitations of the various bus architectures detailed in this chapter.

Understanding the internal bus

You need a good understanding of general bus architectures for the A+ Core Hardware exam. You may not be asked any specific questions from this area, but it helps you understand some of the questions you will be asked.

Concentrate on the various bus architectures used in device I/O (chipsets and expansion cards), which is where you, the repair technician, usually come into contact with the bus. Don't worry about the difference between the specific system bus structures of a 386 processor and the latest Pentium technology.

The internal bus, also known as the *system bus,* is that maze of wires on the motherboard. It provides the internal components of the computer with four necessities:

- ✔ **Power:** Power comes to the motherboard straight from the power supply. The motherboard uses the *system bus* to distribute power to components mounted on or plugged into it.

- ✔ **Control signals:** The control unit within the CPU sends out control signals to coordinate the activities of the system. These signals are carried on the internal *control bus.*

- ✔ **Addresses:** PC components pass data and instructions between one another using memory location addresses to reference the location of the data or instructions in memory. Addresses are transmitted on the internal *address bus.*

- ✔ **Data:** Data and instructions are transferred between components on the internal *data bus.*

PC buses carry data, instructions, or the addresses of data or instructions. Just as a passenger bus stops at different places to pick up or drop off people, a PC bus deposits or collects addresses or data at the different components (such as CPU and memory) to which it is connected. The address carried on the address bus references the source or destination location of the data or instructions carried on the data bus.

The contents of the address and data buses are like a letter in the mail:

- ✔ The envelope (the letter's address bus) has the address of the letter's destination.

- ✔ The message in the envelope (the letter's data bus) is its data.

On Pentium motherboards, the system chipset is the communications controller between all the components that interact with the system bus. The system chipset coordinates with each component or device so that each device properly interacts with every other one.

Defining the external (expansion) bus

For the exam, you need to know what each expansion bus feature is, how each is used, and understand how and why each is applied. This understanding also helps you elsewhere in this chapter.

In the context of the PC, when most people refer to "the bus," they are referring to both the data bus and (without knowing it) the address bus. The external bus must connect and coordinate with these two internal bus workhorses.

Earlier in this chapter, I list the external bus as one of the general bus structures of the PC. This bus, also called the *expansion bus,* allows peripheral devices to communicate with the motherboard and its components, almost like they were a part of the motherboard itself. To add a new device to the PC, the device's adapter card is plugged into the expansion bus via a compatible expansion slot on the motherboard. After it's plugged in, the device is able to communicate with the CPU and other system components.

The expansion slot for any of the supported expansion bus architectures comprises a certain number of small metal spring connectors that line each side of the connector slot. The slot connectors match up with the tabs on the card's edge connectors, as shown in Figure 5-1.

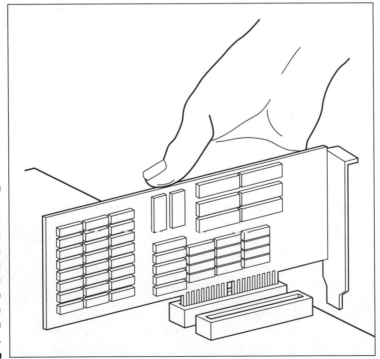

Figure 5-1:
The connectors on an expansion card are aligned to those in the expansion slot.

Like pins in a serial or parallel cable, each connection between the slot and the card form a channel that services a need of the expansion card:

- **Clock signal:** This connection provides the card with the signal of the bus clock so that it can synchronize its communications with the buses of the motherboard.

- **Interrupt request (IRQ):** A request that tells the CPU to interrupt what it's doing to take care of the special needs of the device sending the IRQ. Devices are assigned IRQ numbers so that the CPU knows which device is the rude one. When you install a new device that requires services from the CPU, it is assigned an IRQ number, which enables the CPU to know which device is nagging it and requesting service. On occasion, devices may share an IRQ, provided both devices do not attempt to interact with the CPU at the same time.

- **Direct memory access (DMA):** DMA channels allow certain devices to bypass the processor and access main memory directly. DMA devices have the intelligence to handle their own data transfers to memory. Some bus architectures allow more DMA channels than others, but two devices can't share a DMA channel.

- **Input/Output (I/O) address:** Assigned to a device via its expansion slot. The I/O address, also called an *I/O port* or *hardware port,* allows the CPU to send commands directly to the device by writing them to an assigned area in memory that the device checks frequently. The I/O address is a one-way-only line that works like a reverse IRQ. The CPU uses the I/O address to send a command to the device. If the device responds, it uses the data bus or DMA channel to do so. Only one device can be assigned to an I/O address.

- **Bus mastering:** Allows one device to interact directly with another. Usually, the expansion card plugged into a slot has a bus master processor on the card that directs this activity.

  Most modern motherboards, especially those with the PCI bus (see "Plugging into the expansion bus," later in this chapter), support bus mastering because it improves performance.

Fun with Plug and Play

Plug and Play (PnP) is a configuration standard that allows the system BIOS and the operating system to configure expansion boards and other devices automatically so that the user or PC technician won't have to worry about setting DIP switches, jumpers, and system resources (such as IRQ, I/O, addresses, and DMA). In effect, you just plug in the device or adapter card and play with it.

To use PnP on a system, four requirements must be met:

- ✔ The system BIOS must support PnP.
- ✔ The motherboard and its chipset must support PnP.
- ✔ The operating system running on the PC must support PnP.
- ✔ The bus of the expansion slot used must be compatible with PnP.

All versions of Windows since Windows 95 (including Windows 2000) fully support PnP (although Windows NT only partially supports it). PnP is compatible with ISA, EISA, MCA, PC Card (PCMCIA), and PCI devices and adapters. All PCI devices are PnP, but not all PnP devices are PCI devices.

Plugging into the expansion bus

For the exam, you need to know what differentiates one expansion bus architecture from another and which are the most commonly used types.

One bit of terminology adjustment is needed here: An expansion bus architecture is the same as an expansion slot type.

Several expansion architectures have been used in PCs over the years, including 8-bit, ISA, EISA, MCA, VLB, and PCI. When you open the PC's case and look at the motherboard, the expansion slots you likely see are ISA, AGP, and PCI, as illustrated in Figure 5-2. A motherboard can often support several types of expansion slots.

Here's a brief description of each of the expansion slot architectures that has been used in PCs:

- ✔ **8-bit bus:** Not many of these left around, so don't worry about it for the exam.
- ✔ **Industry Standard Architecture (ISA):** Pronounced "ice-ah," ISA was introduced with the IBM AT and called the *AT bus* in its early days; it provided a 16-bit data bus. As shown in Figure 5-3, the ISA bus is characterized by adding an additional short slot to a slot on the 8-bit bus to create the 16-bit connector. ISA added eight additional IRQs and doubled the number of DMA channels. ISA expansion cards were designated to the appropriate IRQ or DMA numbers through jumpers and DIP switches. The ISA architecture also separated the bus clock from the CPU clock to allow the slower data bus to operate at its own speeds. ISA slots are found on 286, 386, 486, and some Pentium PCs.

ISA/EISA
Slots

PCI Slots

AGP
Slot

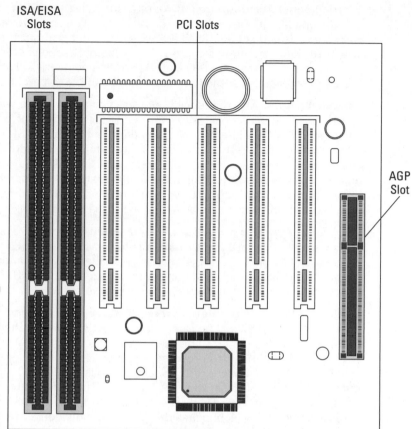

Figure 5-2:
The
expansion
slots most
often found
on a
mother-
board.

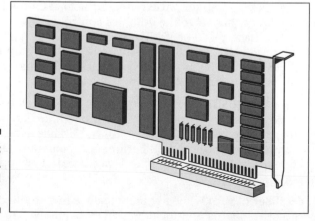

Figure 5-3:
The ISA
16-bit card
and slot.

✔ **Micro-Channel Architecture (MCA):** Introduced with the IBM PS/2, MCA was the first 32-bit option. It featured bus mastering and a 10 MHz bus clock for expansion cards. The MCA expansion slot is about the same size as the ISA slot, but has about twice as many channels. MCA cards are also configured to their IRQ and DMA assignments by software, which is an improvement over the jumpers and DIPs of the ISA architecture.

✔ **Extended ISA (EISA):** Pronounced "ee-sah," this architecture was developed by a group of companies to overcome the limitations of ISA and compete with MCA. EISA takes the best parts of MCA and builds on them. It has a 32-bit data bus, uses software setup, has more I/O addresses available, and ignores IRQs and DMA channels. EISA uses only an 8 MHz bus clock to be backward compatible to ISA boards. (A device that is backward compatible supports all of its previous versions.) In this case, EISA supports ISA expansion boards along with its own.

✔ **VESA Local Bus (VLB or VL-bus):** VLB was used first on 486 systems and grew from the need for the data bus to run at the same clock speed as the CPU. VLB was developed by the Video Electronics Standards Association (VESA) to place a port more or less directly on the system bus with what was called a *bus slot* or a *processor direct slot.*

✔ **Peripheral Component Interconnect (PCI) bus:** Introduced with the Pentium PC, PCI is a local bus architecture that supports either a 32- or 64-bit bus, which allows it to be used with both 486 and Pentium computers. The PCI bus is also processor independent because of a special bridging circuit contained on PCI boards. Its bus speed is 33 MHz, giving it much higher throughput than earlier cards. The PCI architecture and expansion slot, shown in Figure 5-4, also support ISA and EISA cards. PCI cards are also PnP, which means they automatically configure themselves to the appropriate IRQ, DMA, and I/O port addresses.

✔ **Accelerated Graphics Port (AGP):** Based on PCI, but designed specifically for supporting 3D graphics, AGP reduces the load on the PCI bus by providing a direct channel to the graphics controller. AGP uses a 32-bit channel with a base speed of 66 MHz, which translates to twice the PCI bandwidth of 133 MBps at 266 MBps in its 1X (1 times) mode. AGP 2X (2 times) provides 533 MBps, AGP 4X provides 1.07 GBps, and the newer AGP 8X (Pro) provides 2.2 GBps in bandwidth.

✔ **Universal Serial Bus (USB):** The USB connectors are located externally on the PC's case. Almost every newer PC has two to four USB ports available. Compared to other PC bus structures, USB has a few unique qualities: USB provides power to USB peripherals, communicates at data speeds of 1.5 Mbps to 12 Mbps, and USB devices are hot swappable and Plug and Play.

✔ **Audio Model Riser (AMR):** While not technically a bus architecture, many newer motherboards now include AMR slots into which AMR riser cards can be inserted to add support for sound or modem functions. A PCI modem card or a sound card can be inserted into an AMR slot.

✓ **Communications Network Riser (CNR):** CNR, while not a bus architecture, provides an on-motherboard slot through which LAN or home networking, DSL, USB, wireless communications, audio, or modem system can be implemented on a PC. The CNR slot, available on many newer motherboards, connects through the USB bus to accept modems and networking devices configured from CNR slots.

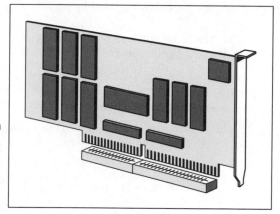

Figure 5-4:
The PCI
card and
slot.

For the exam, remember the bus width in bits for each bus structure, especially the ones that are 32 or more bits. Table 5-1 summarizes the basic characteristics of the bus structures discussed earlier.

Table 5-1		Bus Architecture Characteristics	
Bus	*Bus Width (bits)*	*Bus Speed (MHz)*	*How Configured*
8-bit	8	8	Jumpers and DIP switches
ISA	16	8	Jumpers and DIP switches
MCA	32	10	Software
EISA	32	8	Software
VL-Bus	32	Processor speed (up to 40 MHz)	Jumpers and DIP switches
PCI	32/64	Processor speed (up to 33 MHz)	PnP
USB	Serial	Serial	PnP
AGP	32	66 MHz	PnP

Upgrading notebooks and portables

The *PC Card,* or its original name *PCMCIA (Personal Computer Memory Card International Association) bus,* adds external devices to a notebook or hand-held computer. PC cards (which are about the size of a credit card) add memory, modems, network interface cards, and even hard disk drives to portable computers. These cards slide into slots that are usually on the side of a notebook computer. The three PC Cards standards are

- ✔ **Type I:** Cards that are 3.3 mm thick and used for memory additions. Type I cards have a single row of connectors.

- ✔ **Type II:** Cards that are 5 mm thick and used primarily to add modems or network interface cards (NICs). Type II cards have two rows of connectors.

- ✔ **Type III:** Cards that are up to 10.5 mm thick and used to add an external hard drive to a notebook computer. Type III cards have four rows of connectors.

Expect a test question on the type of devices supported by the PC Card (PCMCIA) types.

You can *hot swap* PC Cards, which means you can remove or insert them with the system's power on.

Using SCSI

The *Small Computers System Interface* (*SCSI,* pronounced "skuzzy") is an interface and not technically an architecture. It connects a wide variety of internal and external devices, such as CD-ROM drives, printers, and scanners. Depending on the SCSI standard in use, up to 7 to 15 different SCSI devices can be attached in a daisy-chain fashion to the host adapter card installed in PC's expansion slot. SCSI is a technology for interfacing multiple devices through a single connection on the motherboard. SCSI adapter cards can be PCI, VL-Bus, EISA, or ISA.

Bus interfacing

Most of the later PC systems (486 and later) support multiple bus interfaces. On these systems, provisions must be made to interconnect the different bus architectures and allow their devices to communicate with one another. This is accomplished using a *bridge*, which connects two dissimilar systems. The most common bridge is the PCI-ISA bridge supplied by the chipset in virtually all Pentium systems. To see the interface bridges on your PC, use the Windows Device Manager and access the System Devices tab, as shown in Figure 5-5. The Windows Device Manager lists the controllers and bridges supplied by the chipset.

Figure 5-5: The Windows Device Manager's System Devices tab shows the device bridges included on the chipset.

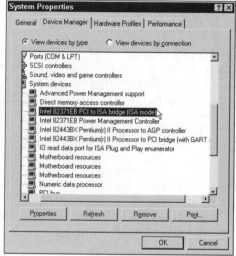

Working with System Resources

In the realm of PC configuration, the term *system resources* refers to the mechanisms used to interface, communicate, and control individual device adapters and controllers, along with the serial, parallel, and mouse ports. Usually, the CPU and the peripheral devices on a PC use the elements of the system resources as a set of communications channels. Any device (including the motherboard, expansion cards, and peripherals) that wants to communicate with the CPU must use at least one of the system resource components: the *IRQ (interrupt requests), I/O (input/output) ports* (also known as *I/O addresses*), and *DMA (direct memory access)* channels.

This area of the Core Hardware exam requires memorization. You must know

✔ The relationships of the primary system resources, especially IRQs are used with which devices (see "Requesting an interrupt, or how to get IRQed"); which devices are assigned to which I/O addresses (see "Using input/output (I/O) addresses"); and the use and common assignments of DMA channels. (See "Accessing memory directly with DMA.")

✔ The physical and logical devices (see "Naming the logical devices") to which the system resources are assigned.

Requesting an interrupt, or how to get IRQed

An *interrupt* is a request from a device (other than the CPU) to the CPU for a service, action, or special action. If you've ever dined at a large coffee shop chain, you've probably seen a form of interrupt processing in use. Usually, above the kitchen service window is a sign with a bank of numbers that can be individually lighted. When the very busy server has an order ready, the cook lights up the server's number on the sign. When the server is able to interrupt what he or she is doing, he or she serves that order to the customer. The server number that alerts the server to the order is much like the interrupt requests used in PC interrupt processing. When a device needs the CPU to perform a task (such as transferring data from memory or issuing an I/O), it sends a signal to the CPU using the IRQ line it is assigned. Each device is assigned a specific IRQ number (much like the food server) so that the processor knows the device to which it must respond.

Interrupt requests are sent to a special system component, called an *interrupt controller,* which is either a separate chip on the motherboard or incorporated into the chipset. The interrupt controller receives and verifies requests and passes them on to the processor. Two interrupt controllers have been on PCs since the 286, each managing eight IRQ lines with each IRQ tied directly to a particular device. The two interrupt controllers are linked, or *cascaded,* through IRQ 2, which is set aside for this purpose.

Conflicting interrupts

For the exam, understand the ramification of IRQ conflicts and how to avoid them.

An IRQ is assigned to one specific device; although two devices can share an IRQ, it just doesn't work to have them active at the same time. Assigning two active devices to the same IRQ creates an *IRQ conflict,* a serious system no-no. If two devices are assigned the same interrupt, the processor could become confused and send its response to the wrong device at the wrong time, causing untold horrors to happen.

An IRQ conflict can cause both devices to perform sporadically (in the best case) or not at all (in the worst case). Similar devices can share IRQs, but they can't be used at the same time. IRQs are assigned by the system BIOS during POST and the boot process. Reassigning an IRQ or changing the assigned IRQ of a device is done differently, depending on the adapter card and perhaps the operating system.

Windows 2000 and Windows XP systems handle IRQs a bit differently than earlier operating systems. Specifically, features like IRQ Sharing, which has been used on PCI devices on earlier systems, is expanded to include other ports and devices on Advanced Configuration and Power Interface (ACPI) motherboards. If you look in the Device Manager on a Windows XP system running on an ACPI motherboard, you should notice that several devices are sharing IRQ 9.

✔ On PCs running DOS and Windows 3.*x*, a device IRQ can be set through either a jumper on its adapter card or proprietary installation software.

✔ On Windows 9*x*, Windows 2000, and Windows XP PCs, a device's IRQ assignment can be managed through the Device Manager.

Lab 5-1 lists the steps you use to access IRQ settings on a Windows PC, a topic that is likely to appear on both of the A+ exams. Although each Windows version may set its IRQs differently, the one thing they have in common is the Device Manager. Lab 5-1 and Lab 5-2 detail the steps to view IRQs on a Windows system.

Lab 5-1   Accessing IRQs from the Desktop

1. **Right-click the My Computer icon on the Desktop to display a shortcut menu.**

2. **Choose Properties from the menu to display the System Properties box.**

Lab 5-2   Accessing IRQs from the Control Panel

1. **From the Start⇨Settings menu, open the Control Panel.**

2. **Click the System icon.**

3. **Choose the Device Manager tab, click the Computer level icon, and then choose Properties.**

4. **From the System Resources display, choose the View Resources tab and click the Interrupt Request (IRQ) option to display the IRQ settings, as shown in Figure 5-6.**

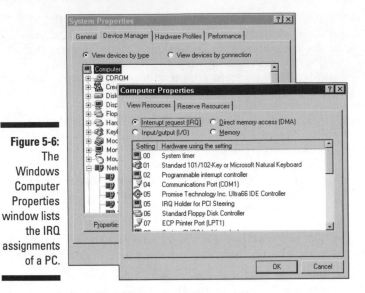

Figure 5-6:
The
Windows
Computer
Properties
window lists
the IRQ
assignments
of a PC.

Using the Windows Device Manager, IRQ settings are changed or assigned in the properties of the individual device.

Assigning IRQs

For the exam, study Table 5-2 carefully. You should know the IRQ assignments for devices standard to all PCs.

Table 5-2		Default IRQ Assignments
IRQ #	*Default Use*	*Description*
0	System timer	Reserved interrupt for the internal system timer.
1	Keyboard controller	Reserved interrupt for the keyboard controller.
2	Bridge to IRQs 8–15	In cascaded interrupt systems, IRQ 2 is used as a link to IRQs 8–15, which means it's not available for general use; if needed by an older system, it's replaced by IRQ 9 (see "Requesting an interrupt, or how to get IRQed" for information on cascaded interrupts). You may also see IRQ 2 assigned to programmable interrupt control.

IRQ #	Default Use	Description
3	COM2 and COM4	Many modems are preconfigured for COM2 on IRQ 3. It's also used as the default interrupt for COM4, if a system has four serial ports in use.
4	COM1	Normally used by the serial mouse. It's also the default interrupt for COM3.
5	Sound card	Often the default IRQ for network interface cards. Used on some older systems for the hard disk drive and is the default interrupt for LPT2 (the second parallel port). Most sound cards are preset to IRQ 5.
6	Floppy disk controller	Reserved for the floppy disk controller (FDC).
7	LPT1	This interrupt is normally used for the first parallel port.
8	Real-time clock	Reserved for the real-time clock timer, which is used by software to track events to "real world" time. (IRQs 8–15 are not available on an 8-bit system.)
9	None	A popular choice for network interface cards, but it's generally available for any use. It replaces IRQ 2 in cascading interrupt systems, so it should not be used if IRQ 2 is in use. Hardware MPEG 2 cards and SCSI host adapters can also use it.
10	None	This IRQ has no specific default settings; it is commonly used for video cards and modems.
11	None	No default assignment; it is used by some SCSI host adapters, PCI video cards, IDE sound cards, and USB controllers.
12	Motherboard mouse (PS/2) connector	On motherboards supporting a PS/2 mouse (mini-DIN connection on the motherboard), this IRQ is reserved for the PS/2 mouse. A PS/2 mouse on this interrupt frees up IRQ 4 (and COM1) for other uses. Some video cards may also use this IRQ.
13	Math coprocessor or floating point unit (FPU)	Reserved for the integrated floating point unit (386DX and later) or a math coprocessor (386SX and earlier).

(continued)

Table 5-2 (continued)

IRQ #	Default Use	Description
14	Primary IDE adapter	Reserved for the primary IDE controller, which controls the first two IDE (ATA) disk drives. On PCs with no IDE devices, it can be reassigned in the BIOS setup for other uses.
15	Secondary IDE adapter	Reserved for a secondary IDE controller, if present. Can be reassigned in BIOS, if needed.

Using input/output (I/O) addresses

For the exam, remember the starting I/O address for devices common to all PCs. Every device must have a unique address. You won't find trick questions in this area.

Every device in the PC uses *input/output addresses* (which are also known as I/O addresses, I/O ports, or I/O port addresses). The address in the I/O address points to the location in memory that's assigned to a specific device to use for exchanging information between itself and the rest of the PC. The I/O address is a device's internal post office box number.

Virtually every device in the PC is assigned an I/O address and a segment of memory to hold messages and data. The size of the memory segment varies with the amount of data a device must pass on to other devices; in general, the memory segment assigned to a device ranges from 1 to 32 bytes, with 4, 8, or 16 bytes being common. These areas of memory allow a device to work without worrying about what other devices or the processor may be doing.

For example, when a modem receives data, it wants to pass the data along to the PC for processing; where can the data be put? The modem writes the data to the I/O address of the COM port to which the modem is attached, and when the CPU is ready to process this data, it knows where to look. This process of using I/O addresses to complete input/output operations is called *memory-mapped I/O.*

I/O addresses are expressed in hexadecimal and written as 3F8h. The lower-case "h" indicates it's a hexadecimal address. When working with I/O addresses, it's not important to determine the size of the memory segment assigned or even decipher the hex address itself. Just remember these addresses are in hexadecimal and ignore the *h.*

For the exam, memorize only the starting addresses of devices that are common to all PCs, such as the keyboard, LPT1, and COM1.

Table 5-3 lists most of the common I/O address assignments used in PC systems.

Table 5-3	Common I/O Address Assignments
I/O Address Range	*Device or Port Commonly Assigned*
000-00Fh	DMA channels 0–3 controller
020-021h	IRQ 0–7 interrupt controller
060h, 061h	Keyboard
0F8-0FFh	Math coprocessor
130-14Fh	SCSI host adapter
170-177h	Secondary hard drive controller
1F0-1F7h	Primary hard drive controller
200-207h	Game port
220-22Fh	Sound cards
278-27Fh	LPT2 or LPT3
2E8-2EFh	COM4
2F8-2FFh	COM2
300-30Fh	Network cards
3B0-3BBh	VGA video adapter
3C0-3DFh	VGA video adapter
378-37Fh	LPT1 or LPT2
3E8-3EFh	COM3
3F0-3F7h	Floppy disk controller
3F8-3FFh	COM1

You can view I/O address assignments on a PC using the Windows Device Manager's Computer Properties dialog box, as shown in Figure 5-7.

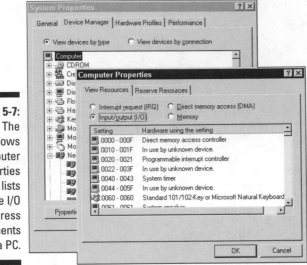

Figure 5-7:
The
Windows
Computer
Properties
window lists
the I/O
address
assignments
of a PC.

Accessing memory directly with DMA

There are no questions on the A+ Core Hardware exam regarding the default assignment of DMA channels. Concentrate your studies on what a DMA channel is and does.

A *direct memory access* (DMA) channel allows a device to bypass the processor to directly access memory. Those devices with a DMA channel assignment gain the advantage of faster data transfers that do not have to pass through the CPU. Not every device on the PC needs or uses DMA channels. DMA use is common in some disk drives, tape drives, and sound cards. Most operating systems handle DMA assignments through PnP configuration. One drawback to using DMA is that while the DMA device is working faster, the CPU may be put on hold, slowing everything else until the DMA data transfer is complete.

A DMA channel can be assigned to only one hardware device. If two devices are assigned to the same DMA channel, both devices will have problems or the PC may crash. Sound cards seem to have the most trouble with DMA conflicts, primarily because they are hard to preset to a particular DMA channel. Most other DMA devices are more flexible; they'll take whatever DMA channel is available.

The best way to avoid DMA conflicts initiated by the sound card is to install it before installing other devices that require DMA channels (such as a scanner or a CD-ROM drive).

Table 5-4 lists common DMA channel usage. However, the assignments on your PC may assign the same devices to different channels, which is common.

Table 5-4	DMA Channel Assignments
DMA Channel	*Assignment*
0	DRAM refresh
1	Sound card
2	Floppy disk drive
3	ECP or EPP parallel port
4	DMA controller
5	Sound card
6	Available
7	ISA IDE Hard Drive Controller

DMA channel assignments can be set using one of these methods:

✔ Preset assignments of a device's adapter card, DIP switches, or jumpers on the device adapter card

✔ Assignments made during PnP configuration

✔ The BIOS setup utility

You can view DMA channel assignments in the Windows Device Manager's Computer Properties dialog box, as shown in Figure 5-8.

To view DMA channel assignments, follow these steps:

1. **On the Desktop, right-click My Computer.**

2. **Choose Properties from the shortcut menu that appears.**

3. **On a Windows 9*x* or Me system, click the Device Manager tab; or on a Windows 2000 or XP system, click the Device Manager button on the Hardware tab.**

4. **Highlight Computer at the top of the device hierarchy shown, and then click Properties.**

5. **Choose Direct Memory Access (DMA) to display the channel assignments on your system.**

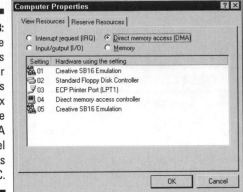

Figure 5-8:
The
Windows
Computer
Properties
dialog box
lists the
DMA
channel
assignments
of a PC.

You can also use these steps to view the status of the other system resources: IRQ, I/O address, and memory assignments.

Naming the logical devices

Many devices are assigned both a physical address and a logical name. Logical device names are assigned to serial ports (which are given the logical names COM1 to COM4) and parallel ports (LPT1 and LPT2). Logical names eliminate the need for software to track what could be the moving target of I/O addresses, not to mention the physical layout of the different motherboard form factors in use.

Logical device names are assigned during the POST process by the system BIOS. The BIOS searches the I/O addresses for devices in a preset order and assigns them a logical name in numerical order each time the system boots.

Table 5-5 lists the default assignments for COM and LPT ports.

Of the tables shown in this chapter, the following table may be the best one to review right before the exam. It's brief and holds most of the information about logical devices you should memorize for the test.

Unfortunately, to see logical device assignments on a Windows system, you must view each device separately. From the Device Manager dialog box, select the logical device from the device hierarchy and choose the Resources tab to see the device's system resource assignments, as shown in Figure 5-9. This window is also good for tracking down any resource conflicts a device may have.

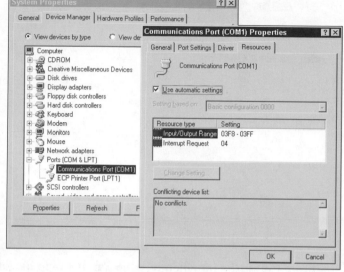

Figure 5-9:
The
Properties
window of
a logical
device
showing its
system
resource
assign-
ments.

Table 5-5	**Logical Device Name Assignments**	
Port	*I/O Address*	*Default IRQ*
COM1	3F8-3FFh	4
COM2	2F8-2FFh	3
COM3	3E8-3EFh	4
COM4	2E8-2EFh	3
LPT1	378-37Fh	7
LPT2	278-27Fh	5

One way to remember at least one IRQ assignment is to add the 1 from COM1 to the 3 from COM3 to get the 4 from IRQ4. This memory aid is fairly complicated, and perhaps convoluted, but it worked for me.

Prep Test

1 The default I/O address for COM1 is

A ○ 2F8-2FFh

B ○ 3F8-3FFh

C ○ 378-37Fh

D ○ 3F0-3F7H

2 The first 32-bit bus was

A ○ PCI

B ○ EISA

C ○ MCA

D ○ VESA

3 A PC has a sound card that locks up whenever the parallel tape backup unit is used on the system. What is the most likely problem?

A ○ A DMA channel conflict

B ○ An IRQ conflict

C ○ The sound card is installed in an incompatible bus slot

D ○ There is no system problem other than a defective sound card

4 To automatically configure a PnP device, a system must have all the following except

A ○ A PnP BIOS

B ○ PnP hardware devices

C ○ A PnP OS

D ○ A PCI system bus

5 COM1 normally uses which IRQ?

A ○ IRQ 2

B ○ IRQ 3

C ○ IRQ 4

D ○ IRQ 5

6 **The CPU uses an IRQ to**

    A ○ Control devices attached to the system

    B ○ Generate a log file containing interrupt requests

    C ○ Identify a peripheral and find the software that controls it

    D ○ Protect the system from hardware device failures

7 **What IRQ is often used for LPT1?**

    A ○ IRQ 2

    B ○ IRQ 10

    C ○ IRQ 7

    D ○ IRQ 5

8 **What should you do about an IRQ conflict?**

    A ○ Reassign the device IRQ settings using the best appropriate method

    B ○ Nothing, if the I/O addresses of the devices aren't in conflict

    C ○ Nothing, if the devices are never used at the same time

    D ○ Always refer to the devices by their logical device names

9 **Bus clock speed refers to**

    A ○ The external speed of the CPU

    B ○ The internal speed of the CPU

    C ○ The speed of the hard drive

    D ○ The speed at which data on the bus moves

10 **A PC Card hard drive fits in which type of slot?**

    A ○ Type I

    B ○ Type II

    C ○ Type III

    D ○ Type IV

Answers

1 **B.** *See "Using input/output (I/O) addresses."*

2 **C.** Micro-Channel Architecture was the first 32-bit expansion bus architecture. *Review "Plugging into the expansion bus."*

3 **B.** When two devices directly affect how the other one works, it's usually a system resource conflict, and probably an IRQ conflict. *Check out "Conflicting interrupts."*

4 **D.** PnP devices are available in just about every bus architecture. All PCI devices are PnP, but not all PnP devices are PCI. *See "Fun with Plug and Play."*

5 **C.** IRQ 4 is the default IRQ assignment for COM1. *Review "Assigning IRQs."*

6 **A.** Interrupts and IRQs (interrupt requests) are used by the processor to communicate and control the activities of peripheral devices. *Look at "Requesting an interrupt, or how to get IRQed."*

7 **C.** LPT1 (the first parallel port) is virtually always assigned IRQ 7. *See "Assigning IRQs."*

8 **A.** IRQ assignments can be made, depending on the device and operating system through a jumper on the card, installation software for the device, or through the operating system (Windows 95). *Check out "Conflicting interrupts."*

9 **D.** The bus clock controls the transfer rate of data on the data bus. *Review "Bus Structure Basics."*

10 **C.** Type I PCMCIA (PC Card) cards are used to install RAM; Type II cards are used to install a modem or network card; and Type III cards are used to install disk drives. *Take a look at "Upgrading notebooks and portables."*

Chapter 6

Microprocessors

● ●

Exam Objectives

▶ Distinguishing CPU chips by their basic characteristics

▶ Distinguishing among popular CPU chips

● ●

*T*he A+ Hardware Technology exam tests your knowledge of the central role that is played by the system's microprocessor, which has become essential knowledge for the professional PC repairperson. At one time, replacing the CPU was nearly as complicated as replacing a house, and I don't mean the kind of house that has wheels. But today's motherboards feature sockets and slots into which several types and versions of microprocessors can be inserted. You still have to watch out for compatibility issues, but it's not uncommon for customers to want you to upgrade their PC instead of replace it.

At least 10 percent of the A+ Hardware Technology exam is comprised of questions about processors, their characteristics, and their compatibilities. For each popular CPU (starting with the Pentium chip), you need to know its general characteristics — including physical size, voltage, caching abilities, and the socket or slot that it uses to mount to the motherboard — as well as details such as the number of pins on its packaging.

You need to memorize a bit in the CPU content area. The good news is that the processors before the Pentium and its clones have been eliminated from the exams. You don't need to worry about when the math coprocessor was integrated into the CPU or the data bus width of the 286 or 486 chip. Pentium-class processors, which include all brands (not just Intel), have steadily moved along a natural evolutionary path with few exceptions. The differences among the processors aren't so great.

Quick Assessment

Distinguishing CPU chips by their basic characteristics

1   The _____ performs all of the arithmetic, logic, and computing actions of a PC.

2   The three primary bus structures on most motherboards are _____, _____, and _____.

3   The _____ is a processor packaging that mounts into a single slot on the motherboard.

4   The Pentium processor generates about _____ degrees Fahrenheit.

5   The motherboard component that regulates the voltage that is fed to the processor is the _____.

6   The socket that mounts Celeron chips with 370 pins is the _____.

7   The slot style that mounts the Pentium II Xeon processor is the _____.

Distinguishing among popular CPU chips

8   The Pentium processor requires _____ volts.

9   The data bus on the Celeron processor is _____ bits wide.

10   The K6 processor is manufactured by _____.

Answers

1   *Microprocessor.* Take a look at "Looking at Microprocessors."

2   *Address, control, and data.* Review "On the CPU bus."

3   *SEC (Single Edge Connector)* or *SECC (Single Edge Connector Cartridge).* Review "CPU packaging."

4   *185.* See "Keeping the processor cool."

5   *Voltage regulator module.* Check out "Feeding power to the processor."

6   *Socket 370.* See "Socket to it."

7   *Slot 2.* Check out "Slot types."

8   *5.* Study the table in "Intel processors."

9   *64.* Review "Intel processors."

10 *AMD.* Take a look at "AMD processors."

Looking at Microprocessors

Everything that a computer can do for you — that is, all its magic — is performed by its microprocessor. The *microprocessor* performs all the arithmetic, logic, and computing actions of a PC. You may see your PC as a word processor, a computer game, a World Wide Web browser, an e-mail tool, or any of the other tasks that you perform on your PC. In fact, each of these tasks is software that is made up of thousands of instructions that the CPU executes one at a time to create the actions that you see and use. The *processor,* which is short for both *microprocessor* and *central processing unit (CPU),* is the electronic circuitry that uses digital logic to perform the instructions of your software.

Technically speaking, a microprocessor is an integrated circuit that contains millions of transistors that are interconnected by small aluminum wires. The microprocessor's processing capabilities control and direct the activities of the PC by interacting with the other electronic components on the motherboard, such as the main memory, bus structures, cache memory, and device interfaces.

You need to know about microprocessors in detail for the exam. This includes nitpicky stuff such as clock speeds, bus widths, features that are included or supported, mountings, packaging, manufacturer, and evolution. The subject of processors is an area where test writers can't resist getting specific. In many areas of the test, a sound, general knowledge of a subject can be enough to get you through, but not here. You need to know this stuff in detail.

On the CPU bus

The *bus,* as it relates to the pathways on the computer and in the processor, carries the various signals, addresses, and data that move about the PC between its components. The bus is a group of electronic transmission lines that interconnect the components of the CPU, motherboard, and expansion cards. Bus structures have different sizes, ranging from 16 to 64 bits on modern microprocessors, which determine the amount of data that can be transmitted. Just as an 8-lane highway carries more traffic than a 2-lane road, a 64-bit bus carries more data than a 16-bit bus.

A PC has several distinct bus structures; the most important are as follows:

✔ **Data bus:** Carries data to and from the CPU, main memory, and peripheral devices. The width (in bits) determines the amount of data that can be transmitted at a time.

✔ **Address bus:** Carries addresses of data and instructions between memory and the CPU. The width (in bits) determines the size of the address (represented as a binary number) that can be passed over the address bus.

✔ **Control bus:** Carries control information, such as the status of the devices, between the CPU and other devices. The information that is passed over the control bus provides data that indicates that data is ready to be read or a device is waiting to use the bus, and indicates the type of operation that a device is requesting (read, write, or interrupt).

Chapter 5 is dedicated to the bus structures of a PC.

CPU packaging

The microprocessor and its associated electronic circuits are packaged in a protective outer packaging. When you look at a processor, you see the packaging, not the microprocessor itself. Typically, the processor's packaging is ceramic or plastic.

The outer covering of the processor protects its core (also called the *die*), which contains the microchip and the wiring that connects the chip to the processor's mounting pins. A variety of packaging types have been used on processors. You should know the following types for the A+ Hardware Technology exam:

✔ **Pin Grid Array (PGA):** Common among early processors, the mounting pins are located on the bottom of the chip in concentric squares. Figure 6-1 contrasts this package to the Single Edge Connector (SEC) package. The earliest chips were packaged in the Ceramic PGA (CPGA). Later chips, including some current ones, use the Plastic PGA (PPGA). The early Pentium chips used a variation that staggered the pin pattern (to cram more pins onto the package) and surprisingly was called the Staggered PGA (SPGA). The Pentium III features a variation of the PGA package with its Slot 370–like Flip Chip–Pin Graphics Assembly (FC-PGA).

✔ **Plastic Ball Grid Array (PBGA):** The primary difference between this packaging technology and the PGA is that the PBGA doesn't have mounting pins projecting from the bottom of the chip; this eliminates the threat of bent pins on the bottom of the processor. Otherwise, these package styles look similar.

✔ **Single Edge Connector (SEC):** You may find a few variations on the name of this packaging technology, including the Single Edge Contact Cartridge (SECC) and others. They all boil down to a packaging style that is mounted perpendicular to the motherboard into a single slot, much like expansion cards and memory modules. The Pentium II was the first processor to sport this new packaging style.

Keeping the processor cool

Before the Intel 486, microprocessors were cooled primarily by the airflow inside the case that was created by a system fan in the power supply. This process was called *radiant cooling*. Any heat that was radiated by the processor was cooled by air being sucked by the fan into the system case. Beginning with the 486, processors are cooled with a *processor cooling fan* or a *heatsink* or both, attached directly to the surface of the processor. In addition, the system fan was reversed to extract the heated air from inside the computer case and force it out.

With the Pentium processors came heat and cooling problems for the PC. The Pentium chip runs much hotter than earlier CPUs and requires special heat dissipation and cooling. You need to know a few things about the heat problems and cooling requirements of the Pentium chips for the exam.

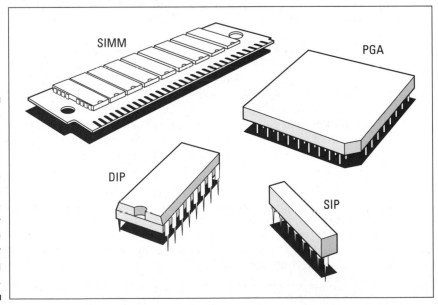

Figure 6-1:
A comparison of the Pin Grid Array (PGA) and the Single Edge Connector (SEC) processor packaging styles.

The Pentium I processor operates at 85 degrees Celsius (about 185 degrees Fahrenheit). The Pentium III processor operates at 100 degrees Celsius (about 212 degrees Fahrenheit, the boiling point of water). The PC's cooling system is designed to keep the processor operating near its optimal temperature. Therefore, you need to keep the PC's case closed to ensure that its cooling system is operating efficiently and as designed. The form factor for the case, motherboard, and power supply that supports a particular processor is designed to provide cooling to keep the processor at or near its optimal operating temperature. At temperatures above its normal operating temperature, a processor begins to perform poorly, shuts down, or becomes permanently damaged. Heatsinks and fans are designed to draw the heat up and out of the processor's packaging and carry the heat away on the tines of the heatsink by the airflow of the fan.

On Pentium and Pentium Pro processors, heatsinks and fans are clipped directly on the processor and attached with a dielectric gel, which is also called *thermal grease*. Later processor models, such as the Celeron, the Pentium II, and the Pentium III (all of which have SEC packaging), have mounting points to attach fans and heatsinks directly to the processor.

In addition to the airflow system of the PC, the Pentium processor also uses special motherboard configurations to help cool it. This may include a fan or a heatsink (or both), mounted directly on top of the processor. The fan sucks the heat away from the chip and up into the PC's airflow. A *heatsink* is a device that looks something like a bed of nails that wicks the heat into its tines, where the airflow removes it. If a processor has both a fan and a heatsink, the fan sits on top of the heatsink.

Thermal grease (also known as heatsink jelly, heatsink compound, thermal gunk, thermal compound, or thermal goo) improves the heat conductivity between the processor and its heatsink. The grease eliminates any gaps between the two devices, working like a denture adhesive, allowing the CPU's heat to transfer to the heatsink more efficiently.

Feeding power to the processor

Most motherboards include a mounting for a voltage regulator module (VRM), which is a device that regulates the voltage that is fed to the processor. The mounting serves the following purposes:

✓ To protect the processor from spikes or other electrical events coming from the power supply

✓ To ensure that a steady flow of power is fed to the processor

Typically, the VRM is located very near the processor mounting slot or socket.

Comparing sockets and slots

Two general types of mountings are used to mount processors to the motherboard: sockets and slots. Most processors are available in only one mounting style, disregarding ceramic versus plastic. Other processors, such as the Celeron, are available in either a PGA-type or an SEC-type package.

Socket to it

A variety of socket types have been used for PC microprocessors. For the exam, pay close attention to those used for Pentium-class processors. You should expect to encounter the following socket types on the A+ Hardware Technology exam:

- **Socket 4:** Mounts the 273-pin PGA package of the Pentium 60 and Pentium 66 processors.

- **Socket 5:** Mounts the 320-pin Staggered Pin Grid Array (SPGA) of early 3V Pentium processors.

- **Socket 7:** A socket type, still in use, that mounts the 321-pin SPGA of the later-release Pentium processors and the chips of AMD, Cyrix, and IDT.

- **Super 7:** An extension of the Socket 7 design that is used for the AMD K6 processors.

- **Socket 8:** A 387-pin SPGA zero-insertion-force (ZIF) socket for the Pentium Pro processor.

- **Socket 370:** Designed for the Celeron processor in Plastic Pin Grid Array (PPGA) packaging, but used for several later processors. Its name comes from the number of pins that it supports. See Figure 6-2.

- **Socket 423 P4:** Along with the Socket 478 Pentium 4 mounting, this is one of two sockets used for the Pentium 4 processor. According to Intel, the Socket 423 P4 mounting is optimized for Windows XP.

- **Socket 478 Pentium 4:** Along with the Socket 423 P4, the Socket 478 Pentium 4 mounting (see Figure 6-3) is one of the two types of sockets used for Pentium 4 processors.

- **Socket A/Socket 462:** This is an American Micro Devices (AMD) 462-pin socket that is replacing the Slot A mounting for the newer Athlon and Duron processors.

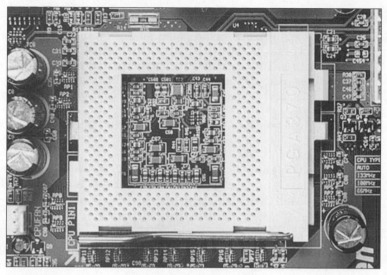

Figure 6-2:
A Socket
370
mounting.

Figure 6-3:
A Socket
478 Pentium
4 mounting.

Slot types

Slot type connections use a single slot mounting on the motherboard that mounts the processor in the same manner that is used for memory modules or expansion cards. The packaging technologies that mount in slot connectors include Single Edge Processor Package (SEPP), Single Edge Connector Cartridge (SECC), and similar types that involve the words *single edge*.

The following types of slot mountings are used to attach microprocessors to motherboards:

- ✔ **Slot 1:** Technically called the SC-242 (Slot Connector — 242 pins) connector, this is a proprietary Intel connector that is used for Celeron, Pentium II, and Pentium III processors.

- ✔ **Slot 2:** Technically the SC-330 connector, the Slot 2 connector is an Intel mounting for its Pentium II Xeon and Pentium III Xeon chips. This slot style enhances the ability of multiple processors that are installed in the same PC to work together.

- ✔ **Slot A:** AMD Athlon processors use this slot style, which is physically the same as a Slot 1 connector. However, the Slot A type uses different pin assignments, making it unusable by Intel processors.

- ✔ **Slot M:** This type is designed to hold the 64-bit Intel Itanium processor.

Intel processors

Most of the PCs that you work on as PC repair technician have processors from Intel Corporation, and because Intel is one of the companies that helped develop the A+ exams, you can expect most of the processor questions to relate to Intel processors.

For the exam, about the only Intel-specific thing that you need to remember are the numbering and naming schemes that Intel uses for its CPUs, and how these schemes contrast with the processors of other manufacturers. You won't be asked to identify the manufacturer of a CPU, but knowing Intel's evolution may help you to identify incorrect answers of a question.

Based on the A+ Hardware Technology exam objectives, you need to know the type of mounting, voltage, clock speed, and bus width for each of the popular (meaning Intel) microprocessors. Table 6-1 includes information for the CPUs that you need to know for the test. The order of the processors in the table is important because it indicates their evolution, although the later processors do overlap a bit.

Table 6-1	Intel Microprocessors				
CPU	**Core Speed (MHz)**	**Voltage (volts)**	**L1 Cache (KB)**	**L2 Cache (KB)**	**Mounting**
Pentium P5	60–66	5	8 WT/8 WB	-	Socket 5
Pentium P5	75–333	3.3	8 WT/8 WB	-	Socket 7
Pentium Pro	166–200	3.3	16	512	Socket 8
Pentium II	233–450	2.8	16 WT/16 WB	512	Slot 1
Pentium II Xeon	400–450	2	16 WT/16 WB	512/1024/2048	Slot 1
Celeron	266–300	2	-	-	Slot 1
Celeron	300–533	2	16 WT/16 WB	128	Slot 1/ Socket 370
Celeron	533–700	1.7	16 WT/16 WB	128	Socket 478
Pentium III	450–1266	1.7–2	16 WT/16 WB	256/512	Slot 1/ Socket 370
Pentium III Xeon	500–1000	2	16 WT/16 WB	256/512/ 1024/2048	Slot 1
Pentium 4	1300–2533	1.75	socket	256	Socket 478 P4

In Table 6-1, the L1 (Level 1) cache is listed in the form of 8 WT/8 WB or 16 WT/16 WB in most places. This indicates that the processor has either 16 or 32K of L1 cache, but the 16 or 32K is divided into halves that perform either write-through or write-back caching operations. (See Chapter 3 for more information on caching.)

Brief descriptions of each of the processors that are included in Table 6-1 are as follows:

- ✔ **Pentium:** This processor features 32-bit multitasking using RISC (Reduced Instruction Set Computer) design techniques and a super-scalar architecture that executes two instructions in the same clock cycle. The Pentium expanded the internal bus to 64 bits and high-speed internal cache.

- **Pentium Pro:** The Pentium Pro was developed as a network server processor. It was specially designed to support 32-bit network operating systems, such as Windows NT, and to be used in configurations of one, two, or four processors, with 1 megabyte of advanced Level 2 (L2) cache.

- **Pentium II:** The Pentium II is the Pentium Pro processor with MMX technology added. The P-II, as it is commonly referred to, is excellent for multimedia work that requires support for full-motion video and 3D images.

- **Celeron:** Developed for use in desktop and portable computers, the Celeron is a low-cost version of the Pentium II processor.

- **Pentium III:** Although recently surpassed by the Pentium 4, the Pentium III has been the highest-powered processor in the Intel arsenal. It features 9.5 million transistors, a 32K L1 cache, 512K of L2 cache, and clock speeds of 450 MHz to 1 GHz.

- **Xeon:** The Xeon processors, both Pentium II and Pentium III, are successors to the Pentium Pro processors. The Xeon is a network server processor that is capable of addressing and caching up to 64GB of memory with its 36-bit memory address bus. Xeon processors can be configured with four to eight CPUs in one server.

- **Pentium 4:** Using the first totally new processor design since the Pentium Pro, the Pentium 4 (P4) processor has clock speeds that exceed 2 GHz, or about twice the speed of the Pentium III.

Caching in on Level 3

The A+ Hardware Technology exam objectives include a reference to Level 3 (L3) cache. Don't panic if this is a new term to you; it is to just about everyone as well.

When the processor manufacturers began including L2 cache on the processor package, any cache that was located on the motherboard — or outside the processor — was demoted to Level 3.

AMD processors

American Micro Devices (AMD) is the manufacturer of the K6, Athlon, and Duron processors, which compete with the Intel Pentium processors. Table 6-2 lists the common AMD processors.

Table 6-2			AMD Microprocessors		
CPU	Core Speed (MHz)	Voltage (volts)	L1 Cache (KB)	L2 Cache (KB)	Mounting
K6	166–266	3.3	32 WT/32 WB	256	Socket 7
K6	266–300	2.2	32 WT/32 WB	256	Socket 7
K6-2	266–550	2.2/2.3	32 WT/32 WB	256	Socket 7
Athlon	500–1800	1.75	64 WT/64 WB	512/256	Slot A/Socket A
Duron	600–1200	1.6	64 WT/64 WB	64	Socket A

Getting Ready for Work

When you are working with processors, especially processors in PGA packaging, it is useful to know how the locking mechanism works on a socket mounting.

As illustrated in Figures 6-2 and 6-3, earlier in the chapter, socket mountings involve many holes into which many pins are inserted. Have you ever wondered just how the processor is retained snuggly on the socket mounting? First of all, it isn't just sitting there. The pins on the back of the processor packaging are locked into place by the locking mechanism on the socket.

The two most common types of locking mechanisms used on sockets are the *zero-insertion-force* (ZIF) and the *low-insertion-force* (LIF) mechanisms. In these two mechanisms, there is little difference between the force that's required to insert the processor in the socket; the LIF just requires slightly more force to seat the processor than the ZIF.

The socket locking mechanism works as follows:

1. The locking arm on the left side of the socket is tucked up under a locking lip. When the arm is pushed down slightly, it releases and can be raised into an unlocked position.

2. At this point, the processor can be inserted into the socket. Typically, one or more locating features help you align the processor with the socket. Be sure that the pins are all aligned properly with the holes in the socket.

3. After the processor is in place, lower the locking arm and tuck it back under its locking lip. The processor should be locked into place and ready to process!

Prep Test

1 Which of the following processors does not include MMX instructions?

- A ○ Pentium
- B ○ Pentium Pro
- C ○ Pentium II
- D ○ Celeron

2 What are the two most common types of locking mechanisms used on processor mounting sockets? (Choose two.)

- A ❑ LIF
- B ❑ NIF
- C ❑ ZIP
- D ❑ ZIF

3 What does VRM stand for?

- A ○ Virtual reality module
- B ○ Voltage regulator module
- C ○ Very real memory
- D ○ Virtually real memory

4 What type of mounting is the most commonly used for a Pentium II microprocessor?

- A ○ Slot A
- B ○ Slot 1
- C ○ Socket 478
- D ○ Socket 7

5 Which CPU packaging form was used for nearly all processors before the Pentium II?

- A ○ Pin Grid Array
- B ○ Plastic Ball Grid Array
- C ○ Single Edge Connector
- D ○ Flip Chip–PGA

6 Which of the following is the CPU packaging type that is used for the Pentium II and Pentium III?

A ○ Pin Grid Array

B ○ Plastic Ball Grid Array

C ○ Single Edge Connector

D ○ Flip Chip–PGA

7 Which of the following is the main chip, found on the motherboard, that executes instructions?

A ○ Math coprocessor

B ○ CMOS memory

C ○ Microprocessor

D ○ ROM chip

8 What are the three primary bus structures on a PC motherboard?

A ○ Address, Instruction, and Information

B ○ Control, Location, and Data

C ○ Memory, Interface, Command

D ○ Address, Data, Control

9 Which of the following is used to keep a Pentium processor cool?

A ○ Liquid nitrogen

B ○ A fan

C ○ A heatsink

D ○ No special equipment is needed

E ○ B and C

F ○ A and C

10 How much memory is the Pentium II capable of addressing?

A ○ 4MB

B ○ 16MB

C ○ 4GB

D ○ 64GB

Answers

1 **B.** The Pentium Pro was designed for use in network servers and did not include MMX capabilities. *See "Looking at Microprocessors."*

2 **A, D.** The two locking arms types used on the most common processor mounting sockets are the zero insertion force (ZIF) and the low insertion force (LIF) locking arms. *Review "Getting Ready for Work."*

3 **B.** The VRM regulates the power that is supplied to the processor. *Look up "Feeding power to the processor."*

4 **B.** A Pentium II processor uses the Slot 1 mounting. *Check out "Intel processors."*

5 **A.** The PGA (Pin Grid Array) remains a very popular CPU processor packaging form. The Celeron processor is available in both the PGA and the SEC (Single Edge Connector) packages. *Review "CPU packaging."*

6 **C.** The SEC packaging provides a better cooling system for the high-end Pentium chips and reduces the space that is required on the motherboard for its circuitry. *Check out "CPU packaging."*

7 **C.** If you answered anything else, go back and read *"Looking at Microprocessors."*

8 **D.** The data bus carries, well, data; the address bus carries, well . . . I think you get it. *See "On the CPU bus."*

9 **E.** Typically, both a fan and a heatsink are used. *See "Keeping the processor cool."*

10 **D.** Although a processor manufacturer claims that the processor can address a humongous amount of RAM, the motherboard or chipset may not make all the RAM available. *Review "Intel processors."*

Chapter 7

Memory Systems

● ●

Exam Objectives

▶ Identifying the type, form factor, and operational characteristics of RAM

▶ Differentiating parity and nonparity memory

▶ Defining DOS/Windows memory management

● ●

About 15 percent of the A+ Hardware Technology exam deals with questions on the motherboard and memory systems. Of that percentage, you can count on about half pertaining to different types of memory, how it's packaged, how it's installed, and how to diagnose its problems.

It's difficult to say how much of the remaining 85 percent of the test touches on memory and subjects like parity, error checking, and other topics that I include in this chapter. But these issues are woven throughout the test, just like they are in real life on the job.

Every professional PC repairperson must have a good understanding of memory systems, how they work, how they're configured, how to avoid problems, and how to identify, isolate, and solve problems.

You should at least review this chapter to make sure that you're familiar with the concepts and terminology of a rapidly changing technology — especially if you're one of the old duffers who, like me, are still clinging to their AT, waiting for the overdrive chip to come out.

Quick Assessment

Identifying the type, form factor, and operational characteristics of RAM

1 Memory that is packaged in the _____ form is installed directly on the motherboard.

2 _____ DRAM is the most common type in use.

3 _____, which is much faster and more expensive than DRAM, is used for memory caching.

4 Memory that loses its contents when its power source is lost is called _____.

5 The three package types of DRAM memory are _____, _____, and _____.

Differentiating parity and nonparity memory

6 _____ involves the use of an additional bit for each 8 bits of data.

7 _____ can detect and correct 1-bit errors in data.

Defining DOS/Windows memory management

8 The first 640K of system memory is called _____.

9 The upper 384K of the first megabyte of memory is called _____.

10 All memory above 1MB is called _____.

Answers

1   *DIP.* See "DRAM packaging."

2   *EDO.* Review "DRAM technologies."

3   *SRAM.* Check out "Static RAM (SRAM)."

4   *Volatile.* Look at "Refreshing Your Memory Basics."

5   *DIP, SIMM, DIMM.* See "DRAM packaging."

6   *Parity.* Review "Understanding parity."

7   *ECC,* or *Error Correction Code.* See "Correcting parity errors."

8   *Conventional memory.* Take a look at "Logically Laying Out Memory."

9   *Expanded or upper memory area.* Check out "Logically Laying Out Memory."

10   *Extended memory.* Study "Logically Laying Out Memory."

Refreshing Your Memory Basics

You can look at memory in the following ways:

- ✔ As the physical chips and modules that mount on the motherboard or in one of a PC's interfaces
- ✔ As the scratch pad space that holds data and instructions before and after their use by the processor

For the two A+ exams, you need to know something about both of these considerations, including the form factors, purposes, and uses of the various types of memory. You also need to know something about memory configuration and a bit more about the troubleshooting processes. (Troubleshooting in general is one of the major focuses of the A+ exams.)

Memory systems are complex and offer a depth of material — the kind of stuff engineers get misty-eyed over. For such a physically small thing, memory is a large subject. But not here! For example, I give no lengthy diatribes on why parity memory is better than nonparity memory. I give you just the facts, along with a small amount of background information to help you understand the exam's questions — quite a trick in itself.

Differentiating RAM from ROM

The PC has the following two basic types of memory:

- ✔ **RAM (random-access memory):** Holds the instructions and data in use by the operating system and software applications before and after the data is passed to the CPU. RAM is volatile; a steady power source is required to hold its contents. Should the power stream be broken, anything that is stored in RAM is erased. No power, no data — pretty straightforward.
- ✔ **ROM (read-only memory):** Is nonvolatile and retains its contents through even the darkest power outage. For more information on ROM, see Chapter 4.

RAM is by far the faster of the two types of memory. In fact, RAM is often used to shadow the BIOS ROM to improve its performance during the boot process. If you're asked what copying the contents of the BIOS ROM into RAM for faster access to the instructions by the CPU is called — the answer is *shadowing*.

When *volatile* memory loses its power source, it also loses its contents. Most types of RAM, especially DRAM, are volatile, and that's why when you turn off the PC's power (or trip over the power cord), everything in RAM is lost. *Nonvolatile* memory, like ROM and other types, does not lose its contents when the power source is lost.

Random-access memory (RAM)

RAM is the primary memory of the PC and is generally installed directly on the motherboard in a variety of package types, which I deal with later. Many types of RAM exist, and you need to know about the following ones for the A+ Hardware Technology exam:

- ✔ DRAM (Dynamic Random-Access Memory)
- ✔ EDO RAM (Extended Data Output RAM)
- ✔ RIMM (Rambus In-line Memory Module)
- ✔ SRAM (Static RAM)

In addition to the types of RAM that are used in primary memory, you should also know about the following types of RAM that are used on video cards:

- ✔ VRAM (Video RAM)
- ✔ WRAM (Windows Accelerator Card RAM)

You need a solid understanding of RAM, its packaging forms, and its technologies for the exam. Many questions assume that you know the types of RAM, their characteristics, and where they are installed. For example, you may be asked which is the fastest of the RAM types (SRAM), or how DIMMs are installed (in vertical sockets on the motherboard).

Dynamic RAM (DRAM)

DRAM (pronounced "dee-ram," but not in the same context as "dee-bears" or "dee-bulls," although it could apply to Marshal Faulk) is the RAM that computer types talk about. DRAM has, until recently, always been the most common type of memory in PCs.

Compared to other forms of integrated circuits, DRAM isn't a complex circuit and, as a result, is not expensive. However, its design also requires that it be refreshed regularly or it loses its contents. This need for constant refreshing gives DRAM its dynamic tag.

DRAM must be refreshed every 2 milliseconds. A special refresh logic circuit reads and then rewrites the contents of each DRAM address, regardless of whether it's in use.

DRAM is also the slowest of the memories, clocking in with access speeds around 50 nanoseconds (ns) or higher (higher, in this case, means slower). Older DRAM had an access speed of about 120 ns.

DRAM technologies

DRAM comes in a variety of popular technologies. The following lists the characteristics of each of the DRAM technologies:

- **Extended Data Out (EDO):** This is the most common type of DRAM. It's common in most Pentium and later PCs, except those with memory buses over 75 MHz.

- **Fast Page Mode (FPM):** This type of DRAM is occasionally called non-EDO RAM. It's generally compatible with motherboards with memory buses with speeds under 66 MHz.

- **Burst Extended Data Out (BEDO):** This DRAM is EDO memory with pipelining technology added for faster access times. BEDO memory allows much higher bus speeds than EDO memory.

- **Synchronous DRAM (SDRAM):** Like its SRAM cousins (see the section, "Static RAM (SRAM)," later in this chapter), SDRAM is tied to the system clock and reads or writes memory in burst mode.

- **Rambus DRAM (RDRAM):** Rambus is a proprietary DRAM technology developed by Rambus, Inc. (www.rambus.com) that has memory speeds of up to 3.2 Gbps. RDRAM comes on a module that is similar to a DIMM, called a RIMM (Rambus In-line Memory Module).

- **Synchronous Link DRAM (SLDRAM):** This is an enhanced version of SDRAM memory that uses a multiplexed bus to transfer data to and from the chips rather than fixed pin settings. SLDRAM has transfer rates as high as 3 Gbps. Unlike RDRAM, this is an open technology.

- **Video RAM (VRAM):** This specialized DRAM is used on video cards and not for main memory. VRAM applies dual porting, which means that it can be written to and read from at the same time. This allows the processor and the refresh circuitry for the monitor to access VRAM at the same time. Another type of video RAM is Windows RAM (WRAM), also called Windows Accelerator RAM, which has essentially the same properties as VRAM.

You will definitely see DRAM technology questions on the A+ exams. Familiarize yourself with the general descriptions that I provide here, which should be enough for FPM, EDO, Burst EDO, RDRAM, and SDRAM. VRAM and WRAM are covered in more detail in Chapter 12.

DRAM packaging

DRAM memory comes in the following package forms:

- DIP (Dual In-line Packaging)
- SIMM (Single In-line Memory Module)
- DIMM (Dual In-line Memory Module)/RIMM

SIMM and DIMM packages are like mini-expansion boards that have either surface-mounted SOJ (Small Outline J-lead) or TSOP (Thin, Small Outline Package) DRAM soldered on one (SIMM) or two (DIMM) sides of a circuit card. Figure 7-1 shows the basic forms of a DIP and a memory module (a SIMM is shown).

SIMMing right along

The memory standard on middle-aged PCs (486s and early Pentiums) is the SIMM (see Figure 7-2). The edge connector on a SIMM has either 30 pins or 72 pins. A SIMM's memory capacity ranges from 1MB to 16MB in either a one-sided or two-sided style, with chips soldered to one or two sides of the board.

Because the Pentium processor uses a 64-bit path to memory, 32-bit SIMMs must be installed in pairs. Each SIMM bank has two sockets and both sockets must be filled before another bank receives a SIMM.

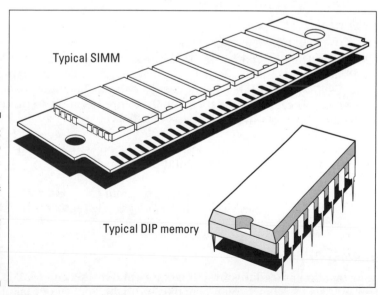

Typical SIMM

Typical DIP memory

Figure 7-1: The two basic package forms of DRAM: a memory module (SIMM) and a DIP chip.

Figure 7-2:
A typical
SIMM.

Moving up to DIMM

The Dual In-line Memory Module (DIMM) is the memory standard on most newer and larger PCs. Because its 64-bit memory matches the 64-bit data path of the Pentium processor, you need to install only one DIMM at a time. In comparison to the SIMM, a DIMM has 168 contact pins as opposed to the 30 and 72 pins of the SIMM. A DIMM looks just like a SIMM, except that it's slightly larger, has memory chips on both sides, and has about twice as many contacts on its edge connector.

DIMMs come in different voltages — 3.3V and 5.0V — and as buffered or unbuffered, which yields four possible combinations.

A smaller version of the DIMM, the 100-pin Small Outline DIMM (SODIMM), which is used primarily in laptop computers, supports PC100 SDRAM. An even smaller DIMM package, the 144-pin MicroDIMM, which is used in sub-notebook portable computers, supports PC100 SDRAM.

On the RIMM

Where SIMM and DIMM are generic names for a type of memory module, RIMM is a trademarked name for the Rambus memory module. A RIMM looks like a DIMM, but the RIMM has 184 pins on its edge connector. RIMMs transfer data in 16-bit chunks. A RIMM is packaged inside an aluminum sheath called a *heat spreader*. The heat spreader covers the entire assembly to protect against overheating. Figure 7-3 shows the parts of a RIMM.

A smaller version of the RIMM, the SORIMM (Small Outline RIMM), is similar to the SODIMM, with the exception of the Rambus technology.

For more information on memory than your brain can possibly hold, check out Kingston Technologies' "Ultimate Memory Guide" at `www.kingston.com/tools/umg`.

Installing DRAM

The installation procedures for DIP memory and SIMMs and DIMMs are quite different. As a PC repairperson, you have probably had an occasion to install a SIMM or DIMM. However, you may not have had to install a DIP memory chip. You need to have some idea of the processes that are used to install memory in a PC.

You do have your ESD (electrostatic discharge) protection on, don't you? You should take steps to protect the PC — and especially memory chips or modules. It doesn't take much of an ESD to severely damage the memory that you're installing. Always perform the following steps before installing memory in the PC (and for any other operation inside the case):

1. **Turn off the PC and disconnect the AC power cord.**

2. **Follow the instructions in the PC's owner's manual on how to locate the memory expansion sockets.**

3. **Before touching anything inside the case or opening the memory's package, make sure that you first touch an unpainted, grounded metal object, such as a chassis wall or support, to discharge any static electricity that's stored on your body or clothing.**

4. **Handle memory modules carefully. Don't bend or flex them, and always grasp them by the edges.**

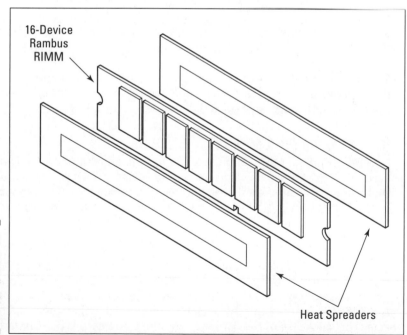

Figure 7-3:
RIMMs are packaged inside of a heat spreader.

Putting in the SIMMs

To install a SIMM, align it with the socket at about a 45-degree angle. As the SIMM is lifted to a vertical position and seated in the socket, the clamping clips on the ends of the socket grab the module and hold it in place. To remove a SIMM, release the clamping clips, push the module to a 45-degree angle, and then lift out the module.

Dropping in a DIMM

A DIMM is installed by inserting the module into an available memory socket. A DIMM is keyed to match the socket, so it only goes in one way. After the DIMM is aligned to the socket slot, firmly press down on the module until it seats in the socket slot and locks into place with a snap.

Nearly all DIMM sockets have ejector tabs. To remove a DIMM, press down on the ejector tabs, and the module should pop up and out of the socket slot. Carefully lift the module out of the socket.

Putting in a RIMM

A RIMM is installed in special RIMM connectors. Check the motherboard's documentation to see whether a pair of RIMM connectors exists on the board. Most likely, they are the connectors that you couldn't identify. Both slots of a RIMM connector set must be occupied by two RIMMs or a single RIMM and what is called a C-RIMM (Continuity RIMM). A C-RIMM doesn't contain memory; it's only a pass-through module that completes the memory channel.

You install a RIMM almost exactly as you would a DIMM — press down until the locking clips snap onto the module. To remove the module, press the ejector tabs outward; this pops the module out of the socket.

Hot-swapping flash memory

Notebook and palmtop computers can have flash memory added with a PC card. A PC card looks like a credit card (see Figure 7-4) and slips into a slot that's usually located on the side of the notebook's base. One feature of PC cards is *hot-swapping*, which allows you to remove and replace the card while the system is running. Chapter 14 covers portable systems and PC cards in more detail.

The Personal Computer Memory Card International Association (PCMCIA) is the standards authority on PC cards. This organization has developed three primary standards for PC cards that define the cards' size and use. PC cards are 85.6 millimeters (mm) by 54 mm (or about 3.4 inches by 2.1 inches) in size. The thickness of the card is set by the three card type standards. See Chapter 14 for more information, but briefly the three standard PC card types are as follows:

- ✔ **Type I:** Up to 3.3 mm thick and used primarily for adding memory

- ✔ **Type II:** Up to 5.5 mm thick and commonly used for I/O devices, such as data/fax modems, network interface cards, and mass storage devices

- ✔ **Type III:** Up to 10.5 mm thick and used for rotating mass storage drives

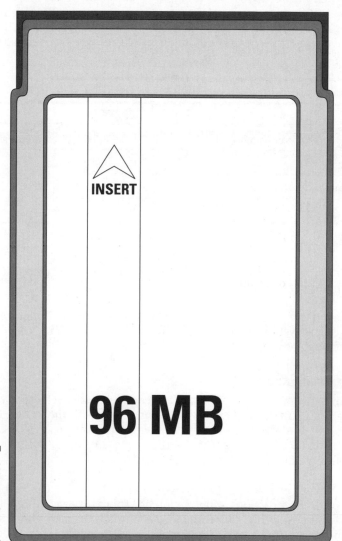

Figure 7-4:
A PC
card flash
memory
module.

Static RAM (SRAM)

SRAM is static, which means that it can retain its data using a very low voltage electrical charge and doesn't need to be refreshed. As long as it has a power stream, SRAM holds its charge and contents. SRAM also has very fast access times, in the range of 15 to 20 ns (comparing to the 50 to 120 ns of DRAM). SRAM in a DIP package is physically two pins longer than DRAM in the same packaging, and because it's a more complex technology, it costs a lot more. Table 7-1 contrasts SRAM to DRAM in terms of their general characteristics.

Table 7-1	DRAM versus SRAM
DRAM	*SRAM*
Slow and must be constantly refreshed	Fast and doesn't require refreshing
Simple	Complex
Inexpensive	Expensive
Physically small	Physically large

SRAM is packaged as either a single DIP chip, on a COAST (Cache On A Stick) module in a variety of increments, or embedded into other chips, such as processors or controllers.

SRAM is available as either synchronous or asynchronous. Synchronous SRAM uses the system clock to coordinate its signals with the CPU, and asynchronous doesn't.

Caching in on SRAM

SRAM is most commonly used on a PC as cache memory. The type of SRAM and the amount that a motherboard supports vary with the motherboard. However, because of its greater cost and bigger physical size, SRAM is most typically used for the Level 2 (outside the processing chip) cache memory that is mounted directly on the motherboard.

Memory caching enables the CPU to work more efficiently. Cache memory stores data and instructions and then fetches them in anticipation of what the CPU will want next. When cache memory is correct, which is about 90 percent of the time, the CPU can get what it needs from the much-faster SRAM instead of the slower DRAM. It is now common for a system to include from 128K to 512K of SRAM cache on the motherboard. Chapter 3 includes information on how caching works.

Comparing DRAM to SRAM

In spite of its constant thirst for power, DRAM works better for PC main memory because it's cheaper and needs less space. SRAM costs too much and takes too much space to be used for main memory. On the other hand, because of its speed and the fact that not much memory is needed, SRAM is perfect for cache memory.

Ensuring Memory Integrity

In addition to all that you should know about memory for the A+ exams, one important aspect of memory that's included in several domains is memory data integrity. It's one thing to store data in memory and quite another to be sure that what's there is still valid, especially if the data hasn't been accessed in eons, or 100 or 200 milliseconds, whichever comes first. As leaky as DRAM is, a mechanism has to exist to verify the integrity of the data.

Lucky for you and me, a mechanism does exist. In fact, two methods are used to ensure the integrity of data that is stored in memory: parity and Error Correction Code (ECC).

First, however, you need to know about the memory controller. The memory controller oversees the movement of data into and out of memory and, in doing so, determines the type of data integrity checking that is used. In both parity and ECC, the memory controller is key to the process. The memory controller generates the signals that are used to control the reading and writing of data to and from memory.

Understanding parity

Parity has been around for a long time, or at least as long as the PC. DRAM that implements parity checking has one additional bit for every 8 bits of data. This extra bit allows the system to verify the data format using two parity protocols — odd parity and even parity — that work similarly. In a nutshell, if the system is using even parity, the extra bit is used as necessary to make the total number of positive (1) bits an even number. In an odd parity world, the extra bit is used to create odd-number totals. Parity is achieved when the total number of 1 bits in a byte adds up to either an even or odd number, depending on the parity technique that's in use.

When a character fails to have the appropriate number of bits, a parity error occurs. A parity error can be the first signal of a host of problems, ranging from one-time anomalies to faulty memory. Faulty memory can be the cause of repeated memory parity errors.

The limitation of the parity method for data integrity checking is that it can only detect an error. It has no mechanism to fix the error. It doesn't know which of the bits are wrong and which are correct. When the parity method detects a parity error, it knows only that the count is wrong.

Nonparity memory

Nonparity memory systems don't perform data integrity checks. You can't use nonparity memory in a parity system. Doing so generates a parity error as soon as the system boots up. You can turn off parity checking on some systems in the BIOS setup. Parity memory works fine in a nonparity system — the extra bit is ignored.

You can count on being asked about the difference between parity and nonparity memories. Parity memory contains an extra bit that is used to check the integrity of the data stored in each byte, and nonparity memory does not.

Correcting parity errors

Error Correction Code (ECC) is a data integrity method that is used in place of parity memory on many systems. The difference between ECC memory and parity memory is that ECC can detect errors like parity memory, but ECC can also correct errors to a point. ECC memory can detect up to a 4-bit memory error, but it can correct only 1-bit errors. This isn't a big deal because a 4-bit error (that's not the same as a 50-cent error) is rare, and 1-bit errors are more common. Like the parity method does with all errors, when ECC sees a multiple-bit error, it reports it as a parity error. Believe me, if your memory has a 4-bit error, you want to know about it, and any attempt to fix it would be only sheer guesswork. Expect to see a question on the A+ Hardware Technology exam about the difference between ECC and parity memory systems.

Logically Laying Out Memory

You should know how Windows divides memory into logical divisions for both A+ exams. In fact, it may be the most important thing that you should know about memory. The logical memory divisions of RAM are the subjects of direct and specific questions and are referenced in questions in other domains. Spend the time to memorize the information that's included in this section.

Memory on the PC is divided into four basic areas, as shown in Figure 7-5 and discussed in Table 7-2.

Table 7-2	Logical Memory Layout
Memory	*Description*
Conventional memory	The first 640K of system memory. Used by operating system kernels and standard DOS programs, device drivers, and TSRs.
Upper memory area	The upper 384K of the first megabyte of memory, located right above conventional memory. Reserved for the system BIOS and device drivers and special uses such as ROM shadowing. Also called *expanded memory* or *reserved memory*.
High memory area	The first 64K (less 16 bytes) of the second megabyte of memory. Although it's the first 64K of extended memory, it can be accessed in real mode.
Extended memory	Technically, this is all memory above 1MB, but in practice, it is any memory that's above the high memory area. Used by Windows for programs and data that are running in protected mode.

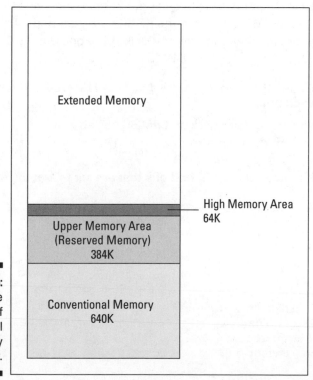

Figure 7-5:
The divisions of the logical memory layout.

Prep Test

1 What type of DRAM is based on the Rambus technology?

A ○ EDO DRAM

B ○ SDRAM

C ○ RDRAM

D ○ VRAM

2 Which of the following are types of DRAM packaging?

A ○ DIP

B ○ SIMM

C ○ DIMM

D ○ RIMM

E ○ All of the above

3 Why must SIMMs be installed in pairs in a Pentium PC?

A ○ They are matched memory cells that cannot operate independently.

B ○ It takes two 32-pin SIMMs to match the 64-bit data path of the Pentium.

C ○ A Pentium requires a minimum amount of RAM to operate.

D ○ It takes two SIMMS to equal one DIMM.

4 Parity memory validates the integrity of the data that is stored in RAM by doing which of the following?

A ○ Checking the header of each packet of data received

B ○ Checking every eighth bit for errors

C ○ Checking the RAM table in BIOS

D ○ Counting the number of even or odd bits that are set to 1 in the data

5 BIOS programs are most often loaded to which area of memory?

A ○ Conventional memory

B ○ Upper memory

C ○ Extended memory

D ○ Virtual memory

6 Which of the following memory types is most commonly used for L2 cache?

A ○ DRAM

B ○ SRAM

C ○ SDRAM

D ○ PCMCIA

7 What is the name for all memory that is above 1MB?

A ○ Extended memory

B ○ Expanded memory

C ○ Upper memory

D ○ Base memory

8 What is the first 640K of memory called?

A ○ Upper memory

B ○ Extended memory

C ○ Conventional memory

D ○ Expanded memory

9 Which of the following types of memory is able to correct 1-bit parity errors?

A ○ EDO

B ○ BEDO

C ○ Rambus

D ○ ECC

Answers

1 **C**. Rambus is a proprietary DRAM technology that is installed on RIMMs. *See "DRAM technologies."*

2 **E**. All of these are DRAM packages. In fact, DIP is the packaging for SRAM as well. *Review "DRAM packaging."*

3 **B**. SIMM assemblies must be installed in pairs, because they have only a 32-bit data bus. On the other hand, a DIMM has a 64-bit path and can get by with a single module installed. *Check out "SIMMing right along."*

4 **D**. Parity checking involves using an additional bit with each 8 bits to set the total number of 1 bits to either an even or odd number, depending on the protocol that's in use. *Take a look at "Understanding parity."*

5 **B.** The upper memory area is used to hold BIOS programs and memory-resident drivers. *Study "Logically Laying Out Memory."*

6 **B**. SRAM, because it is larger in size and costs more, is used primarily for cache memory on the motherboard. *Review "Static RAM (SRAM)."*

7 **A**. Memory above 1MB is called extended memory. *See "Logically Laying Out Memory."*

8 **C**. The first 640K of memory is conventional memory. *See "Logically Laying Out Memory."*

9 **D**. Error Correcting Code (ECC) technology can identify 4-bit errors and correct 1-bit errors. *See "Correcting parity errors."*

Chapter 8

Storing Data

• •

Exam Objectives

▶ Identifying basic terms, concepts, and functions of storage systems

▶ Formatting and partitioning hard drives

▶ Installing and configuring ATA (IDE) drives

▶ Installing and configuring SCSI devices

▶ Identifying portable USB storage devices

• •

*S*everal different ways exist to store data with a PC. Some are familiar to everyone and some are not so well known. One problem with an industry-wide certification exam is that it expects you to know about all the various devices and FRMs (field-replaceable modules) you may find in a customer's computer. I've crammed all of the stuff you need to know about storage devices into this chapter, focusing on those devices you're likely to encounter on the A+ Core Hardware exam.

The exams won't necessarily test you on the latest or greatest up-to-the-minute technologies available when you take the test. The A+ exams are written against a generic objective set that attempts to include the PC components you are likely to encounter as a working PC repair professional. Don't spend your time reading the latest issues of PC magazines to bone up on the newest revelations in storage devices. Expand your knowledge of the storage devices in general and focus on the topics included in this chapter.

It's assumed that you understand how bits are organized into bytes and that bytes can store both text and numeric data. It's also assumed that you know that data stored in memory is temporary and that to store data permanently, you must use permanent storage media (such as a hard drive). These are the assumptions of the A+ Core Hardware exam as well. If those assumptions are correct and you know this much, you're off to a good start.

Quick Assessment

Identifying basic terms, concepts, and functions of storage systems

1 ATA and IDE stand for _____ and _____, respectively.

2 A hard drive cluster is a collection of _____.

Formatting and partitioning hard drives

3 A(n) _____ should never be low-level formatted.

Installing and configuring ATA (IDE) drives

4 You can connect _____ hard drives to a single ATA IDE cable.

5 RAID level _____ provides for disk striping without parity.

6 The two general translation modes used on ATA IDE disk drives are _____ and _____.

7 LBA refers to _____.

8 The interface used with CD-ROM, DVD, and tape drives is the _____.

9 You must install _____ at the beginning and end of the SCSI chain.

Installing and configuring SCSI devices

Answers

1 *AT Attachment* and *Integrated Drive Electronics.* Review "IDE technology."

2 *Sectors.* Look at "Organizing data on disk."

3 *IDE disk drive.* Check out "IDE technology."

4 *Two.* See "IDE technology."

5 *0 (zero).* Review "Raid!?!."

6 *PIO* and *DMA.* See "IDE protocols and modes."

7 *Logical block addressing.* Check out "Moving bigger blocks of data."

8 *ATAPI.* Look at "CD and DVD interfaces."

9 *Terminating resistor pack,* or *terminators.* Look at "SCSI technology."

Understanding the Basic Terms

You may not think of the floppy disk as a removable storage system, but it is — so are CD-ROMs, DVDs, optical disks, tape cartridges, and USB storage devices. Removable storage, also known as removable media, allows for expansion of the permanent storage space whenever it's needed and the ability to store the media and its data outside of and away from the PC.

Hard drive technologies

Five types of hard drive technologies have been used in PCs over the years:

- ST506
- ESDI (Enhanced Small Device Interface)
- IDE (Integrated Drive Electronics)
- EIDE (Enhanced Integrated Drive Electronics)
- SCSI (Small Computer System Interface)

ST506 and ESDI are outdated hard drive technologies, along with the AT computer where they were used. Most PCs used today have either an IDE/EIDE or a SCSI hard drive.

The A+ Core Hardware exam includes questions on IDE, EIDE, and SCSI (including RAID) drive technologies. Focus your review on hard drive storage in these technology types.

IDE technology

IDE (Integrated Drive Electronics) gets its name from the fact that its controller board is integrated into the disk drive assembly itself, which contrasts to earlier technologies that used a controller board mounted in a motherboard expansion slot. IDE was originally developed as an inexpensive alternative to the expensive SCSI technology (see "SCSI technology" later in this chapter). IDE is one of the most popular disk drive interfaces in use.

IDE is a simple interface technology compared to its predecessors. The IDE interface connects hard drives, CD-ROMs, DVDs, and tape drives to a PC. With the interface controller built into the disk drive itself, only a pass-through board is needed to connect the device to the motherboard. The interface card that's plugged into the motherboard for an IDE disk drive is often a multifunction card supporting such peripheral devices as the floppy drives, game ports, and serial ports. Most of the newest motherboard designs (see Chapter 3) incorporate one or two IDE/EIDE controllers into the motherboard, which eliminates the need for the pass-through card.

You should also know that IDE uses a 40-pin connector to connect the drive to the pass-through card or to the motherboard via a 40-wire ribbon cable. That cable must be less than 18 inches long (to protect the integrity of the data signal passing through it). An IDE interface supports either one or two 504MB drives.

IDE drives are low-level formatted at the factory. A *low-level format* is one that scans the disk storage media for defects and sets aside sectors with defects so that they aren't used for data, preventing later problems. IDE drives should never be low-level formatted by a user or a technician. Only a *high-level format,* such as that performed by the DOS/Windows command `FORMAT` or the Windows Explorer Format function, shown in Figure 8-1, prepares the disk partitions for use by the operating system and stores data. (See the "Formatting the disk" section, later in this chapter.)

IDE, or the interface that is called IDE, is really the *ATA (AT Attachment)* interface. In fact, the standard that defines the IDE interface for CD-ROMs, DVDs, and tape drives is called *ATAPI (AT Attachment Packet Interface).*

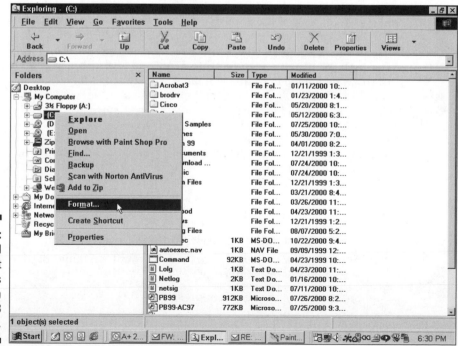

Figure 8-1:
A high-level format function is available in Windows 98 Explorer.

IDE protocols and modes

The ATA IDE interface standard defines several features and translation modes that interact with the disk drive and the internal systems of the PC. Here are the two you should be aware of for the A+ Core Hardware exam:

- ✓ **PIO (programmed input/output) modes:** This is the standard protocol used to transfer data over an ATA IDE interface.

- ✓ **DMA (direct memory access) modes:** This data transfer protocol, which is also called *bus mastering,* allows the hard drive's built-in controller to control the transfer of data into the PC's main memory without involving the CPU, as is true for a PIO transfer.

A drive usually uses either PIO or DMA and rarely both. (Using both is inefficient because both the CPU and the disk controller vie to move data to and from RAM.)

ATA-2 (EIDE) technology

If your computer and those on which you work are relatively new (1995 or later), the interface in use probably is EIDE (Enhanced IDE), which is more correctly called *ATA-2.* This interface enhanced the original ATA IDE standard to take advantage of the fact that newer BIOS systems could handle disk drives much larger than the 504MB capacity that the ATA IDE standard was limited to. This ability to work with larger drives was possible because of translation modes that allowed the BIOS to talk to the hardware differently than it talked with software.

For both A+ exams, remember that ATA-2 and EIDE are interchangeable. ATA-2 is an ANSI (American National Standards Institute) standard, which makes it a real and official standard. The many variations of the ATA-2 standard (such as EIDE, Fast ATA, and Fast ATA-2) are marketing names, not variations of the standard.

The ATA-2 standard (which is backward compatible to ATA IDE drives) has these features:

- ✓ Larger disk volumes and faster data transfers

- ✓ Additional and faster PIO and DMA modes (see the "IDE protocols and modes" section, earlier in this chapter)

- ✓ Ability to block transfer data (which groups a number of data reads and writes into a single interrupt)

- ✓ Support for logical block addressing (LBA)

Moving bigger blocks of data

Logical block addressing (LBA) is an enhanced feature that extends the capability of the device to address larger data blocks than was possible in standard ATA IDE drives that used traditional *cylinder/head/sector (CHS)* addressing or the *ECHS (extended CHS).* ECHS translation, which is also called *large mode* by some BIOS systems, is the translation mode that helped to break the 504MB barrier for some IDE drives.

Instead of the standard CHS type of addressing, LBA uniquely identifies each sector on the disk with a sector number. CHS addressing is much like standard postal addressing schemes that use a street address, city, and state to locate a home. LBA is more like the "Plus Four" zip code scheme used in the U.S., which attempts to uniquely number each delivery point within a zip code. LBA assigns each sector a unique number that is used to locate, read from, and write to the sector. Most of the BIOS systems sold since 1995 include support both LBA and ECHS (large mode) address translation.

Moving ultra fast

The ATA interface standard continues to be improved with additional error correction, self-monitoring and reporting capabilities, and faster speeds.

For example, the ATA-3 interface includes logic called *S.M.A.R.T.,* which stands for *Self-Monitoring Analysis and Reporting Technology.* This gives the disk drive the ability to send information to the PC's operating system when its operation is degrading for any reason.

ATA-4 defines the variation of the ATA-2 standard that is called the *Ultra ATA interface.* Like the other ATAs, Ultra ATA has a few aliases: Ultra DMA or *UDMA,* ATA-33, DMA-33. Ultra ATA adds one new DMA mode that supports a data transfer speed of 33 MBps per second. It also includes special error detection and correcting code that helps maintain the integrity of the data as it moves at high-speed over the standard ATA IDE 40-wire ribbon cable, which has yet to be upgraded.

ATA-5 and ATA-6 have added DMA data transfer speeds of up to 66.6 MBps and 100 MBps, respectively.

Floppy disks and drives

Unless you have been repairing computers in Elbonia for about twenty years, I'm confident that you know what a floppy disk is and how it's used. You may even know that the most popular size of floppy disk is 3½ inches. There have been larger floppy disks, but I'll bet that you haven't even seen anything bigger than a 3½-inch floppy disk anyway.

A floppy disk is perfect for transporting files of around 1MB in size between computers that aren't directly or indirectly connected by a local or wide area network (a technique known as *sneaker net*). Multiple floppy disks can also be used to record large files or backups. However, there are some dangers involved in using a floppy disk in many computers (such as computer viruses, which I discuss in Chapter 16). I cover the organization of a floppy disk in the section, "Organizing data on disk," later in this chapter.

CD-ROM and DVD technologies

CD-ROM (Compact Disc-Read-Only Memory) and DVD (Digital Versatile Disc or Digital Video Disc) are optical storage technologies that use a laser to read data from (and in some cases, store data to) its media. For purposes of the A+ Core Hardware test, it isn't important to know all of the ins and outs of how CD-ROM and DVD drives read or write data to their media. The Core Hardware exam deals with these devices as forms of storage units that are installed in a PC or may need troubleshooting and diagnostics at some point. So don't spend much time dissecting CD-ROM or DVD drives to learn their inner workings or how their media are constructed.

CD-ROM drives

A CD-ROM has the capability of storing up to 650MB of data. Its data is recorded in reverse of the old vinyl phonograph records — the ones you see at yard sales a lot. Data on a CD-ROM is recorded in one long continuous strand beginning on the inside edge and winding to the outside edge. Today, PCs often have a CD-ROM drive that also records data to the CD. These drives as a group are called *CD-R* (Recordable) or *CD-RW* (Read/Write) depending on whether they can be written to once (CD-R) or rewritten or written over several times (CD-RW).

CD-ROM drives are available in a wide range of transfer speeds. The transfer speed of a CD-ROM drive sets its type. CD-ROM types are stated as *X* factors. Each increment of the X is worth 150K in transfer speed. For example, a 1X CD-ROM has a transfer speed of 150K, an 8X CD-ROM has a transfer rate of 1200K, and a 24X CD-ROM has a transfer rate of 3600K.

1X represents the speed of a CD-A (Audio).

DVD drives

DVD is a family of optical disc storage technologies. DVD uses an optical disc (meaning it uses a laser to read or write the disc) that is the same size of a CD; that's where the similarities end. A DVD is double-sided; which means that at least it should hold twice as much data as a CD. Depending on the format used to record its data, a DVD-ROM (the kind used with a PC) can hold from 4.7GB to 17GB; that's the equivalent of 7 to 26 CD-ROMs. Two added features of a DVD drive are that

✔ DVD drives read CD-ROMs

✔ DVD drives play DVD-Video movies on your PC (because DVD-ROM and DVD-Video have the same format)

CD and DVD interfaces

Internal CD-ROM and DVD drives usually use the ATA IDE interface as defined in the ATAPI (ATA Packet Interface) standard, but drives using a SCSI interface are also available. If the drive is a SCSI drive, most, but not all, come with its own host adapter card. Before installing a SCSI drive, verify that the PC already has a SCSI host adapter installed.

An external CD and DVD drive may also use the SCSI interface, but it's more common for an external CD or DVD drive to connect to the PC using a USB or IEEE 1394 (FireWire) interface.

SCSI technology

The *Small Computer Systems Interface (SCSI)* is a collection of interface standards that covers a wide range of peripheral devices, including *hard drives, tape drives, CD-ROMs,* and *disk arrays (RAID).* (SCSI is pronounced *skuzzy.* It rhymes with fuzzy and not *scoozy,* which would sound like the Italian word for *pardon me.*) SCSI is less common in small office and home PCs because its components cost more and these PCs don't need the flexibility and high-end performance of this interface. ATA IDE is by far the most common interface in those environments.

SCSI is actually not an interface. It is more like a system bus structure on which many SCSI devices can connect to a single SCSI controller by sharing a common interface, called the *SCSI bus* or *SCSI chain* (see Figure 8-2). Each device connected to the SCSI bus is assigned a unique device number. These numbers are configured to the device with jumpers, DIP switches, or rotary dials located on the device. Most BIOS systems that support Plug and Play also include a feature called *SCSI Configured Automatically* or *SCAM* that sets SCSI device IDs automatically by software. For this to work, the BIOS, the host adapter, and the peripheral device must support the SCAM adapter.

When the SCSI controller (which counts as a numbered device) wants to communicate with a device on the bus, it sends a message encoded with the unit's device number. Any reply to the SCSI controller includes the sender's number. Like IDE/EIDE devices, SCSI devices also have their controllers built in; they can both control their own data access and capture activities and interpret requests from the PC that are passed to SCSI device from the SCSI controller.

SCSI devices are connected in what is called a *daisy chain,* which means that each device is connected in series with the next device on the bus. That is, of course, unless the device is the last device, in which case it uses a DIP switch setting or a resistor block to terminate the bus. Internal SCSI devices attach to a ribbon cable that can connect multiple devices. The ribbon cable is connected to a single port that provides service to all of the devices attached to the cable. The internal SCSI cable serves as the common bus media for all internal devices. External devices usually have two ports: one for the incoming cable, another to connect to the next device in line or for the terminator (if it is the last device on the bus). Figure 8-2 shows the SCSI bus. As shown, the devices on each end of a SCSI chain terminate the bus.

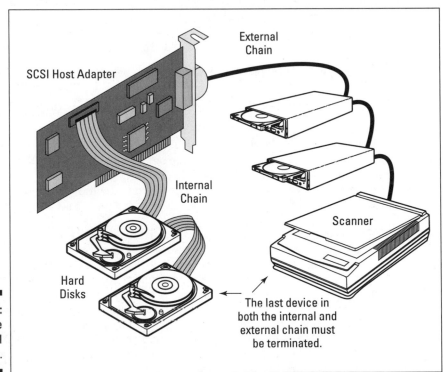

Figure 8-2:
An example of a SCSI bus system.

Just as World War I was not given a number until World War II began, the original SCSI interface is now SCSI-1. This implementation of the SCSI standard has a 5MB transfer rate, uses either a Centronics 50-pin or a DB-25 connector, and has an 8-bit bus. Major improvements have been made to the original SCSI-1 interface in the succeeding versions: SCSI-2 and SCSI-3.

SCSI-1

The original SCSI standard, developed in 1986, defined the basic specifications of the SCSI bus structure, including its commands, transfer modes, and cabling. SCSI-1 supported 8 devices on an 8-bit bus that supported up to 5 MBps of data transfer. SCSI-1 was not universally accepted and devices from different manufacturers were not always compatible.

SCSI-2

The extensive advancements in SCSI-2 solved many of the problems of SCSI-1. SCSI-2 established the foundation of the SCSI bus on which all future enhancements have been built. SCSI-2, which is also called *Fast-Wide SCSI,* defines two separate protocols:

- **Fast SCSI:** Features data transfer speeds of up to 10 MBps over the SCSI-1 8-bit cabling.
- **Wide SCSI:** Provides for 16-bit and 32-bit SCSI bus structures.

It's important to note that these two protocols can be used together to create a Fast and Wide SCSI bus. SCSI-2 also increased the number of devices that could be supported on the bus to 16. SCSI-2 is also backward compatible with SCSI-1 devices; the SCSI-1 devices can only operate at their original speeds.

SCSI-3

Also known as Ultra SCSI, SCSI-3 defines data transfer speeds up to 20 MBps over an 8-bit bus or higher speeds over the Wide SCSI bus. Table 8-1 details the various SCSI specifications, including the newer Ultra SCSI and its variations.

Table 8-1	SCSI Specifications			
SCSI Type	*Bus Width*	*Maximum Devices*	*Transfer Speed (MBps)*	*Connector Size (Pins)*
SCSI-1	8	8	5	25
SCSI-2	8	8	5	50
Fast SCSI	8	8	10	50

(continued)

Table 8-1 *(continued)*

SCSI Type	Bus Width	Maximum Devices	Transfer Speed (MBps)	Connector Size (Pins)
Wide SCSI/ Fast Wide SCSI	8	16	20	68
Ultra SCSI	8	8	20	50
Wide Ultra SCSI	16	16	40	68
Ultra2 SCSI	8	8	40	50
Wide Ultra2 SCSI	16	16	80	68
Ultra3 SCSI/ Ultra160	16	16	160	68
Ultra320	16	16	320	68

For more information about the various SCSI specifications, visit the Web site of the SCSI Trade Association (SCSITA) at www.scsita.org.

All SCSI devices should be powered on before the PC to allow the SCSI host adapter (usually inside the system) to detect and interrogate each of the devices on the SCSI bus.

RAID!?!

Though not specifically listed in the blueprint of the Core Hardware exam, you need some understanding of RAID technology in case it's included in a situational question or as an answer option.

A *Redundant Array of Independent Disks (RAID)* is a storage technology that uses at least two hard drives in combination for high availability, fault tolerance (error recovery), and performance. RAID disk drives are used often on servers but generally aren't necessary for a personal computer.

Data striping is a fundamental concept of RAID drives. In this process, data files are subdivided and written to several disks. This technique allows the processor to read or write data faster than a single disk can supply or accept it. While the first data segment transfers from the first disk, the second disk is locating the next segment, and so on.

Another common feature of RAID systems is data mirroring. This feature involves writing duplicate data segments or files to more than one disk to guard against losing the data should a hard drive fail.

Ten different RAID levels exist — 0 through 7, 10, and 53, each more complicated than its predecessor. The RAID levels you should know for the A+ Core
Hardware exam are

- ✔ **RAID 0 — Data Striping:** Interleaves data across multiple drives. Doesn't
  include mirroring, redundancy, or any other protection against device
  failure. RAID 0 is not fault tolerant.

- ✔ **RAID 1 — Data Mirroring:** Provides fault tolerance by completely duplicating data on two independent drives. This provides a failover disk if a
  mirrored disk fails.

- ✔ **RAID 5 — Disk Striping with Parity:** RAID 5 stores parity bits from two
  drives on a third drive to provide for data stripe error correction. This is
  the most popular RAID technology implemented.

Working with Disk Storage

You'll find questions that are either directly or indirectly about disk storage
directly throughout the A+ exams. It's hard to predict how many questions
you can expect on the exam versions you'll see, but my guess is between
three and five on the Core Hardware exam and perhaps fewer on the
Operating Systems Technologies exam.

Organizing data on disk

Just as you need an organization scheme to file documents in a file cabinet
so you can find them later, the disk also needs one. If you aren't interested in
finding the data later for some reason, then you really shouldn't worry about
organization. This is called the *FISH* file-organization technique — First In
Stays Here. But if you do care, you need some organization scheme.

Even before you can get your data organized, the PC and disk drive must have
an organization technique that helps them place and find data stored on the
media. The following are the building blocks of disk media organization and
some basic disk storage terms you absolutely should know for the exam:

- ✔ **Tracks:** A track is a concentric circular area of the disk that is discrete to
  all other tracks (see Figure 8-3). A length of a track is one circumference
  of the disk. On a hard drive, there may be more than 1000 tracks. When
  data is written to the disk, it begins with the outermost track first.

✔ **Sectors:** A sector, shown in Figure 8-3, is a single segment of a disk created by cross-sectioning divisions that intersect all the tracks. In addition to dividing each track into manageable pieces, sectors provide addressing references. Data can be addressed by its track and sector numbers, much like directions to a building located at the intersection of two major streets.

✔ **Clusters:** Groups of sectors used by operating systems to track data on the disk. There are normally about 64 sectors to a cluster; the size of the disk drive determines the actual number of sectors in a cluster.

✔ **Cylinders:** This addressable feature is unique to hard drives. A cylinder is a logical grouping of the same track on each disk surface in a disk unit. All of the tracks with the same track number on all of the hard drive's surfaces form a cylinder. For example, if a hard drive has three platters, it has six surfaces and six track 52s, as shown in Figure 8-4. All six of the track 52s make up cylinder 52. This feature allows data to be written to each platter on the same track, eliminating the need to move the read/write heads.

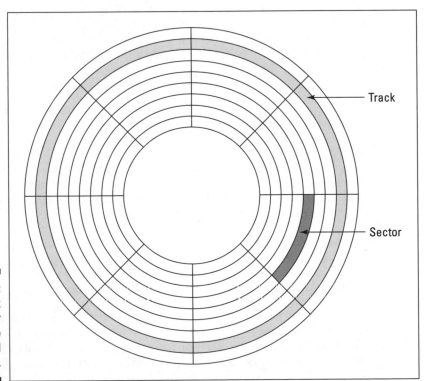

Figure 8-3:
A disk platter divided into tracks and sectors.

Track

Sector

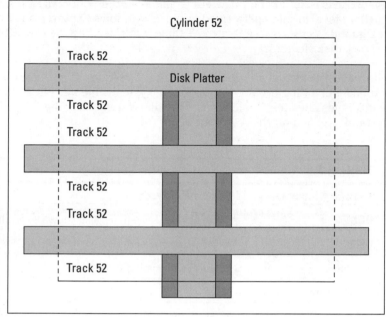

Cylinder 52

Track 52

Disk Platter

Track 52

Track 52

Track 52

Track 52

Track 52

Figure 8-4:
A cylinder
logically
groups the
tracks with
the same
number
from each
disk.

Formatting the disk

The processes included in this section are described in generic terms. You need to know the particular process used to format, partition, and create a file system in the specific operating systems included on the A+ Operating Systems Technologies exam (such as Windows 9*x,* Windows NT, Windows 2000, and Windows XP). Book II, Chapters 2, 3, and 4 cover these actions for the operating systems.

A disk drive undergoes two levels of formatting before it's installed in the PC. The low-level format shouldn't concern most PC repair technicians because it's done at the factory during manufacturing. Low-level formatting accomplishes two major outcomes:

- ✔ Builds the sector identification on a disk that is used by the drive to find sectors during read or write operations
- ✔ Physically scans the disk media for defects and records the location of any unusable areas found

During the procedure to install an operating system on a disk, the disk is prepared by performing a high-level format of the disk. The command to perform a high-level format varies from one operating system to the next, but in general the process is about the same. For example, in the Windows 9*x* installation, the high-level format (performed from the Windows Explorer, as shown back in Figure 8-1) creates a separate FAT table that's used by the operating system to track disk clusters.

Different operating systems use different file systems to manage disk storage. A high-level format creates the operating system's file system and management tables and files. Table 8-2 lists the file systems used by the operating systems you find on the A+ exams.

Table 8-2	File Systems
Operating System(s)	*Primary File System*
DOS	File Allocation Table (FAT); also known as FAT16
OS/2	High Performance File System (HPFS)
Windows 3.*x*	Virtual File Allocation Table (VFAT)
Windows 9*x*	FAT32
Windows NT/2000/XP	NT File System (NTFS)

Partitioning the hard drive

For the test, you should know

- ✔ The reason for partitioning the hard drive
- ✔ Something about the partitions themselves
- ✔ That FDISK is the command used in both Windows and DOS

  The FDISK utility partitions the hard drive into logical subdivisions, which are seen by the operating system as separate logical (as opposed to physical) hard drives.

Specialized software utilities can be used to format and partition hard drives, such as PartitionMagic Pro from Power Quest (www.powerquest.com) or Partition Commander from V Communications (www.v-com.com). These tools provide a graphical interface that provides disk volume and partition information beyond the basic data provided by the FDISK command.

You partition the hard drive to do the following:

- ✔ Divide the disk into logical subdrives that are addressed as separate drives; for example, C, D, and E
- ✔ Create separate areas of the disk to hold multiple operating systems, such as Windows and Linux, in their own partitions
- ✔ Separate programs from data into separate partitions to ease the backup process

Hard drives are divided into primary and extended partitions. Typically, one of the *primary partitions* is set as the active partition and is the one used to boot the system. A hard drive can have up to four primary partitions. Or in place of a primary partition, an *extended partition* can be created. An extended partition can be logically subdivided into as many as 23 logical disk drives. Although a hard drive can be divided into as many as four primary partitions, only one of the primary partitions can be active at a time.

The two types of partitions, primary and extended, can be allocated to be

- ✔ **System partitions:** The disk volume that contains the files needed to boot an operating system on a particular type of hardware. On most systems, the "active" partition is the system partition.
- ✔ **Boot partition:** The operating system's executable and support files. The boot partition can be (and often is) the same as the system partition, which in turn can be the primary partition.

Partitioning disks can improve disk efficiency. Under DOS and Windows, cluster sizes are automatically assigned in proportion to the disk size. The bigger the disk, the bigger the clusters, and large clusters can result in slack space (wasted disk space). Reducing the size of the disk through partitioning also reduces the cluster size.

Remember these partition facts for the A+ Core Hardware exam:

- ✔ Windows 95 OSR2 and Windows 98, which implement FAT32, can create a primary partition of 8GB.
- ✔ Windows 2000 supports FAT32 partitions of 2TB (terabytes or trillion bytes), but can only create a partition up to 32GB using the tools available with the operating system. A wide range of software tools is available to help partition a hard drive effectively.

After a hard drive is partitioned, the first sector on cylinder 0 (the outermost track) is reserved for the master boot record that contains the partition table. All partition types have a partition table that's used to track its contents.

However, the partition table in the master boot record contains the mapping for all partitions on all drives. The master boot record uses the partition table to locate and use the active primary partition to boot the system.

Installing and Configuring Storage Devices

The same basic process is used to install and configure a floppy disk, hard drive, CD-ROM, DVD, or tape drive. Only a few subtle and specific tasks differentiate these tasks. The A+ Core Hardware exam focuses on aligning and attaching a device's cabling. As you review the procedures used for each device in the following sections, pay attention to how the cabling is aligned and installed for each device.

Installing floppy disk drives

There are three considerations when installing a floppy disk drive in a PC:

- **Media:** Which diskette sizes has the user been using to back up data or install software? Don't do the customer a favor and upgrade the system to a 3½-inch floppy drive when all of his files are on 5¼-inch floppies.

- **Physical size:** Three package sizes (also called *form factors*) for floppy disk drives exist:

    - A *full-height drive* (which is big, bulky, and takes about two expansion slots) is common in older PCs.

    - The *half-height drive* is half as tall as a full-height drive. It's the size of one expansion slot on a PC case. This drive is the de facto standard in use today.

    - The *combination half-height drive* fits both a 3½-inch and a 5¼-inch drive into a single half-height drive.

- **Capacity:** Floppy disks range in their storage capacity. Depending on how many sides and the media density of the disk, 5¼-inch floppy disks hold between 360K to 1.2MB. Depending on the same variables, 3½-inch disks hold from 720K to 1.4MB.

Installing a floppy disk drive

To install a floppy disk drive in a computer, you must install the floppy disk drive controller card in the motherboard. Three types of floppy disk controller interfaces are used in PCs:

- ✔ **Standalone cards:** Usually not a single purpose card, floppy controller cards install into an expansion slot on the motherboard. For example, many floppy controller cards also include a game port, a serial port or two, a parallel port, and the disk interface.

- ✔ **Disk controller cards:** It has been common for a single card to provide the interface for the hard drive and the floppy disk since the days of the 286. This practice reduces the number of expansion slots needed to install what are considered system necessities.

- ✔ **Built-in controllers:** On most newer systems, the motherboard includes an interface adapter that is supported through its chipset for a floppy disk.

Cabling the floppy disk drive

The common floppy disk cable is a 34-wire ribbon cable that is usually light blue in color with one edge painted either red or blue. Usually three connectors are on the cable, as shown in Figure 8-5. The three connectors connect to the controller card and up to two floppy disk drives.

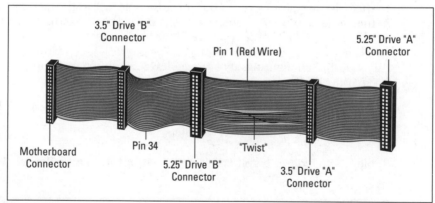

Figure 8-5: A floppy disk connector cable.

To be sure you have the floppy cable installed correctly, you can use two tricks:

- ✔ Remember "Big Red Is Number One"
- ✔ In most cases, the red edge should point toward the AC power cord.

A floppy cable is installed in a specific way. In addition to worrying about the alignment of the cable and getting Pin 1 installed on the controller card (Pin 1 is either marked with a "1" or a white dot on the controller card connector), you must also make sure that you use the correct connector with the proper disk drive. Some computer manufacturers go one step further to make this even easier. For example, Compaq uses a keyed cable connector for its floppy and IDE drives that can be connected in only one way.

As shown in Figure 8-5, two two-connector sets for floppy disk drives are on the cable:

✔ The first set of connectors, in the middle of the cable, is for the B floppy disk drive.

✔ After the twist in the cable (that is, at the end of the cable) are the A floppy disk connectors.

The floppy drive is connected to the power supply via a special 4-pin flat power connector (usually a Berg connector). Most power supplies provide at least two of these connectors.

Configuring the floppy disk drive

The drive cable takes care of any configuration problems you may have, unless you're installing a used drive. The drive select jumpers that assign an identity to the drive are usually set to DS2, or drive select 2, at the factory. The twist in the cable near the A: connector tricks the system into thinking that the drive connected after the twist is DS1, or drive select 1.

A key part of configuring any storage device, including a floppy disk drive, is ensuring that

✔ Correct system resource settings (IRQ, DMA, and I/O ports) are used

✔ Other devices don't have conflicts

Table 8-3 includes the system resource settings used for a floppy disk drive.

Table 8-3	System Resource Assignments for Floppy Disks	
Resource Type	*Resource Assigned*	*Comment*
IRQ	IRQ6	Default setting for floppy disk drives
DMA	Channel 2	Default setting for floppy disk controller (FDC)
I/O Address	03F0–03F7	Default for FDC (excludes address 03F6)

Installing ATA hard drives

Don't low-level format an IDE/EIDE or SCSI drive. If you low-level format one of these drives, you may render it totally useless by wiping out its sector translation information.

Mounting the disk drive

Hard drives share two physical sizing characteristics with floppy disks: The overall physical dimensions of the disk drive itself and the size of the drive bay into which it can be mounted. Many of the newer system case form factors include both *externally* accessible drive bays into which hard drives can be mounted and *internal* drive bays that are not accessible without opening the system case.

Hard drives have two form factors:

- **5¼-inch:** This larger form factor usually fits into the standard half-height drive bay on most system cases without other mounting hardware.

- **3½-inch:** This form usually must be installed in a tray to accommodate the oversize half-height bay. If a case includes an internal drive bay, it is usually a smaller bay for the smaller form factor.

Orienting the cable

You can expect one or two questions on these topics:

- Number of drives supported by ATA or IDE (2) and ATA-2 or EIDE (4)
- How the cables are aligned

Two cables must be attached to the disk drive: a data cable and a power cable. The power cable is attached to the power supply and is a keyed 5-pin cable that attaches directly to the drive in a matching connector port.

ATA drives are connected to either an adapter card or the motherboard with a 40-pin ribbon cable that must also be aligned to pin 1. The alignment is performed the same as for the floppy ribbon cable. Only two ATA IDE drives can be installed in a system, with one the master and the other the slave. Up to four ATA-2 or EIDE drives can be installed in a system with two drives on each of the two cables. One of the cables is designated as the primary and the other as the secondary interfaces. There is a master and a slave on each interface; you will see references to primary master, primary slave, secondary master, and secondary slave on the exam.

Configuring a hard drive

ATA drives must be designated either as a master or a slave. The *master* is the primary disk drive from which the system is normally booted. The slaves are not. Whether you install two IDE or four EIDE drives, one drive on each cable should be designated as the master. Set any other drives as slaves. This is done with jumpers on each drive controller. This step is important because two masters will fight each other to the death. The result is no disk access. Read the manuals for the drives to locate and set the jumpers appropriately.

Hard drives themselves are not directly configured with system resource assignments during their installation. However, the interface (IDE, SCSI) or its host adapter is. Table 8-4 lists the system resources used by the IDE and SCSI interfaces on a PC.

Table 8-4	System Resource Assignments for Hard Drives	
Resource Type	*Resource Assigned*	*Comment*
DMA		Not used for IDE or SCSI interfaces
IRQ	IRQ14	Reserved for the primary IDE controller (first two IDE (ATA) drives)
IRQ	IRQ15	Reserved for the secondary IDE controller (second two IDE (ATA) drives)
I/O Address	1F0–1F7	Primary HDC (hard drive controller)
I/O Address	170–177	Secondary HDC
I/O Address	370	IDE Controller

Installing and configuring optical drives

CD-ROM and DVD drives are installed using the same process as hard drives and usually occupy a half-height bay on the front panel of a PC so the user has access to the disk tray and drive controls. These drives are usually ATAPI devices and install on an ATA IDE data connection to one of the following:

- ✔ A proprietary adapter card
- ✔ A multipurpose adapter card
- ✔ Directly to the motherboard IDE connectors

Internal CD-ROM or DVD drives should also be connected to the PC's sound card (if a sound card is installed). A thin three-wire cable is usually included with the CD or DVD drive that interconnects these two devices. Check the documentation for your sound card to determine where a brand of CD or DVD drive should be connected. The power connector used is one of the same 5-pin Molex connectors used for a hard drive.

When installing an IDE CD-ROM drive to a system that has an IDE hard drive installed, you must configure the CD-ROM as a slave. See the drive manual for the correct setting. If no IDE hard drive exists, the CD-ROM can be the master, but some CD-ROMs run only as slaves.

CD-ROM and DVD drives are configured to the interface and are not directly assigned system resources. For a list of the system resources assigned to the IDE (ATA) interface, refer to Table 8-4.

To operate a PC's CD-ROM drive in a DOS environment, its device driver must load from the CONFIG.SYS file during the boot process. If the CD-ROM drive will be installed internally, you have the choice of either an IDE or SCSI. The IDE is less expensive, but the SCSI offers greater expandability.

Installing and configuring a SCSI hard drive

SCSI devices have new importance on the latest A+ Core Hardware exam. Expect a question or two about the idiosyncrasies of how a SCSI bus chain is installed and configured — a lot differently than the relatively simple process used for ATA devices.

Configuring the SCSI adapter

Many SCSI host adapters are configured via a block of DIP switches located on the adapter card. For example, an Adaptec SCSI host adapter is configured by setting its switches to the settings listed in Table 8-5. Some SCSI adapters are Plug and Play and do not require physical configurations on the card before installation.

Table 8-5	Sample Switch Settings for Configuring a SCSI Host Adapter	
Switch	*On/Off*	*Setting Represented*
1	On	Plug and Play disabled
	Off	Plug and Play enabled

(continued)

Table 8-5 (continued)		
Switch	*On/Off*	*Setting Represented*
2	Off	Together with Switches 3 and 4 sets default I/O address
3	Off	
4	Off	
2	On	Together with Switches 3 and 4, sets alternative I/O address
3	On	
4	On	
5	Off	Disables FDC defaults
6	Off	Together with Switches 7 and 8, sets BIOS default address
7	Off	
8	Off	

Driving Miss SCSI

Most SCSI host adapters require a device driver to be installed. On a Windows system, the device driver for a SCSI adapter can usually be located in the list of supported SCSI host adapters to be automatically installed and configured on the system.

Lab 8-1 lists the general steps used to install the device driver for a SCSI host adapter on a Windows NT or 2000 system.

Lab 8-1	Installing a SCSI Host Adapter Device Driver

1. **Log on to the system as either the administrator or a user with administrator privileges.**

2. **Open the Control Panel by choosing Start⇨Settings⇨Control Panel.**

3. **Activate the SCSI Adapters window from the SCSI Adapters icon.**

4. **Click the Drivers tab.**

5. **Ensure that a driver for the SCSI Adapter is not already installed.**

   If the driver is already installed, it doesn't need to be reinstalled.

6. **Click the Add button, and then select the driver from the Driver list.**

   Make sure the driver is available on the Windows system media or on the hard drive.

7. **Close the windows when completed and restart the system.**

Problems of the cabling kind

Up to 16 devices can be attached to a SCSI bus, so the cabling that connects them can be the primary source of problems on the chain. One problem is the cable can be too long. SCSI-1 chains cannot be more than six meters long, which is about 19 feet. Not six meters for the internal bus and six meters for the external bus, but six meters total for both. The cables inside external SCSI devices count, too!

SCSI-2 and SCSI-3 bus chains (because they're fast and wide) are limited to only 3 meters (just under 10 feet) and have the same rules of inclusion as SCSI-1. One other limitation is that a SCSI cable in any SCSI chain should not be less than 6 inches (approximately 0.15239 meters) as a general rule.

Terminating the bus

You can use two types of termination to terminate a SCSI bus:

- ✔ **Passive termination** can be used only with a SCSI-1 system because this system does not include voltage regulation and passive termination can cause problems on longer chains.

- ✔ **Active termination,** which regulates voltage at the termination point, should be used whenever possible. Don't mix active and passive termination on the same system.

On an external chain, the termination is a plug or cap that is attached to the open port on the last device on the chain. Internal chains are terminated through a jumper or a resistor block.

The SCSI chain is terminated at each end, internal and external. The last device on the internal SCSI chain should usually be a disk drive.

Avoiding conflict

Each SCSI device must be assigned an ID number. The number is assigned through a jumper or a DIP switch block. Because the SCSI bus, depending on the standard in use, supports 8 to 16 devices, including the host adapter, the numbers range from 0 to 7 and 8 to 15. Device ID 7 is reserved for the SCSI host adapter. You can assign the other devices any of the other numbers, but slower devices, such as CD-ROMs, should be assigned a higher SCSI ID. This gives them lots of time to process data on the SCSI bus. A SCSI hard drive used to boot the system is assigned SCSI ID 0.

SCSI devices are accessed in a priority scheme. Device ID 7 has the highest priority, as it should, followed by devices 6 through 0 and then devices 15 through 8, if they are in use and supported.

If you have both an ATA IDE disk drive and a SCSI disk drive on a system, the IDE drive should be the boot drive. The SCSI host adapter is set to 7; the boot hard drive is set to 0.

Getting Ready for Work

The odds of you running into a PC that has SCSI hard disk drives or other types of peripheral devices get better everyday. Even many factory PCs now include SCSI controllers and drives for disk, tape, CD, or DVD devices. So, to help you get ready both for the job and the exams, Lab 8-2 details the steps to use to troubleshoot problems on the SCSI bus.

When problems appear on a SCSI bus, especially after you have added or removed a SCSI device either internally or externally, use the steps in Lab 8-2 to try to pinpoint the problem.

Lab 8-2   Troubleshooting SCSI Device Problems

1. **Determine the total length of both internal and external (including any cable inside external devices) to verify that you haven't exceeded the maximum length for the interface type you're using.**

2. **Verify that each SCSI device has been assigned a unique address.**

3. **Only the last device on both the internal and external chains should be terminated.**

4. **Check all cables and connectors for defects and fit.**

5. **Verify that any new devices added to the system are not providing termination power.**

   Only the adapter card should provide termination power for a system terminated with active termination.

6. **Check the settings of the host adapter.**

7. **Verify that the terminators aren't damaged.**

Carrying Portable Data Storage

The early 20MB and 40MB portable hard drives were six to eight inches in diameter, weighed at least five pounds, and had to be mounted inside the PC's case for general protection. The latest development in disk storage are portable systems that range from pocket-sized 40GB hard drives to data storage devices that look more like key fobs than disk drives.

Many available newer and smaller storage devices include a biometric security device to unlock the storage unit for access, such as a fingerprint recognition unit.

These portable hard disk and compact flash devices connect to the PC through several connections, including USB (the most popular), FireWire (IEEE 1394), and serial. Portable hard disk devices usually use a connecting cable that can connect directly to a USB port or through a USB hub. Smaller, finger-sized flash storage devices usually plug directly into the USB port.

Prep Test

1 Which RAID level provides for disk striping with parity?

   A ○ 0

   B ○ 1

   C ○ 4

   D ○ 5

2 When should high-level formatting be done on an IDE hard drive?

   A ○ By the manufacturer at the factory

   B ○ Before it's partitioned with FDISK

   C ○ After it has been partitioned with FDISK

   D ○ IDE drives should never be high-level formatted

3 Which of the following are ATA IDE data transfer modes? (Choose two.)

   A ❑ PIO

   B ❑ IRQ

   C ❑ DMA

   D ❑ ISA

4 Which of the following is not an addressing scheme used by ATA and ATA-2 devices?

   A ○ LBA

   B ○ CHS

   C ○ WKRP

   D ○ ECHS

5 How many devices are supported on a Wide Ultra SCSI chain?

   A ○ 3

   B ○ 8

   C ○ 16

   D ○ 32

6 **DVD and CD-ROM drives use an IDE interface as defined in which standard?**

A ○ MAPI

B ○ CDAPI

C ○ ATAPI

D ○ ATARI

7 **Which of the following is required for each device on a SCSI chain?**

A ○ Termination

B ○ Unique device ID

C ○ Discrete cabling to host controller

D ○ Priority coding

8 **A hard drive cluster is made up of**

A ○ Cylinders

B ○ Tracks

C ○ Sectors

D ○ Hard drives

9 **When installing IDE/EIDE disk drives, at least one drive must be assigned as the**

A ○ Slave

B ○ Host

C ○ Controller

D ○ Master

10 **How many SCSI devices can be attached to a SCSI-2 chain?**

A ○ Two

B ○ Seven

C ○ Fifteen

D ○ Thirty-one

Answers

1 **D.** RAID 5 provides data striping at the character level and implements stripe error correction. *See "RAID!?!."*

2 **C.** IDE disk drives never need low-level formatting, but they should be high-level formatted after being partitioned to load the operating system to the drive. *Review "IDE technology."*

3 **A & C.** Although DMA is the transfer mode most commonly used in PCs over the past few years, PIO devices are still in use. *See "IDE protocols and modes."*

4 **C.** Although one of my favorite TV shows features the fictional radio station *WKRP in Cincinnati,* it's not an addressing scheme used by ATA devices. *Look at "Moving bigger blocks of data."*

5 **C.** "Wide" SCSI standards support 16 devices. *Review "SCSI technology."*

6 **C.** ATAPI (AT Attachment Packet Interface) is the standard that defines the interface used for CD-ROM, DVD-ROM, and some tape drives. *See "CD and DVD interfaces."*

7 **B.** Each SCSI device must be assigned a unique device ID number. *Review "Getting Ready for Work."*

8 **C.** Clusters are groups of sectors. Normally about 64 sectors are in a cluster, but the size of the disk drive determines the actual number of sectors in a cluster. *Look at "Organizing data on disk."*

9 **D.** When installing IDE/EIDE drives, you must designate one disk drive on each channel as a master. Designate the other drive on each channel as a slave. *See "Installing ATA hard drives."*

10 **C.** Up to seven devices (plus the SCSI adapter) can connect to a SCSI-1 bus, and a SCSI-2 bus supports up to 15 (plus the SCSI adapter). *Review "SCSI technology."*

Chapter 9

Powering and Cooling the PC

Exam Objectives

▶ Recognizing PC power supply terms, concepts, and functions

▶ Explaining PC power supply safety procedures

▶ Detecting common PC power supply problems

▶ Reviewing PC cooling systems

▶ Using a multimeter to troubleshoot power problems

*O*ne of my favorite you-never-can-tell stories is the "Case of the Fibbing Sibling." Anyone who has had the pleasure of being a brother or a sister (or parent) has experienced the "Not me's." This happens when your loving sibling has done something worthy of parental consternation and when asked about it says, "Not me!" This translates to mean that *you,* the innocent bystander, must have done it.

This story reminds me of a power supply that was also a fibbing sibling. A brand-new computer gave a POST disk drive error right out of the box. A new disk drive was sent for and installed. When the system was rebooted, it had the same error. The hard disk cables were replaced, but to no avail. The motherboard was replaced, and the system finally booted. However, a few days later the problem returned. Eventually, with no other parts to swap, the power supply was replaced. End of problem!

The power supply has one of the highest failure rates of any PC component. In spite of this, it's often the last component suspected for a problem. A faulty power supply can cause untold damage to the computer and, as the preceding story relates, can send the PC repairperson on a wild goose chase.

Quick Assessment

Recognizing PC power supply terms, concepts, and functions

1 The PC power supply converts _____ power into _____ power.

2 The power supply also contains the main cooling _____ of the PC.

3 The PC power supply generates five voltages: _____, _____, _____, _____, and _____.

Explaining PC power supply safety procedures

4 A(n) _____ happens when disturbances create a temporary high-voltage burst that travels down the power line.

5 _____ are small variations in the voltage of the power line.

6 A(n) _____ reduces power problems by absorbing spikes and smoothing line noise.

7 A Green Star device reduces its power consumption by _____ in sleep mode.

Using a multi-meter to troubleshoot power problems

8 Placing one probe on a pin at an end of a serial cable and the other probe on a pin at the other end of the cable checks for _____.

Answers

1 *AC, DC.* See "Power to the 'Puter" and "Internal power."

2 *Fan.* Study "Cooling it."

3 *+5V, −5V, +12V, −12V, +3.3V.* See "Converting power."

4 *Power surge.* Look at "The paradox of external power."

5 *Line noise.* Review "The paradox of external power."

6 *Surge suppressor.* Check out "Suppressing the surge."

7 *99 percent.* See "Saving the planet."

8 *Continuity.* Check out "Measuring resistance."

Power to the 'Puter

In spite of the power supply's importance, there aren't many questions on the A+ exam specifically about it. When you boil it down, it just supplies power and provides for the general cooling of the case. However, expect questions on system and processor voltages, the cooling system, surge suppressors, UPSs (Uninterruptible Power Supplies), and why they are needed.

Two basic facts of computer power are that much of the computer runs on either 5 or 12 volts of direct current (DC) power internally, and the electrical outlet on the wall supplies alternating current (AC) at about 110 to 115 volts. The PC's power supply bridges these incompatible worlds by converting raging AC power from the wall into the docile DC power used by the computer.

Obviously, the computer can't run without a power supply, which

✔ Supplies power to all the components in the computer

✔ Regulates incoming power voltage to eliminate the spikes and electrical noise common to most electrical systems

✔ Includes the primary components of the cooling system

To the PC power supply, two types of power exist: external and internal.

The paradox of external power

External power from your home or office wall outlet is the power everyone tends to take for granted — if it's there, it's fine. You may be surprised at the number of problems external power can have: line noise, spikes, surges, brownouts, and blackouts, among the major ones. Most of these problems go unnoticed, because they are usually small enough that the computer's power supply can deal with them (all except a blackout, of course). But these power problems can lead to reliability problems in your computer.

When you plug your PC directly into the wall socket, you are subjecting the PC to several problems. Some of these problems your computer can handle, but over time, even unnoticed problems can take their toll and result in major damage. You should know for the test the kinds of problems that the PC can experience from external power:

✔ **Line noise:** Small variations in the voltage of the power line. A small amount of line noise is normal in just about every system, and all but the cheapest power supplies can handle it. If you have the PC plugged into its own circuit (unshared line), you should have little trouble from line noise. However, if your computer shares an extension cord with the pop machine or its circuit with a megaton air conditioner, line noise is a certainty, and it will soon cause some major problems. Usually, the line noise eventually burns out the power-regulating circuits in a PC's power supply. After that, any line noise on the power line could pass through the power supply to the motherboard, disk drives, and other internal PC components.

- ✔ **Power surges:** A power spike (which the power company calls an *overvoltage event*) happens when disturbances in the electrical supply grid (such as distant lightning strikes or other anomalies) create a voltage spike that travels down the line to your wall plugs. The surge lasts only a few thousandths of a second, but that's plenty of time for the voltage to increase to 1000 volts or higher. High voltage spikes can degrade a PC's power supply. Multiple surges over time can destroy it.

- ✔ **Brownouts:** Called an *undervoltage event* by the power company, a brownout is the opposite of a power surge (overvoltage event). A brownout is a sudden dip in the power line voltage. A brownout doesn't usually last long, but it can. In most cases, the power level drops below normal levels for a time and then returns to normal. Brownouts are extremely common during periods of heavy load on the electrical system, such as hot afternoons or cold mornings. The reduced voltage level causes many devices to run slower than normal or malfunction in other ways. Low voltage for an extended time can do just as much damage as spikes.

- ✔ **Blackouts:** A blackout occurs when the power fails completely. The problems caused by a blackout are usually more frustrating than damaging, but the fluctuation of power surrounding a blackout can harm your system. If you're in the middle of a long document (that you hadn't yet saved), or were defragmenting or fixing other hard disk problems (and the allocation tables weren't completely rebuilt) when the power goes out, you probably have problems. More often, the damage occurs when the power returns suddenly (usually as a huge spike).

- ✔ **Lightning strikes:** This is the big spike. It can deliver more than a million volts.

  I have witnessed what a lightning strike can do to a building. Everything plugged in was completely destroyed or melted down: computers, copiers, fax machines, telephones, and more. A strike even in the vicinity can result in a very high voltage spike.

Internal power

The PC runs on DC. The computer's power supply converts AC power into the various DC voltages and signals used by the PC's components and circuits. The computer power supply, like that shown in Figure 9-1, is a switching power supply. It reduces the 110V incoming voltage to the 3.3V, 5V, and 12V charges used by the PC by switching the power charge off and on.

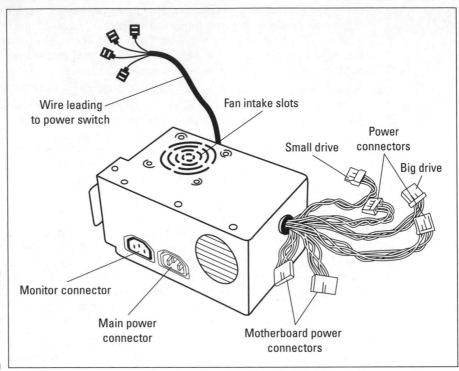

Wire leading
to power switch

Fan intake slots

Power
connectors

Small drive

Big drive

Figure 9-1:
A personal
computer
power
supply.

Monitor connector

Main power
connector

Motherboard power
connectors

The PC power supply functions only when it has demand. It has to know how much power to produce from the switching process used to generate its DC voltages. A power supply without some demand will not function properly and may even damage itself. Never "test" a power supply without connecting it to at least one 12V line — for example, a disk drive.

Internal power on portable PCs

Portable PCs, such as notebooks, palmtops, and PDAs (Personal Digital Assistants), are powered by batteries, which supply DC voltage directly to the PC. Several battery technologies are used in portable devices, some good and some better, but the tradeoff is made for convenience and portability. Chapter 14 details portable PCs, including their power systems.

Protecting against Power Evils

There are certainly ways you can fight back against the evils of external power. In fact, several levels of protection exist, ranging from none to too much, that you can use to protect your computer system from power problems. It's all in how much you want to spend, with costs up to several hundred dollars or more.

For the A+ Core Hardware exam, be very familiar with the benefits and limitations of the various types of power protection devices described in this section. The exam has few trick questions, but one that you might look for is, "Which of these devices provide surge suppression?" The answer is that almost every one of these devices provides surge suppression. So don't be tempted to quickly choose "surge suppressor;" also consider the other answers.

Two types of damage can be done to the PC by electrical forces:

- ✔ **Catastrophic damage:** The device is destroyed in a single event.
- ✔ **Degradation:** The device is damaged over repeated instances and begins to fail or has intermittent problems.

In the following section, I discuss some of the ways you can practice safe power.

Never, ever, never cut the grounding pin off a PC power plug cord. This is like looking the power monster in the face and smugly daring it to bite you.

Suppressing the surge

Most users plug their computers into a power strip or surge suppressor. These devices, which provide protective levels ranging from psychological to pretty good, are generally available at most computer stores or electronics departments. At the psychological level is the less-than-ten-dollars power strip, which basically is a fancy extension cord. At the pretty-good level are full surge suppressors that include line conditioning. Usually, the more you pay, the better the protection.

The primary component of a surge suppressor is a Metal Oxide Varistor (MOV). The MOV protects the computer by taking the hit from voltage spikes. The problem with MOV is that one big spike or an accumulation of small surges over time can knock it out. Some surge suppressors have a light to indicate that the MOV is still all right.

A surge suppressor reduces power problems by absorbing spikes and surges and by smoothing out line noise (this is called *line conditioning*). Surge suppressors at the high end of the cost range offer more protection, but some protection is always better than none. Unfortunately, how much protection you have really depends on how much you pay.

Know the following two main features when choosing a surge suppressor for the test:

- **Clamping voltage:** The voltage at which the suppressor begins to protect the computer.

- **Clamping speed:** The time lapse before the protection begins, or how much time elapses between detection and protection.

Not all surge suppressors include line conditioning. Check the box and any literature carefully when buying one.

A few other characteristics you should look for when comparing surge suppressors are (familiarize yourself with the units of measures — Joules, decibels, and watts — used in the following descriptions):

- **Energy Absorption:** Surge suppressors are rated in Joules, which measures their capability to absorb energy. You should be familiar with Joules for the test. The higher the rating, the better the protection: 200 Joules is basic protection, 400 is good protection, and 600 is superior protection.

- **Line Conditioning:** The line conditioning capability of a surge suppressor is measured in decibels. The more decibels of noise reduction, the better the line conditioning.

- **Protection Indicators:** If you have a surge suppressor, you're familiar with the LED that indicates you are protected. How reliable the indicator is depends on how much you paid. Less-expensive units will absorb enough power over time to degrade them. This is certain — if the LED is out, get a new suppressor. You can't know whether you're protected if a suppressor has no indicator.

- **Levels of Protection:** Surge suppressors have three levels of protection that indicate the maximum number of watts the suppressor allows to pass through to anything plugged into it. The standard ratings are 330 (best), 400 (better), and 500 (good).

Underwriters Laboratories (UL) has established a standard (UL 1449) for surge suppressors. A suppressor with UL approval has met this standard and should protect your system.

Conditioning the line

Line conditioners filter the power stream to eliminate line noise. Because true line conditioners usually are expensive, few PC users use them, preferring to purchase this capability in other devices (such as surge suppressors).

Hedging your bet

An uninterruptible power supply (UPS) tries to live up to its name by providing a constant (uninterrupted) power stream to the computer. Under normal conditions, a surge suppressor can also handle brownout conditions. When the power drops below a certain level or is disrupted completely, the UPS kicks in and provides power for a number of minutes (or hours in some cases). Expect a question or two on UPSs.

All UPS units have two sets of circuits:

- ✔ One circuit is the AC circuit; it's like an expensive surge suppressor.

- ✔ The other circuit is the battery and *DC to AC conversion*. That's right — DC to AC conversion. The batteries store a DC charge that must be converted to AC because AC is what the PC expects.

Two types of UPS units are available and differ in the following ways:

- ✔ **Standby UPS:** Operates normally from its AC side. When the power drops, it switches over to its battery backup side.

- ✔ **In-line UPS:** Operates normally from its DC or battery backup side. The AC side is used only if there is a problem with the battery-powered circuits.

UPS units are often confused with a standby power supply (SPS), or battery backup, which supplies power only when none is available and has no power-conditioning capabilities.

Never plug a laser printer into a conventional PC UPS:

- ✔ Laser printers draw a lot of power at startup and use power in "gulps" during their fusing processes; few UPS units can handle the demand.

- ✔ Laser printers inject noise back into the UPS or surge suppressor.

Saving the planet

The A+ Core Hardware exam tests you on environmental issues surrounding the PC and its peripherals, including the hazards and safeguards.

To reduce the amount of electricity consumed by computers, the U.S. Environmental Protection Agency (EPA) established guidelines for energy efficiency under a program called *U.S. Green Star,* also known as *Energy Star.* On Green Star systems, the power supply works with the computer's components and some peripherals to reduce the power they use when idle.

Green Star devices have a standby program that puts them into sleep mode after the device has been idle for a certain period. In sleep mode, the device reduces 99 percent of its power consumption and uses no more than 30 watts of power.

The Power Supply

This section concentrates on the first exam objective listed at the beginning of the chapter: recognizing PC power supply terms, concepts, and functions. This section covers a few questions you should expect on the test.

The power supply is a black or silver box with a fan inside and cables coming out of it. It's located either at the back of a desktop case or at the top of a tower or mini-tower case. The power supply is distinctive because of its big yellow warning label with scary-looking symbols and warnings. The purpose of this label is to warn you not to try to fix a power supply.

A caution sticker (you'll know it — it says "Caution") on an electric or electronic device in a PC alerts you to possible equipment damage. A warning label (says "Warning" and has lightning bolts, a skull and crossbones, or the like) alerts you to possible electrocution, which could hurt you.

Just to quench your curiosity, inside the power supply, one part should keep you out: a 1000-microfarad capacitor. Capacitors store electricity, even when the power is off. This capacitor performs line conditioning by absorbing any power coming in above the normal level and using it to replace power below normal levels. If you were to touch the capacitor, it would shock you — potentially with bodily harm or worse. Because you can buy a new power supply in the range of $25 to $80, I'm not sure it's worth risking your life to open up the power supply to try to fix it. A good quality power supply should last for years, providing the computer with stable electrical current, if it has been protected adequately. On the other hand, a low quality, faulty, or overloaded power supply can cause all kinds of problems in a system. A bad power supply can cause hard disk drives to develop bad sectors and affect memory to cause what seem like software bugs — problems that are usually hard to pin on the power supply.

Anatomy of the power supply

Be familiar with the parts of the power supply for the exam.

The features you can access on the outside of the power supply are incredibly standard even between form factors. The primary power supply components are

- ✔ **Power cord:** I think you know what this is.
- ✔ **Passthrough connectors:** Located on the back of the power supply. In the past, these connectors were used primarily to plug a monitor into the power supply, which enables you to turn the monitor on and off with the computer's power switch. This feature has all but disappeared from PCs, because it's no longer necessary to plug the monitor into the power supply.
- ✔ **Power switch:** Where the main power switch is located on a PC depends on its form factor and its age:
  - • On older PCs, this switch extended through the case wall from the power supply on a back corner of the PC.
  - • In the newer ATX power supply, the switch is electronic, not physical. You don't so much turn on or off the computer as you request the motherboard to do it.
- ✔ **110V/220V Selector switch:** Allows you to select between the two voltages. If a power supply has one, be sure it's set correctly. This switch is handy when you jaunt to Europe with your PC.

When a monitor is plugged into the power supply's passthrough connector, the monitor is not being powered by the PC's internal power supply. It's called a *passthrough plug* because it passes the AC power through. You have only gained the convenience of turning the monitor on and off with the PC.

Cooling it

The power supply also contains the main cooling fan that controls airflow through the PC case. The power supply fan is the most important part of a PC's cooling system. Air is forced to flow through the computer case and over the motherboard and electronic components, which generate heat as they work. Any interruption to the airflow can cause sensitive components to degrade or fail. The power supply fan should be kept clean and clear.

Only with the case closed and intact does the PC cooling system function at its optimum level.

If a power supply's wattage rating is sufficient to supply the computer's electrical requirements, the fan should be adequate to handle the computer's cooling needs, although Pentium-class processors require additional cooling or heatsinks of their own.

As I cover in more detail later in this chapter, two popular form factors for power supplies exist: the Baby AT and the ATX. I bring up form factors here only because these two types of power supplies cool the system differently. A form factor defines the size, shape, and fit of the components of a case, motherboard, and power supply combination:

- ✔ The Baby AT, which has been the standard until the past year or two, cools the system by pulling air into the case and blowing it out through the fan. You can feel the air blowing out of the fan on this type of power supply. If you've ever opened up an old PC AT computer that has been in use for a while without the case being opened, you know firsthand a primary problem with this type of cooling. Room dust, smoke, chalk in school settings, and all else are sucked into the computer to accumulate on internal components such as grills, wires, circuit boards, memory modules, and so on. This buildup can affect the cooling system's capability of cooling the motherboard and drives by restricting the airflow. Buildup also can possibly short out the motherboard or other components.

- ✔ The ATX form of power supply sucks air into the case. This method helps keep the case clean by pressurizing the inside of the case. The power supply is situated on the board so that air blows straight over the processor and RAM. This was originally intended to eliminate the need for a CPU fan, but nearly all Pentium-class processors include their own fans and heatsinks.

In either case, all expansion slot filler slides should be in place and the case should be in place and intact to allow the cooling system to do its job.

Cooling it beyond cold

Liquid cooling systems usually use ordinary water; some use liquid nitrogen, which is about the coldest liquid there is (except maybe for Lake Tahoe in the early spring), around –196 degrees Celsius.

- ✔ Water cooling systems, called *waterblocks* (see Figure 9-2), are available for CPUs, video processors, and chipsets. They do what you expect: circulate water in a closed system through a cooling agent and over the processor, where the water absorbs heat from the processor.

Figure 9-2:
A CPU
waterblock
is the
component
of a water-
cooling
system that
attaches to
the heat
sink and
CPU.

Image courtesy of Swiftech

✔ The most sophisticated systems used liquid nitrogen to cool the heat sinks and the processor. Just to frame a reference for you, water freezes solid at 0 degrees Celsius (32 degrees Fahrenheit) and boils at 100 degrees Celsius (212 degrees Fahrenheit). So –196 degrees Celsius is nearly 200 degrees (Celsius) colder than the temperature needed to freeze water. Obviously, this is not something you want to just cobble together for your PC.

See Chapter 6 for more information you need to know for the exam about the methods and devices used to cool a microprocessor.

Converting power

What the power supply does is simple: It converts AC to DC. Many devices can convert current; for example, the power converter I plug into my van's dashboard so my kids can watch videotapes as we motor along. Another type allows my portable CD player to plug into the wall when the batteries are dead. Another lets my notebook PC run from an AC supply while it charges the batteries. If only it were as simple for the desktop PC as it is for the notebook PC. The PC power supply must provide several voltages at different strengths and manage some power-related signals for the motherboard.

Standard voltages

Know this stuff for the test. The power supply provides the following voltages to the motherboard and drives:

- **+5V:** The standard voltage of motherboards with all processors below 100 MHz (such as early Pentium, 486, and 386) and many peripheral boards.

- **+12V:** Used primarily for disk drive motors and similar devices. Modern motherboards also pass this voltage to ISA bus expansion slots.

- **–5V and –12V:** Included in most power supplies for compatibility with older systems. Most modern motherboards don't use either of these voltages. Power supplies that produce these values do so at very low (less than 1 amp) amperage. Check the label on your power supply.

- **+3.3V:** This is the standard voltage level for motherboards compatible with 100 MHz processors and faster. Upgraded motherboards must convert the 5V signal from the power supply into 3.3V for the processor, requiring a voltage regulator on the motherboard. Newer power supplies provide the 3.3V power for the CPU directly.

Concentrate on which voltages are used with which types of devices, especially the voltage of all Pentium-class processors, listed in Table 9-1. For example, disk drives use the +12V lines, the Pentium processor uses 3.3V, and the other lines (+/–5V and –12V lines) are primarily used for backward compatibility.

Processor voltages

Processors use two levels of power:

- **External voltage or I/O voltage:** Powers the devices mounted to motherboards compatible with a certain processor.

- **Internal voltage:** The voltage level used by the micro-components of the processor. The internal voltage number is important; because the higher the voltage, the more heat the processor generates.

Table 9-1 shows a trend of smaller internal voltage levels for the Pentium-class processors.

Table 9-1	Processor Voltage Levels		
Processor	*Version*	*External*	*Internal*
Pentium	60–66	5	5
Pentium	75–200	3.3/3.52	3.3/3.52

Processor	Version	External	Internal
Pentium	MMX	3.3	2.8
6x86		3.3	3.3
AMD	K5	3.52	3.52
Pentium Pro	150	3.1	3.1
Pentium Pro	166+	3.3	3.3
Pentium II	(Klamath)	3.3	2.8
Pentium II	Deschutes/Celeron/Xeon	3.3	2.0
Pentium III	Katmai	3.3	2.0
Pentium III	Coppermine/Xeon	3.3	1.65–1.75
Celeron II	Coppermine 128	3.3	1.5–1.65
Pentium IV	423-pin	3.3	1.75
Pentium IV	478-pin 256KB L2	3.3	1.75
Pentium IV	478-pin 512KB L2	3.3	1.5–1.525
AMD Athlon	Socket A	3.3	1.6–1.8
AMD Athlon	XP	3.3	1.75
AMD Duron	Socket A	3.3	1.6
AMD	K6-2+/K6-III+	3.3	1.8–2.0
AMD	K6-III	3.3	2.2
AMD K6-2	w/3DNow	3.3	2.2
AMD K6	266/300	3.3	2.2
AMD K6	233	3.3	3.2
6x86 MX		3.3	2.9

Regulating power to the processor

Virtually every motherboard has a voltage regulator to control the flow of voltage to the microprocessor. On some motherboards, a replaceable module, called a *Voltage Regulator Module,* or VRM, is used and on others the voltage regulator is a built-in component of the motherboard itself.

Fitting it in the box

Form factor refers to the shape and dimensions of a device. PC cases are designed to hold a power supply form factor. The power supply must match both the designed form factor of the case and the motherboard's power requirements. The form factor of a power supply is seldom an issue (except for upgrades and build-your-owns) because the power supply is usually purchased already installed in the case. The form factor of the case is usually more of an issue.

In general, the form factors of the motherboard are the same for the case and the power supply. The most common form factors used today are

✔ **Baby AT:** The oldest standard that has been used for PCs until recently

The Baby AT is what most people think of as the standard desktop case and power supply. Figure 9-3 shows the back of a Baby AT power supply. On the left side of the power supply is the power switch intended to extend through a hole in the system case.

✔ **ATX:** The newest form factor

The ATX form factor has essentially replaced the Baby AT for new systems. The ATX power supply differs from the Baby AT power supply in three primary ways:

• ATX has additional voltage and power lines that signal and control the power supply.

• The fan blows into the case instead of out as with the Baby AT, which helps keep the case clean.

• The ATX power supply turns on and off with electronic signaling and not a physical power switch. It can also be switched on and off by software, such as a Windows shutdown.

Figure 9-4 shows the back of an ATX power supply.

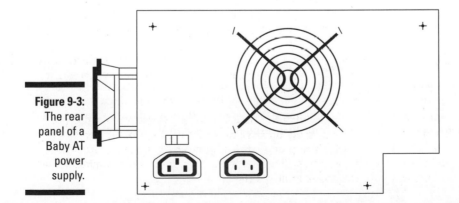

Figure 9-3:
The rear panel of a Baby AT power supply.

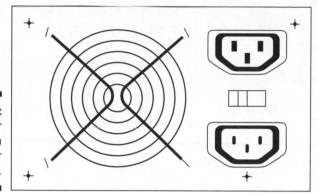

Figure 9-4:
The rear panel of an ATX power supply.

Connecting the Power

The Core Hardware exam includes power questions that relate to the mother-board, disk drives, and other devices. Some of these questions may appear to be about the device; they're actually power and power connection questions. Review this section carefully.

The bundles of wire hanging from the power supply are what the power supply is all about. They carry juice to the parts of the computer. Depending on the form factor, four or five bundles of wire come from the power supply.

Always be sure that the power supply is unplugged by removing its power cord from its back before you attach its connectors inside the PC.

Motherboard connectors

Don't expect any questions on the A+ Core Hardware exam on the specific pinouts (pin assignments) of power supply connectors. However, questions may deal specifically with the power supply and the motherboard connections of specific form factors. The only form factors mentioned specifically in the test objectives are the Baby AT and the ATX; I recommend you study these.

You can definitely tell which form factor you have by the motherboard power connectors. The Baby AT power supply has two 6-wire connectors, and the ATX has a single 20-wire keyed connector.

- **Baby AT:** The two connectors of the Baby AT power supply attach to the motherboard next to each other. Sometimes, the connector blocks are labeled P8 and P9, the plug position numbers for their mates on the motherboard. But you're still left with the dilemma of which side is 8 and which is 9, and they look almost identical.

The P8 and P9 connectors are oriented correctly if all four of the black (ground) wires (two on each plug) are together in the middle. Any other orientation will likely damage the motherboard.

✔ **ATX:** The ATX power supply must be used with an ATX motherboard. Together, they eliminate any confusion with the power connection through a single 20-wire keyed connector. A keyed connector usually has a prong, lip, or finger that prevents it from being connected incorrectly. The ATX power supply also has power connectors for the front panel.

The ATX power supply is always on. Power is supplied to the motherboard even when the system power is off. Always disconnect the power cord from the back of the case before working on one.

Drive power connectors

Most power supplies have either three or four four-wire power connectors for internal drives. Two types and sizes of connectors exist and are easy to tell apart.

The larger power supply connector shown in Figure 9-5, which is also called a *Molex connector,* connects almost all hard drives, CD-ROM and DVD drives, and 5¼-inch floppy drives.

Figure 9-5:
Some drives use the larger (Molex) power supply connector; others use the smaller (Berg) power supply connector.

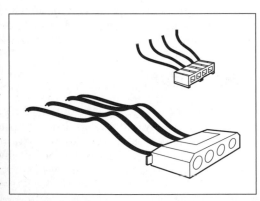

The smaller plug shown in Figure 9-5, which is also called a *Berg connector,* is used by 3½-inch floppy drives, some tape drives, and a few others. These connectors are keyed, so they can't be installed backwards, try as you might.

Getting Ready for Work

One of the skills you should have to be truly effective as a PC repair professional is the ability to use a multimeter, whether digital or analog, to troubleshoot PC electrical problems. On the exam, you can expect to see at least one question that deals with the use of a multimeter to measure the voltage of the power coming from the power supply or into the motherboard or a hard disk drive. So this section is worth reviewing, if for no other reason than it may help you get that question right.

Meeting the multimeter

The A+ Core Hardware exam expects you to know how to use, when to use, and what to measure with a multimeter. Expect questions in the troubleshooting area that ask which settings to use when measuring volts, amps, and ohms. If you don't have much experience with a multimeter, get one and either read the booklet that comes with it or ask a more experienced PC service technician to explain it you.

A *multimeter* measures the properties of AC and DC electrical power circuits. The range of capabilities available on multimeters is wide; even the simplest (and cheapest) have features you will rarely (or never) use.

A multimeter has two probes: a red (positive) probe and a black (negative) probe. When you test a device, place the red probe on the *hot point,* or high point, of the current and place the black probe on the *ground,* or low point. The voltage of the circuit is calculated as the difference in the readings of these two points.

The two major categories of multimeters are *analog* and *digital*. Here's a brief description of these two types of multimeters:

- **Analog multimeter:** An analog multimeter performs the same measurements as a digital multimeter, but uses a scaled dial and a needle to register the value measured.

- **Digital multimeter:** Digital refers to the fact that the output numbers that represent the results of a measurement are displayed on an LCD (liquid crystal diode) screen. In other words, the results are displayed as digits.

Never, I repeat, *never* connect a multimeter to the main (building) electrical supply line, which carries at least 20 kilowatts of power. This is bad for your multimeter and it won't do you much good, either.

Using a multimeter

You can make four measurements on a PC using a multimeter:

- ✓ **Amps:** Measure the strength of an electrical current
- ✓ **Farads:** Measure the capacitance of an electrical device
- ✓ **Ohms:** Measure the resistance in an electrical medium
- ✓ **Voltage:** Measure the electrical potential of a circuit

Table 9-2 lists the type of problems that can be identified in some systems and the property that is measured.

Table 9-2	Troubleshooting with a Multimeter	
Component/System	*Property*	*Potential Faults*
Power supply connectors	Volts	Defective power supply, cables, or connectors
Cable connections	Ohms	Broken or defective cable
Cable shielding	Ohms	Broken or defective cable sheath or insulation
Electrical FRMs	Volts or Ohms	Improper electrical operation to specifications

Probing for power

When preparing a multimeter for use, you must set three things:

- ✓ **The type of current you're measuring:** AC or DC (also known as VDC — voltage direct current).
- ✓ **What you're measuring:** Set the appropriate indicator or dial to voltage (volts), current (amps), or resistance or continuity (ohms).
- ✓ **The range of values expected:** If you're measuring voltage from the power supply, the voltage range is 3V to 12V, and for the AC wall plug's output, the range is around 105V to 125V. You can find Autorange multimeters that sense the incoming power and set the range automatically.

Remember to put on your ESD wrist strap and connect it to either a static ground mat or the PC case.

Measuring volts

Voltage is the easiest and most common measurement that is made with a multimeter on a PC. Here are the general steps to follow when measuring voltage:

1. **Set the dial to measure DC voltage.**

2. **Choose the voltage range. Usually, this will be 20V or lower, based on what you are measuring.**

3. **Hold the black (negative) probe to a grounding point on the circuit.**

4. **Touch the red (positive) probe to a hot point on the circuit.**

Measuring resistance

The amount of resistance, or *continuity,* a circuit has to allow an efficient flow of electricity is measured in ohms. The general steps to measure resistance are

✔ Be sure the circuit (power connector, trace, or cable) has no power running through it. If the circuit to be tested is inside the PC, turn off the PC's power supply. You could damage your multimeter if you test a circuit that has power running through it.

✔ Set the multimeter to test ohms and set an appropriate range.

✔ Touch the multimeter's probes to two metal points on the circuit. If you get a zero value, set the range higher or lower.

The multimeter should give a reading, buzz, or beep to indicate continuity in the cable. If you do not get buzzed or beeped, then either no continuity exists in the cable, or you have not made a good connection. Try a few more times — if you still get no reading, probably there is no continuity and you have discovered a bad cable. Before you chuck out the cable, try testing all of the remaining pins, using the cable's pinout for which pins are connected to each other.

Prep Test

1 A device that can supply backup power to a PC when the electricity fails and provides for line conditioning as well is called a(n)

A ○ SPS

B ○ UPS

C ○ Surge suppressor

D ○ Line conditioner

2 A device that protects a PC against overvoltage is called a(n)

A ○ UPS

B ○ Power conditioner

C ○ Surge suppressor

D ○ A, B, and C.

3 While you repair a PC with an ATX motherboard, it should be

A ○ Plugged in

B ○ Unplugged

C ○ Turned on

D ○ Powered up

4 A PC conforming to the Green Star standard reduces what percentage of its power consumption in Sleep mode?

A ○ 99

B ○ 90

C ○ 92

D ○ 96

5 What electronic component in the PC power supply absorbs most power spikes?

A ○ Resistors

B ○ Varistors

C ○ Coils

D ○ Capacitors

6 **What are two important factors to consider when selecting a surge suppressor?**

A ○ Switching rate and Joules dispersed
B ○ Switching speed and clamping speed
C ○ Clamping speed and clamping voltage
D ○ Joules dispersed and wattage

7 **Which of the following devices should not be connected to a UPS?**

A ○ A laser printer
B ○ A monitor
C ○ A PC power supply
D ○ You can connect any device to a UPS

8 **When the electrical power system fails completely, it's called a(n)**

A ○ Brownout
B ○ Blackout
C ○ Overvoltage
D ○ Undervoltage

9 **What procedure is used to measure continuity between two points with a multimeter?**

A ○ Set the meter to ohms and test the circuit with power to it.
B ○ Set the meter to ohms and test the circuit without power to it.
C ○ Set the meter to amps and test the circuit with power to it.
D ○ Set the meter to amps and test the circuit without power to it.

10 **What are the two types of uninterruptible power supplies?**

A ○ Standby and interactive
B ○ In-line and out-line
C ○ Standby and in-line
D ○ In-line and interactive

Answers

1 **B.** A battery backup supplies only backup electricity. A surge suppressor and a true line conditioner provide only line conditioning protection. The uninterruptible power supply (UPS) does both. *See "Hedging your bet."*

2 **C.** Overvoltage is the same as a power surge or a spike. A surge suppressor absorbs the spike and prevents it from damaging your computer. *Review "Suppressing the surge."*

3 **B.** ATX form factor power supplies should be unplugged because they provide power to the motherboard even when the power supply itself is turned off. *Check out "Connecting the Power."*

4 **A.** A device that conforms to the U.S. Green Star standard reduces its power consumption to less than 30 watts and reduces its overall consumption by 99 percent. *Try "Saving the planet."*

5 **D.** A capacitor is used to absorb a power spike and can be used to provide power to bring up an undervoltage condition. *Charge over to "The Power Supply."*

6 **C.** The clamping voltage is the voltage level at which the surge suppressor engages; the clamping speed is how soon after detection suppression begins. *Consider "Suppressing the surge."*

7 **A.** Laser printers draw a lot of power at startup, and few UPS units have enough power to handle the demand. *See "Hedging your bet."*

8 **B.** A blackout is the complete loss of power from the general electrical power supply system. *Review "The paradox of external power."*

9 **B.** Set the meter to ohms and test the circuit without power to it. Continuity is measured in ohms. With power running through a cable, you're testing current or power. Without the power on, you're testing continuity. *Review "Using a Multimeter."*

10 **C.** The standby UPS is like a big surge suppressor with a battery backup; the in-line UPS is a big self-charging battery that runs your computer with an emergency AC line, just in case. *Look at "Hedging your bet."*

Part III
Outside the Box

The 5th Wave   By Rich Tennant

"I can tell a lot from your resume. You're well educated, detail oriented and own a really tiny printer."

In this part . . .

A significant portion of the A+ Core Hardware exam is on the information you find in this part of the book. In this part is the coverage on input/output ports and connectors, printers, monitors, keyboards, mice, and even portable PCs.

The devices covered in this part of the book provide the human computer interface, or the audible, visual, and tactile ways the human, you, and the computer, it, are able to communicate and work together to solve problems and find entertainment, information, and even a movie or two.

Chapter 10

Input/Output Ports

● ●

Exam Objectives

▶ Identifying common peripheral ports, cabling, and connectors

▶ Listing the system resource assignments of standard port types

▶ Explaining the troubleshooting procedures for the common port types

● ●

*I*f you've spent hours trying to get a parallel port to accept a serial printer connected to a serial-to-parallel converter in hopes of salvaging a customer's old system printer, you have a deep appreciation for the differences among input/output ports and their communications. To oversimplify, parallel ports are used for printers and serial ports are where modems plug in. As way oversimplified as this may be, it isn't an altogether bad summarization of the differences of these two ports. However, you should know more about the subtleties of these port types and a couple of other kinds of ports for the A+ Core Hardware exam.

You should understand the ins and outs of each of the port types described in this chapter. Don't worry about the finite details of each port and its connectors, such as the electronic specifications or the exact pinout assignments of the connector. But you should know the best use of each port type, the type of connector it uses, and the number of pins in or the shape of its connector. When it matters (I'll point it out when it does), you should also know the standards that specify or define the usage of each connector or port type.

Review the information on ports in this chapter and in Chapters 11, 12, and 13 to gain some background and understanding of the terminology, their function, and their system resource assignments, such as COM and LPT ports, IRQs, and I/O address linkages.

Quick Assessment

Identifying common peripheral ports, cabling, and connectors

1 Serial data is transmitted _____ bit(s) at a time.

2 A(n) _____ cable is used to connect two computers directly via their serial ports.

3 Serial devices are controlled by a(n) _____.

4 The _____ standard covers bidirectional communications through a parallel port.

5 _____ ports are commonly used for printers on most PCs.

6 FireWire and i.Link are proprietary names for the _____ interface.

7 A(n) _____ port can support up to 127 devices.

Listing the system resource assignments of standard port types

8 COM1 is commonly assigned to IRQ _____.

9 LPT1 is usually assigned I/O address _____.

Explaining the trou-bleshooting procedures for the common port types

10 Serial port problems are usually caused by _____ conflicts.

Answers

1   *One.* Check out "Understanding Serial Devices."

2   *Null modem.* Take a look at "Cabling the connection."

3   *UART* or *Universal Asynchronous Receiver/Transmitter.* Peek at "Is that UART?"

4   *IEEE 1284.* See "Keeping up to standard."

5   *Parallel.* Review "Looking at Parallel Devices."

6   *IEEE 1394.* Check out "There's fire in the wire: IEEE 1394."

7   *USB.* Look over "Connecting with USB."

8   *4.* See "Setting up a serial port."

9   *378h.* Take a look at "Troubleshooting a parallel port."

10   *System resource.* Review "Troubleshooting a serial port."

Defining Ports and Connectors

In the life of the PC repair technician, the really fun stuff (such as replacing the motherboard, upgrading the processor, or tracking down a transient error in memory) is only a small part of the job. The real work involves more mundane tasks, such as installing a new printer, connecting an external modem, rigging a nifty new mouse or keyboard, or adding the pizzazz of a digital camera. In spite of my feeble attempts to make these tasks sound exciting, they're not much more than connecting the device's cable and connector to one of a PC's ports. That's the stuff that fills your hours. That's why the A+ Core Hardware exam emphasizes knowing different types of ports in use, the types of connectors used with them, and the proper way to connect.

You should know these characteristics about ports and connectors for the test:

- ✔ The types of devices that use each port type
- ✔ The system resources used to configure serial and parallel ports
- ✔ The standards that define each of the common port types
- ✔ The connectors, meaning their sizes and shapes, and cabling used with each port type

You should know these *port types* for the test: IEEE 1394/FireWire, infrared (IR), parallel, serial, and USB.

Understanding Serial Devices

Serial communications, which are conducted through serial ports, involve sending bits in a serial fashion, one bit a time. *Serial* means that the bits are sent in a series, a single-file stream. This contrasts to parallel, where several bits are sent at the same time side-by-side.

Serial and parallel devices, cables, ports, and communications are all based on the same basic premises:

- ✔ Serial data is transmitted one bit at a time.
- ✔ Parallel data is transmitted at least eight bits at a time.

These fundamental differences characterize all comparisons between these two communications modes. To transmit a single ASCII character via a serial port, eight separate one-bit transmissions are needed. On the other hand, a parallel port needs only one 8-bit wide transmission. In some ways, serial communications are like a single-lane country road, while a parallel transmission is like I-90 with eight lanes. Obviously, parallel communications can handle more data in less time.

Here are some facts you may not know about serial ports and communications (if you already know this information, this is still a good review for the test):

🖙 A serial transmission moves less data than a parallel transmission, but it can travel a greater distance. A serial cable can be up to 50 feet long (compared to the standard 15-feet limit of a parallel cable). Beyond that distance, the data begins to lose its oomph and data errors can occur.

🖙 Most serial devices are external devices that plug into the PC via a *serial port*. Serial ports are also called *COM ports* or *RS-232 ports*.

RS-232 stands for IEEE (Institute of Electrical and Electronic Engineers) "Reference Standard number two hundred thirty-two," and the term *COM* is used these days to mean serial port, although it's rumored to be an abbreviation for communications port.

Serial and parallel ports are almost always located on the back panel of a PC. Be sure you know which is which.

🖙 Serial ports on the back of the computer are always *male connectors* (either 9-pin or 25-pin D-type).

🖙 Parallel ports are always *female connectors.*

Male plugs have pins, female plugs don't; no gender jokes, please!

🖙 Serial connectors are called *DB-9* and *DB-25.* The *DB* stands for *data bus,* and the number is the number of pins in the connector. There are different configurations for serial connectors that use differing numbers of pins; rarely are all the pins used. All serial connectors are DB type D-shaped connectors, but not all DB connectors are serial.

🖙 PCs use only nine pins in a serial connection, which is why many PCs use the DB-9 connector in place of the DB-25 with its way-too-many and wasted pins. You will find the DB-25 plug on many older PCs, multipurpose adapter cards, and some modems, although it's becoming more and more rare.

Serial ports are also called COM (short for communications) ports:

• Nearly all PCs include the serial ports designated as COM1 and COM2, which are assigned to interrupt requests IRQ4 and IRQ3, respectively.

• Some PCs also support COM3 and COM4 serial ports, which by default are also assigned to IRQ4 and IRQ3.

On systems with all four serial ports, you may need to switch I/O port and IRQ assignments to accommodate them (especially if you plan to use them simultaneously).

✔ When serial ports are added to the PC via an expansion card (or cards), COM1 usually uses a DB-9 connector and COM2 usually uses a DB-25 connector. However, there's no standard for this; you may need to look at the card to see how the connections are labeled. It should come as no surprise that COM1 is labeled *COM1*.

Setting up a serial port

Every PC technician should understand how serial devices and ports operate to ensure the proper installation of serial devices. For the A+ Core Hardware exam, you should know *serial communications terminology,* its *system resource assignments,* and the *purpose of a serial port's components.*

Table 10-1 lists the system resource assignments for the common serial ports found on most PCs. Be sure you have these assignments engraved into your brain before the test.

Table 10-1	Serial Port System Resource Assignments	
Logical Device	*IRQ*	*I/O Address*
COM1	IRQ 4	3F8h
COM2	IRQ 3	2F8h
COM3	IRQ 4	3E8h
COM4	IRQ 3	2E8h

I don't have any cute little sayings to help you remember these assignments, so you just have to memorize them. However, the *8h* part of the I/O address is the same for all COM ports. Here's all you need to remember about COM ports and their IRQ assignments:

✔ Odd-numbered ports (COM1 and COM3) have the odd I/O addresses (3F8h and 3E8h)

✔ Even-numbered ports have the even I/O addresses (2F8h and 2E8h)

In both of the preceding cases, the IRQ is one more than the first number of the I/O port.

You may find these serial-speak key words lurking on the exam:

- ✔ **Data bits:** Indicates the number of bits used in the character coding scheme, or data word. Some systems use seven bits and others eight bits, with no other choices available.

- ✔ **Flow control (handshaking):** The embodiment of the protocol used to control the dialog of two serial devices. In general, flow control manages the data flow by sending a character or signal to stop it. Usually the flow control method used also has a means for restarting the data flow. See the "DTE to DCE, over" section for more details.

- ✔ **Parity:** A group of five choices: *even, odd, space, mark,* or *none.* Parity is a way of checking whether the correct number of bits was sent and received. Most modems in use today do not use parity (a parity setting of none). Regardless of the setting, both devices in a serial communications must be set the same.

- ✔ **RTS/CTS (request-to-send/clear-to-send):** Sends signals to specific pins to stop and start the data flow. The CTS signal indicates that a device is ready to accept data, and the RTS signal indicates when a device is ready to send data.

- ✔ **Stop bits:** Used in certain serial communications to indicate the beginning and end of data words.

- ✔ **XON/XOFF:** One of the two most common forms of flow control, it sends control characters to stop the flow of data (XOFF) and restart it again (XON). This is the software method of flow control.

DTE to DCE, over

After a serial device such as a modem is connected to the PC, each is designated as either the *Data Terminal Equipment (DTE)* or the *Data Communications Equipment (DCE)*. When you connect a modem to a PC, the modem becomes the DCE and the PC is the DTE. These designations determine which device initiates and controls the conversation between the two devices at various points in their interaction.

Table 10-2 lists the pin assignments of a serial connection.

Don't waste your time memorizing these pinouts. Instead, pay attention to what each pin is assigned to do and the role it would play in passing data back and forth to another device.

Table 10-2	Serial Connection Pin Assignments	
Pin Number	**Designation**	**Activity**
1	Carrier Detect (CD)	Indicates a connection is established.
2	Receive Data (RD)	All incoming data is received on this pin.
3	Transmit Data (TD)	All outgoing data is sent on this pin.
4	Data Terminal Ready (DTR)	The host device (such as the PC) is ready to communicate.
5	Signal Ground	Not used on PC systems.
6	Data Set Ready (DSR)	The connected device (such as the modem) is able to communicate.
7	Request to Send (RTS)	Host device wants to communicate.
8	Clear to Send (CTS)	Connected device is ready to communicate.
9	Ring Indicator (RI)	The telephone is ringing.

The serial connector's pins send signals to create what amounts to a conversation (the *handshaking*) between two serial devices. Picture that each pin is a light that's turned on to indicate the next of a sequence of events. Handshaking accomplishes the hardware flow control (the most common method) between the PC and the modem, as follows:

1. The DTE (Data Terminal Equipment), or PC, turns on the DTR (Data Terminal Ready) signal, indicating that it's good to go.

2. The DCE (Data Communications Equipment) acknowledges this message by turning on the DSR (Data Set Ready) that says, "Me too."

3. The DTE turns on its RTS (Request to Send) signal to let the DCE know it is ready to receive data.

4. The DCE acknowledges this request with a CTS (Clear To Send) that replies, "Here it comes!"

5. The data flows one bit at a time until a device stops it. This stopping is indicated by either the RTS or CTS being turned off. The flow starts again when the applicable indicator is turned back on.

Review the preceding steps until you have a good idea of what happens in a serial communications handshake. Expect a question that asks you about all or part of this sequence of events.

Cabling the connection

The cable used to connect a PC to a modem is called a *serial cable,* a *modem cable,* or a *straight-through cable.* In this cable, all the pins are connected one to one without any twists, crosses, or other fancy arrangements (unless you need to use a 9– to 25-pin converter should the modem cable come with a 25-pin connector and the PC has a 9-pin serial port).

There are a few serial port questions on the A+ Core Hardware exam. Expect at least one with "null modem cable" as its answer. On occasion, two PCs are connected in a DTE-to-DTE arrangement. When this happens, the cable's pinout is changed to simulate the action of the modem by cross-connecting a number of the pins and creating what is called a *null modem,* or *modem eliminator,* cable. Both the modem cable and the null modem cable are generic, and you can purchase them at any electronics store.

Is that UART?

Serial devices are controlled by a *Universal Asynchronous Receiver/ Transmitter (UART).* This specialized integrated circuit is found either on the device adapter card or on the motherboard (if a serial port is mounted on it). The UART chip controls all actions and functions of the serial port, including:

✓ Controlling all the connectors' pins and their associated signals

✓ Establishing the communication protocol

✓ Converting the parallel data bits of the data bus into a serial bit stream for transmission

✓ Converting the received serial bit stream into parallel data for transmission over the PC's internal data bus

The UART usually is a close-but-no-cigar answer on at least one question, so be careful not to confuse it with the port itself. You may be asked something like, "Serial communications are controlled by what device?" And if you're not asked, you should be!

Troubleshooting a serial port

If you're having a serial port problem, the cause is usually a system resource conflict. System resource conflicts include problems such as a serial device that fails intermittently or doesn't work at all, another device that stops working when the serial device is installed, or the PC locking up during the boot sequence.

The test requires that you know how to troubleshoot various situations, and you may encounter a question on troubleshooting a serial port. Don't worry; there isn't that much to it. Here, let me help you out. To determine the source of the problem, check the following:

- ✔ **Inspect the port for bent pins.** Certain pins must be absolutely straight for the device to work properly.

- ✔ **Ensure that the cable is the appropriate cable for the device.** Some serial devices can't use a straight-through or null modem cable.

- ✔ **Check the Windows Device Manager for system resource conflicts.** An IRQ conflict is the most common error in this area. Remember, only one customer to an IRQ at a time.

- ✔ **Be sure that the serial cable is not more than 50 feet long.** Beyond this distance, you lose data integrity, which appears many ways; none are good.

Looking at Parallel Devices

For the exam, know how parallel data is transmitted (eight bits at a time), the standard covering parallel port technologies (IEEE 1284 — see the section "Keeping up to standard"), and that parallel ports are used primarily for printers. This section provides you with additional background material.

Parallel data moves much faster than serial data, which is why the internal bus structures of the PC use a parallel format. Parallel ports were originally designed specifically for printers. However, other devices have been adapted to them, including other types of output devices, input devices, and storage devices, all taking advantage of the bidirectional capabilities of IEEE 1284 parallel devices. These include some external CD-ROMs, external tape drives and Zip drives, and file transfer software over proprietary cabling.

Parallel cables shouldn't be more than 15 feet in length.

Keeping up to standard

You're asked about the fact that IEEE 1284 is the standard for parallel ports, bidirectional parallel communications, and perhaps the ECP protocol.

In 1984, the IEEE (Institute of Electrical and Electronic Engineers) standardized parallel port protocols. The standard, formally titled "IEEE Standard Signaling Method for a Bi-directional Parallel Peripheral Interface for Personal

Computers," or IEEE 1284 as it's known, incorporated the two existing parallel port standards into a new protocol, creating an all-encompassing port model. The standards included in IEEE 1284 are

- ✔ **Standard Parallel Port (SPP):** Allows data to travel one way only — from the computer to the printer.

- ✔ **Enhanced Parallel Port (EPP):** Allows data to flow in both directions, but only in one way at a time. This lets the printer communicate information to the processor or adapter such as that the printer is out of paper or its cover is open.

- ✔ **Enhanced Capabilities Port (ECP):** Allows bidirectional simultaneous communications over a special IEEE 1284–compliant cable. Many bidirectional cables are EPP cables, which do not support ECP communications.

IEEE 1284 established the standard for bidirectional communications on the parallel port, and the ECP protocol allows for full-duplex (simultaneous communications in two directions) parallel communications.

Troubleshooting a parallel port

Trouble with a parallel port is usually in the device attached to it. Because a parallel port is virtually featureless, it either works or it doesn't (and it usually does). Problems are either in the connector (bent pins or blocked holes), the cable (wrong type — SPP, EPP, or ECP), the parallel port's BIOS configuration, or the device itself.

A problem may be a system resource conflict, but only if more than two parallel ports are on the PC.

Check for system resource conflicts when troubleshooting non-printer parallel port problems. Printers don't use IRQs or DMA channels, but other parallel port devices do. Table 10-3 lists the common system resource assignments for parallel ports.

Table 10-3	Parallel Port System Resource Assignments		
Port	**IRQ**	**I/O Address**	**DMA Channel**
LPT1	IRQ 7	378h	DMA 3 (ECP capabilities)
LPT2	IRQ 5	278h	n/a

Making High-Speed Serial Connections

When the standard PC only connected a printer and a modem to its ports, a serial port or two and a parallel port or two were enough. In today's PC world, standard serial and parallel ports aren't fast enough. Enter two new higher-speed serial data interconnection standards: USB (Universal Serial Bus) and the IEEE 1394 (FireWire).

Connecting with USB

The Universal Serial Bus (USB) is a newer hardware interface that supports both low-speed devices (such as keyboards, mice, and scanners) and higher-speed devices (such as a digital camera). USB, while still a serial interface, provides data transfer speeds of up to 12 Mbps (1.5 MBps) for faster devices and a 1.5 Mbps (188 KBps) sub-channel speed for lower-speed devices. A newer version of the USB standard, USB 2.0, which is also known as the Enhanced Host Controller Interface (EHCI), supports up to 480 Mbps for data transfer speeds.

USB uses a unique pair of connectors and ports, as shown in Figure 10-1. USB Type A connectors connect devices directly to a PC or USB hub. You'll find USB Type A connectors on devices with permanently attached cables. USB Type B connectors are found on those devices that have a detachable cable. The cable uses a squarish Type B port on the device and connects to either a Type A or Type B socket (the cable usually has both on the other end) on the PC or hub.

The USB interface supports up to 127 devices on a system. These devices connect both to the PC directly or into at least one USB hub, as shown in Figure 10-2. Each USB port carries .5 amps of electrical power (which is enough to power most low-power devices, such as a mouse or keyboard), which provides a lot of flexibility for adding additional devices to the system, regardless of its location. USB devices that require more power usually use their own AC adapters.

There's fire in the wire: IEEE 1394

The IEEE 1394 standard defines a high-speed serial interface bus. This standard is also known as the *i.Link* (Sony), *Lynx* (Texas Instruments), and the *FireWire* (Apple), which are proprietary, licensed versions of the IEEE 1394 standard. The generic version is *High Performance Serial Bus (HPSB)*. The IEEE 1394 standard defines a serial bus protocol that provides data transfer speeds between 100 Mbps to 400 Mbps (around 12 MBps to 50 MBps), depending on how the standard is implemented. The IEEE 1394 connector looks a bit like a USB connector, except that it's a bit larger and about halfway between rectangular and square — see Figure 10-3.

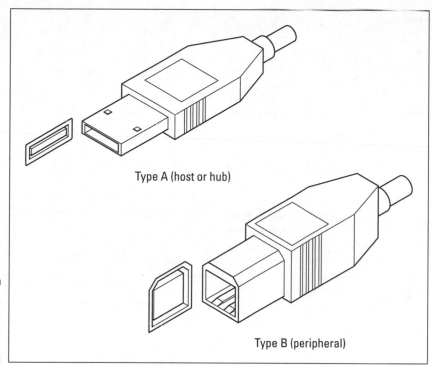

Type A (host or hub)

Type B (peripheral)

Figure 10-1:
USB
connectors
and ports.

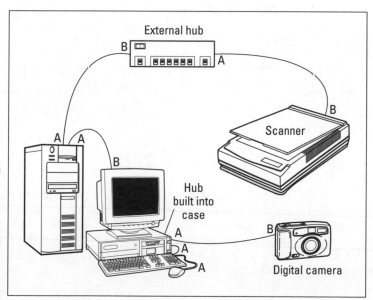

External hub

B   A

Scanner   B

A   A

B

Hub
built into
case

A
A
A

B

Digital camera

Figure 10-2:
Multiple
USB
devices
connected
to a
single PC.

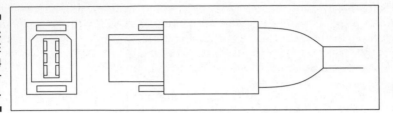

Figure 10-3:
The IEEE 1394 connector and plug.

The IEEE 1394 bus is similar to the USB interface (see "Connecting with USB," earlier in the chapter) in that it is a high-speed, Plug and Play bus that eliminates the need for devices to have their own power supplies. It goes USB one better by providing for *isochronous* (real-time) data transfers — data is transferred within certain time constraints (such as multimedia data where the audio and video must arrive together).

An IEEE 1394 port supports up to 63 external devices and is considered the link between PCs and consumer electronics. For example, through a 1394 port, a digital video camera can be used to both capture video content and then play back the video after it's been edited on the PC.

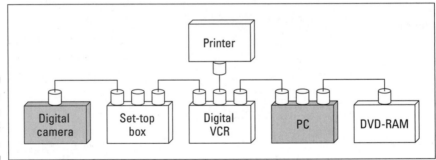

Figure 10-4:
A sample IEEE 1394 bus.

Working with Infrared Ports

The *infrared (IR)* port uses an invisible band of light at the low end of the electromagnetic spectrum. You'll never see this PC connection unless you have super powers. IR light stops just short of the beginning of the visible light part of the spectrum. Infrared contrasts with ultraviolet (UV), which is another invisible band at the other (high) end of the light spectrum. UV light erases an EPROM after about ten minutes of exposure.

Using this invisible beam, IR devices (which are also called *IrDA,* or *Infrared Data Association,* devices) can be connected to a PC without a physical cable. IrDA ports are common on portable computers. IrDA is the trade organization for the infrared device industry that has established a number of standards defining and prescribing the use of the IR connection.

IR devices are line-of-sight devices; they must have a clear, unobstructed path between their transmitters and receivers. (IR is the wireless mode most often used by TV remotes and other wireless controllers.) If anything blocks the path, you must move the obstruction or the controller to reopen the line of sight. Using an IR connection, a portable PC or a PDA (personal digital assistant) can connect to another PC, a keyboard, mouse, or a printer without a physical cable connection. The IR connector on your PC or notebook is a small plastic window located usually on the front or side of the case. External IR connections can be attached to the PC via a serial port.

Here are some tips for working with IR devices:

- ✔ Two IR devices need a clear, unobstructed line of sight between them.

- ✔ The devices you are trying to connect via IR must be at least 6 inches apart, but not more than 3 feet away.

- ✔ The IR signal transmission pattern is a cone about 30 degrees wide. The devices must be oriented to each other inside the transmission cone.

- ✔ Make sure that there are no competing IR devices in the vicinity that may interfere with the connection, such as a TV remote control.

Configuring PC Ports

If trouble arises with a PC's port, whether it's a serial, parallel, USB, IEEE 1394, or IrDA port, the problem probably is with the system resource settings. This usually happens when you add new devices to a PC that already supports many peripheral devices. See the documentation for your device and device drivers for the correct system resource settings.

Depending on the devices already installed on the PC and the system resources already in use, you need to watch for resource conflicts (usually with IRQs). USB and IEEE 1394 devices are usually assigned to IRQ 11, but you can't count on that. An IrDA port is usually configured as either COM3 or COM4 and uses the usual default values of those ports (refer to Table 10-1).

Prep Test

1 **A parallel port transmits data**

- **A** ○ One data bit at a time
- **B** ○ Four data bits at a time
- **C** ○ One sector at a time
- **D** ○ Eight data bits at a time

2 **A UART chip is used to control**

- **A** ○ The Plug and Play BIOS
- **B** ○ A parallel port
- **C** ○ A serial port
- **D** ○ The processor

3 **A serial port is almost always**

- **A** ○ A female port
- **B** ○ A male port
- **C** ○ A DB-15 connector
- **D** ○ A 36-pin connector

4 **An IrDA port requires which of the following conditions?**

- **A** ○ Line of sight between transmitting and receiving devices
- **B** ○ Digital phone lines
- **C** ○ Clear radio frequency signals
- **D** ○ Low humidity and a clean operating environment

5 **Equipment such as the PC and the printer are designated as**

- **A** ○ DCE devices
- **B** ○ DTE devices
- **C** ○ XON devices
- **D** ○ RTS devices

6 **The I/O address of COM1 is**

- **A** ○ 2E8h
- **B** ○ 3E8h
- **C** ○ 2F8h
- **D** ○ 3F8h

7 The two most common connectors used for serial ports are

A ○ Centronics 25- and 36-pin

B ○ DB-9 and DB-15

C ○ DB-9 and DB-25

D ○ Berg and Molex

8 Which of the following are IEEE 1394 type ports? (Choose two.)

A ❑ FireWire

B ❑ USB

C ❑ Flaming Geyser

D ❑ i.Link

9 Which of the following parallel port protocols allows bidirectional simultaneous communications?

A ○ ECP

B ○ SPP

C ○ EPP

D ○ TCP

10 The most common form of software flow control is

A ○ RTS/CTS

B ○ XON/XOFF

C ○ Stop bits

D ○ Handshaking

Answers

1 **D.** A parallel port carries an entire data character using parallel wires to carry each bit. *See "Looking at Parallel Devices."*

2 **C.** A UART (Universal Asynchronous Receive/Transmit) chip controls the functions and protocol of a serial port. *Review "Is that UART?"*

3 **B.** Serial ports are usually a male connector, whereas parallel ports are female connectors. *Check out "Understanding Serial Devices."*

4 **A.** Infrared (IR) devices require a clear, unobstructed line-of-sight between them. *Take a look at "Working with Infrared Ports."*

5 **B.** If the device could have been a terminal on a mainframe, it's Data Terminal Equipment (DTE). If it's used for communications purposes, like a modem, it's Data Communications Equipment (DCE). *Link up with "DTE to DCE, over."*

6 **D.** If you're having trouble remembering the I/O addresses for the IRQs and COM ports, just remember that COM1 comes first and gets the highest address (3F8). *Study "Setting up a serial port."*

7 **C.** These two connectors are common on the PC, especially for serial ports. *See "Understanding Serial Devices."*

8 **A, D.** FireWire (Apple) and i.Link (Texas Instruments) are proprietary versions of the IEEE 1394 standard interface. *See "There's fire in the wire: IEEE 1394."*

9 **A.** SPP and EPP are parallel port standards that allow for one- and two-way communications, but both allow communications only one way at a time. TCP is either the stuff in the gasoline or the Internet protocol. *Review "Keeping up to standard."*

10 **B.** RTS/CTS is a hardware flow control method. Handshaking and flow control are synonymous terms, and stop bits are a part of the serial data transmission protocol. *Check out "Setting up a serial port."*

Chapter 11

Input Devices

Exam Objectives

▶ Identifying common input devices

▶ Defining input device terms, concepts, and functions

▶ Cleaning and caring for input devices

▶ Troubleshooting common symptoms and problems

*1*nput devices are included on the A+ Core Hardware exam primarily under installing, configuring, and upgrading field-replaceable modules (FRMs). You may also run into preventive maintenance and troubleshooting questions about input devices. Don't expect to find many questions like "How many keys are on the keyboard?" or "How does a mouse work?" The keyboard and mouse, the major input devices, are essentially throwaway technology. It's a lot cheaper, in terms of both labor and parts, to simply replace a problem keyboard or mouse with a new module than to waste the time needed to repair one.

I can't quote statistics as proof (and I looked for them), but I bet that after power problems ("It worked fine this morning before the power failure") and printer problems ("What does online mean?"), the most common service problem involves a keyboard ("I spilled my Mountain Dew on it and for some reason it stopped working") or mouse ("The foot pedal doesn't seem to work anymore"). If I'm right, and I can't be too wrong on this, then as a certified PC repair technician, you should understand how input devices work, connect, and fail. You especially need to know how to plug in the replacement unit.

Quick Assessment

Identifying common input devices

1 The most commonly used PC keyboard format is the _____ keyboard.

2 The mouse type that uses captured digital images to detect movement is a(n) _____ mouse.

3 A(n) _____ mouse uses a ball and sensor mechanism to detect movement.

Defining input device terms, concepts, and functions

4 A(n) _____ mouse connects to a mini-DIN-6 connector.

5 The bus mouse attaches to its own _____.

Cleaning and caring for input devices

6 To remove paper bits and food crumbs from a keyboard, you turn it upside down and _____ it.

7 _____ and _____ are best for cleaning the ball of a mouse.

Troubleshooting common symptoms and problems

8 A 300-range error code displayed during the boot sequence indicates a(n) _____ error.

Answers

1   *Enhanced.* Check out "Keyboards."

2   *Optical.* Click on "Sighting the optical mouse."

3   *Mechanical.* See "Rolling along with mechanical mice."

4   *PS/2.* Peruse "Connecting the mouse."

5   *Adapter or expansion card.* Review "Connecting the mouse."

6   *Shake.* Review "Cleaning the keyboard" for the common keyboard preventive maintenance actions.

7   *A swab, mild soap.* Take a look at "Taking good care of your mouse."

8   *Keyboard.* See "Solving boot sequence problems" for information on common keyboard errors during POST.

Keyboards

The A+ exam focuses on three areas of keyboards: *connectors, preventive maintenance,* and *troubleshooting.* If you're confident that you know how a keyboard works, skip to the section, "Connecting the keyboard," later in this chapter. Otherwise, review the following sections for background and terminology.

The obvious place to begin your review of input devices is with the most common input device of all — the keyboard. The keyboard's role on a PC system should be obvious: The keyboard enables the user to communicate with the computer by using keystrokes.

Keyboard styles

The keyboard formats found on any DOS or Windows PC is typically one of three keyboard styles:

- ✔ **Enhanced (also known as AT Enhanced):** 101 keys, including 12 function keys, separate cursor and screen control keys, and a numeric keypad (see Figure 11-1). This style keyboard may even include buttons for controlling a CD-ROM drive, the sound, and other built-in features of the PC. Enhanced is still the most common keyboard type in use.

- ✔ **Windows:** 104 keys, including keys to pop-up the Windows Start menu and a key to show the pop-up shortcut menu.

- ✔ **Natural:** Enhanced keyboard with a built-in wristrest and an arched or bowed keyboard shape; this keyboard may also separate into segments (see Figure 11-2). The Microsoft Natural keyboard is probably the best known of the natural-style keyboards, but there also are many clones on the market.

- ✔ **Ergonomic:** Although the natural keyboards also claim to be ergonomic, truly ergonomic keyboards are available, such as those from DataHand (www.datahand.com) and Kinesis (www.kinesis-ergo.com).

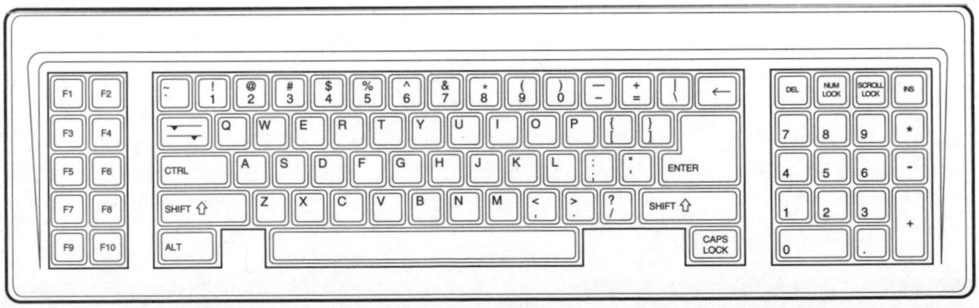

Figure 11-1: The AT Enhanced keyboard.

Figure 11-2:
The natural
style
keyboard.

Connecting the keyboard

Connect a keyboard to the computer by plugging its connector (located at the end of the cable attached to the keyboard) into a matching port on the PC. You also can connect the keyboard through a wireless *infrared (IR)* or *radio frequency (RF)* system. Chapter 10 contains specific information on the various connectors used on the PC.

Physically connecting

Unless a keyboard is a wireless model (see the section, "Connections of the wireless kind," later in this chapter), it must be physically connected to the computer. This connection is made with one of three connector types: a DIN-type 5-pin connector (shown in Figure 11-3); a mini-DIN 6-pin, also known as a PS/2 connector (shown in Figure 11-4); or a Universal Serial Bus (USB) connector (shown in Figure 11-5).

DIN connectors are also called *DIN-5* and *mini-DIN-6* connectors, representing the number of pins they use. The mini-DIN connector gets its name due to its smaller overall size. Some proprietary keyboards connect with the RJ-11 style plug, but they are disappearing. DIN connectors have a notch or key slot that prevents an incorrect connection.

Connections of the wireless kind

That little red plastic window on the front of your desktop or notebook computer is actually a "port" through which a keyboard, mouse, or other specially equipped device can be attached. Systems with the little red window have a small infrared receiver built-in, but you can add one to the system through the standard keyboard and mouse (or touch pad) ports.

In general, IR keyboards are "line of sight" devices, which means the keyboard must be directly in line (without obstruction) with the receiver port to operate properly. However, some IR devices now use broadbeam IR technology that frees you from having to be directly in front of the system case and its receiver port. Broadbeam IR allows you to use the keyboard with a wide range of operating angles. The operating range of most IR systems is between 1 and 50 feet, but you can usually adjust the operating power to fit the distance at which you plan to use the keyboard.

The keyboard is usually assigned IRQ 1 and I/O address 060h. You need to memorize all of the IRQs, the I/O addresses for the COM and LPT ports, and all the DMA channel assignments for the exam.

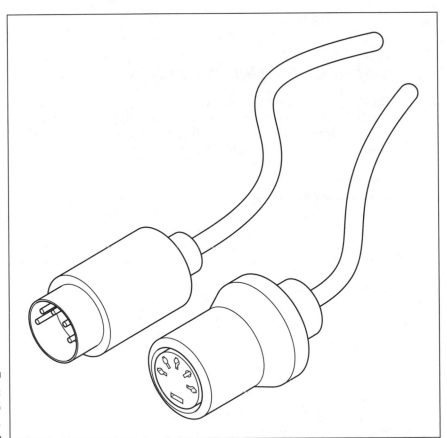

Figure 11-3:
The DIN-5
connector.

Figure 11-4:
The mini-
DIN-6
connector.

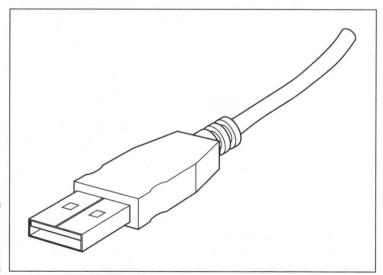

Figure 11-5:
The USB
connector.

Troubleshooting the keyboard

Keyboards can be repaired, but why bother? A keyboard is far less valuable than the time it would take to troubleshoot and repair it. Individual keyswitches may be replaced on a mechanical keyboard, but that should be the prudent limit.

To determine whether you have an electrical failure in the keyboard or on the system board, use the following steps:

1. **Turn off the computer.**

2. **Unplug the keyboard connector from the motherboard.**

3. **Turn on the computer.**

4. **Use a digital multimeter to check the voltages of the connector pins.**

If any of the voltages are out of range (near +2 volts to +5.5 volts, depending on the pin), the problem is likely in the keyboard circuits of the motherboard. See the keyboard's documentation for the specific voltage and pinouts. Otherwise, the problem is probably in the keyboard.

As a professional PC repair technician, always listen carefully to the user's explanation of the problem and avoid jumping to conclusions as to whether you are servicing a keyboard or dealing with a motherboard malfunction. Don't assume that you know the problem or its solution ahead of time. Don't waste the customer's time or your energy troubleshooting a keyboard problem that would be solved less expensively with a new keyboard.

Solving boot sequence problems

Keyboard-related problems may occur during the POST (Power-On Self Test) process. As I explain in Chapter 4, the boot process has two means of indicating the source of the problem:

- ✔ **Early in the POST process:** Before the POST completes its system check phases, the video BIOS has not been loaded. As a result, only the system speaker is available to signal the operator. The POST produces a series of beeps of particular duration and sequence to the system BIOS installed on the PC, and the error is detected.

- ✔ **Later in the POST process:** After the video system is available for use by the POST or boot processes, the system can display error messages on the monitor. No standard exists for any of the error codes used by any of the BIOS systems. Each uses its own set of error codes, which, thankfully, are similar. In most cases, if a keyboard failure occurs, an error code in the range of 300 to 399 displays, indicating the keyboard error. The most common reason for a keyboard POST or boot error is a keystroke detected during the POST processing. This could be a stuck key, an accidentally-pressed key, someone leaning on the keyboard, or the corner of your *Scientific American* lying on the keyboard. The remedy is to simply clear the problem and reboot the computer.

Don't waste time memorizing POST error beep codes relating to keyboards or anything else. Each BIOS system has its own set of codes and some are lengthy. As far as keyboard problems go, knowing that the 300 series error codes relate to keyboard problems is enough. For a list of the beep codes you should know for the exam, see Chapter 4.

The Mouse and Other Pointing Devices

Like the keyboard, a mouse can be found on nearly every PC in use and most definitely on every PC sold today. Some diehards still refuse to move to a Windows environment, clinging to their command line interfaces, and so they don't have a mouse on their PCs. The time when you could get by without a mouse on your PC is fading fast. Systems without a mouse or other type of pointing device will eventually go the way of the dinosaurs.

You may encounter exam questions that cover at least one of these areas:

✔ Connecting the mouse to the computer

✔ The internal parts and operation of the mouse

✔ Common preventive maintenance procedures

Rolling along with mechanical mice

Most mouse units in use are the mechanical type, although optical units are making a comeback. The mechanical mouse uses a rubber ball, which moves as the user rotates the mouse. As the ball moves, it rotates a set of rollers, which in turn drive sensors that translate the ball's movement to move the screen pointer around the display. As the user moves his hand, the distance traveled and the speed of the ball is detected by the rollers and sensors, and the screen pointer moves a relative distance and speed accordingly.

An upside-down version of the traditional, mechanical mouse, called a *trackball,* puts the ball on the top of the mouse. The user manipulates the ball with her fingers or thumb. However, any mouse questions you'll see on the Core Hardware exam deal with the standard mechanical mouse; so don't worry about trackballs for the test.

Sighting the optical mouse

The *optical mouse,* also known as the opto-mechanical mouse, uses either optical sensors and LEDs or a digital capture "eye" to sense the distance and speed of the mouse's movement. This type of mouse "sees" its movement over a surface and translates it into movement of the on-screen pointer.

Early optical mouse units required a special mouse pad, which was usually hard, shiny plastic or metal that had a grid of intersecting lines printed on it. As the mouse moved, an LED (light-emitting diode) reflecting off the shiny surface and grid lines were used to detect direction, speed, and distance. This mouse worked great, unless you lost the special mouse pad and couldn't use the mouse (or computer) at all.

The latest optical mouse works with a digital capture apparatus that literally takes around 2,000 pictures per second of the surface under the mouse to determine its movement. This means that any surface — such as the top of the desk, your jeans, the wall, or the box it came in — can now be your mouse pad. A mouse pad is no longer needed, let alone a special optical mouse pad. Inside the optical mouse is a *digital signal processor (DSP)* that compares the captured images to detect even the slightest movement.

Unlike its mechanical predecessors, the optical mouse has no moving parts to pick up dirt that can impair its performance. This also means that you don't have to clean it.

Summarizing pointing devices

Table 11-1 lists other pointing devices that can be attached to the PC. For the test, you should be familiar with what they are.

Table 11-1	PC Pointing Devices
Device	*Use*
Joystick	Popular with flight and navigation games, and as a backup mouse
Trackball	In effect, an upside-down mouse where the ball is rotated to move the screen pointer
Touchpad	A reliable alternative to the mouse that can be integrated into the keyboard
Digitizing tablets	Used with drawing or CAD (computer-aided design) software to create line or vector graphics

Connecting the mouse

In case you've been on a remote desert island or in a deep dark cave for about fifteen years: A mouse is a pointing device commonly used on the PC. It's safe to say that every desktop PC sold today comes with a mouse as standard equipment.

The mouse is available in five different units. These units differ in how they connect to the computer. The different units and their connectors are

- **Serial:** Connects via a 9– or 25-pin serial port usually with a DB-9 or DB-25 connector.

- **PS/2:** Connects with a mini-DIN 6-pin plug to a port usually mounted on the motherboard.

- **Combination:** Connects with either a mini-DIN (PS/2) 6-pin connector to a port on the motherboard or with a DB-9 or DB-25 connector through an adapter card to either a DB-9 or DB-25 serial port.

- **Bus:** Connects to its own adapter card. Bus mouse units usually connect with a mini-DIN-6 plug to an adapter added to the PC specifically to support the mouse.

- **USB (Universal Serial Bus):** A USB mouse is a hot-swappable device that can be added and removed from the PC without restarting the system. A USB mouse also shares the system resources of the USB port and does not require additional IRQ and I/O port resources.

- **Radio Frequency (RF):** RF mice are, along with IR mice, one form of a wireless mouse. Although few systems have RF support built into the system case, adding RF support is not difficult.

- **Infrared (IR):** If the PC has built-in IR support, in many ways the support of the mouse is provided directly from the motherboard and chipset. If the IR system is an add-on, it connects either via a serial or mini-DIN-6 port.

The most commonly used connector for a mouse is the PS/2. You should never connect a PS/2 mouse (or any other PS/2 device) to the PC while the PC is powered up. This could damage the port or the motherboard. And this is on the test, too!

Installing Sound

You probably think of sound playback when you consider sound and the PC, but devices also capture sound. Sound capabilities (both input and output) are installed in a PC through a *sound card* (a special type of expansion card). Usually, a sound card has connection ports for both microphones and speakers.

Sound cards act like a modem of sorts, in that they are involved in the conversion of analog sound to digital data, and vice versa. Grossly simplified, sound capture involves grabbing a piece of the sound every so often to build a digitally reproducible facsimile of the original sound, also known as *sampling*. The sampled sound file is stored as a digital file on the computer, usually as a WAV or similar file type.

The sound card is generally assigned to IRQ 5 and I/O address 220h. A sound card can use up to three DMA channels: channels 0, 1, and 3 for an 8-bit card, and channels 5, 6, and 7 for a 16-bit card.

Getting Ready for Work

Keyboards and mice, especially mechanical ones, must be cleaned periodically. The following two sections show you how to properly clean a keyboard and a mouse as preventive maintenance.

Cleaning the keyboard

You can clean a keyboard with the computer turned off by using the following steps:

1. **Turn the keyboard upside down and shake out any paper, potato chips, jujubes, cookie crumbs, paper clips, lint, cat hair, or the like.**

2. **Use an aerosol can of compressed air to dislodge any stubborn bits.**

3. **Spray some all-purpose cleaner onto a soft cloth and wipe key tops with the dampened cloth.**

4. **Use a lint-free swab dampened with the cleaner to clean between the keys.**

If soda pop or some other sticky stuff spills on your keyboard, you can rinse the keyboard with water, soak it in a sink or tub, or even put it through a dishwasher rinse cycle — just don't use dishwasher detergent or any other kind of soap. If you have really gunky water, use distilled water or Perrier or such to rinse the keyboard. Just make absolutely sure that the keyboard is *completely* dry before you reconnect it to the computer.

Taking good care of your mouse

If you have a mechanical mouse, you should periodically clean its moving parts — the ball and rollers inside the ball housing. Cleaning should be part of routine maintenance because a dirty mouse can cause the screen pointer to move erratically or not at all.

In any case, use the following steps to clean the mouse:

1. **Open the ball access cover.**

   You usually do this by either rotating or sliding the locking collar that holds the mouse ball in place. Usually, large arrows show the direction you must push or twist.

2. **Clean the ball with a swab and a mild soap.**

   Don't rub the mouse with a pencil eraser to clean it. And don't use anything that could react with the rubber to cause flat spots or make the mouse ball out-of-round, such as contact cleaner or alcohol.

3. **Clean the ball rollers using a swap and mild soap.**

   Often the problem with a dirty mouse is that the rollers deep inside the mouse have become dirty or clogged with lint. First use tweezers to remove any lint on the rollers and then use the same cleaner you used for the ball to clean the rollers with a clean swab.

4. **Blow into the ball housing.**

   Use aerosol compressed air, not your breath. Compressed air contains fewer germs and usually less moisture. Replace the ball and reinstall the retaining ring, and you're back in business. Test the mouse immediately, and correct any problems that appear.

Prep Test

1 **The keyboard and mouse are considered**

   A ○ Throwaway technology

   B ○ Shop-repairable items

   C ○ Factory-only repairable items

   D ○ Not repairable

2 **The technology used to detect movement on an optical mouse is**

   A ○ A low-grade laser beam

   B ○ A digital capture "eye"

   C ○ A video detection system that detects movement in the mouse ball

   D ○ Static electricity sensors

3 **Which mouse type is the most commonly used? (Choose two.)**

   A ❏ Trackball

   B ❏ Mechanical mouse

   C ❏ Touch pad

   D ❏ Optical mouse

4 **What keyboard style attempts to relieve strain on the hands, wrists, and arms of the typist?**

   A ○ AT standard

   B ○ Ergonomic

   C ○ AT enhanced

   D ○ Windows

5 **Which of the following are connectors used by mouse units? (Choose two.)**

   A ❏ USB

   B ❏ Mini-DIN-6

   C ❏ DIN-5

   D ❏ Parallel

6 **What is the most commonly used PC keyboard format?**

A ○ Ergonomic

B ○ Natural

C ○ XT

D ○ Enhanced

7 **What type of mouse connects to either a serial port or a port mounted on the motherboard?**

A ○ Serial

B ○ PS/2

C ○ Bus

D ○ Combination

8 **A keyboard error code displayed during the boot sequence would be in what number series?**

A ○ 1700–1799

B ○ 300–399

C ○ 100–199

D ○ It may be a number from any series

9 **Which of the following is not a system resource normally assigned to a sound card?**

A ○ IRQ 5

B ○ I/O address 220h

C ○ 128 MB of RAM for buffering

D ○ Up to three DMA channels

10 **The joystick is**

A ○ A special tool used for RAM

B ○ The lever on a ZIF socket

C ○ A type of pointing device

D ○ A type of output device

Answers

1 **A.** The cost of repairing a keyboard or mouse for anything but the simplest problems can be more expensive than just replacing it with a new one. *See "Troubleshooting the keyboard."*

2 **B.** You might see a question about an optical mouse unit on the exam, so connect the words optical and eye to be safe. *Check out "Sighting the optical mouse."*

3 **B & D.** Others may come and go, but the little mechanical mouse keeps on going, and going, and going. And the optical mouse could show up on the exam at any time. *Review "Rolling along with mechanical mice."*

4 **B.** Ergonomic keyboards are designed with the comfort of the operator in mind. *See "Keyboard styles."*

5 **A & B.** The other types of connectors used are serial and infrared (IR), but, at least so far, the parallel port has not been used. *Review "Connecting the mouse."*

6 **D.** The newer natural, ergonomic, and separating keyboards are essentially enhanced keyboards in new packages. *Take a look at "Keyboard styles."*

7 **D.** The combination mouse can be adapted to fit either type of connector, which allows it to work with just about any system. *See "Connecting the mouse."*

8 **B.** Any POST error code in the 300 to 399 range is a keyboard fault. Check with the BIOS manual for the specific error. *Look at "Solving boot sequence problems."*

9 **C.** Sound cards carry their own buffering memory. *See "Installing Sound."*

10 **C.** The joystick is perhaps better than the mouse for playing many games. *Review "Summarizing pointing devices."*

Chapter 12

Output Devices

Exam Objectives

▶ Identifying common output devices and their normal operation

▶ Identifying output device connectors

▶ Using preventive maintenance products

▶ Disposing of environmentally hazardous equipment

▶ Following safety procedures for high-voltage equipment

*U*nlike their input device cousins, which are adapted to gather data at their myriad sources, output devices are limited by sight and sound. As a result, the PC is designed to provide its users with things they can read, watch, or hear. Outputs that we can taste and feel will undoubtedly be out in the near future, don't you think, HAL? Output devices have only one purpose: To display (or print or sound) the results of instructions and data entered by the user and processed by the PC.

On a PC you are likely to repair, usually only two or three types of output devices exist: monitors, printers, and sound systems. Therefore, the A+ Core Hardware exam includes questions focused primarily on monitors and printers because virtually every PC has them. Sound is still somewhat new to the A+ world, but you may see a troubleshooting question or two on sound cards.

On the A+ Core Hardware exam, monitors and displays are included in three separate parts, but are primarily in the domains of "Installation, Configuration, and Upgrading" and "Diagnosing and Troubleshooting," with a slight mention in "Preventive Maintenance." I interpret the configuration part to include picking the device for the customer's needs, setting the jumpers or DIP switches, and configuring software. Troubleshooting means isolating and repairing output device problems, and the preventive issues surround proper disposal and cleaning of monitors.

This chapter also quickly reviews PC sound devices and monitors that can be both input devices and (technically) output devices. Printers covered are in Chapter 13 because they have their own domain on the A+ Core Hardware exam.

Quick Assessment

Identifying common output devices and their normal operation

1   The _____ is the primary component of the PC monitor.

2   A CRT monitor paints its image using _____, which are tiny clusters of color dots.

3   The picture quality of a monitor is determined by its _____.

Identifying output device connectors

4   The VGA/SVGA standard connector has _____ pins.

5   A sound card usually uses IRQ _____.

Using preventive maintenance products

6   The monitor's glass builds up _____ and holds dust on its surface.

Disposing of environmentally hazardous equipment

7   A Green monitor is one that reduces its power by _____ in sleep mode.

Following safety procedures for high-voltage equipment

8   A CRT monitor has a large _____ inside that holds an electrical charge.

9   You should not wear a(n) _____ when working inside a monitor.

10 A process called _____ eliminates most of the magnetization inside the CRT monitor.

Answers

1   *CRT.* See "Looking Inside the Monitor."

2   *Pixels.* Check out "Looking Inside the Monitor."

3   *Resolution.* Review "Sizing up the display."

4   *15.* Look up "Making the connection."

5   *5.* Take a look at "Connecting to sound."

6   *Static electricity.* Charge to "Cleaning the monitor."

7   *99 percent.* Boldly go to "Saving the planet."

8   *Capacitor.* Mosey over to "Keeping the lid on."

9   *ESD grounding strap.* Zap to "Keeping the lid on."

10   *Degaussing.* Review "Exorcising the magnetic evils."

Looking Inside the Monitor

The PC's monitor is not an item that PC service technicians are often called on to fix. The A+ exam includes few questions on the internal workings of the monitor. Study this section as background material for the terminology and concepts concerning monitors in general.

You don't need to know the inner workings of a CRT to install and configure a monitor, but you need a general idea of how it works. After the system unit or a laser printer, the monitor is the customer's next largest investment; it's the only part of the system that actually holds its value. Your focus for the A+ Core Hardware exam should be the technologies that enable the monitor to work at its best.

The primary component in the PC monitor is the cathode ray tube (CRT). Although its name makes it sound a little like a weapon from a cheesy old science fiction movie, it's actually the technology used in most computer monitors (and televisions) to produce the displayed image.

Lighting up the world

A CRT monitor works by projecting an electron beam onto a screen of phosphor dots inside a glass tube. The beam works from top to bottom and left to right, one row at a time. The dots are illuminated in patterns that create images on the CRT's face. It takes only a fraction of a second to create the image on the CRT. However, the brightness of the illuminated dots fades just as fast, requiring the entire display to be refreshed by repeating the laser and dot illumination process many times per second to keep the image on the CRT's screen.

On a color monitor, each dot carries one of three colors: red, green, or blue. Three dots (one of each color) are arranged together to create a *pixel* (a *picture element*). Three electron beams illuminate a pixel's dots in varying degrees, and this mixture of color intensities produces different color shadings on the screen. When all the pixels on the screen are lit up, a picture forms in living color.

Speaking the language of the monitor

Here are a couple of monitor terms you may find in monitor-related questions on the exam:

✔ **Refresh rate:** This rate represents the time it takes the CRT's electron beam to paint the screen from top to bottom. Refresh rates are expressed as Hertz (Hz), which is one complete screen refresh cycle. Different monitors have different refresh rates. For example, VESA (Video Electronics Standards Association) has set the minimum refresh rate as 70 to 75 Hz for the Super Video Graphics Array (SVGA) monitor. See "Setting the refresh rate," later in this chapter.

✔ **Interlacing:** Interlaced monitors use two passes to draw the screen, drawing only the even count lines on the first pass and only the odd count lines on the second pass. An interlaced monitor usually has more screen flicker than a noninterlaced monitor, which draws the entire screen in each pass.

Inside the monitor is a controller board that communicates with the adapter card, directs the drawing of the CRT's display, and responds to the adjustment controls on the monitor to adjust the display. The monitor's internal controller also determines the technology used in creating the display.

The names of the technologies that control the illumination of the CRT's phosphor sound like a bad old movie title or a song by the Eagles: the *shadow mask* and the *aperture grill.*

Here's how they work:

✔ **Shadow mask:** A metal screen with thousands of holes. The mask is placed so that the holes are directly in line with the dots of each pixel. The shadow mask absorbs unwanted electrons and prevents the phosphor material between the pixels from being illuminated, which leaves a black border around each pixel.

✔ **Aperture grill:** Very thin vertical wires let more electrons through than the shadow mask, creating a deeper color display. Horizontal wires hold the vertical wires in place to keep the verticals from vibrating.

The Video Adapter Card

The video card, also called the *graphics adapter,* converts the graphic images from a software application or operating system into a series of instructions that tell the monitor's internal controller how to draw the image on the screen and the colors to use. Back when monitors displayed only monochrome, the video card was simple, leaving most of the heavy work to the PC's CPU and RAM. However, graphics adapters now have their own onboard processor (a *graphic processing unit,* or GPU) and their own special video memory. These produce better and faster graphic images.

The video card and monitor must use the same graphics standard to work properly.

Connecting to adapter card standards

Here are the different video adapter card standards you will want to know:

- ✔ **Monochrome Display Adapter (MDA):** Does just what its name says — displays mostly text on a monochrome monitor. This digital adapter is still used for servers, process control, and monitoring systems where the display contains only text and a color display is not needed. Resolution is not an issue on MDA monitors. It works just like a dot matrix printer, using illuminated dots to form letters on each line of the display. A variation of the MDA that integrates graphics is the Hercules-based Monochrome Graphics Adapter (MGA).

- ✔ **Color Graphics Adapter (CGA):** This digital adapter was the first color adapter. It's capable of displaying four colors. CGA monitors support 320 x 200 (four colors) or 640 x 200 (two colors). In this case and those that follow, as the number of colors increases, the resolution usually decreases. This trade-off must take place so that the video RAM is not exceeded. More on this later (see "Sizing up the display").

- ✔ **Enhanced Graphics Adapter (EGA):** This digital adapter supports 16 colors at a resolution of 640 x 350.

  Don't worry about this one for the exam. I only include it for continuity and comparison. EGA cards (and for the most part CGA) are obsolete.

- ✔ **Video Graphics Array (VGA):** VGA is the de facto standard for video adapters on Windows and several other operating systems. The VGA standard supports up to 640 x 480 with 16 colors or lower resolutions with 256 colors.

- ✔ **Super VGA (SVGA):** Most of the video standards that followed VGA and support resolutions and color depths higher than those of the VGA standard are grouped under the SVGA standard. The SVGA standard was developed by VESA (a group of monitor and graphics card manufacturers and other companies interested in video standards). SVGA video cards support several resolutions, including 800 x 600; 1,024 x 768; 1,280 x 1,024; 1,600 x 1,200; and higher, and SVGA supports up to 4 billion colors (although 16.7 million colors is commonly used as the standard).

Table 12-1 lists the more popular video graphic adapter standards.

Table 12-1	PC Video Adapter Standards	
Video Standard	*Resolutions*	*Colors*
VGA (Video Graphics Array)	640 x 480	16
	320 x 200	256
SVGA (Super VGA)	800 x 600	16
	1,024 x 768	256
	1,280 x 1,024	256
	1,600 x 1,200	256

Sizing up the display

Exam questions that relate to video cards often use definitions of resolution — dot pitch, color depth, and aspect ratio. Review the following sections closely.

Resolution

The number of pixels available to generate an image is key to the quality of the images produced — regardless of the technology that lights the pixels. *Resolution* means the number of pixels that are available to produce an image.

The more pixels available for use in creating the display, the higher the resolution, which results in a much better display. Resolution is stated as the number of pixels available horizontally on the screen by the number of rows of pixels available vertically on the screen. For example, 800 x 600 represents 800 pixels in each horizontal row and 600 vertical pixel rows (of 800 pixels each) on the screen. Table 12-1 lists the common resolutions of color monitors.

The resolution is important for two reasons: It determines the size and quality of the image displayed on the monitor, and it is a major factor in determining the amount of video RAM that should be on the video card to support the display. Each pixel in a monitor's resolution requires a certain amount of data to encode exactly how the pixel should appear. For example, nearly 6MB of video RAM is required to generate a true color image using 1,600 x 1,200 resolution.

The size of the monitor's display (such as 15 inch or 17 inch) has some bearing on the number of pixels available and the resolutions supported. A monitor using 640 x 480 resolution uses 307,200 pixels to create its display. The same monitor set to a resolution of 1,280 x 1,024 uses 1,310,720 pixels in the same display space. As the pixel count increases, the size of each pixel and the amount of space around it decreases. For more information on how this works, see "Getting Ready for Work," later in this chapter.

Dot pitch

The distance between pixels on the CRT is the *dot pitch*. Technically, the dot pitch is the distance in millimeters (mm) between dots of the same color in two adjacent pixels (for example, the distance between two adjacent green dots); in effect, it is the distance between the pixels. Common dot pitch sizes on color monitors range from .15 mm to .30 mm. (You usually see the dot pitch expressed without the "mm" unit of measure.) The smaller the dot pitch, the better the picture quality. It also stands to reason that a smaller dot pitch makes room for more pixels, which gives the monitor a higher resolution.

Color depth

The number of colors that a video card or monitor can display is the *color depth*. It is also commonly called the *bit depth,* because the color depth is expressed as the number of bits used to define the colors of a video standard's color depth.

The color depth represents the number of individual colors that each pixel on the screen can display. It is always expressed as the number of bits used to describe each color in the color set. The common color depth settings are 8-bit, 16-bit, 24-bit, and 32-bit color. Figure 12-1 shows the settings available on a Windows 98 PC and its monitor.

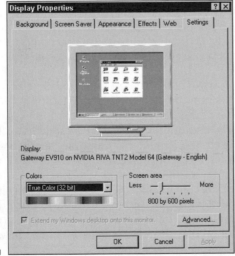

Figure 12-1: The color depth settings available on a Windows PC.

The number of bits in the color depth determines the number of colors a video card or monitor can display. For example, 8-bit color uses 8-bits to number each of the colors. In binary numbers, the range of numbers available is 00000000 to 11111111, or the range of decimal numbers 0 to 255. In other words, an 8-bit color depth can display 256 colors.

The number of colors that a color depth supports is the largest binary number that can be displayed in its bit depth plus one. A 16-bit color depth can display 65,536 colors (2^{15} + 1), the 24-bit color depth has 16.7 million colors and 32-bit color supports over 4 *billion* colors. Depending on the PC, video card, and monitor, either 24-bit or 32-bit will be designated as the True Color setting.

The human eye can only discern around 16 million colors and has trouble distinguishing the color of adjacent pixels at about that level.

Aspect Ratio

The aspect ratio of a monitor describes the relative number of horizontal pixels to vertical pixels in the resolutions it supports. The standard aspect ratio for nearly all monitors and resolutions is 4:3 (read as 4 to 3). This is the aspect ratio of 640 x 480; 800 x 600; 1,280 x 768; and several other resolutions. This number indicates the monitor's ability to display certain shapes and graphics, such as a circle, on the screen.

Sizing up the video memory

Most video cards come with 8MB to 64MB of video RAM, but there are high-end 3D graphic cards that have as much as 256MB. Some people think that 64MB is far more than is needed, but others, especially the 3-D crowd, think that you can never have enough.

Table 12-2 shows the amounts of video RAM required by several common graphics settings.

Table 12-2	Common 2-D Video RAM Requirements	
Resolution	*Color Depth*	*Video RAM Required*
640 x 480	8-bit	307K
1,024 x 768	16-bit	1.57MB
1,024 x 768	24-bit	2.36MB
1,600 x 1,200	24-bit	5.76MB
1,600 x 1,200	32-bit	7.68MB

A 3D video card requires more video RAM than a 2D card, even when it uses the same resolution and color depth. In addition to the 2D (down and across), a third dimension of depth is added. 3D graphic cards use three buffers to hold the graphics data: a front buffer, a back buffer, and a Z-buffer. For example, a 2D video card with 4MB of video RAM can support a 1,600 x 1,200 16-bit display, but the same card can support a 3D game only on an 800 x 600 16-bit setting. The Z-buffer consumes enough of the available RAM to require the resolution to be reduced.

The sizes of the front and back buffers are each the size required by the color depth. The Z-buffer uses 16-bits (2 bytes).

Looking at the Video RAMs

The memory (RAM) on the video card is also called the *frame buffer,* because it holds graphic instructions about each scene or frame to be displayed on the monitor. The first form of video RAM was standard DRAM, the same kind of RAM found in early PCs. Because DRAM requires constant electrical refreshing to hold its contents, it didn't work well for video memory. For one reason, it could be accessed while it was being refreshed and the video system had to wait, which meant that its performance suffered. Since then, several memory technologies have been used, each one more efficient and faster than the last.

The most common RAM technologies used with video cards are

- ✔ **Dynamic Random Access Memory (DRAM):** The DRAM used on early PCs.

- ✔ **Extended Data Output DRAM (EDO DRAM):** Provides a higher bandwidth and handles read/write cycles better than standard DRAM.

- ✔ **Video RAM (VRAM):** VRAM, not to be confused with the generic "VRAM," is a special type of DRAM that doesn't need to be refreshed as often. VRAM is *dual-ported,* which means it has two access portals, and the processor and RAMDAC (RAM digital to analog converter) can both be accessing it at the same time. As the saying goes, two doors are better than one, and dual-porting doubles the memory's speed.

- ✔ **Windows RAM (WRAM):** Called *Windows Accelerator Card RAM* on the A+ Core Hardware blueprint, WRAM is a dual-ported memory that runs a bit faster than VRAM.

- ✔ **Synchronous DRAM (SDRAM):** SDRAM is EDO DRAM that it is synchronized to the video card's processor and chipset. SDRAM is single-ported (one door) memory that is common on video cards.

✓ **Double Data Rate SDRAM (DDR SDRAM):** DDR SDRAM has twice the data transfer speed of standard SDRAM. DDR memories are becoming more commonplace on video cards, especially on 3D graphics accelerators.

✓ **Synchronous Graphics RAM (SGRAM):** An improvement on standard SDRAM adds features that support faster graphics performance:

  • *Block write* copies the contents of a color register into memory in a single clock cycle.

  • *Write per bit* allows a single bit of a data block to be changed without rewriting the entire data block.

  SGRAM, which is a single-ported memory, is found only on video cards with chipsets that support it.

✓ **Double Data Rate SGRAM (DDR SGRAM):** DDR does for SGRAM exactly what it did for SDRAM: doubles its data transfer rates.

✓ **Direct Rambus DRAM (DRDRAM):** A newer general-purpose memory type that is used for the PC's main memory (and on video cards) that runs about 20 times faster than conventional DRAM. DRDRAM includes bus mastering and dedicated channels between memory devices. *Bus mastering* allows the video card to take control of the PC's system bus and transfer data into and from system RAM. This improves the performance of some video operations that use primary RAM for certain calculations, such as 3D acceleration.

✓ **Unified Memory Architecture (UMA):** Many lower-cost systems intended for home use integrate graphics support and the video system into the motherboard. UMA is so named because it uses system RAM for video memory. This technology almost always produces inferior graphics performance.

Interfacing with the video system

A large amount of data moves between the video card and the PC's CPU and RAM to create each frame of the video display. What you see on the monitor is actually a series of still images rapidly displayed. Each frame requires a lot of information to be sent from the PC to the video card. The pathway that the video information data travels must have more bandwidth than any other peripheral device interface on the PC. This is why either the *PCI (Peripheral Components Interconnect)* or the *AGP (Accelerated Graphics Port)* interfaces are used for most modern PC video systems.

There are some ISA (Industry Standard Architecture) video cards hanging around, but the A+ Exam doesn't care about them; neither should you.

Avoid the myth that the number of bits used on the video card's internal bus is also the number of bits used for the video card's interface. A 128-bit video card usually uses a 32-bit interface. The width of the interface is 16-bits (ISA/EISA cards), 32-bits (VL-Bus, PCI, or AGP), or 64-bits (PCI).

The two most popular video system interfaces in use today are

- **Peripheral Component Interconnect (PCI):** All Pentium-class motherboard chipsets support the PCI interface bus. PCI is commonly used for 2D graphics cards, sound cards, network interface cards, and other expansion cards that attach directly to the motherboard. Of course, a PCI card slot is also required.

- **AGP (Accelerated Graphics Port):** The AGP interface was designed specifically for use as a video system interface. AGP also has a direct link to system RAM, which makes it possible for the video system to use system RAM for calculations and temporary storage. An AGP video card will fit only in an AGP slot.

Because of its faster transfer rates, AGP is quickly replacing the PCI interface as the interface of choice. In fact, AGP has evolved into several versions, each designated as a multiple of the original standard's speed. Table 12-3 lists the versions of AGP and the data transfer rate associated with each.

Table 12-3	AGP Versions
Version	*Data Transfer Rate*
AGP 1X (meaning 1 times)	266 Mbps
AGP 2X	533 Mbps
AGP 4X	1.07 Gbps
AGP 8X (Universal AGP Pro)	2.1 Gbps

One reason for AGP's increased speed, compared to PCI's 133 Mbps, is that AGP is a port and supports only one device (the video card); PCI is a true bus structure over which the PC communicates with a number of devices.

Dealing with driver software

The software device driver is a major component of the modern video system. The device driver interacts between the video card's BIOS and any application software or operating system generating images to be displayed on the monitor. The driver software decides the most efficient way to use the features of the graphics processor and translates what an application wants to display into instructions that the video card can understand. A video card usually has a separate software routine in the device driver for each resolution or color depth combination.

Making the connection

Expect a question about the sizes of the different plugs that connect the monitor to the system. The monitor connects to the system through a connector on the back of the adapter card or through a connector on the motherboard. Different plugs are used, each with a different number of pins. The number of pins on the connector is somewhat indicative of the adapter card's capabilities. Here are the different connectors for monitors:

- ✔ **15-pin:** The HD-15 connector (the HD means high-density) is the standard monitor connector on virtually all newer monitors and video cards, especially VGA and SVGA. The video card has the female connector into which the male plug of the monitor is attached. The HD-15 is a DB-style plug and connector.

- ✔ **9-pin:** Most older monitors (usually digital displays, such as CGA, EGA, and early VGA) use a 9-pin connector.

- ✔ **BNC connector:** Some very high-end monitors use a special cable that connects with a standard 15-pin connector at the video card and a 5-pin BNC connector at the monitor.

Monitor Power and Safety

Two areas of concern to the CompTIA that are strongly reflected in the A+ Core Hardware exam are safety and environmental issues of monitors. Expect at least one question on these issues on the Core Hardware exam.

Cleaning the monitor

Dust collects on the glass of the monitor and is held there by the static electricity, accumulating over time. Never clean the monitor's glass with any liquid solution while it's powered on. A danger of personal injury and equipment damage exists. The static electricity built up on the screen can be conducted straight to you by the liquid cleaner when you wipe it off. If you want to use a spray cleaner, turn off the monitor, spray a cloth, and then wipe the monitor. You can also find antistatic wipes that are made just for this purpose.

Saving the planet

PC monitors contain high levels of lead. In fact, the average CRT contains from 5 to 8 pounds of lead, which can pose a threat if released into the environment. Many states now have laws stating that if the CRT's screen is still intact, the monitor can be safely recycled. Some public and many private recyclers can handle the special requirements of PC monitor disposal.

In active mode, the monitor uses more power than the entire PC system. However, reducing the power consumption of monitors in their idle state is a focus of the United States Environmental Protection Agency (EPA) program called *Energy Star,* or *Green Star.* The purpose of this program is to certify PCs and monitors that use less than 30 watts in all power modes and reduce their power consumption by 99 percent in sleep or suspend mode. PCs that meet this standard can display the Energy Star logo.

Monitors meeting the Green standard must reduce their power consumption by 99 percent in suspend mode.

VESA's *Display Power Management System (DPMS)* protocol shuts down the parts of the monitor or motherboard that have been inactive for a certain period of time. PCs with both a motherboard and a monitor supporting the DPMS protocol significantly reduce the system's power consumption.

Protecting against electromagnetic evils

CRTs produce strong electrical and electromagnetic emissions, which are formidable and can wreak havoc on other electrical or magnetic systems. Debates are ongoing within the computing and health worlds regarding the possible threat of these emissions to humans. Some people believe that extended exposure can increase a person's risk of cancer; others believe no risk at all exists. Everyone agrees that limiting your exposure to electromagnetic emissions can't hurt. So it's not a good idea to hold a monitor to your ear for long.

Keeping the lid on

For the exam, memorize this section word for word. Even if you don't find this on the test, the information may save your life.

Don't open a monitor to work on it. Chances are that you

✔ Don't have the foggiest idea what you're doing in there.

✔ Don't have the tools or equipment to fix it.

✔ Will kill yourself. The monitor holds at least 20,000 volts and *all* of that voltage is still present even when the power is off.

If you must open the case to work on a monitor, *do not* wear an ESD grounding strap. Also, unplug the AC cord from the power source and use the buddy system (never work alone on a monitor). Do you get the impression that maybe you shouldn't work on monitors?

To be safe, send the monitor to the manufacturer or a repair company specializing in monitors or a salvage company to dispose of it properly.

Monitors use very high voltages and hold other hazards that can cause serious injury or even death, even when the power is off and disconnected. Never use a regular multimeter or other test equipment to measure the voltages on a monitor. Much like the PC's main power supply, some large *capacitors* inside the monitor hold some big nasty charges, and you don't want any part of them.

Exorcising the magnetic evils

Because preventive maintenance is an important part of the PC repairperson's job, the A+ Core Hardware exam requires you to know about monitor cleaning and preventive maintenance techniques.

The powerful electromagnetic forces in the monitor or any placed nearby can cause the internal components of the monitor to become magnetized. When this happens, the image resolution and color quality produced by the monitor can be distorted or faded, especially in the display's corners.

A process called *degaussing* eliminates most of the magnetization inside the CRT. Most color monitors have a built-in degaussing protocol that can usually be accessed from the monitor's front panel. A monitor should be degaussed fairly regularly, but be careful not to overdo it. Degaussing a circuit too much can damage it.

Getting input from an output device

Touchscreen monitors are becoming more common as their prices fall. They may be popular in information kiosks, automatic teller machines, and car washes, but they also are used in homes and offices. The A+ Core Technologies exam wants you to be familiar with how a touchscreen knows it's been touched; how it accepts input.

There are three primary systems used to detect a touch on the screen:

- ✓ **Capacitive:** This system places a capacitive layer over the glass face panel of the monitor that holds an electrical charge. When an object touches the screen (such as a human finger), the charge of the spot that was touched transfers to the other object; therefore, there's less charge at that location. Circuits in the corners of the monitor screen calculate the location of the touch exactly using the relative differences in the charge amount at each corner. A capacitive monitor transmits almost 90 percent of the light from the monitor compared to only about 75 percent of the light from a resistive system.

- ✓ **Resistive:** This touchscreen system uses a normal glass panel covered with conductive and resistive metallic layers, which are kept apart with spaces. A scratch-resistant layer covers all of these layers. When a user touches the screen, using a human finger I hope, the conductive and the resistive layers are forced together and the coordinates of the contact result in an exact X (horizontal) and Y (vertical) location. Unfortunately, the metallic layers restrict the amount of light emitting from the monitor.

- ✓ **Surface acoustic wave (SAW):** This type of touchscreen system is indicated by the tiny holes along the top and side of the monitor's front bezel. Behind the holes are two sets of transducers, one to send and one to receive signals from each other. If the receiving transducer sees that the signal has been interrupted by some object touching the screen, it can locate it precisely. Because the SAW system places no metallic or conductive layers on the screen, it is able to emit 100 percent of the monitor's light.

The stimuli that make contact with the screen can be almost anything on a resistive or SAW system. However, on a capacitive system, the object must be able to absorb an electrical charge, which means it must be conductive.

Adding Sound to the PC

You may see an exam question directly related to sound reproduction and capture technology, outside of the IRQ that's usually occupied by the sound card (IRQ5), or where the CD-ROM's audio cable connects (to the sound card).

Sound, beyond the little system speaker on the front of the system unit, is added through an adapter card in an expansion slot. Most newer computers come with a sound system (a sound card, a CD-ROM or DVD, and a set of speakers). For older systems, sound can be added to a PC with a multimedia upgrade kit (CD-ROM, sound card, microphone, and speakers) or as a single card and speakers.

Hearing all about the standards of sound

Essentially, three sound card standards have existed: the 8-bit AdLib, the better SoundBlaster, and the General MIDI (musical instrument digital interface). Most sound cards in use today support both the SoundBlaster and General MIDI standards for recording and playback. The AdLib card has all but disappeared. Most sound cards are CD quality, which means that they capture and reproduce digital audio at the same resolution (CD-A) used for audio CDs.

The two standards in use are SoundBlaster and MIDI.

A CD-ROM drive produces sound through a headphone jack on its face, or sound can be piped through the sound card for broadcast to the PC's speakers. You can find an audio cable on the CD-ROM that connects to the sound card for this purpose.

Components of a PC Sound System

These components are common to PC sound systems:

- ✔ **Sound card:** The sound card combines all the inputs, outputs, and signal processors required to convert audio information into and from digital form into a single card. Sound cards are either ISA or PCI adapter cards or can be integrated directly on the motherboard through an audio chip.

- ✔ **Amplifier:** After the sound card has converted digital audio into an analog (audible) signal, the signal must be amplified before it can be played back on speakers. Most sound cards include a weak amplifier that is capable of driving a set of headphones or a set of small PC speakers. Some PC speakers include an amplifier in one or both of the speakers, which takes the burden off the sound card.

- ✔ **Speakers:** PC speakers are available as small passive systems that are powered from the sound card's headphone output or as active (amplified) 3-way surround-sound systems that rival many home theatres and somewhere in-between. Some computer monitors have speakers that are integrated into their bezels or that snap onto their sides. USB speaker systems do not require a separate sound card — all the sound processing is contained inside the speaker itself.

Turning on to sound cards

The sound card combines the components required to transfer sound into and out of a PC, including:

- **Analog input jacks:** Most sound cards have two kinds of inputs:

  - *Line-level* inputs accept signals from electronic sources such as a CD player or directly from a musical instrument like a synthesizer.

  - *Mic-level* inputs accept the signal from a microphone or an unamplified electric guitar.

- **Analog output jacks:** Nearly all sound cards have two kinds of analog output jacks:

  - The *speaker out* jack is driven by a small amplifier. Its output power is appropriate for headphones or small PC speakers.

  - The *line out* jack provides a line-level signal that can be used as an input to another sound device, such as a stereo receiver.

- **Analog to Digital Converter (ADC):** The ADC converts analog audio data, such as a live voice or a musical instrument, into digital data that can be stored on a PC.

- **Digital I/O jack:** Directly connects digital devices to the PC and passes digital audio signals without converting to analog.

- **Digital Signal Processor (DSP):** Reduces the load on the PC's CPU for processing audio. This is common on most newer sound cards.

- **Digital to Analog Converter (DAC):** Converts stored digital audio data into audible (analog) information that can be played on speakers or headphones.

- **Game/MIDI port:** This connector can serve two functions:

  - Connect game controllers, such as joysticks

  - Connect to an external MIDI device (through a special cable)

- **Synthesizer:** Many of the sounds that a sound card produces are generated on the card using a synthesizer chip.

Interfacing to the sound card

Sound cards are installed in expansion card slots on the motherboard using one of these standard interfaces:

✔ **ISA (Industry Standard Architecture) bus:** ISA sound cards usually require some manual configuration to set their system resource settings, such as the I/O address, DMA, and IRQ. These values are set with either a series of jumpers or DIP switches on the card. Some cards also require you to enter a few commands into the AUTOEXEC.BAT and CONFIG.SYS files.

✔ **PCI (Peripheral Component Interconnect):** PCI sound cards are usually Plug and Play and will be configured automatically by the BIOS or operating system, like Windows 9x, Widows 2000, or Windows XP. In most cases, system resources, such as the IRQ and DMA, cannot be set manually.

Connecting to sound

For the exam, know which IRQ (interrupt request), DMA (direct memory access) channel, and I/O address are usually assigned to the sound card.

SoundBlaster-compatible sound cards, the current standard, are normally configured to support

✔ DMA Channel 1

✔ IRQ 5

✔ I/O address 220

However, you may find that PCI sound cards can take as many as three DMA channels, if they are available.

Listening to sound files

Several audio file types can be stored and played on a PC. Audio file types usually go by their file extensions. These audio file types are common:

✔ **AAC:** *AAC* is the compression standard expected to succeed MP3. *AAC (Advanced Audio Coding)* is another name for MPEG-2, which should not be confused with MP2.

✔ **AIFF:** *AIFF (Audio Interchange File Format)* is the Macintosh equivalent of the Windows' WAV format. This format can be played on a PC with the Windows Media Player.

✔ **AU:** *AU* is the UNIX audio file standard. Most Web browsers have built-in AU support, and newer versions of the Windows Media Player can play back AU files.

✔ **MID:** *MID* aren't really digital audio files; they contain MIDI data, which includes such information as the *pitch* and *duration* of each note.

✔ **MP3:** Short for MPEG-1 Layer 3, *MP3* is an audio compression standard developed by the Moving Pictures Experts Group (MPEG). MP3 compression has become popular because file sizes can be greatly reduced while retaining most of the original WAV file's sound quality.

✔ **RA or RAM:** Real Networks developed these file formats for streaming audio files. Real Audio files require either a dedicated Real Audio player or a browser plug-in for playback.

✔ **WAV:** *WAV* is the standard Windows audio file format with recording and playback support built into the Windows operating systems.

✔ **WMA:** *Windows Media Audio* is Microsoft's answer to Real Audio. WMA files can be played back on Windows Media Player and many other sound players.

Interfacing to a CD-ROM or DVD

CD audio is unique among PC audio formats because the CPU does not process the output from an audio CD. Instead, both CD-ROM and DVD drives send their output directly to the sound card via a specialized cable. Although it may appear that the computer is processing CD audio because volume levels can be adjusted with a software mixer, all that is being controlled is the sound card's output level.

Cabling between a CD-ROM or DVD drive and a sound card is straightforward, especially if the drive shipped with its own audio cable (and most do). The analog output is always at the rear of the drive, often to the left of the IDE or SCSI connector, and is usually well marked, both on the card and in the documentation. Older drives and those that ship without an audio cable can be a bit more complicated, because there is no single standard for the cabling between a CD-ROM or DVD drive and a sound card. Sound card and drive manufacturers often use proprietary connector types; in these cases, a "Panasonic to Sound Blaster" or "Sony to Pro Audio Spectrum" cable might be required. Fortunately, inexpensive (less than $10) universal cables are now available with multiple connectors that will fit almost any combination of drive and sound card.

Getting Ready for Work

Often the problem with a user's PC is either the adjustments on the monitor itself or the video settings of the operating system.

Use Lab 12-1 to practice changing the settings for a PC's monitor.

Lab 12-1   Setting the Display Resolution on a Windows PC

1. **Access the Display Properties dialog box by right-clicking an empty space on the Windows desktop and choosing Properties from the shortcut menu that appears.**

2. **Select the Settings tab to display the Screen Area and Colors boxes (refer to Figure 12-1).**

3. **Move the slide selector from side to side to adjust the size of the Screen Area to a new setting.**

4. **From the drop-down list of Colors, choose a different color setting.**

5. **Click Apply to change the settings for your video system.**

   The Compatibility Warning dialog box (shown in Figure 12-2) appears, giving you the option of restarting the system to make the change. The choice is yours, but the restart is usually not needed.

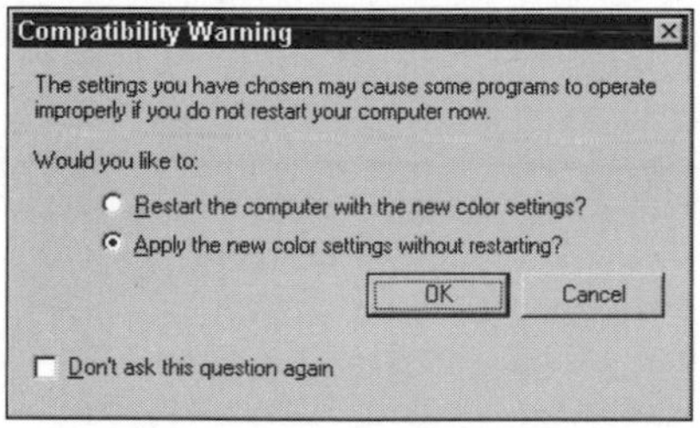

Figure 12-2: This warning appears when you make video settings changes.

6. **Another warning lets you know that the change may take a second or two (15 seconds is what it says). Click OK to proceed.**

7. **If you increase the resolution on your display, the images become smaller; if you decrease the resolution, they become larger.**

8. **Change the settings in the opposite direction to demonstrate the resolution range of your system.**

9. **Reset the settings back to your original settings, or if you found a new setting to your liking, keep it.**

The higher the resolution, the smaller each pixel appears on the screen. If a user complains that Windows icons are too small on a new monitor, lower the resolution.

Another setting that affects the performance of the video card and monitor is the refresh rate. Lab 12-2 details the steps that set the refresh rate on your monitor or to check the setting.

Lab 12-2   Setting the Refresh Rate

1. **Follow the steps used in Lab 12-1 to display the Display Properties dialog box.**

2. **On the Settings tab, click the Advanced button to display the Properties dialog box for the video adapter in your PC.**

3. **Select the adapter tab. The Refresh rate is selected from a drop-down list that is located about in the middle of the window. On most Windows 9*x* or Windows 2000 PCs, the refresh rate is likely set to Optimal.**

If you change the refresh rate and the result is a distorted or blurry image, reboot your PC into Windows Safe Mode and reset the refresh rate using the steps in Lab 12-2.

Prep Test

1 The sound card normally uses which IRQ?

A ○ IRQ 2

B ○ IRQ 5

C ○ IRQ 11

D ○ IRQ 9

2 To support a monitor with a resolution of 1,024 x 768 pixels and 65,000 (16-bit) colors, a video card with at least how many MB of video RAM is needed?

A ○ 2

B ○ 4

C ○ 8

D ○ 1

3 A customer calls you claiming that his or her floppy disk drive must be going bad because files are often missing or corrupted after they're saved to the floppy disk. When you arrive at the customer's site ready to troubleshoot the floppy disk drive, you discover a stack of floppy disks sitting on top of the monitor. What do you think may be the problem?

A ○ The customer is not actually saving the data to the disks.

B ○ The cause may be a bad box of disks, which the customer should throw out and replace with new disks.

C ○ The floppy drive is bad and you need to replace it.

D ○ Magnetic emissions from the CRT are possibly erasing the disks.

4 A monitor that uses two passes to draw the entire screen, drawing every other line on each pass, is what type of monitor?

A ○ Noninterlaced

B ○ Interlaced

C ○ Interleaved

D ○ Multiscan

5 Which of the following is not a type of video RAM?

A ○ WRAM

B ○ VRAM

C ○ SGRAM

D ○ ZRAM

6 **The audio wire that connects to the sound card is attached to**

A ○ The ground lead of the motherboard's power connection

B ○ The audio jumper on the motherboard

C ○ The CD-ROM drive

D ○ Nowhere, it is a never-used extra wire

7 **A monitor conforming to the Energy Star standard reduces its power by what percentage in sleep or suspend mode?**

A ○ 99

B ○ 80

C ○ 100

D ○ 96

8 **An ESD grounding strap should always be worn when working on the PC, except when working on a**

A ○ Memory board

B ○ CRT

C ○ Hard drive

D ○ Motherboard

9 **The distance between pixels on the CRT screen is measured as**

A ○ Resolution

B ○ Interlacing

C ○ Dot pitch

D ○ Dot triad

10 **Which of the following is not a type of video adapter card?**

A ○ CGA

B ○ VGA

C ○ LPGA

D ○ SVGA

Answers

1 **B.** A sound card that is SoundBlaster compatible, the current standard, supports DMA channel 1, IRQ 5, and I/O address 220. *See "Connecting to sound."*

2 **A.** This is calculated as $1,024 \times 768 \times 16 \div 8$. *Check out "Sizing up the video memory."*

3 **D.** The CRT produces electrical and magnetic emissions strong enough to corrupt the floppy disks. *Look at "Protecting against electromagnetic evils."*

4 **B.** An interlaced monitor uses two complete screen cycles to completely build the display or refresh the display. *Review "Looking Inside the Monitor."*

5 **D.** WRAM, VRAM, and SGRAM are all types of memories used on a video card. *See "Looking at the Video RAMs."*

6 **C.** The audio wire is actually a part of the CD-ROM assembly and is connected to the sound card to provide sound audio support. *Look up "Interfacing to a CD-ROM or DVD."*

7 **A.** The EPA Energy Star standard certifies equipment that reduces power consumption by 99 percent in sleep or suspend mode. *Check out "Saving the planet."*

8 **B.** Never work on the internal system of a monitor without proper equipment, but if you decide to do so, please don't wear an ESD wrist strap. *Zap over to "Keeping the lid on."*

9 **C.** Dot pitch is the distance between two dots of the same color in adjacent pixels. *Slide up to "Looking Inside the Monitor."*

10 **C.** LPGA may mean anything, but it definitely is not a video adapter card type. *Review "Connecting to adapter card standards."*

Chapter 13

Printers

● ●

Exam Objectives

▶ Identifying printer ports, cabling, and connectors

▶ Explaining printer concepts, operations, and components

▶ Troubleshooting common printer problems

▶ Identifying common printer care procedures

● ●

*A*lthough society cherishes the idea of a paperless society, it churns out more paper with thousands (or millions) of numbers, letters, and symbols to be interpreted as information. People thought that the computer would create a paperless society but as near as I can tell, the opposite has happened. More paper is printed today than ever before, and computer printers are doing most of the printing. Printers come in many models, but they all essentially perform the same task — printing information on paper.

The printer is a very important device to the PC system. Its importance makes its failure all the more disrupting. I can live without my sound card for a while, but when will you have my printer fixed?

In my experience, at least four in ten service calls involve a printer. Even if the number is actually only 20 percent of the calls, of the ten major subsystems of the PC, the printer is still responsible for a disproportionate share of the problems, which is probably why the A+ Core Hardware exam has an entire domain devoted to printers.

Quick Assessment

Identifying printer ports, cabling, and connectors

1 The most common connection type used for PC printers is _____.

2 The default I/O address of _____ is 378-37Fh.

3 A printer that includes a NIC is said to be _____.

Explaining printer concepts, operations, and components

4 Bidirectional parallel interfaces are defined in the _____ standard.

5 A(n) _____ printer uses an array of printwires to form and print a character.

6 Most laser printers use the _____ process or a derivative of it to print.

7 The _____ is used to uniformly charge the photosensitive drum.

8 The six steps of the laser printer process are _____, _____, _____, _____, _____, and _____.

Trouble-shooting common printer problems

9 Paper jams in a laser printer usually occur in the _____ area.

Identifying common printer care procedures

10 Laser printer toner consists of _____ -coated iron particles.

Answers

1 *Parallel.* See "Getting directly connected."

2 *LPT1.* Look at "Getting directly connected."

3 *Network-ready.* Check out "Connecting to a network."

4 *IEEE 1284.* Check out "Keeping up with standards."

5 *Dot matrix.* Review "Dot-matrix printers."

6 *EP (Electrophotographic).* Scan "Laser printers."

7 *Primary* or *main corona.* Look at "Inside the laser printer."

8 *Cleaning, conditioning, writing, developing, transferring,* and *fusing.* See "Printing with a laser printer."

9 *Paper pickup* or *paper feed.* Review "Troubleshooting Common Printer Problems."

10 *Plastic resin.* Take a look at "Inside the laser printer."

A Printer Is a Printer Is a Printer . . .

Computer users get rather animated and emotional when their printers don't work. Whatever type of printer is involved, at some point it just stops working. The true definition of a nanosecond is the length of time it takes the user to dial your number after the printer has not immediately spewed forth a document in perfect form. A significant portion of the exam is devoted to printers and their function, problems, and care. Most of the questions are about laser printers, but prepare for questions on dot matrix and inkjet (bubble jet) printers too.

Getting directly connected

Although some printers connect through several port types, most PC printers connect through a parallel port, which is designated as LPT1, LPT2, or perhaps LPT3. (If LPT ever had a meaning, it is lost to the lore of the PC. My guess is that it was something like *line print terminal,* but don't sweat it.) LPT ports are designated and numbered according to their I/O addresses during the boot sequence by the system BIOS. See Chapter 10 for more information on connectors and port types, and Chapter 4 for more information on the boot sequence and BIOS.

Table 13-1 lists the IRQ and I/O address assignments usually assigned to the LPT ports. A PC printer interacts with the system through the memory area at the I/O address assigned to the LPT port to which it is connected. However, most PC printers don't actually use an IRQ, especially those attached to a PC running Windows 9*x* or later. Some parallel devices use interrupts and IRQs, such as an external tape, a storage drive, or cables associated with file transfer software. No default DMA assignments are made to the LPT ports, but DMA channel 3 is used by some types of LPT ports.

Table 13-1	LPT Port System Resources	
Parallel Port	*I/O Address*	*IRQ*
LPT1	378-37Fh	7
LPT2	278-27F	5
LPT3	3BC-3BFh	7 or 5

The most often used connectors that connect printers directly to a PC are

✔ **25-pin DB (data bus) female connector:** The parallel port on the back of a PC is a 25-pin female connector into which the male connector counterpart on the printer cable (see Figure 13-1) is connected. Most computers today have only one LPT port; it's usually mounted either on the motherboard or an expansion card.

✔ **36-pin Centronics:** This connector, shown in Figure 13-1, is used at the printer end of the connecting cable. The PC end of the cable is a 25-pin male connector, as described in the preceding item. The Centronics connector is also the standard connector for the HP-IB (Hewlett Packard Interface Bus). This general style of connector has become known as the Centronics connector because Centronics Corporation produced a large share of the printers used for the earliest PCs. Ampenol produced the original design. Other types of Centronics connectors are used on the PC (such as the 50-pin SCSI), but the 36-pin is the one used with printers.

✔ **Mini Centronics:** This connection, which is used primarily for Hewlett Packard laser printers, is a smaller version of the standard Centronics connector, shown in Figure 13-1. On the mini Centronics connector, the 36-pins are moved closer together, which allows the size of the connector head and jack to also be smaller in overall size.

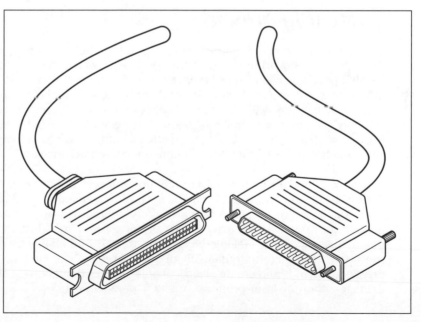

Figure 13-1: The Centronics connector (left) and the parallel connector (right) are the two most common connectors that connect a printer to a PC.

✔ **USB:** Some of the latest printers now feature a USB connection in addition to the standard parallel connector. But, if the printer you're working on is a bit older, it can still be connected to the PC via a USB port using a USB to a parallel adapter cable. This cable has a Centronics connector on the printer end and a USB connector on the PC end. Why would you connect your printer via the USB port? You may want to free your parallel port for another use (such as a scanner or a Zip drive) or connect the printer to a USB hub.

✔ **IR (infrared) or IrDA (Infrared Data Association):** Some adapters, such as the one made by Extended Systems (www.extendedsystems.com), can connect a parallel printer to a PC through its IrDA connection, which frees the parallel port on the PC for other uses. A number of hand-held-size printers designed for use with notebooks and PDAs that interface with an IrDA connection are also available, but these are not covered on the exam.

A general rule for how long a parallel cable can be is that older Centronics cables should not be more than 15 feet in length; between 9 and 12 feet is best. Newer IEEE-1284 cables extend up to 30 feet in length; 50-foot high-end cables are available. Typically, if you must be more than 10 feet away from a printer, connect into a network.

Switching around

You can use a switchbox (either manual or automatic) to connect more than one nonlaser printer or any other parallel device or devices to a single parallel port. You can also use them to allow multiple PCs to share a single printer. A dial designates which PC or device is to be connected to the primary device of the switchbox. The devices on the switchbox are called *A/B switches* because the station designations are generically labeled alphabetically — such as A, B, and C. An automatic switchbox senses activity on a line and switches to it when its device connection becomes available.

Before you flood me with e-mails saying how successful you've been with your laser printer and your automatic switchbox, remember that the following is just a caution. Because they are highly interactive with the printer, many laser printer device drivers (not all) have problems with switchboxes due to electrical noise. Taking the laser printer on- and off-line by changing the active location (either manually or automatically) can interrupt device driver commands and create electrical noise spikes that could possibly damage either the laser printer or the PC's parallel port.

Conforming to standard

The IEEE 1284 standard, especially bidirectional communications on a parallel port, is definitely on the test. IEEE 1284 defines three operating modes for parallel port communications: forward (from the PC to the peripheral device), backward (from the peripheral device to the PC), and bi-directional (both ways, but only one at a time).

Chapter 10, which covers parallel ports, includes a section on the IEEE 1284 parallel port and protocol standards. Thoroughly study that chapter and its "Keeping up to standard" section.

Connecting to a network

As the businesses continue to focus on the cost of computing and printing, sharing expensive resources, such as a high-end color laser printer, with several PCs by integrating the printer into the local area network (LAN) is a good idea. The printers often found in business settings, which are usually shared over the network, are typically purchased network-ready or can be adapted to connect to a network.

Printers that are network-ready have a network interface card (NIC) already installed into which an RJ-45 network connector can be inserted. Chapter 18 covers the process that configures printers to the network, but it is becoming easier every day. Operating systems are starting to recognize that nearly all computing environments include a printer, that there are literally hundreds of printers to choose from, and that including the printer drivers is a good thing.

If a printer is not network-ready, some network printer interface devices (such as Hewlett Packard's JetDirect) can connect at least one printer to the network. These devices connect to the printer through its parallel port and provide a built-in NIC that connects to the network with a network connector (usually an RJ-45).

Figure 13-2 shows both a network-ready printer that is connected directly to the network and the use of a printer to network interface device to connect a printer that is not network-ready.

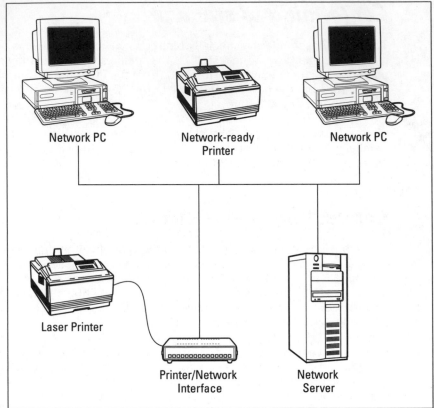

Figure 13-2:
Printers
can be
connected
into a
network and
shared by
many users.

A Plethora of Printers

You can connect many different types of printers to a PC. If you always have the latest and greatest hardware, you probably have a distorted view of the kinds of computers that most users actually have — not the latest and greatest. Many dot-matrix, inkjet, bubble jet, and even some noisy, old daisy-wheel printers are still in use. Not everyone has a laser printer.

The printers that are listed in the objectives of the A+ Core Hardware exam (the ones you are supposed to know) are

✔ **Dot-matrix:** These printers create characters by forming a group of hard-wire pins into the pattern of the letter, number, or special character and then striking the entire pin group through a ribbon, forming the character on paper.

✔ **Inkjet or bubble jet:** Inkjet printers are probably the most popular printer type in use for home users. They produce a better-quality print without the noise of the dot-matrix printer and at a lower price than a laser printer. Inkjet printers produce an image by heating ink into steam and then "jetting" it onto the paper.

✔ **Laser:** These printers use a complex printing process to produce high-quality documents. Laser printers are becoming more common on the desktop, especially with prices continuing to decline.

✔ **Other printer types:** The A+ Core Hardware exam objectives list three other printer types that are becoming more commonplace: dye sublimation, solid ink, and thermal printers.

Dot-matrix printers

You may see questions on the exam about preventive care of dot-matrix printers, how they form characters and drive paper, and how their resolution is measured.

The dot-matrix printer is an impact printer that creates its printed characters using a matrix of very fine printwires that produce a pattern of dots. As the number of printwires that create the character increases, so does its resolution and the quality of the printed image. Each pin, chosen from a matrix of pins, forms a dot on the page, and the pattern of dots creates the printed character. The resulting character is less sharp than a character created by a laser printer, but the trade-off of cost and flexibility makes this acceptable for many documents.

Resolution is the number of dots that are printed in a square inch (dots-per-inch or dpi).

The most common numbers of printwires (pins) in the dot-matrix printer's printhead are 9, 18, and 24. A 24-pin printhead produces *near-letter quality* (NLQ) print. Printers with less than 24 pins are only capable of *draft quality* print, which produces characters with lots of wide-open spaces between the dots. If the print produced by a laser printer is Los Angeles, then draft quality is North Dakota.

To produce a character, the print mechanism extends all the printwires needed to create a character's pattern. Behind each printwire is a solenoid coil that causes the pin to extend and impact the inked ribbon. A spring then pulls each printwire back into the printhead. Because of the impact that strikes the ink of the ribbon onto the page, dot-matrix printers are commonly used in situations where forms or documents with many carbon copies are created.

The typical dot-matrix printer uses continuous feed paper (in contrast to the cut sheet paper used in laser and inkjet printers). Much like a typewriter, dot-matrix printers use a platen (a large rubberized roller), under which the paper is fed. The platen provides spring tension to hold the paper in place and move it through the printer. When the platen motor rotates the platen, the paper is pushed up and past the printhead. If *typewriter* is a new term to you, visit Joanne and Ben Batchelor's History of the IBM typewriter site at www.etypewriters.com/history.htm.

Dot-matrix printers support *form tractors,* or *pin-feed tractors,* which attach to the platen and are driven by the platen motor. Form tractors provide a more consistent feed mechanism by using the pin-feed holes along the side of the paper to pull the paper and multiple part forms through the printer.

The speed of a dot-matrix printer is rated in characters per second (CPS). Common speed ratings for dot-matrix printers range from 32 to 72 CPS. The actual speed realized from the printer depends largely on its mode of operation. Dot-matrix printers operate in either *font* (normal text, numbers, and symbols) or *dot-addressable* (graphics and charts) modes.

The printhead in a dot-matrix printer can get extremely hot and should not be touched while in use. Be gentle when cleaning and handling the internal parts of a dot-matrix printer, particularly with the printhead and its print-wires (especially in aging dot-matrix printers). If you are too rough with the printhead, you can damage its tracking or its printwires.

Inkjet printers

Expect questions on the Core Hardware exam about inkjet printers, particularly about the way they form characters.

Inkjet, also known as bubble jet, printers are probably the most popular printer type in use. They are quiet and use an ink reservoir instead of a messy ribbon. The inkjet printer is a nonimpact printer. Except for the rush of the printhead moving back and forth, it makes little noise. The ink reservoir is included in a disposable cartridge that contains the printing mechanism. This means that each time the ink reservoir is replenished, a new print mechanism is supplied.

Inkjet printers form characters by squirting ink using an elaborate ink-stream process, which utilizes as many as 50 tiny nozzles. The print quality of an inkjet printer is rated in dots per inch (dpi). The more dots in the image, the better the image. Inkjets range from 150 dpi to over 1400 dpi on photo-quality printers.

Inkjet printer speeds are rated in pages per minute (PPM) rather than characters per second (CPS) because the inkjet doesn't form each character separately. Rather, it prints one line at a time across the page. Each printed line contains only a portion of the print image oriented top to bottom. It takes several passes across the page to complete a complete line of text. Inkjet printer speeds range from 2 PPM to 20 PPM, with their speeds varying between the number of pages produced in color versus black ink.

The paper feed mechanism of an inkjet printer is simple. A cut sheet of paper is fed from a stacked supply past the printhead by a series of rollers that also clamp the paper in place. The paper is advanced one print line at a time past the printhead, which moves back and forth across the paper. The printed pages are then stacked in a separate tray from the original paper supply.

Laser printers

Laser printers are VIT (very important technology) on the A+ Core Hardware exam. Have a good understanding of general laser printer operations and the six steps of the laser printer's printing process.

Laser printers are considered page printers because they form and print all the text and graphics for one full sheet or page at a time. Three different printing processes are used in laser printers, each directly attributable to one or more manufacturer(s):

- **Electrophotographic (EP) process:** This process, which was the first laser printer technology, was developed by Xerox and Canon. It is the technology used by all laser printers in one form or another. A laser beam produces an electrostatic charge and a dry toner to create the "printed" image.

- **Hewlett-Packard (HP) process:** The HP process is essentially the same as the EP process, with the exception of some minor operating procedures. It's similar enough to be considered the same process, yet different enough to get its own name.

- **Light-emitting diode (LED) process:** From outward appearances, you can't distinguish an LED printer from a laser printer. The difference boils down to the fact that an LED printer uses an array of about 2,500 light-emitting diodes instead of a laser to produce an electrostatic charge. An LED printer with a 600 dpi resolution has 600 LEDs per inch.

Inside the laser printer

Laser printers use toner to create the image on the printed page. Toner is a dry powder that consists of iron particles coated with a plastic resin that bonds to the paper during the print process. Toner is supplied to the printer in a removable cartridge that contains many of the most important parts used in the printing process. The toner cartridge contains the photosensitive drum (a mechanism that places a charge on the drum), a roller to develop the final image on the page, and, of course, the toner.

Very few PC vacuums can be used to clean a laser printer. The toner in a laser printer can severely clog any vacuum not specifically designed to handle it. Be sure that your vacuum can handle toner before you use it for that purpose. Plan on understanding just about everything there is to know about laser printers for the test, including the following list of major components. Expect questions about both the overall laser printing process and the specific role of key components.

In addition to the toner cartridge, eight standard assemblies exist in a laser printer:

- ✔ **The drum:** The drum inside the toner cartridge is photosensitive, which means it reacts to light. The drum holds an electrostatic charge (except where it is exposed to light). The laser beam is reflected onto the surface of the drum to create a pattern of charged and not-so-charged spots, representing the image of the page to be printed.

- ✔ **High-voltage power supply:** The EP process uses very high voltage to charge the drum and transfer and hold the toner on the paper. The high-voltage power supply converts AC current into the higher voltages used by the printer.

- ✔ **DC power supply:** Like a computer, most of the electronic components in the laser printer use direct current. For example, logic circuits use +/–5V DC (volts direct current), and the paper transport motors use +24V DC. Also, like the computer's power supply, the laser printer DC power supply also contains the cooling system fan.

- ✔ **Paper transport:** Inside the laser printer are four types of rollers that move the paper through the printer. Each rubberized roller or set of rollers is driven by its own motor. The four roller types in the paper transport system are the *feed roller* (or the *paper pickup roller*), the *registration roller,* the *fuser roller,* and the *exit roller.*

Most paper jams in a laser printer occur in the *paper transport* area.

- ✔ **Primary corona:** Also called the *main corona* or the *primary grid,* this device forms an electrical field that uniformly charges the photosensitive drum to –600V to reset it prior to receiving the print image and toner.

- ✔ **Transfer corona:** This mechanism moves a page image from the drum to the paper. The transfer corona charges the paper; the charge pulls the toner from the drum onto the paper. As the paper exits the transfer corona, a static charge eliminator strip reduces the charge on the paper so that it won't stick to the drum.

I cover the transfer corona in detail elsewhere in this chapter.

Not all printers use a transfer corona; some use a *transfer roller* instead. When working on a printer with a transfer roller, be careful not to touch the roller with your bare hand or arm. The oils from your skin can spot the transfer roller and cause improperly charged paper, which appears as defects in the printed image.

✔ **Fusing rollers:** The toner is melted permanently to the page by the fusing rollers that apply pressure and heat (between 165 and 180 degrees Celsius) to it. The fuser — not the laser — makes the printed pages hot.

✔ **Controller:** This is the motherboard of the laser printer, and it has architecture and components like a PC motherboard. The controller communicates with the PC, houses the memory in the printer, and forms the image printed on the page. Memory expansion is possible on virtually all laser printers. Adding memory allows the printer to reproduce larger documents or graphics in higher resolutions or to support additional soft fonts.

A printer that experiences frequent memory overflow errors has a bad memory board, a memory board that was installed incorrectly, or a memory board that needs additional memory. Diagnose this problem by eliminating these conditions in this order.

Printing with a laser printer

Six major steps are involved in printing a page on a laser printer. It's important that you remember the sequence and activities of each step in the process. A catch phrase I've devised to help you remember the sequence is

California Cows Won't Dance The Fandango (CCWDTF)

The first letter in each word represents a step in the laser printing process: Cleaning, Conditioning, Writing, Developing, Transferring, and Fusing. (You may also see cleaning as the last step in other references, but on the exam, it's listed first.) Also be ready to list the steps in backward order. You need to develop your own shortcut for remembering the process backwards because I still have a headache from the last one.

Here is what goes on during each step of the EP laser printing process:

✔ **Cleaning:** Before a new page is printed, any remnants from the previous page are cleared away. The drum is swept free of any lingering toner with a rubber blade, and a fluorescent lamp removes any electrical charge remaining on the drum. Any toner removed in this step is not reused but is put into a used-toner compartment on the cartridge.

✔ **Conditioning:** The entire drum is uniformly charged to –600V by the primary corona wire (also known as the main corona) inside the toner cartridge. This charge conditions the drum for the next step.

✔ **Writing:** The laser printer controller uses a laser beam and a series of mirrors to create the image of the page on the drum. The laser beam is turned on and off in accordance with the image to be created on the drum. At the spot where the laser's light contacts the photosensitive drum, the charge is reduced to about –100V. After the image has been transferred to the drum this way, the controller also starts the page sheet through the printer, stopping it at the registration rollers.

✔ **Developing:** The developing roller, located inside the toner cartridge, has a magnet inside of it that attracts the iron particles in the toner. As the developing roller rotates near the drum, the toner is attracted to the areas of the drum that have been exposed by the laser, creating the print image on the drum.

✔ **Transferring:** The back of the paper sheet (the one that has been waiting patiently at the registration rollers) is given a positive charge that attracts the negatively charged toner from the drum onto the paper as it passes. After this step, the paper has the image of the page on it, but the toner, which is held only by simple magnetism, is not yet bonded to it.

✔ **Fusing:** The fusing rollers apply heat and pressure to the toner, which melts and presses it into the paper to create a permanent bond. The fusing rollers are covered with Teflon and treated with a light silicon oil to keep the paper from sticking to them.

Other printers and ink types

Yes, there are other types of printers beyond the dot matrix, inkjet (which are also called *ink dispersion* printers), and laser printers. Perhaps the better known of the lesser-known printer types are

✔ **Dye sublimation:** This type of printer produces photo-processing-lab-quality prints at home or at the office. The dye part of this process is on rolls of transparent film with red (magenta), blue (cyan), yellow, and gray (black) dyes embedded in the film. The printer head is heated and then passed over the film, causing the dyes to vaporize and permeate the glossy face of the special print paper and turn back to solids. Dye sublimation printing is done in smooth forms of color, not pixels. Like in other printer types, heat is an important part of the printing process.

✔ **Solid ink:** The inks used in this process are like large rectangular coloring crayons that are inserted into individual "tanks" on the printer. The process that prints an image on a solid ink printer is like that used in the laser printer process. The solid ink blocks are melted by the print head onto the print drum and after the image is formed, paper is passed over the print drum, and the image is transferred to the paper. Because the inks are transferred first to the drum and then to the paper, the printer is able to achieve a high degree of registration.

✔ **Thermal:** Thermal printers use specially treated paper that changes color in reaction to the heat of the print head. There are both monochrome (gray) and color thermal printers:

- **Monochrome thermal printers:** If you have been to a bar or restaurant lately, you probably received a receipt printed on a little *thermal printer* (which is popular in these businesses because they are very quiet). Monochrome thermal paper is chemically treated to darken when heat is applied. However, this can be a problem should you leave your receipt in the bright sunlight.

- **Color thermal printers:** If you can afford their operating costs, color thermal printers are very high quality and very quiet. Like monochrome thermal printing, these printers use chemically treated paper that reacts to absorb color from a color ribbon when heated. This paper currently costs about 25 cents a sheet. As the paper passes through the printing mechanism, it is pressed against a multi-colored ribbon that has banks of cyan, magenta, yellow, and black (CMYK). As heat is applied, small dots of the dyes on the ribbon are pressed onto the paper, a variation of the solid ink printing process. However, only one color is applied at a time and the paper makes additional passes through the printer for other colors to be applied.

Technically, both dye sublimation and solid ink printers use a form of thermal (heat) process to create images.

Adding memory and disk space to a printer

Given the explosion of graphics that are begging to be printed, your laser printer may need additional memory (RAM), hard disk space, or even an internal print server added to it so it can handle anything you may send it.

Adding memory

Adding RAM or expanding the memory on your laser printer improves its ability to process large image files sent to it and allowing the PC's CPU to be freed sooner in the print transfer and go on about its business. Most manu-facturers of mid- to high-end laser printers have optional memory upgrades available for their printers.

Adding a printer disk drive

Most of the better-known laser printer manufacturers offer an optional hard disk drive that can be installed inside or through a PCMCIA slot on the printer to provide additional storage space for the printer. For example, fonts and the print queue can be stored on the printer's hard disk drive to both free the main system hard drive and reduce the transfer time between the PC and the printer.

Preventive Maintenance and Supplies

Regular preventive maintenance and proper care of a printer extends its life.

Expect at least one question on the A+ Core Hardware exam about the clean-ing, protection, and preventive maintenance of a printer (probably a laser printer).

General printer housekeeping

Here are a number of common-sense and technical procedures that keep a printer working and reliable:

- ✓ Plug the printer into a surge protector or UPS (uninterruptible power supply). On a laser printer, first make sure that the UPS is capable of handling the power demands of the printer at startup; few conventional PC UPS units can.

Under the heading of *you heard it here first* (but you will again later): Never plug a laser printer into a conventional PC UPS. Laser printers draw a lot of power at startup, and few UPS units have enough power to handle the demand. If you use a UPS for your laser printer, be sure the UPS can handle the peak loading (peak power requirements) of the laser printer.

- ✓ Always use the type and weight of paper recommended for the printer to avoid print feed path jams. Some printers prefer laser paper that is finished on one side. Check the printer's documentation. Also check and remember the heaviest paper recommended for your printer (and never use anything heavier than that) to avoid paper jams and possible damage to the paper-handling mechanism of the printer.

✔ Clean dot-matrix printers regularly by vacuuming or blowing them out with compressed air. If you want to vacuum a laser printer, be sure you use only a vacuum and dust bag specially made for that task. The toner can really clog a regular vacuum cleaner.

✔ Use a wire brush or rubber-conditioning product to clean and maintain the paper transport of an inkjet or laser printer. When trying to clear the paper path, never put anything inside a laser printer while it's running and always wait until the fusing area has cooled down before working in this area of a laser printer. It generates a lot of heat to melt the toner to the paper and stays hot for some time afterward.

Keeping the printer firmware up-to-date

Using a process something like that used to flash the BIOS (see Chapter 4), the firmware on a printer can be upgraded to correct bugs and add features, just like a BIOS update for the PC. The process is somewhat unique to each manufacturer, but in general it involves downloading a compressed or self-extracting file and running the utility with the printer online. Having the printer online while you are attempting to update it is an important part of this process.

Keeping the laser printer clean, tidy, and operating

Laser printers have their own special needs when it comes to maintenance, which you should know, test or no test. For the A+ Core Hardware exam, you must know about toner and the cleaning of the primary corona wire. The following list helps you properly address these special needs:

✔ The toner in a laser printer is really nasty stuff. If you have ever accidentally dropped a toner cartridge or ignorantly turned one over and shaken it, you know what I mean. If you ever have a toner spillage accident or see toner spilled inside the laser printer, don't use a regular vacuum to clean it up. Toner is fine particles of iron and plastic. The particles are so fine that they seep through the walls of most vacuum bags and get into the motor, where the plastic particles melt. Special types of vacuums and vacuum cleaner bags are made for working with toner.

✔ If you get toner on your skin, never use warm or hot water to clean it off. Warm water may cause the toner to fuse to your skin. First wipe off as much of the toner with a dry paper towel or soft cloth, rinse with cold water, and finish by washing with soap and cold water.

- Usually packed with the toner cartridge is a cleaning brush or cotton swab that you can use to clean the transfer corona wire and the primary corona wire. (Be careful not to break these wires while cleaning them.)

- During the print process, the laser produces a gas called *ozone*. Most laser printers have an ozone filter that also captures toner and paper dust. Replace or clean this filter in accordance with the manufacturer's instructions in the printer's manual.

- Inside the laser printer are at least two mirrors that reflect the laser onto the drum. Using clean, lint-free cloths, periodically clean the laser mirrors — with the power off, of course. Never, I repeat, never look directly at the laser and never operate the printer with its cover off. Most printers will not power up with the cover open, anyway.

- The fuser cleaning pad and the fusing roller can also become dirty and leave unwanted toner blobs on the paper. Check these printer parts regularly and clean them as necessary.

Troubleshooting Common Printer Problems

The A+ Core Hardware exam may include situational questions that require you to choose the action that should be taken *first* or *next* in a set of events. The troubleshooting sequence for a printer problem is routine for experienced PC service technicians; you probably have your own. Review the following steps to refresh your memory for the test.

The first real sign of a printer problem is that paper with printing on it isn't coming out of the printer. When this happens, look in four places:

- **Printer:** These suggestions may seem like bonehead stuff, but they are often the problem:

  - Check whether the printer is powered on, and then check whether it's online.

  - Make sure that the printer has paper and that the feed tray, roller, or slide is in its proper position for operation.

  - Check for a paper jam; if you find one, clear it, but also notice the point at which the jam occurred and check the rollers and paper feed mechanism carefully.

    Most paper jams happen in the paper pickup area, so look there first.

✔ **Cable:** If the printer seems all right, ensure that the cable is the proper type of cable. Nearly all laser printers and the newest inkjets and dot-matrix printers require an IEEE 1284 cable. If the cable is the right kind, then make sure that it's solidly connected at each end.

✔ **Port:** To check the port, use loopback plugs and diagnostic software. After the printer itself, the parallel port has the next highest failure rate.

✔ **Software:** In the Windows environment, printers stall for just about any reason. If the printer status shows no problems, and you can't find any other problem, try restarting the system.

Beyond a printer not printing, the most common failure is a bad print image. Regularly cleaning the printer and its printing mechanism or printhead as directed by the printer's manuals helps to avoid this problem. As a professional PC repairperson, it is worth your while to show customers how to clean their PC and its peripherals themselves.

Getting Ready for Work

In addition to the fact that you should expect a question or two about the process to set up a printer on a Windows PC on the Operating Systems Technologies exam, you should also be familiar with this process as a part of your preparations for the workplace. Familiarize yourself with the process used by doing it a few times using different ways to access the Printer group on the Control Panel.

Before you can set a printer in a Windows environment, you must obtain the printer driver for that printer under the specific version of Windows that you operate. Regardless of which Windows operating system version you use, you should install a printer driver designed for that version. Usually, you can find the correct printer driver on the manufacturer's Web site.

Windows 9*x*, Windows Me, Windows NT, Windows 2000, and Windows XP each include a remarkable number of printer drivers on their installation CD. To be absolutely sure you have the latest driver for the PC's operating system, visit the manufacturer's Web site. Some printers come with a separate printer driver included on a floppy disk or CD-ROM. Plus, you don't know how long the operating system, or the printer itself, has been sitting on the shelf.

Add new printers through the Printers function found on the Control Panel or on the Settings option of the Start menu. In either case, the Printers dialog box displays the Add Printer wizard icon (see Figure 13-3). Lab 13-1 details the steps to add a printer.

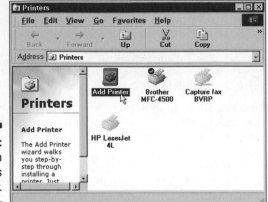

Figure 13-3:
Printers in
the Printers
folder.

Lab 13-1   Adding a New Printer

1. **From the Windows desktop, click the Start button to display the Start menu. Access the Settings menu and choose the Printers option.**

   Or double-click the My Computer icon to display the My Computer folder. Open the Control Panel and choose the Printers icon.

2. **With the Printer folder open, click the Add Printer icon shown in Figure 13-3 to display the Add Printer dialog box (Windows 95) or start the Add Printer wizard (Windows 98, Windows Me, Windows 2000, and Windows XP).**

3. **If the printer you are adding is not included in the supported printers list, use the floppy disk or CD-ROM that came with the printer to supply the device driver by clicking the Have Disk button when appropriate.**

   After the printer driver loads, an icon for the new printer displays in the Printers folder.

Prep Test

1 The paper continuously jams in a laser printer. Where would you look first?

A ○ Pressure roller area

B ○ Transfer roller area

C ○ Fuser roller area

D ○ Paper pickup area

2 What happens in the conditioning phase of a laser printer?

A ○ The image is created on the drum.

B ○ The erasure lamps neutralize the drum.

C ○ The primary corona applies a uniform charge to the drum.

D ○ The paper is charged by the transfer corona.

3 The correct order of operations in the laser printing process is

A ○ Conditioning, cleaning, writing, developing, fusing, transferring

B ○ Cleaning, conditioning, writing, developing, transferring, fusing

C ○ Conditioning, cleaning, writing, developing, transferring, fusing

D ○ Cleaning, conditioning, writing, developing, fusing, transferring

4 On a system on which printing has been working well, the user gets an error message when he or she tries to print. No changes have been made to the system. After checking whether the printer is powered on, what do you check next?

A ○ Is the printer online?

B ○ Is the printer designated as the default printer?

C ○ Is the correct printer driver installed?

D ○ Will the printer print when attached to a different PC?

5 Reducing the negative charge on the areas of the drum that represent the image to be printed is done in which step of the laser printing process?

A ○ Transferring

B ○ Conditioning

C ○ Fusing

D ○ Writing

6 The toner is deposited onto the drum surface in which step of the printing process?

A ○ Writing

B ○ Conditioning

C ○ Developing

D ○ Transferring

7 Toner is bonded with the paper during which phase of the laser printing process?

A ○ Writing

B ○ Transferring

C ○ Conditioning

D ○ Fusing

8 Which of the following forms the electrical field that charges the drum?

A ○ Transfer corona wire

B ○ Primary corona wire

C ○ Fusing roller

D ○ Cleaning blade

9 A dot-matrix printer with a 24-pin printhead is capable of producing

A ○ Letter-quality print

B ○ Daisy-wheel quality print

C ○ Near-letter quality print

D ○ Graphics only

10 Bidirectional communications on a parallel cable was standardized by

A ○ IEEE 232

B ○ VESA

C ○ Laser printers

D ○ IEEE 1284

Answers

1 **D.** Most paper jams happen in the paper pickup area when more than one sheet, a crumpled sheet, or a twisted sheet of paper tries to feed into the paper pickup rollers. *See "Troubleshooting Common Printer Problems."*

2 **C.** In this step of the laser printing process, the drum is put into the right condition to receive the print image. *Charge over to "Printing with a laser printer."*

3 **B.** Remember "California Cows Won't Dance The Fandango." *See "Printing with a laser printer."*

4 **A.** I know this seems pretty basic, but forgetting the basics gets many PC technicians in trouble. *Check out "Troubleshooting Common Printer Problems."*

5 **D.** This step "writes" the blips on the drum where toner will be placed during the developing step. *Read "Printing with a laser printer."*

6 **C.** I include this question to drive home the comment I make for Prep Test Question 5. Putting toner on the drum "develops" the print image so that it can be transferred to the paper. *Review "Printing with a laser printer."*

7 **D.** Okay, this is the last question of the laser printer's process steps. In the fusing step, the toner is heated to about 350 degrees Fahrenheit and pressed down hard by the fusing rollers. *Take one more look at "Printing with a laser printer."*

8 **B.** To separate the two corona wires in your mind, just remember that the primary corona goes first and charges the drum. The transfer corona is second and charges the paper. *Look at "Inside the laser printer."*

9 **C.** About the best a dot-matrix printer can do with round dots is getting the print near the quality of print produced with a solid typeface. *Review "Dot-matrix printers."*

10 **D.** IEEE standard 1284 defines the operating modes that include bidirectional communications. *See "Keeping up with standards."*

Chapter 14

Portable Systems

• •

Exam Objectives

▶ Identifying the unique components of portable PC systems

▶ Installing and upgrading components

• •

*A*lthough the early laptop computers were smaller than the desktop devices of their time, they filled your lap completely and then some. The so-called portables that first came on the market were much too big for airline meal trays, not to mention too heavy to carry far — sure killers in the business market. Today, the *notebook computer* has finally established a package size that the market accepts as usable almost everywhere. You can play Solitaire anywhere, anytime, anyplace!

The latest evolution in portable systems is the ultimately small palmtop. Technology has finally developed a full-fledged Windows computer that you can literally hold in your hand or fit in your briefcase — or even conveniently tuck into your little zippered day planner. Even smaller systems are becoming available that, while fitting more into the category of personal digital assistants (PDAs) and generally still considered personal electronics, are on the verge of redefining a portable computer.

The exact role of the professional PC service technician with these devices has yet to be defined. Portable systems are evolving largely as disposable technology, which probably explains why the A+ Hardware Technology exam has only a few questions on portable systems and deals mainly with notebook PCs.

Quick Assessment

Identifying the unique components of portable PC systems

1   _____ is the most popular type of portable PC today.

2   A(n) _____ is the power system that allows a notebook computer to be portable.

3   Because of its weight and long life, the _____ type of battery is probably the best choice for a portable PC.

4   Portable PCs use a special kind of memory module called a(n) _____.

Installing and upgrading components

5   Before physically installing a larger internal hard drive in a notebook computer, you can add _____, _____, or _____ by using an existing port.

6   The type of LCD that supports each pixel with its own transistor is called _____.

7   Type I PCMCIA cards are used to add _____ to a notebook computer.

8   A modem is an example of a(n) _____ PC card.

9   Type III PCMCIA cards can be up to _____ millimeters thick.

10   Changing a PC card while the system is running is called _____.

Answers

1   *Notebook.* Flip to "Checking Out Portable PC Types."

2   *Battery.* Look at "Portable PC power systems."

3   *Lithium Ion.* See "Portable PC battery types."

4   *SODIMM.* Take a look at "Adding memory."

5   *Zip, Jaz,* or *tape drive.* Review "Upgrading the hard drive."

6   *Active matrix.* Scan "Comparing active and passive liquid crystal displays."

7   *Flash memory.* See "Focusing on PC cards."

8   *Type II.* Check into "Focusing on PC cards."

9   *10.5.* Take a look at "Focusing on PC cards."

10 *Hot-swapping.* Look at "Expanding capacity on the fly."

Relating Portable Systems and the A+ Exam

Study the following portable system areas:

- ✔ AC/DC power sources, including battery power supplies
- ✔ Hard drives
- ✔ Keyboards
- ✔ Mice
- ✔ Motherboards
- ✔ Memory
- ✔ Video and other adapter cards
- ✔ Displays
- ✔ Docking stations and port replicators

The next few sections cover a little history and terminology. To cut to the chase on portable PCs for the A+ Hardware Technology exam, go to the section, "Expanding capacity on the fly," later in this chapter.

Powering the Portable

Adaptable, lightweight, and long-life power sources play a large part in the usability of a portable PC system. Essentially, three general types of power sources, described as follows, are available for portable PCs — each designed to provide it with power either in the office or on the road:

- ✔ **AC/DC adapter:** This adapter works much like the power supply in a desktop computer to convert the wall socket AC power into DC power. AC adapters are also used to recharge the portable PC's battery. You are probably familiar with this type of device because it's used on a wide range of electronic products — including games, calculators, and external computer peripherals.

- ✔ **Battery:** The battery is an integral part of any portable PC because without it, the PC would not be as portable. Instead, users would need very long extension cords and would have to depend on having an AC outlet everywhere they go.

> ✔ **Docking station:** In addition to the power that it provides the PC, the docking station enables the PC to connect to full-sized expansion cards and additional ports, and allows the portable PC to connect to and drive the peripherals (such as monitors and printers) that are usually connected to a desktop computer. A *port replicator* is typically a smaller version of the docking station that provides only additional I/O ports.

Portable PC power systems

The power supply of a portable PC is focused on power conservation rather than power regulation; the latter is the aim of a nonportable PC power supply. A portable PC runs on DC power like other PCs, but the portable runs straight from a battery. This means that the portable PC supply does not convert AC to DC to power the motherboard, processor, video display, and peripheral devices. AC power recharges the battery, but it does not power the PC.

Managing portable PC power

Virtually all portable PCs now have some kind of a power-management system, most often as a software battery monitor. This system tracks the reserve power of the battery and reports the battery's strength as a percentage. A report of 70 percent means that you've used only 30 percent of the battery's capacity. Many power-management systems also check whether the PC is in use; if it's not, the power-management system suspends the PC to conserve the battery's power. Conserving a battery and extending its life is a much better — and less expensive — choice than replacing the battery.

ACPI and APM

Power management is a major concern for all portable computing device owners. Nearly all notebook PC and portable device owners look for and take advantage of anything that will help save battery power.

Nearly all notebook PCs are configured with either the Advanced Configuration and Power Interface (ACPI) or the Advanced Power Management (APM) technologies. ACPI is the newest of these technologies and APM is a legacy technology.

ACPI is configured in the BIOS and APM is implemented through an application programming interface (API). ACPI is a collection of BIOS code routines, where APM is an operating system directed configuration and power management technology for portable PCs, as well as desktop and server computers.

The benefit of ACPI is that it lets the PC control the power supply to peripheral devices, such as the CD-ROM, printer, and other external devices. In a turn about is fair play twist, the peripherals also have the ability to use ACPI to power on the PC. For example, if you insert a CD-ROM into a CD-ROM drive, the PC automatically boots up from a power off state.

Portable PC battery types

Expect a question about portable PC battery characteristics on the A+ Hardware Technology exam.

Portable PCs use the following types of batteries:

- **Alkaline:** These are the same batteries that are common for your calculator, TV remote control, and portable tape player.

  This type of battery is used in some palmtop computers.

- **Nickel Cadmium (NiCad):** This is the most popular and durable type of rechargeable battery. This battery is also the heaviest, yet least expensive, of the portable PC battery types. It is also quick to charge and has a reasonable life of around 700 charge-and-discharge cycles.

- **Nickel-Metal Hydride (NiMH):** Unlike NiCad batteries, these batteries are environmentally friendly because they don't contain heavy metals that can be toxic. They also store up to 30 percent more power than NiCad batteries of the same weight.

  Some of the disadvantages of NiMH batteries are that they have a shorter life (around 400 charge-and-discharge cycles) and cost about 30 percent more than NiCad batteries.

- **Lithium Ion (Li-Ion or LiON):** Very lightweight with a long battery life, this type of battery is made with one of the lightest available metals (lithium). LiON batteries hold about twice the power of a NiCad battery in about half the weight. Compared to a NiMH battery of equal weight, a LiON delivers twice the run time from each charge. The LiON battery type has about the same life cycle as NiCad and NiMH batteries. LiONs are not generally available for all models; they're usually more expensive than other battery types.

  A LiON battery is probably the best choice for a portable PC, but it can be more expensive than the other choices.

Running off fuel cells

Fuel cells are a new objective of the A+ Hardware Technology exam. They are a power source for portable PC systems. However, I doubt that you will see an exam question about fuel cells.

Fuel cells have been talked about for some time, but always in the future tense. However, Toshiba now has a prototype direct methanol fuel cell (DMFC) battery for its portable PCs. The primary advantages offered by fuel cells are that they have a longer life, which means they can run the portable system longer, and they don't need recharging, which could be a real cost savings in the long run. The Toshiba DMFC (Direct Methanol Fuel Cell) battery offers a small form factor with an average output of 12 watts and a maximum output of 20 watts, for up to 5 hours. The DMFC battery fits in the same space and uses the same connectors as the lithium-ion battery.

A fuel cell battery produces electricity like an ordinary battery — using electrochemical reactions. The difference between the two is in the fuel cell's ability to produce electricity as long as it has a fuel source (such as methanol, aluminum, hydrogen, and other substances), while an ordinary carbon battery must be recharged periodically. Fuel cell batteries don't store electricity and can't run down like an ordinary battery. Fuel cells convert fuel into electricity; ordinary carbon batteries store electricity that's provided from an external source.

Looking Inside the Portable PC

Portable PCs resemble their nonportable computer cousins only in their functions. Their internal components, such as processors, motherboards, and memory, vary in size, capacity, speed, mounting, and other characteristics that contribute to a PC's portability.

Intel's Pentium family of processors includes the most popular CPUs used in notebook computers. Among these are mobile versions of its Celeron, Pentium III, and Pentium 4 processors, plus the latest Centrino mobile technology bundle, which includes the Pentium M processor.

AMD is gaining in popularity among portable system manufacturers with its Athlon XP-M and XP-M Berton, Mobile Athlon 4, and Mobile Duron processors.

When producing a mobile version of a processor, the manufacturers are primarily concerned with reducing _size, power usage,_ and _heat generation._ The packaging of a mobile CPU provides much of the cooling for the processor (nonportable systems normally handle heat with fans and heat sinks).

Upgrading the Portable PC

The two main disadvantages of notebook PCs are that they are difficult to work on and upgrades are expensive. Upgrade parts are expensive because they are usually proprietary and not generally interchangeable between manufacturers — or even between models from the same manufacturer, in many cases.

You can assume the following three guidelines about questions regarding repairs on a portable PC:

- ✔ The type of portable PC in question is a notebook computer, unless otherwise stated.

- ✔ The notebook computer has a Pentium or higher CPU.

- ✔ The only upgrades that are performed internally are to the RAM and hard drive.

Adding memory

RAM upgrades (at least on most high-end and name brand portable PCs) are accomplished through a porthole or trap door on either the bottom or the side of the portable PC. Many different memory technologies can be inserted into a portable PC, but the first rule is not to mix memory types. The module sizes are now large enough that memory types shouldn't need to be mixed. See Chapter 7 for more general information on memory types.

After installing new RAM in a notebook PC, if the RAM doesn't appear in the BIOS POST display, the RAM probably isn't properly seated. Shut down the notebook and reseat the RAM.

Notebook PCs and many other portable computers use *Small Outline Dual In-line Memory Modules (SODIMMs)*. A SODIMM is a smaller, narrower, and taller version of the DIMM that is used in desktop PCs. On most newer notebook designs, memory is added through the bottom of the PC's case, as shown in Figure 14-1. The SODIMM is mounted flush to the main board and lies flat to save space.

For information on how a SODIMM module is installed, see the section "Getting Ready for Work," later in the chapter.

Working with smaller portable devices

Palmtop computers and other handheld computing devices don't have the overall physical size or internal case space to accommodate full-sized memory modules. For these systems, smaller memory modules have been developed, such as the microDIMM. Such a module is shown in Figure 14-2.

Installing memory in older portables

Older notebook PCs may use Single In-Line Memory Modules (SIMMs), which are installed in much the same manner as the SODIMM. However, a portable system often prescribes both the total memory that it can support and the increments that you can use to add it. Consult the owner's manual to determine the right choices.

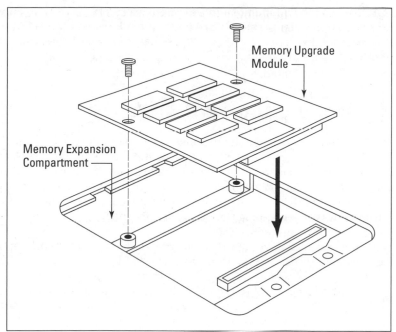

Figure 14-1:
Some newer portable PCs have openings on the case into which a memory module (a DDR SODIMM is shown) is installed.

Memory Upgrade Module

Memory Expansion Compartment

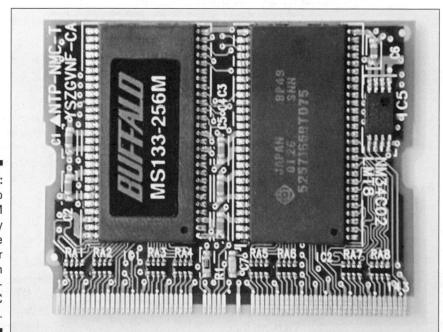

Figure 14-2:
A micro DIMM memory module designed for use in subnotebook PC systems.

Another way to add memory to a PC is to insert a PC card, also known as a Personal Computer Memory Card International Association (PCMCIA) card. (See the section "Focusing on PC cards," later in this chapter, for more information on PC cards.)

Upgrading the hard drive

The secondary storage units of some notebook models are under the keyboard for easy interchange or replacement. In these models, replacing the hard drive is a snap: Snap out the old and snap in the new. On other models, however, the hard drive is internally blended into the notebook's system. If you really want to increase the hard drive space, you may want to use a less arduous way of increasing the PC's storage capacity.

The following is a list of options that you should try before attempting to replace an internal hard drive on a notebook PC:

- ✔ You can easily add removable storage through an existing port. For example, you can add a Zip, Jaz, or tape drive via a serial, parallel, or USB port.

- ✔ You can add a hard drive card in a PC card slot or add a USB-port drive or compact flash (CF) card.

- ✔ If a portable PC supports it, you can interchange the floppy disk or CD-ROM drive with a second removable hard drive.

- ✔ You can use disk space compression utilities to increase the effective space of the hard drive.

Notebooks and other portable computers don't have standard internal layouts and designs like those provided by the form factors of desktop and tower PCs. Because of this, you need an upgrade kit to change the hard drive in a notebook PC. The upgrade kit usually includes the new hard drive, a PC card, and data transfer cables. The PC card and cables are used with data transfer software that is also included in the kit to temporarily hold and transfer the data from the old hard drive to the new one.

Focusing on PC cards

PCMCIA offers a standard for adding more memory and peripherals to portable computers using credit card–like cards — also called *PC cards*. All PC cards are 85.6 mm long and 54 mm wide, or approximately 3.4 inches by 2.1 inches, and use a 68-pin connector. PC cards are matched to designated slots on the portable PC, and each is defined to one of the three types and sizes of cards.

The three types of PC card slots are as follows:

✓ **Type I:** At 3.5 mm thick, these slots have one row of sockets and are used primarily to add *flash memory,* or SRAM (static RAM). This type of memory is common on PCMCIA cards because it requires less power. You can read more about flash memory in Chapter 4.

✓ **Type II:** At 5.5 mm thick, these slots have two rows of sockets and are used to add modems and NICs to a notebook computer. These cards usually have a pop-out connector for an RJ-11 or RJ-45 connector.

✓ **Type III:** At up to 10.5 mm thick, these slots have three rows of sockets and are used to install hard drives or support adapters for external CD-ROM, DVD, and tape drives.

More information is available on PC card standards from PCMCIA's Web site (www.pc-card.com).

The magic of the PC card

Adding a function through the PC card slots of the notebook PC is as easy as pressing the card (firmly) into its slot. You can even do this while the notebook is running. The card's function is instantly recognized by the PC — provided that the card services and sockets are running.

PC card sockets and services

Portable PCs contain the following layers of software to detect and support a PC card when you insert it into the computer:

✓ **Socket services:** A layer of BIOS-level software that detects when a card is inserted or removed

✓ **Card services:** Software that manages the assignment and allocation of system resources to the PC card, such as IRQ and I/O addresses, after the socket services software has detected the card

Expect at least one of the following questions about PC card types:

✓ The higher the type number, the thicker the card. Hard drives (Type III) are thicker than modems (Type II), which are thicker than memory (Type I).

✓ Remember which card type supports which device type. Type I cards are typically memory cards; Type II cards are commonly communications-oriented, such as a modem or a NIC; and Type III cards are secondary storage, such as a hard disk drive, or an adapter interface for an external peripheral device.

Expanding capacity on the fly

Hot-swapping lets you change PC cards without shutting down the system. You can remove an existing card from its slot and install a new card while the PC is on and the operating system is running.

Expect a question on hot-swapping, such as, "What is changing a PC card without powering off the system called?"

PC cards use the 32-bit CardBus standard, which is essentially identical to the PCI bus architecture with some minor electrical differences. CardBus supports bus mastering, accommodates cards at different voltages, and includes advanced power-management features that can idle or turn off PC cards to increase battery life.

Adapting the PCI bus to portable PCs

The PCI bus, the major crosstown bus of the desktop PC, has been adapted to the smaller footprint of the portable system. The following two primary PCI adaptations are used on systems with smaller physical sizes:

- **Compact PCI (CPCI):** This PCI adaptation is used primarily for industrial computer applications that need a smaller and more robust form factor than is used with desktop PCs. CPCI, an open standard developed and supported by the PCI Industrial Computer Manufacturer's Group (PICMG), is well suited to small, high-speed industrial applications with several high-speed card interfaces.

- **Mini-PCI:** This is a smaller version of the standard desktop PC PCI form. The mini-PCI has all the same features and functions of a standard PCI card while being only about one-fourth the size of the larger standard card. Adapters are available that allow full-sized cards to fit into the mini-PCI slot and vice versa. The mini-PCI is commonly used for internal wireless network adapters on portable PCs and hand-held devices.

Comparing active and passive liquid crystal displays

Liquid crystal displays (LCDs) are used on notebook computers because LCDs have lower power requirements than the CRT-style monitor and can be configured into a flat panel.

Exam questions about notebook computer displays often explore the following major types of LCDs:

✔ **Active matrix:** If you have an LCD on your watch, you have an active matrix display. This type of LCD has a transistor for each pixel and creates a crisp image that is easy to read from an angle and has sharp resolution. The downside is that all those transistors take a lot of power. An active matrix display can run down a battery in less than 2 hours. Active matrix displays are TFT (Thin-Film Transistor).

✔ **Passive matrix:** This type of LCD has two groups of transistors: one along the top edge of the display, containing one transistor for each vertical column of pixels, and the other along the left side of the display, containing one transistor for each horizontal row of pixels. Wires form a matrix that interconnects the transistor rows and columns. To darken a particular pixel, power is sent to the transistors on the same row and column as the pixel and down the wires to the intersection point where the pixel sits. This method uses much less power, but it is much slower and produces a lower-quality image. Passive matrix displays are usually either the older *Double-Layer Supertwist Nematic (DSTN)* or the newer *High-Performance Addressing (HPA)*. HPA improves the response of the display over DSTN, but both produce an inferior image compared to active matrix (TFT) screens.

Both types of LCDs are flat and about ½-inch thick. TFT displays produce the best image and cost the most. HPA and DSTN screens are hard to see except by looking straight at the display. An HPA screen has one advantage: Only the operator has a clear view of the screen. People trying to see the screen from the side are out of luck, which may be desirable when working with secure data.

Because LCDs are covered with a thin sheet of plastic, avoid any abrasive cleaners and cloths. Use a mild detergent or a low-sudsing, general-purpose cleaner and a lint-free soft cloth.

Looking into graphics standards

The graphics display resolution standards supported on portable PCs are the same as those available on desktop monitors and PCs. For the most part, four standards are the primary standards supported on active displays. The four standards supported on portable PCs are:

✔ **Super video graphics array (SVGA):** This is an extension of the video graphics array (VGA) standard, that supports 1024 x 768 and higher resolutions.

✔ **Extended graphics array (XGA):** The standard in use today is actually XGA-2, based on the original IBM XGA standard introduced in 1990. This standard supports non-interlaced resolution of 1024 x 768 and higher.

   ✔ **Super extended graphics array (SXGA):** An extension of the XGA standard that can support 1280 x 1024 with 1.3 million pixels in the display.

   ✔ **Ultra extended graphics array (UXGA):** A further extension of XGA that supports 1600 x 1200 resolution.

Introducing Tablet PCs

You knew it couldn't be too long before the stylus and touch-screen technologies that are available on personal digital assistants became available on portable PCs. However, this iteration of the portable PC has arrived in the Tablet PC, which is a cross between a notebook computer and an electronic writing tablet. You can display your documents and images on the screen that covers nearly all of the top of the unit, and you can either type data into the PC or use a stylus to hand-write information straight into the system. Special software converts your handwriting into text for storage purposes (or you can store the handwriting, or both the handwriting and the text).

Don't expect many questions on the A+ exams about Tablet PCs. However, watch for touch-screen questions. Chapter 12 has more information on displays and touch-screen devices.

Getting Ready for Work

Follow these general steps to install a SODIMM in a notebook PC:

| Lab 14-1   Installing a SODIMM Module in a Notebook PC |

1. **Remove the old SODIMM. Push the plastic retaining clips outward and tilt the SODIMM up and out of the socket.**

2. **Install the new SODIMM by aligning the edge connector notches to the slot.**

3. **Place the SODIMM in the slot at a slight angle.**

   The retaining clips prevent the module from laying flat in the socket.

4. **Gently but firmly press the SODIMM into the slot until the detents on the retaining clips line up with the notches on the module.**

5. **Press the SODIMM until the plastic clips snap.**

   The plastic clips lock the SODIMM into place and hold it flat in the mounting.

Prep Test

1 **A Type I PC card is used to do which of the following?**

   A ○ Add SRAM to the system

   B ○ Add network capabilities to the system

   C ○ Add a device, such as a modem, to the system

   D ○ Connect an external device, such as a CD-ROM drive, to the system

2 **A PC card hard drive fits into a what slot type?**

   A ○ Type I

   B ○ Type II

   C ○ Type III

   D ○ Type IV

3 **Which of the following defines hot-swapping?**

   A ○ Installing new devices without the need for a driver

   B ○ Removing and adding internal devices without rebooting

   C ○ Removing and inserting PCMCIA cards while the system is running

   D ○ All of the above

4 **SODIMM stands for which of the following?**

   A ○ Special Operations for Digital Image Multimedia

   B ○ Some Other Dual In-line Memory Module

   C ○ Small Outline Dual In-line Memory Module

   D ○ None of the above

5 **After inserting a PC card into a notebook computer, the system does not recognize the card. Which of the following could be the problem?**

   A ○ No drivers were installed for the card.

   B ○ The card was inserted in the wrong slot type.

   C ○ The notebook computer does not support PCMCIA.

   D ○ Socket or card services have not recognized the card.

6 **A modem generally fits in what PCMCIA slot type?**

   A ○ Type I

   B ○ Type II

   C ○ Type III

   D ○ Type IV

7 **PC card socket services software does which of the following?**

A ○ Allows PC cards to emulate ISA devices

B ○ Traps PC card internal errors

C ○ Detects the insertion and removal of PC cards

D ○ Is used to eject PC cards

8 **Which of the following are types of passive matrix displays? (Choose two.)**

A ❑ TFT

B ❑ DHCP

C ❑ HPA

D ❑ DSTN

9 **Which of the following resolution standards are used for notebook computer displays? (Choose three.)**

A ❑ UGA

B ❑ SVGA

C ❑ XGA

D ❑ SXGA

10 **What type of power supports the video display on a portable PC?**

A ○ AC power only

B ○ DC power only

C ○ AC power when the PC is plugged in or DC power when it is not plugged in

D ○ Either AC or DC at the user's choice

Answers

1 **A.** Type II cards are used to add network adapters and modems, and Type III cards are used to plug in external drive adapters. *See "Focusing on PC cards."*

2 **C.** Type III slots support hard drives. *Review "Focusing on PC cards."*

3 **C.** Hot-swapping is removing and inserting PC cards (PCMCIA) without shutting down the system. *Take a look at "Expanding capacity on the fly."*

4 **C.** Because they must mount flush to the main board of the portable computer, specially designed modules (SODIMMs) are built for each make and model of notebook computer. *Visit "Adding memory" one more time.*

5 **D.** Unless the socket services software detects the card, card services will not allocate its system resources. *Refer to "PC card sockets and services."*

6 **B.** Type I cards are used for memory, Type II cards are used for modems, Type III cards are used to add hard drives and NICs, and Type IV cards do not exist. This is the last question on the PC card types, I promise. *Review "Focusing on PC cards."*

7 **C.** Socket services software detects when a PC card is inserted or removed. *Check out "Focusing on PC cards."*

8 **C & D.** Passive displays produce a lower-quality display that does not adapt to rapid changes quickly, but they produce a good image and don't use much power. *Look at "Comparing active and passive liquid crystal displays."*

9 **B, C, & D.** Depending on the size of the display, different resolution standards are used to produce the best possible image for the dots per inch (dpi) resolution available on the notebook computer. *Check out "Comparing active and passive liquid crystal displays."*

10 **B.** All systems in a portable PC are powered with low-power DC current. AC is converted to DC by the AC/DC converter. *See "Portable PC power systems*

Part IV
Remembering Why It's Called Hardware

The 5th Wave   By Rich Tennant

It's another cow box mutilation, Sheriff. Look how cleanly the case has been severed. And if my hunch is right, you won't find the motherboard within a thousand miles of here.

In this part . . .

The chapters in this part of the book provide information for a significant portion of the Core Hardware exam and across just about every domain on the exam objectives including, the "Installation, Configuration, and Upgrading," "Diagnosing and Troubleshooting," PC Preventive Maintenance, Safety, and Environmental Issues," "Motherboard/Processors/Memory" and "Basic Networking" domains of the exam.

The part of the Core Hardware book reviews the procedures used to disassemble a PC, put it back together again, upgrade key components, connect it to a network, determine the source of a problem and fix it, and care for the PC. This part summarizes the technical tasks associated with working as a PC service technician and the safety precautions used to protect both you and the PC in the process.

Chapter 15

Taking a PC Apart (And Putting It Back Together Again)

● ●

Exam Objectives

▶ Identifying electrostatic discharge (ESD) safeguards
▶ Removing and replacing field-replaceable modules (FRMs)
▶ Identifying system modules and their normal operations
▶ Working safely with high-voltage modules

● ●

*Y*ou don't have to worry about being asked to list the steps to disassemble (or reassemble) a PC on the A+ Hardware Technology exam. However, you need background knowledge of the process that is used to remove (or install) a field-replaceable module (FRM) and the safeguards that are used to protect FRMs and you from electrostatic discharge (ESD). The best way to review the procedure for removing and replacing PC FRMs (such as hard drives, adapter cards, and the motherboard) is to go step by step through the processes.

Taking the PC apart isn't difficult, but being able to remove the modules without disrupting everything else separates the professional PC repair technician from the hobbyist. The essential skill that is involved in this process is knowing the difference between an FRM (such as the power supply) and other modules. In addition to your personal safety, your primary concern is to keep working parts working.

When you disassemble a PC, you can see all the modules that you must remove. When you put a computer back together, however, you start with a pile of pieces and must reassemble them in the correct order. If the computer isn't assembled correctly, it will probably have serious problems functioning.

Review this chapter for the following important factors about FRMs: removing, protecting, and replacing FRMs, and the ESD issues that are involved.

I haven't included a "Getting Ready for Work" section in this chapter because the whole chapter serves that purpose.

Quick Assessment

Identifying electrostatic discharge (ESD) safeguards

1 You should always wear a(n) _____ when working on the PC system unit.

2 You should have _____ and _____ available when working inside the PC so that you can note or diagram the identifying features, orientation, and position of components.

Removing and replacing field-replaceable modules (FRMs)

3 You should handle adapter cards and other circuit boards by their _____ to avoid touching the electronic contacts.

4 _____ and _____ memory modules are installed in stand-up edge connector sockets.

5 Controller card failures are likely to be a result of the card not being _____.

Identifying system modules and their normal operations

6 Ribbon cables, used to connect data connections for hard drives, have a color stripe that identifies pin _____ on the cable.

7 If you detached the CMOS battery during disassembly, you must update the _____.

8 Not installing a(n) _____ can result in a boot disk failure.

Working safely with high-voltage modules

9 Not installing the _____ can cause the power supply to explode.

10 The cable that provides power to the front panel of the PC carries _____ power.

Answers

1 *Antistatic protection device* or *ESD wrist strap*. Zap over to "Avoiding shocking developments."

2 *Paper, pen*. Review "Checking in: Is the patient ready, nurse?"

3 *Edges*. Peruse "Taking out the adapter cards."

4 *SIMM, DIMM*. See "Reinstalling memory modules."

5 *Seated properly*. Review "Testing the Results."

6 *1 (one)*. Become one with "Relating to the Zen of ribbon cable."

7 *CMOS configuration information*. See "Checking the CMOS and Configuration Data, or Where Did the Battery Go?"

8 *Drive power connector*. Check out "Stating your preference: The adapter or the drive first?"

9 *Motherboard power connectors*. Take a look at "Testing the Results."

10 *110V AC*. Charge over to "Grasping the power and removing it."

Getting Ready and Taking Precautions

Two important preparations must be made before working on the PC, regardless of what you are planning to do: ESD preparations and general surgery preparations.

A person can feel a static charge beginning at about 3,000 volts, but electronic circuits can be damaged by a charge of only 30 volts.

Avoiding shocking developments

I can't overemphasize the importance of protecting the PC and yourself from ESD and its potential damage and hazards. You can do this in the following ways:

- For use in emergencies only — not recommended for general use: If you are trapped inside a system case without another form of ESD protection, keep yourself in contact with the metal frame of the PC at all times.

- The minimum precaution against ESD is to wear an antistatic wrist strap and keep the strap attached to the metal PC chassis with an alligator clip. When working inside the PC, you cannot avoid becoming a grounding circuit for static electricity that is built up in the system. The ESD strap contains a resistor that slows the discharge and protects you and the PC. In addition to wearing the ESD strap, use an antistatic mat under the PC case. That way, if you accidentally knock off the clip, you won't pass along a charge to whatever you're holding at the time. Several mat and strap combinations are available.

- Keep a supply of antistatic bags on hand to protect cards and smaller FRMs outside the case. ESD lurks everywhere. Never let your guard down, and always protect your computer parts.

- Remove the power plug from the electrical source when working on newer Pentium-class PCs. In the past, you could leave pre-Pentium PCs plugged into an AC power source, which provided a connection to an earth ground. These systems did not provide fast power-up or instant-on motherboards.

Checking in: Is the patient ready, nurse?

A year or two ago, I would have said that it's rare for a PC repair technician to completely disassemble a PC — especially at a customer's site. Today's customers, however, are trying to maximize their investment in PC hardware by upgrading their older units. Replacing the motherboard, processor, power supply, and adapter cards when upgrading an older PC isn't unusual. The information that I give you in this chapter goes beyond preparing you for the A+ Hardware Technology exam.

I use the word *disassemble* (and as many derivatives as I can get away with) to mean the disconnection of cables, extraction of fasteners, and removal of a module to a location outside the case — for example, onto a workbench or in a box. *FRM* (field-replaceable module) is used on the A+ Hardware Technology exam to refer to any component that is replaced as a whole unit and can be installed at a customer site.

You will remember this information better if you have a PC that you can use as a model as you review this chapter. Nothing compares to hands-on experience.

Before beginning surgery on your PC, take the following actions:

- ✔ Have your tools standing by and ready for use. If you are lucky enough to have a surgical assistant for this process, all the better — but you're probably on your own. So, to avoid the hassle of clipping and unclipping your wrist strap (and the possibility of forgetting to clip up again) as you run off for a forgotten tool, have your tools nearby and ready to go.

- ✔ Have paper and pen standing by so that you can write down or diagram the placement, orientation, and identifying features of the modules, cables, cards, and other vital organs that you remove. Your notes and diagrams are your guide when it's time to reassemble the PC.

- ✔ Use any system that works for you to sort, store, and secure the screws and other fasteners that you remove from the patient. They can easily get lost, scratch the case, or worse. (You hear an awful screeching sound if you drag the case across the workbench with a fastener trapped underneath.)

- ✔ Gather all the support and reference disks for the devices that are installed in the PC. You may need these to reconstruct the system, especially device drivers and system resources, should you catastrophically lose the BIOS configuration settings.

Taking inventory

As a precaution against the unlikely event that you accidentally disconnect or dislodge the CMOS battery (which would unfortunately result in losing the CMOS setup information), you should boot the system and write down the system setup configuration data, such as its RAM size and its CMOS setup information.

If you are working on a 286 or newer PC, do not disconnect the battery from the motherboard; you will lose the CMOS setup information if you do.

Before you begin to disassemble the PC, enter the CMOS setup information and record the following information:

- ✔ Floppy disk drive size and density
- ✔ Hard drive type and configuration in cylinders, heads, sectors, capacity, and other unique attributes, such as the landing zone (LZone)
- ✔ RAM size by type
- ✔ Time and date
- ✔ Parallel port type
- ✔ Serial port type and status
- ✔ Other stuff that's specific to your system

After you have written down the CMOS information, you can begin the disassembly process. Record the model and serial numbers of each major FRM as you go — especially in the shop environment.

As you reassemble the PC, verify that the parts that came out are the ones going back in. Inadvertently replacing a good part with a faulty one, and thus introducing new problems to a system, is a bad thing.

Always close all running programs, shut down the operating system, and turn off the computer before disassembling it.

Removing the Major Components

You need to remember only a few general procedures for disassembling a PC. Each procedure relates specifically to a particular FRM, such as the *case, power supply, adapter cards, RAM,* and *motherboard.*

Opening the box

The logical place to begin the disassembly of the PC is the case of the system unit. To remove the case from a PC, the only tool that you need is a Phillips screwdriver. Some newer cases allegedly don't require tools.

Unless you are the warranty service provider, be sure not to void the warranty on someone's PC by opening the system unit. Some manufacturers place stickers over the edges where the case parts fit together to warn you that you may be voiding the warranty by removing the cover.

Be sure to wear your ESD protection and to avoid touching any of the internal parts when removing the cover.

System cases come in a variety of types and sizes, and each is opened using a slightly different technique, as follows:

- **Disconnect the cables.** Remove all peripheral device connectors, and get them out of the way. Disconnect the parallel, serial, game, and video port and other cables that are connected to the back of the unit; unplug the mouse and keyboard. You may want to use masking or other light tape to label the cables and plugs to help you reconnect them properly. Some manufacturers color-code their connectors, which is appreciated. (Now, if they could only do that for the rest of my life.)

- **Clean the case.** Although not the most technical step, this is a practical one. While the case is intact and with peripheral devices removed from its top (desktop models, of course), clean the dust bunnies from the top, back, and sides of the unit. This eliminates the chance that any accumulated gunk will fall inside the case when you remove the top.

- **Remove any protection or appearance bezels.** Some older desktop cases and full-size tower cases have plastic panels that are mounted on either the back or front. If you have a PC that has such a panel, you should be able to pull it off. You may need to encourage it with a screwdriver to get it started. Check the back of this panel for dust, clean it if needed, and set it aside.

- **Remove the case cover.** Manufacturers are always designing new ways to open and close cases. In general, the common cases are opened in the following ways:

  - **Tower cases:** These cases have the most variations, such as a screwless case, a case with a removable single side panel, or a two-piece case that consists of a base and a U-shaped cover. On other cases, you can find usually two to four Phillips screws or thumbscrews on the back edge of the case. Release the fasteners and remove the case. Check the PC's documentation to be sure that you are disassembling the case properly and not removing the power supply screws.

  - **Standard desktop case:** This is the case type that has been around since the original PC, but it's fading away. The two pieces of this case fit together in an "L7" fashion, with the front panel attached to the case top and the back panel attached to the case bottom. In some variations of this design, just the top of the case is popped off by depressing clips on the sides. On older cases, be sure that you know which screws are case screws and which screws hold the power supply. After you remove the case screws (if you must remove screws), either push the top forward and lift it off or continue pushing forward (depending on the case type). When in doubt, check out the PC's documentation.

Be careful not to remove screws that connect internal components (such as the power supply or some connectors) to the inside of the case. Always verify what a screw is attached to before removing it.

- **Screwless case:** These cases have a release mechanism on the front or top so that the front or side can be removed without a screwdriver. This type of case, available as either a tower or desktop, can be opened without tools (except for the occasional need to pry a panel loose with a screwdriver). The screwless case comes apart in a number of pieces (front, side, and top panels) that slide/lock into place.

Taking out the adapter cards

After the case cover is off and stored in a safe place, remove the adapter cards. Lab 15-1 is a typical process for removing adapter cards.

Lab 15-1	Removing Adapter Cards

1. **Write down or diagram the expansion slot and type (such as ISA, VL-Bus, PCI, or AGP) that the adapter card occupies before you pull it out.**

   This saves you time when you reassemble the PC. Label any cables that are attached to the card before you disconnect them.

2. **If possible, record all jumper settings and DIP switch settings before removing the adapter card.**

   A small dental mirror is handy for this step. If you wait until after you've removed a card and handled it, can you guarantee that you haven't accidentally changed a setting?

3. **Remove the mounting screw that holds the adapter card in place.**

4. **Examine the card for any cables or wires that may be attached to it.**

   In addition to diagramming any cables or wires that you find, tag any cables or wires with a small piece of tape. (Small address labels are good for tagging parts and cables.)

5. **Grasp the card along its front and back edges, and gently rock it front to back until it releases.**

   Avoid touching other circuit boards and the contacts on the bottom of the board with your hand. Handle cards and circuit boards only by their edges or port mountings, and avoid touching the edge connectors.

6. **Lift the card out slowly and look for attached wires or cables that you may have overlooked.**

7. **If you're not going to replace the card, insert a port spacer.**

   A *port spacer* is a flat metal space holder that's used to block port openings on the back of the case. The cooling system needs all of these slots filled to do its job efficiently.

8. **Store the card in an antistatic bag; do not stack the cards on top of each other.**

If an ESD wrist strap or ankle strap is not available, rest your forearm on one of the metal beams that run across the chassis, and leave your arm in constant contact with the chassis while you lift out the adapter cards.

Undocking the bay

On a case that has been manufactured in the past 5 or so years, the hard drives are usually installed in metal enclosures called *drive bays*. The standard drive bay, designed to hold a variety of drives, is referred to as a *half-height* drive bay. These enclosures allow drives to slip into place either from the front or the back. Removing a floppy disk, tape, or CD-ROM drive is much easier than installing one. Installing a hard drive can involve mounting problems, cabling considerations, and formatting (see Chapter 8 for more information). However, removing a hard drive requires only that you disconnect a few cables, remove a few screws, and slide it out.

You must consider the following three facts when removing a hard drive or tape drive from the PC:

- ✔ The drive is powered by the power supply through a connector.
- ✔ The drive is controlled by either an adapter board or a connection that's directly on the motherboard through at least one cable.
- ✔ The drive is attached to the chassis, so it won't move when in use or when the PC is moved.

Removing the power connections

The power connections for hard drives and tape drives are easy to find. The wires of their connectors extend back to the power supply. You will encounter the following two types of connectors:

- A larger, white, four-wire connector (usually a Molex connector).
- A smaller, white four-wire connector (a Berg connector) that probably has a clip latch to hold it in place.

Follow these guidelines to remove power connectors:

- **Molex connector:** Grasp the connector and gently move it from side to side to slip it out of the plug. Don't yank on it, because you can break the connector off the drive circuit board (and then you have to install a new drive).
- **Berg connector:** Pry it open gently and slide it apart. Use a small screwdriver to lift the latch tab just enough to pull the connectors apart. Again, don't pull on the wires. If you must, use your needle-nose pliers to grasp the plug to pull it out.

You don't need to label drive power connectors (unless you feel compelled to do so). Drive power connectors come in only two types (each device takes only one type), and they may already be labeled. You can use only the connectors that you have on the power supply, and the plugs are keyed so that you can't install them incorrectly.

Removing adapter cables

Depending on the drive and the form factor of the motherboard (see Chapter 3), a hard drive is connected either to an adapter card inserted in an expansion slot or directly to the motherboard. In either case, remove these cables before proceeding further in disassembling the PC. Label each cable and its orientation to the power supply (which is always a good landmark inside the case). Recording the orientation of a hard drive cable means to note the location of the color-striped edge (on which side of the cable) and its orientation to the power supply. If the cable doesn't have an edge reference, use a permanent marker to create one.

Gently pull out the drive adapter cables, keeping them level. In other words, don't yank them off, and pull in the direction of the pins to avoid breaking or bending the pins on the connector.

Detaching a drive from the chassis

When detaching a drive, you should first note the size, height, and placement of the bay where the hard drive is installed. The location of and access to drive bays vary with the case. Although two cases may be of the same form factor, the bays may be accessed differently. In some of the newer mid- and full-tower cases, many 3½-inch drive bays are hidden inside the case.

Some XT cases are still around; these have one full-height bay. Two half-height devices can be stack-mounted in this bay by using a side bracket. This bracket holds one drive above the other with enough space between them so that the electronics don't contact each other and to provide sufficient airflow. When removing a drive (or a pair of drives) from an XT case, don't forget the retaining screws in the bottom of the drive bay. XT drives pull out through the front.

AT cases have two (or more) half-height bays that receive drives from the front. A drive is held in place with a pair of small L-shaped retaining brackets, which are fastened with a single screw on each side of the drive. To remove the drive, use a screwdriver to extract the retaining brackets and slide the drive forward out of the bay.

Taking out the motherboard

If you're not wearing your ESD wrist strap, put it on now! At this stage of disassembling a PC, you can do some major and expensive damage if you're not wearing it. Worse yet, the damage may not appear immediately. It may appear later, after the damaged component is stressed further, causing an intermittent or misleading error condition.

At this stage, the only item of significance left inside the case should be the motherboard. Depending on the PC's vintage, the remaining steps range from extremely easy to slightly complicated. Note or diagram all jumpers, DIP switches, and connectors that require special orientations on the motherboard. After the motherboard is removed, it should be carefully protected in an antistatic bag and be placed away from other circuit boards, preferably in a protective box or case.

PC XT motherboards have one small plastic connector that joins the motherboard to the speaker. Disconnect the speaker connector, and remove the two or three screws that mount the motherboard to the chassis, and the motherboard is out.

The IBM AT and its clones have both a speaker connector and a keylock connector. Remove the speaker and keylock connectors slowly, because they are adjacent to the memory-size jumper on the AT motherboard. Be careful not to dislodge any jumpers on the board.

AT and related motherboards also have a lithium battery or a pack of AA batteries that are usually attached to the side of the chassis or case with Velcro. The battery or battery pack should be removed with the board and kept connected to the board. Newer AT boards have the battery mounted directly on the motherboard, so be careful that you don't dislodge it. If this connection is broken, the CMOS chip loses the system setup configuration information.

Newer AT, Baby AT, ATX, LTX, NLX, and other form-factor motherboards are mounted on plastic spacer anchors and are held in place by two or three screws that are attached to the chassis. To remove these motherboards, extract the mounting screws and then slide the motherboard laterally toward the open end of the case to disengage the spacers, and then lift the motherboard from the case by its edges. Leave the spacers in the motherboard.

Pulling out the memory modules

When removing memory modules — which would be mostly Dual In-Line Memory Modules (DIMMs) or Rambus DIMMs (RIMMs) in the latest PCs, Single In-Line Memory Modules (SIMMs) in older systems, and Dual In-Line Packages (DIPs) in extremely old systems — be sure that you are electrically grounded. When working with memory, just touching the case or power supply may not protect memory modules from ESD damage. See Chapter 7 for more information on memory systems.

If a PC has RIMMs installed, Continuity Rambus In-Line Memory Modules (CRIMMs) are installed in any unused memory slots. CRIMMs (which are a kind of memory circuit placeholder for RIMMs) are thin, plain-looking, green-colored circuit boards.

Follow the steps in Lab 15-2 to remove memory modules.

Lab 15-2	Removing and Installing Memory Modules

1. **After ensuring that you are grounded, open the system case and ground yourself once again to an unpainted metal part inside the case.**

2. **Locate the memory slots on the motherboard.**

   The memory slots on a desktop PC (the type in question here) are usually colored black and have *ejector clips* at each end of the memory module slot.

3. **Remove any existing memory that is to be replaced. If the DIMM/ RIMM slot is empty, skip to Step 4.**

   a. Press down and slightly outward on the ejector clips at each end of the module card.

    b. After the ejector clips are released, remove the module from the slot with firm pressure without jerking the card up.

    c. Depending on your plans for the memory card that you just removed, you may want to place the card in a protective bag or other container.

4. Holding the new memory module carefully by its edges, place the module in the lowest-numbered slot available.

If you aren't sure which is the lowest-numbered slot, use the slot that's closest to the processor or other filled memory slots.

    a. Align the notches in the bottom edge of the card with the keys in the memory slot. You may need to reverse the card to fit the key pattern and the card.

    b. With the card aligned to the slot, use your thumbs to firmly press the top edge of the card straight down into the slot. The card is firmly inserted into the slot after you hear a click or a snap and both of the side ejector clips are in their full vertical positions, gripping the card's edge.

5. Test it before you close it up.

Before replacing the system cover, boot the system to determine whether the new memory is being seen by the BIOS and operating system.

Grasping the power and removing it

These days, the power supply and case are usually purchased as a single unit. Rarely would you remove the power supply, but you may find it necessary on occasion. For example, the power supply or cooling fan in an older AT or XT PC can wear out and need replacement. Or you may find yourself removing a system's modules one at a time in an attempt to isolate the source of an intermittent problem. Unless you have a compelling reason to remove the power supply from the case, however, it is usually better to leave it in.

Treat the power supply and the main cooling fan as a single module, and don't open it for any reason. If any part of the power supply is not working, remove the power supply, dispose of it properly, and install a new one. A new power supply is not expensive enough to risk injuring yourself. Inside the power supply are big, nasty capacitors that pack a wallop and can hurt you seriously if you touch them — even if you're wearing an ESD strap.

ATX and later form-factor motherboards contain power at all times, even when the power supply is turned off. Be sure that you know this for your safety and for the A+ Hardware Technology exam.

Lab 15-3 takes you through the process of removing the power supply.

Lab 15-3	Removing the Power Supply

1. **Turn off the power supply.**

   I'm sure you did this long before getting to this point, but I feel obligated to mention it.

2. **Remove the power cord from the power supply.**

3. **Diagram the orientation of the power supply, or use a grease pencil to mark and orient the edges of the power supply connectors to the PC's front panel, motherboard, and hard drives, and then disconnect these components in that order.**

   Use rubber bands to bind the motherboard and hard drive connectors in separate groups.

   The thick black cable that extends to the front panel from the power supply in many AT and ATX PCs carries 110V AC power straight from the wall socket! This power is passed through the power supply directly to the cable that connects to the front panel.

   If your system has this cable, be sure to draw a diagram of this connector configuration (illustrating where each of the four wires is connected by color). If you connect the wrong wire in the wrong place, the system can catch fire, not to mention shocking you big time.

4. **Locate and remove the screws (either Phillips or hex-head) that hold the power supply to the back of the case, the side wall, and the chassis.**

5. **Inspect the power supply for faulty, frayed, or broken wires or connectors, and use compressed air to blow out the fan and vents.**

Putting Everything Back in Its Place

If you have built or reassembled many PCs, you are probably reasonably prepared for the A+ Hardware Technology exam. For review, then, write down the steps that you use to build or reassemble a PC, along with any safeguards and safety and performance checks that you use along the way. Then jump to the last section of this chapter — "Testing the Results" — and review it for common device failure modes. You can expect to see several common device failure modes on the exam.

For the exam, make sure that you know the general sequence of assembly and the relationship of the major FRMs to each other. Questions either assume knowledge or directly ask how FRMs are installed and ask how associated cables and wires are attached. You won't see questions that directly ask how a PC is assembled.

FRMs are reassembled in essentially the reverse order that they were removed. Assuming that the power supply wasn't removed from the system case (a wise decision), the motherboard (with its memory reinstalled) goes in first, then the hard drives, the adapter cards, and finally, the case parts. If the power supply was removed, it must be reinstalled first, with the other components following in their natural sequence.

Selecting the tools for the job

You need more tools to reassemble the PC than to disassemble it: an *ESD grounding strap,* a *Phillips screwdriver,* a *slotted screwdriver,* a pair of *needle-nosed pliers,* and a small *flashlight.* Mature eyes may also want a small *magnifying glass.* The most important tool, however, is patience. Take your time. If something isn't right, and no smoke was involved in reaching that decision, take the computer apart and do it again.

Protecting the PC and its FRMs from ESD damage is as important when reassembling the system as when taking it apart. Use your grounding straps, or take other appropriate precautions. Together, you and ESD are the most threatening element to a PC. Whatever you can do to reduce this threat gives additional life to the PC. Makes you feel kind of powerful, doesn't it?

The greatest threat of ESD damage to the PC is working on the PC with its case open without proper ESD protection in place.

Putting back the power supply

It's easy to reinstall the power supply. Just line up the fan with its hole in the case, match the power supply to the screw holes, and then insert the screws. The only required safeguard take is to make sure that the power supply's cables are not trapped under the case or along its sides.

This may sound obvious, but when you install the power supply, it shouldn't be plugged into an AC power source. After you install the power supply, plug it in and operate it briefly to test the fan — and the fan only. If the fan turns, all is well. If the fan doesn't operate, determine whether the power supply's voltage selector is set correctly and whether the power cord is seated tightly.

Do not use a screwdriver, your finger, or anything else to turn the fan blade. If all is well, and the fan still doesn't turn, replace the power supply.

Reinstalling the motherboard

As you reassemble the PC, pay your greatest attention to the motherboard and its cables and connections. Putting a floppy disk drive in backward is a mistake that's easily corrected and normally does no harm, but some of the connectors on the motherboard can do extreme damage to the motherboard and other components if they are installed incorrectly. So take care as you work.

Do not begin to reassemble the PC without first putting on your ESD ground strap and connecting it to the PC case or ground mat. Do you get the impression that I think this is important?

If you are installing a new motherboard in an existing system case, you must verify several conditions, including the fact that the motherboard is compatible with the form factor of the case and power supply, and that the devices in the PC are compatible with the motherboard and its BIOS and chipset. Most of this information is available in the motherboard's documentation or on the manufacturer's Web site. Look up this information before you try to install the new motherboard; it saves you and your customer money in the end.

Lab 15-4 shows you how to reinstall the motherboard.

Lab 15-4	Reinstalling the Motherboard

1. **Orient the motherboard so that its spacers (also called *standoffs*) are aligned with the slots in the bottom of the case.**

2. **Laterally slide the motherboard toward the power supply until the standoffs are firmly snug in their slots.**

3. **Reinsert the mounting screws to anchor the motherboard in place.**

   Most motherboards are attached to the case with screws. Some new case designs allow the motherboard to be attached to a hinged plate with only the spacers locking it into place. If screws are used, use either Teflon or plastic washers under the mounting screws when attaching the motherboard to the system case; this prevents the screw heads from contacting circuitry on the motherboard. Be sure that the electronic contacts and cut pins on the motherboard are not in contact with the metal case lining. Contact will give you trouble — if it doesn't short out the motherboard. Look under the motherboard to verify that it is not touching the case.

4. **To complete the installation, reattach the speaker, keylock, and battery connectors.**

   If the motherboard has a separate battery supply, keep it connected to the motherboard throughout this process. If it was removed, or if the system battery was removed, you must set the system's configuration (by using the CMOS setup utility) the first time that you boot the PC.

Connecting the power source

The procedure and the level of caution that you should use to connect the motherboard to the power supply depends on its form factor. You use a different process and different connectors for AT form-factor motherboards than for ATX or later motherboards. The differences are as follows:

✔ **AT motherboards:** The two six-wire power supply connectors for AT form-factor motherboards should be labeled as P8 and P9. These two connectors are installed side by side into a 12-pin connector on the motherboard. It is possible to reverse the positions of these two connectors. If you reverse them, you will need a new motherboard. However, because you labeled them and drew a diagram when disassembling the PC, you know exactly which goes on the right and which goes on the left of the connector.

   Remember: The four black wires (two on each plug) must be aligned together in the middle.

   If you forget to connect the motherboard power connectors (P8 and P9), when you turn on the power, the power supply may explode — or at the least make loud, ugly noises. So don't forget to install these plugs!

✔ **ATX (and later) motherboards:** You can easily distinguish the power connector on these form-factor motherboards by its unique size and shape, and installation is easy because of its connector key. The connector has 2 rows of 10 pins in a rectangular shape. You should have it labeled and included on your diagram.

See Chapter 3 for more information on motherboard form factors.

Connecting the front panel

If the PC has a power cable for the front panel, which means that it has a main power switch on the front of the PC, unplug the PC for the duration of this operation. The front-panel cable that comes from the power supply carries 110V AC power that is passed straight from the AC wall socket. This isn't something with which you should take chances. Even if you diagrammed the front panel power switch connector during disassembly, check the power supply's documentation, if available, for the wire color scheme.

The power switch on the front panel closes a circuit that allows the AC power to flow to the power supply. To allow this flow, the power switch has both hot (live) and return (to the power supply) leads.

Stating your preference: The adapter or the drive first?

Some technicians prefer to install the hard drives before the adapter cards, and others like to do the reverse. Whichever you do first, the same rules apply, just in a different order. Follow your diagram, and reinstall the adapter cards and drives, keeping the cables and cards spaced evenly to allow good airflow. Place the hard drive as far from the power supply as possible to allow maximum air circulation inside the cabinet.

You may want to take this opportunity to clean the edge connectors of the adapter cards with an edge connector cleaner and protector. You can find these products at most computer supply stores.

Expect questions on how cables are connected to adapter cards and the power supply. For the A+ Hardware Technology exam, it doesn't matter which you install first (drives or adapter cards).

A common installation error is forgetting to attach the power cables to hard drives. This error can be a result of the full attention that is required to align the drive in the bay correctly, making sure that round-headed screws anchor the drive in the bay and that the data connection (the dreaded ribbon cable) is attached correctly. If you don't attach the power connector to the drive, a POST (Power-On Self-Test) boot disk failure usually results.

Relating to the Zen of ribbon cable

In general, ribbon cables connect the same way on either end. However, this versatility can get you into trouble. You must connect the cable so that the wires connect to their counterparts on both connections. To help you with this connection, the wire representing pin 1 on the cable and connector is usually marked with a red or dark blue stripe along the edge of the cable.

You may have two or more ribbon cables to reinstall. The cable for the floppy disk drive is slightly different from the cable for the hard drive or other drives. Be sure to reattach the correct cable to the correct device, although this shouldn't present a big problem, because usually they won't attach to the wrong device anyway.

Excuse the veiled sports metaphor here, but an easy way to remember the orientation of a ribbon cable is the phrase "Big Red is Number 1." If you forget this phrase, ask anyone from Nebraska who's Number 1. You'll be reminded that the red-stripe edge of the ribbon cable aligns to pin number 1. For ribbon cables with a dark blue edge, you'll have to find somebody from Michigan or Duke to help you.

Finding pin 1 on the circuit board is the next step to completing the match. How do you tell which end of the connector is pin 1? A small numeral 1 should be printed next to or above the end of the connector that is pin 1. A magnifying glass may be handy in this situation, along with a flashlight. If you can't find the printed number, examine the solder pads on the back of the circuit board where the connector is attached. Pin 1 has a square solder pad. These general rules are not universally applied, though, which is why your diagrams are so important.

Watch out for the following common ribbon cable connection errors:

- The connector is reversed. This can do major damage, so chant the mantra "Big Red/Blue is Number 1" as you connect ribbon cables.

- The connector is attached to only one row — it's easy to do this, given the size of the connector and the pins. If you catch this error before the power is turned on, no damage should result.

- The connector is shifted to the left or right, missing a pair of pins — this is also easily done and just as dangerous.

Closing the lid

Reattach the case top. You may want to put the top in place, but leave the screws out until after you've had a chance to test the results. When reattaching the case top, don't snag or trap cables. Cables can get damaged by little nicks or breaks. They may also pull out of connectors if dragged or dinged by the case top. If the case lid doesn't slide freely into place, investigate the problem.

When reassembling the case parts, ensure that they line up properly and that the seams fit the same as before you disassembled the case. The case is an integral part of the cooling system of the PC. Misaligned case parts could create air leaks that could cause the difference between a great-running system and one with overheating processors and memory.

Checking the CMOS and Configuration Data, or Where Did the Battery Go?

If you were zealous about disassembling every possible FRM in the PC and you removed the battery pack or the lithium battery from the motherboard, you are now faced with the challenge of resetting the CMOS setup configuration data. If the system boots okay, press the appropriate key (depending upon your BIOS version) to open the CMOS setup utility and enter the appropriate data.

You wrote down the CMOS information, didn't you?

CMOS stands for *complementary metal oxide semiconductor,* which is a common integrated circuit technology. For more information on CMOS, see Chapter 4.

Okay, so you removed the CMOS battery. Now you reenter the CMOS information that you captured before you started the disassembly of the PC (see "Taking Inventory," earlier in the chapter).

If you didn't write down your CMOS settings before you removed the CMOS battery, do some research to reconstruct the settings accurately. Most newer system CMOSs can detect some of the configuration of the PC (such as RAM size), but you need the manuals for the motherboard and peripherals to get all the settings right.

Testing the Results

The real proof that you have reassembled the PC correctly comes when you turn on the power and everything works. However, don't panic if you don't get these results — unless, of course, smoke or flames billow from the PC.

The following common problems are associated with reassembling a PC:

- ✔ **Motherboard power connector(s) not installed:** This error is by far the most disastrous and can result in a damaged motherboard or an exploded power supply.

- ✔ **Motherboard solderside contacts touching the case:** On the back side of any circuit board (called its *solderside*) are the clipped contacts (cut pins) of the electronic components that are installed on the board's circuit side. If these contacts touch the metal case lining, some or all of the board may short out.

✔ **Reversed data and control cables:** This error can damage a device and changes how the computer operates — if it operates at all. Align the colored edge to pin 1.

✔ **Drive power connectors not installed:** This one isn't so bad; it usually just gives you a boot error beep code or disk boot failure.

✔ **Speaker, keylock, and battery connectors not installed:** This is a minor problem that comes under the heading of "What a nuisance."

✔ **Hard drive, video display, and other peripheral failures:** The adapter card may not be seated properly, may not be anchored with a mounting screw, or may be installed in an incorrect architecture slot.

✔ **Floppy drive failure:** The ribbon cable may not be connected properly. The first floppy disk drive (A) should be connected after the twist, or at the end of the cable.

✔ **Keyboard failure:** The keyboard connector may not be installed or is not pushed in all the way. Also, if the PC has a PS/2 mouse and its connector is not installed properly, the keyboard may not function.

✔ **No lights, no action:** Did you plug it in?

Always be sure that the power supply is switched off before changing any power supply or signal cable connections.

Prep Test

Disassembly and Assembly

1 When removing an adapter card circuit board, which of the following actions is taken after you detach any connectors and remove the retaining screw?

A ○ Ensure that the power is off

B ○ Grasp the card's front and back edges, and rock the card gently back and forth

C ○ Grasp the card's top edge and pull straight up

D ○ Grasp the card's front and back edges, and rock the board gently from side to side

2 When servicing a PC, to which of the following would you not attach the ESD ground strap?

A ○ The inside of the case

B ○ The ground mat

C ○ The static shielding bag that came with the computer

D ○ A wall outlet

3 After a circuit board is removed from the system, where should it should be stored?

A ○ A cool, dry, dark place

B ○ An antistatic bag

C ○ A stack with other circuit boards

D ○ A clean, zippered plastic bag

4 What does the term *FRM* refer to?

A ○ Front or rear module

B ○ Fully replaceable modem

C ○ A slang term that's used by PC technicians to confuse customers

D ○ Field-replaceable module

5 Forgetting to attach which motherboard cable can cause damage to the power supply?

A ○ The power supply connector

B ○ The front panel power connector

C ○ The speaker connector

D ○ The keyboard connector

6 What is the likely result of forgetting to attach the power connector to a hard drive during reassembly?

A ○ The power supply explodes.

B ○ A disk boot failure.

C ○ A 601 POST error.

D ○ The hard drive dies an agonizing death.

7 The colored edge of the ribbon cable represents which of the following?

A ○ Pin 40

B ○ Pin 1

C ○ The Cornhuskers

D ○ The power connector

8 You installed a hard drive, but it's not working. Which of the following could cause this problem?

A ○ It is connected to the wrong IDE controller.

B ○ The floppy disk drive is not connected properly.

C ○ The ribbon cable is aligned to pin 1 on the drive.

D ○ The ribbon cable is aligned to pin 40 on the drive.

9 What is the biggest threat to a PC when it is being serviced?

A ○ ESD

B ○ Accidental breakage of a component

C ○ Improper tools damaging a component

D ○ Placing components on the wrong type of work surface

10 Where is the motherboard is mounted?

A ○ On brass standoffs

B ○ On plastic standoffs

C ○ On copper mounting brackets

D ○ Directly on the case's metal lining

Answers

1 **B.** Answer A is not a bad first step, but that should have been done before you opened the system case. You must avoid stressing the card by bending it side to side or harming the edge connectors by yanking the card straight up. *See "Taking out the adapter cards."*

2 **C.** Unless the static shielding bag is connected to a solid ground, it won't do you much good. If you have the type of grounding system that plugs into the third (round) hole of an AC wall outlet, be careful when plugging in the grounding system. *Charge over to "Avoiding shocking developments."*

3 **B.** Never stack circuit boards on top of each other (even if they are in antistatic bags), and never store a circuit board where it can gather static electricity. *Look at "Taking out the adapter cards."*

4 **D.** CompTIA uses this term to refer to all components of the PC that can be replaced at a customer site. *Check out "Checking in: Is the patient ready, nurse?"*

5 **A.** The power supply must have an electrical load, which means that at least one device must be drawing power from it, to prevent the power supply from being damaged. *Visit "Connecting the power source."*

6 **B.** The BIOS looks to the hard drive to boot from and, not finding the drive, displays a disk boot failure. *Check out "Stating your preference: The adapter or the drive first?"*

7 **B.** The colored edge indicates how the cable's connector should be oriented to the adapter or motherboard connector. *Look up "Relating to the Zen of ribbon cable."*

8 **D.** The ribbon cable, which provides the data connection to the drive, must be correctly connected for the device to work properly. *Review "Relating to the Zen of ribbon cable."*

9 **A.** Besides the technician, the biggest threat to the PC when being serviced is electrostatic discharge (ESD). *Take a look at "Selecting the tools for the job."*

10 **B.** Also called *spacers,* the plastic standoffs permit the motherboard to sit up off the case, allowing airflow under the board. *Check out "Reinstalling the motherboard."*

Chapter 16

Keeping the PC Running

● ●

Exam Objectives

▶ Performing preventive maintenance procedures

▶ Identifying the purpose of preventive maintenance products and knowing when to use them

▶ Using preventive maintenance products appropriately

▶ Complying with environmental guidelines for cleaning products

▶ Detecting and removing viruses

▶ Creating data backups and storing backup media

● ●

*1*t has always seemed somewhat foolish to me for someone to invest a couple of thousand dollars in a computer system, run it until it dies, and then call the repair technician to perform a Lazarus miracle and raise it from the dead. I'm not talking about the usual, everyday kinds of stuff — you know, the 44-ounce soft drink that's dumped on the keyboard, the flower vase that spilled water inside the monitor, or the metal fingernail file that somehow slipped inside the case. I'm talking about the truly scary abuse.

I've seen power supplies so choked with dust and smoke residue that they looked like miniature replicas of Carlsbad Caverns. I've also seen a virus that devoured an entire hard drive and half of Cleveland. I won't mention any others for fear that children may read this book. Where's the Computer Protection Services Agency when you need it?

About 5 percent of the A+ Hardware Technology exam is devoted to the Preventive Maintenance domain. This means that you can expect questions on the test that challenge your knowledge and skills of protecting, cleaning, and caring for the PC while protecting yourself and the environment. You should expect the emphasis of the questions from this domain to deal with preventive maintenance issues or computer viruses. So, on a test where every question is equally important, you can't afford to dismiss this chapter. You need to know this stuff!

I haven't included a "Get Ready for Work" section in this chapter, because the number of labs that I include should provide you with plenty of job skills practice.

Quick Assessment

Performing preventive maintenance procedures

1 The purpose of a(n) _____ is to prolong the life of the computer.

2 _____ is used to check a hard drive for possible surface errors.

3 You should never wear an ESD grounding strap when working on a(n) _____.

Identifying the purpose of preventive maintenance products and knowing when to use them

4 _____ is used to blow out the dust and debris that are found in the keyboard and in many other FRMs.

5 To clean a mouse ball, use a(n) _____.

6 A(n) _____ is used to clean the floppy disk drive.

Using preventive maintenance products appropriately

7 Do not use _____ on a mouse ball, because it may shrink or misshape the ball's rubber material.

Complying with environmental guidelines for cleaning products

8 A(n) _____ lists the hazards, proper handling, and storage procedures for a chemical solution.

Detecting and removing viruses

9 A(n) _____ contains a virus program but is not suspected because it imitates a legitimate application.

Creating data backups and storing backup media

10 Tapes and other backup media should be stored in a(n) _____ and _____ location.

Answers

1 *Preventive maintenance program.* Review "Applying regular maintenance."

2 *ScanDisk.* Zip over to "The hard drive."

3 *Monitor or CRT.* Check out "The monitor."

4 *Compressed air.* Scoot over to "The keyboard."

5 *Damp cloth.* See "The mouse."

6 *Floppy drive cleaning kit.* Check out "The floppy disk drive."

7 *Alcohol.* Take a look at "The mouse."

8 *MSDS.* Review "Using the right cleaning supplies."

9 *Trojan horse.* See "Horses, worms, and germs."

10 *Cool, dry.* Take a look at "Storing data on tape."

Housekeeping, Safeguarding, and Other Chores

When your computer is worth more than your car, as mine is, you should want to keep it in good running order by performing regularly scheduled maintenance inspections. Just like a car needs regular oil changes, lubrication, and cleaning, a PC also benefits from a preventive maintenance program that's regularly applied. Without regular care and maintenance, your PC won't perform as it should — it may even stop working, just like a car would without some form of regular attention.

Experienced with preventive maintenance programs and how the PC and its components are cleaned and checked for wear and tear? You can skip most of this chapter. However, it won't hurt you to quickly review the material to remind you of some helpful hints that you may have forgotten.

Applying regular maintenance

The purposes of any *preventive maintenance (PM)* program are to reduce the need for repair and to extend the life of the computer. You can accomplish these goals only if you perform PM on a regular basis following a well-defined procedure. Virtually all PC owner's manuals include a chart or table that details the maintenance, adjustments, inspections, and cleaning that should be performed at specific, periodic intervals. For example, if you look in any automobile owner's guide, you can find such a guide that's based on the car's mileage. Like the car, every computer should have a similar guide.

Using the right cleaning supplies

The liquid cleaning compounds that are used to clean or condition the computer's components, case, and glass surfaces present safety and environmental problems to the user, the technician, and other people. Many of the chemical solvents and cleaners — and their containers — may require special handling because they're poisonous (or harmful in other ways).

Finding the right information

The best tool for finding out whether a chemical solution poses a threat to you, the user, or the world in general is a *Material Safety Data Sheet (MSDS)*. An MSDS, which is used in the United States, Europe, and most of Asia, is available for every potentially hazardous chemical product. I use the following two Web sites to look up any product that I'm not sure of:

  ✔ **MSDS Search National Respository:**

   www.msdssearch.com

  ✔ **Vermont Safety Information on the Internet (SIRI):**

   http://siri.org/msds/index.php

In Canada, the product safety information is referred to as Workplace Hazardous Materials Information System, or WHMIS. Visit its Web site at the following URL:

www.ccohs.ca/oshanswers/legisl/intro_whmis.html

However, the label is the first place to look for safety information on a product. Usually, if a problem may exist for either you or the PC in using the product, the label cautions you.

An MSDS lists the proper handling and storage procedures for chemical cleaning solutions.

Performing Preventive Maintenance

The process that is used to clean and maintain a PC and its components are one of the focuses of the A+ Hardware Technology exam. Review this section to remind yourself of the general steps and cleaning products that are used on each field-replaceable module (FRM).

Before you do anything else, you should perform one often-overlooked step — make sure that the PC works! When I was young and foolish and still searching for each computer's bit bucket, I once cleaned a PC until it shined, only to find that it didn't have a motherboard. It may not have worked so well, and my time was surely wasted, but it sure did sparkle!

The following sections concentrate on the preventive maintenance steps of various FRMs. Review this information to get a general understanding of the steps, materials, and products that are used to clean and protect the PC and its parts. Most of the cleaning questions on the A+ Hardware Technology exam deal with the kinds of products (for example, a mild cleaner) and materials (for example, a lint-free cloth) that are used to clean a particular device.

The keyboard

Other than the monitor, you probably clean the keyboard more often than the rest of the PC. This is because it sits open-faced most of the time and collects debris, flotsam, jetsam, and all the other gunk that floats by or falls in.

To clean the keyboard, use the steps shown in Lab 16-1.

Lab 16-1	Preventive Maintenance on the Keyboard

1. **To get the keyboard clean or to do a close visual inspection of the keyboard, remove its cover.**

   Otherwise, you can open a cleaning hole by removing the key caps of the –, +, and Enter keys in the numeric keypad at the far-right end of the keyboard. You can remove the key caps by using a small screwdriver or tweaker and gently prying off the key caps.

2. **Using compressed air, blow out the keyboard, sweeping with the air toward the removed key caps, or use a keyboard vacuum to clean the keyboard.**

   If you removed the cover, you can turn the keyboard over, shake it out, and then use compressed air to clean the internal and cover pieces.

   Special small vacuums can be used to clean the keyboard as well as other small parts of the PC. These vacuums usually have a small brush head attached with a gooseneck that can be bent to provide the best angle for cleaning.

3. **Use nonstatic brushes or probes to loosen any large or stubborn pieces.**

   If the keyboard has had soda pop or something similar spilled into it, you may need to wash it. If so, use warm, nonsoapy water to rinse the guck away. Just be sure that the keyboard is completely dry before you power up the PC.

4. **Replace the key caps or reassemble the keyboard cover.**

   You can replace the key caps by gently pressing them back onto their mountings.

5. **To clean the keys and keyboard case, use a soft, lint-free cloth and isopropyl alcohol, or use a nonsudsing, general-purpose cleaner to wipe away any guck, ink, or other indescribable yuckies.**

   Isopropyl alcohol is good because it evaporates quickly, reducing concern about the keyboard being wet. Again, be sure that the keyboard is dry before you send power to it.

6. **Reboot the system, observing the POST for keyboard errors, and test the keyboard by pressing every key and verifying its action.**

The mouse

Just as it's the mud puddle's fault that the kid is dirty, it's the mouse pad's fault that the mouse gets dirty and needs cleaning. Like the keyboard, the mouse pad sits in the open most of the time and gets dusty, wet, and slimed like most other things that sit on your desktop. The mouse then rolls over what has collected on the mouse pad, and it gets inside the mouse, gumming up the works.

To clean the mouse, follow the steps that are listed in Lab 16-2. To clean the mouse pad, wipe it off occasionally with a damp cloth, or just get a new pad.

Lab 16-2   Preventive Maintenance for the Mouse

1. **Make sure that no open applications are running on the PC, roll the mouse gently onto its back, and without tickling, remove the ball-access slide cover.**

2. **Be sure that your hands are clean, and remove and closely examine the ball for pits, cracks, or canyons. Also check to see whether the ball is lopsided or oval-shaped.**

   If the mouse ball has any of these problems, replace it or the entire mouse unit (recommended). Inspect the hole in which the ball sits for gunk, lint, hair, string, ant colonies, or beaver dams. I'm only kidding about the last two, but you can find some pretty weird and extremely yucky stuff inside a mouse.

3. **Inspect the rollers that are inside the mouse for debris or sticky or greasy buildup.**

   To clean the rollers, use a small, flat-blade screwdriver or tweaker (you know, the little pocket screwdriver) to scrape off the gunk.

4. **Blow any dust from inside the mouse using compressed air.**

   Don't blow the dust out with your mouth for two reasons: You can accidentally spit inside the mouse, and you can get dust in your eyes.

5. **Use a damp, lint-free cloth to clean the mouse ball. Don't soak it or scrub it, just wipe it clean and let it dry before reinserting it in its hole.**

   Don't use alcohol to clean the mouse ball. Alcohol may shrink the ball or dissolve the mouse-ball material and cause flat spots and distortion, just like it does to humans.

6. **Place the mouse ball back into its hole, replace the slide cover, and lock the cover in place.**

   If needed, you can use isopropyl alcohol or a general-purpose cleaner to clean the exterior of the mouse or the mouse pad. Check the mouse pad to see whether it's worn, frayed, torn, or hollow in its center. A beat-up mouse pad can cause lint, bits of rubber, or other gunk to get inside the mouse. Mouse pads are cheap, and you can usually garner freebies from stores or manufacturers or at trade shows (one good reason to go). Your employer may even have some promotional mouse pads for you to give your customers.

7. **Test the mouse, using something other than Solitaire or another game — it just doesn't look right to the customer.**

The monitor

Monitors are usually covered with a special coating that can be permanently streaked if the wrong solutions are used to clean them. Ammonia-based cleaning products can dissolve the coating on the monitor, which may damage the display. You can find antistatic cleaners that are specially designed for cleaning monitor and LCD screens.

You shouldn't wipe the screen while it is on and warm. This can generate static electricity that can be harmful to the monitor and to you. The best way to clean your monitor's screen is to dry-dust it with a lint-free cloth. Remember that water, which most liquid cleaners are made of, is an excellent conductor of electricity. Another caution is that because of the mechanics and high voltage inside the monitor, you should never open the monitor's cover.

Lab 16-3 shows the proper cleaning procedure for the monitor.

Lab 16-3   Preventive Maintenance for the Monitor

1. **Turn the monitor off and unplug it.**

   Wait a few minutes before you begin, and *do not* wear an ESD grounding strap. As I explain in Chapter 12, an ESD grounding strap, whether worn on a wrist or ankle, is a dangerous thing to wear while working on a monitor.

2. **Using compressed air or a slightly damp, lint-free cloth, clean any dust from the top of the monitor, being careful not to blow the dust into the open vents.**

   Never open the cover of the monitor! Mean and nasty high voltage lurks inside.

   You can use either isopropyl alcohol or a general-purpose cleaner to wash the outside of the monitor case. Alcohol is probably the better choice, if you can stand the fumes, because it doesn't create a safety hazard if dripped inside the case.

3. **Use an antistatic cleaner to wash the glass of the monitor.**

   Never wash the monitor glass with the power on. You can buy antistatic cleaning packets that come individually wrapped, just like the moist towelettes that you get from the fried-chicken place.

4. **Reconnect the monitor and test the video.**

   If nothing displays, check that the power switch is on, and check the power cord and video connections and the brightness and contrast settings. These connections and settings may have been inadvertently loosened or changed during the cleaning.

The case

Not a lot needs to be done to the PC case itself to keep it functioning properly. After all, the case doesn't do a heck of a lot — it mostly just gets dusty. However, you can perform some preventive maintenance activities at the system (or case) level to keep the general system functioning as it should.

Lab 16-4 lists the activities that you can use to keep the system case in working order.

Lab 16-4   System-Level Preventive Maintenance

1. **Turn off the PC, remove the power cord, and carefully remove the case cover.**

   Visually inspect the inside of the case to assess any problems that may be written in the dust. Normally, the inside and outside vents have dust accumulated on them, but if dust is gathering in a place that it shouldn't, the case may have a crack in it, a part may be missing, or some other problem may have developed. A common problem is that one or more of the slot covers that should be filling empty expansion ports on the case are missing.

   Look over the case thoroughly for dust, corrosion, leaking battery acid, dead bugs, moose droppings, and birds' nests. If the case is only lightly dusty, use compressed air to blow it out, using caution not to blow the dust into your eyes. If you must remove boulders and other chunks, pick them out with tweezers, or if big enough, with your fingers. Because you are working inside the case, you must use ESD protection and safeguards.

2. **Check cables and wires for loose connections.**

   Using compressed air, blow out the outside vents of the power supply first, and then clean the case's inside vents, drive bays, adapter cards, and outside vents.

   You can also use a small vacuum cleaner to clean the inside of the case. In fact, for some systems, a vacuum cleaner may be better than compressed air. Blowing the dust around can merely move it from one place to another inside the case. Sucking out the dirt and grime is sometimes better than blowing the dust under the edge of a loose component or connector.

3. **Replace the case cover (and be sure not to snag any cables).**

4. **With your bucket of isopropyl alcohol or the general-purpose cleaner, swab down the case, being careful not to slop the mop inside the case.**

5. **Power on the PC and watch the POST process for errors.**

Anytime you open a PC, perform a little preventive maintenance. If nothing else, vacuum the system case to remove all the dust bunnies that have accumulated inside since the last time it was cleaned (if ever). Several small vacuum cleaners designed specifically for PCs are available in both AC and battery-powered models. Most have either a small brush head or a relatively short hose on which brush attachments are mounted.

The floppy disk drive

To perform preventive maintenance on a floppy disk drive or to clean it when it begins to fail, use the steps that I list in Lab 16-5.

Lab 16-5	Preventive Maintenance for the Floppy Disk Drive

1. **Verify that the floppy disk drive works.**

2. **Using a floppy disk drive cleaning kit, follow its directions to clean the read/write heads.**

   This is an excellent place to use a small handheld vacuum with a brush head to remove any dust from the opening of the floppy disk drive.

3. **Test the drive.**

The hard drive

The preventive maintenance tasks for the hard drive deal more with optimizing its storage than with physical cleaning tasks. You have no cleaning tasks to perform, because the hard drive is a sealed unit. The PM tasks for a hard drive involve the following:

✔ **Backing up the data:** Creating frequent backups can help ensure that in any slight to catastrophic data disaster, you are able to restore a user's data files.

✔ **Running diagnostic software on the hard drive:** ScanDisk, Norton Utilities, or other diagnostic software tools should be used to check the surface of the hard drive for errors. Although extremely rare, disks can develop physical property problems. Power problems are typically the cause of the read/write heads making contact with the disk surface and damaging its recording capability. Running a diagnostics program on the hard drive can identify and set aside the bad sectors before they can become operating problems.

✔ **Defragmenting the hard drive:** Running the Disk Defragmenter, Norton Speed, or an equivalent disk-optimization program can help improve the disk drive's read/write efficiency and response times.

Saving the earth

Several components in a PC require special handling when you dispose of them. The list includes batteries, mercury switches, the CRT in the monitor, and more.

Disposing of dead batteries

PC batteries, such as the lithium battery that provides power to the CMOS memory, shouldn't be disposed of in either fire or water. Batteries should be disposed of according to local restrictions and regulations covering the disposal or recycling of all batteries.

Leaking batteries should be handled carefully. Make sure that you don't get the electrolyte, the stuff on the inside of the battery, in your eyes.

Getting rid of a monitor

A monitor contains the following contaminants: solvents and solvent vapors, metals (including a very high level of lead), photoresist materials, deionized water, acids, oxidizers, phosphor, ammonia, aluminum, carbon slurry, and a long list of other chemicals and caustic materials. For this reason, a monitor shouldn't just be thrown in the dumpster. In fact, federal regulations require monitors (actually CRTs in general) to be encased in concrete before being disposed of in water or a landfill. The best way to discard a monitor is through a disposal service that handles computer equipment.

Handling other PC problem components

Other items that are related to the PC must be disposed of carefully. Most are common-sense items, but you may see a question on the exam that groups them as hazardous PC waste. Included in this bunch of items are laser-printer toner cartridges, refill kits, and the used or empty containers of chemical solvents and cleaners.

Use the documentation that comes with a device to find out how the device should be disposed of. Also, refer to the MSDS or WHMIS information on a particular chemical product (see the section, "Finding the right information," earlier in this chapter).

Virus Detection and Protection

Viruses are nasty pieces of software that have taken on the characteristics of an infectious disease, spreading germs that infect unsuspecting and unprotected PCs. You can expect a couple of questions on the exam that deal with what a virus is, how it spreads, and how it is detected.

The following characteristics define a computer virus:

- ✔ A virus attaches itself to another piece of programming code in memory, on a floppy disk, or on a downloaded file, or it has the form of an executable file and runs when opened on the target system.

- ✔ A virus replicates itself and infects other systems, propagating itself from one computer to another.

Horses, worms, and germs

Not all viruses do catastrophic damage to a system. Many viruses are just nuisances or pranks, playing music, simulating system meltdowns, or displaying misinformation during the system boot. Viruses that are malicious can cause considerable damage in the form of lost data.

Many types of viruses exist. The following list describes common viruses:

- ✔ **Trojan horse:** Like the gift horse that hid the attacking army, the viral Trojan horse hides a virus program by camouflaging itself as or imitating a legitimate application. When executed, the virus program springs the virus, often creating other Trojan horses to avoid detection.

- ✔ **Worm:** This is a self-contained program that spreads itself to other systems, usually over a network connection. Worms create many different nasty effects when they run.

- ✔ **Virus impostor or gag programs:** These are demented jokes created by programmers with not enough to do, obviously. These programs simulate the effects of a virus, scaring users into believing that they've been infected. It's not unusual for users to hear the truth from the jokester, about halfway through the apparent reformatting of their hard drive.

Some of the nastiest viruses are not viruses at all. Virus hoaxes spread through the rumor mill (especially on the Internet) and tell of untold horrors of what will happen at 13 minutes after midnight on the day that the creator of a certain candy bar was born, or something like that. Before it gets started, I just made that one up.

Viruses and how they spread

Computer viruses are a form of electronic warfare that was developed solely to cause human misery. The evil, sick, and talented minds that develop computer viruses would like nothing better than to have your boot sectors catch cold or have your drives develop dysentery.

The following four major virus classes exist, each with many subclasses:

✔ **Boot sector viruses (system viruses):** These viruses target the boot program on every bootable floppy disk or hard drive. By attaching itself to the boot sector program, the virus is guaranteed to run when the computer starts up. Boot sector viruses spread mostly by jumping from disk to disk.

✔ **File viruses:** File viruses modify program files, such as .EXE or .COM files. Whenever the infected program executes, the virus also executes and does its nastiness. File viruses spread by infected floppy disks, networks, and the Internet.

✔ **Macro viruses:** The newest general class of viruses, macro viruses take advantage of the built-in macro programming languages of application programs such as Microsoft Word and Microsoft Excel. Macro languages allow users to create macros, which are script-like programs that automate formatting, data entry, or frequently repeated tasks. A macro virus, most commonly found in Microsoft Word documents, can cause as much damage as other viruses and can spread by jumping from an open document to other documents.

✔ **E-mail viruses:** This is the latest trend in viruses and is getting most of the press these days. For example, the Melissa virus was an e-mail virus that spread by e-mailing itself from one computer to another using the PC's e-mail address book.

Because a virus is a program, it can only infect programs. A virus can't hide anywhere that it doesn't blend into the scenery. Viruses that infect graphic files, e-mail, or text files are just myths. It would be like trying to hide a bright red ball among bright white balls. However, viruses can be attached to text files or e-mail and transmitted or copied to a new host system.

Playing hide-and-seek with viruses

As virus-detection software becomes more sophisticated, so do the viruses. Most antivirus software works by recognizing a predefined pattern of characters that are unique to individual viruses — a sort of fingerprint, called its *signature*. As viruses get more devious, they include new ways to elude the virus detectors. These tricks, as a group, are called *cloaking*. Some of the cloaking techniques used are as follows:

✔ **Polymorphing:** Allows viruses to change their appearance, signature, and size each time that they infect a system.

✔ **Stealth virus:** Hides its damage in such a way that everything appears normal.

✔ **Directory virus:** Hides itself by lying. It changes a directory entry to point to itself instead of the files that it is replacing. No actual change is made to the affected files, and they appear normal in directory lists and Windows Explorer lists; this allows the virus to avoid detection.

Combating viruses

Viruses manifest themselves on a PC in a wide variety of ways. Some examples are as follows:

✔ Spontaneous system reboots

✔ System crashes

✔ Application crashes

✔ Sound card or speaker problems

✔ Distorted, misshapen, or missing video on the monitor

✔ Corrupted or missing data from disk files

✔ Disappearing disk partitions

✔ Boot disks that won't boot

In spite of the efforts of the virus developers, the best defense against virus infection is antivirus software, also called *scanners* or *inoculators*. Don't you just love all this medical talk?

The general types of antivirus software in use today are as follows:

✔ **Virus scanner software:** This run-on-demand software scans the contents of memory and the hard drive, directories, and files that the user wants to check. This type of software is the most common form of antivirus program.

✔ **Memory-resident scanner software:** This kind of scanner stays in memory, automatically checking the environment, including incoming e-mail and browser documents, for viruses.

✔ **Behavior-based detectors:** A more sophisticated form of memory-resident scanner, a behavior-based detector looks for suspicious behavior that is typical to virus programs. Some stereotyping is involved, and some good processes may be interrupted, but safe is better than sorry.

✔ **Startup scan antivirus software:** This software runs when the PC boots and does a quick scan of boot sectors and essential files to detect boot sector viruses before the PC boots.

Most antivirus software uses a database of virus profiles and signatures for reference, commonly referred to as *DAT,* which stands for data or database, files. This database should be updated frequently; most antivirus packages include a provision for a set number or an unlimited number of updates.

Maintaining Your Integrity

Although you won't see it referred to as data integrity on either of the A+ exams, where it is more likely to be called *data backups,* be ready to answer at least one question on when data backups should be created and where you should store the backup media.

Data backups are a form of preventive maintenance. They ensure that, should a problem develop with your PC or system that jeopardizes your data, you have a copy of the data to restore when the problem is solved. On top of that, backups just make good sense. Any number of threats can compromise the integrity of your data: hardware failures, beta-test software, operator error, and viruses. It may seem a bit paranoid, but just because I'm paranoid doesn't mean that they aren't trying to get me.

Creating a data backup

Tape is a good medium to use for creating a backup of hard drive data. Making a backup of files is a safety precaution that's taken to ensure that data outlives the device on which it's stored. Here's a cardinal rule of computing: Back up files regularly, and then back up the backups.

Most operating systems include utilities for creating a backup, and backup software is usually included with tape, recordable CD, and other writable media drives. Of course, you can purchase a variety of software packages that are specifically designed to perform backups.

Backup software offers some advantages over just copying a file to a removable medium. Most software offers data-compression techniques to reduce the number of disks or tapes that are needed to hold the archived data. Many software packages also offer cataloging routines and single-directory or file-restore capabilities.

You can create the following different types of backups:

✔ **Archival (or full):** Contains every file, program, table, and so on from the hard drive.

✔ **Incremental:** Contains only those files that have been modified since the previous full or incremental backup. When a file is created or modified, an archival bit is set in the file header block that indicates the file should be included in the next backup. Full and incremental backups reset the archival bits when a file is copied to the backup media.

✔ **Differential:** Copies all the data that was added or modified since the last full backup. Differential backups don't reset the archival bit, so if differential backups are created daily between full or incremental backups, the size of the backup grows each day to include any file modified since the last backup.

✔ **Copy:** Uses a COPY or XCOPY command to write a duplicate of a file, directory, or disk to another media. The XCOPY command will also copy all subdirectories and reset the archival bit if desired. The COPY command has no effect on the archival bit.

Storing data on tape

Tape is a somewhat unique medium in comparison to the other writable permanent data storage media that are available to PC users today. Whereas most of the other media are direct access, tape is a serial — or physically sequential — access media. For example, to hear the third song on a music cassette, you must first fast forward through the first two songs. The same holds true for accessing the third record of a tape file.

Tape is primarily a backup media today, and many larger systems, especially network servers, have either an internal or external tape drive. This is a good use of the media, its serial nature, and its relatively compact size. Some problems exist with using tape, but they're avoidable with proper care and diligence. You should rotate your tapes regularly; store them in a cool, dry place (look for this tidbit on the test); and replace them at least once a year. It's a very good idea to occasionally test your backups by restoring a few random files to the hard disk. You should test each backup immediately after creating it as well as periodically during its storage time.

If intermittent problems begin showing up in a rotated group of tapes that are used for daily backups, the problem could be the age of the tapes or that the tape drive heads need cleaning.

Prep Test

1 Where should backup media, especially tape cartridges, be stored?

  A ○ Warm, humid location

  B ○ Warm, dry location

  C ○ Cool, humid location

  D ◉ Cool, dry location

2 Which of the following provides information on the hazards of a chemical solution and the safe handling and storage of the solution?

  A ○ MSSC

  B ○ MSDS

  C ○ MSCE

  D ○ DHCP

3 Which of the following would you remove to open a hole on the keyboard through which you could blow out dirt and debris?

  A ○ Tab, Caps Lock, Shift, and Ctrl keys from the left end of the keyboard

  B ○ Spacebar

  C ○ Arrow keys

  D ○ Minus, Plus, and Enter keys from the right end of the keyboard

4 When should you clean the monitor glass?

  A ○ When the monitor is on

  B ○ When the monitor is off

  C ○ Anytime, using a wet cloth

  D ○ Never

5 Which of the following are the major steps for preventive maintenance on a hard drive?

  A ○ Defrag, ScanDisk, Backup

  B ○ Fdisk, Format, ScanDisk

  C ○ Backup, ScanDisk, Defrag

  D ○ Disassembly, blow dust out, reassembly

6 E-mail-transferred viruses are transmitted in what form?

A ○ Text messages

B ○ Binary data hidden in text messages

C ○ An e-mail attachment that contains executable code

D ○ All e-mail viruses are hoaxes

7 You should never wear ESD grounding attachments when working on which of the following FRMs?

A ○ Memory module

B ○ Monitor or CRT

C ○ Motherboard

D ○ Expansion card

8 Which of the following backup types capture files that have been changed since the last backup? (Choose two.)

A ❏ Incremental

B ❏ Partial

C ❏ Differential

D ❏ Copy

9 What is the unique data image that's used by antivirus programs to detect and remove a virus?

A ○ Profile

B ○ Fingerprint

C ○ Mug shot

D ○ Signature

10 Which type of cleaner is used to clean the contacts of a memory module or expansion card?

A ○ Nonsudsing cleaner

B ○ Clean, lint-free cloth

C ○ Contact cleaner

D ○ Ammonia

Answers

1 **D.** In fact, just about all recordable media should be stored in a cool and dry location, although some are less affected by the environment than others. *See "Storing data on tape."*

2 **B.** Material Safety Data Sheets contain information on all aspects of using, handling, and storing chemical products. *Take a look at "Using the right cleaning supplies."*

3 **D.** These three keys open up a slot on the end of the keyboard through which the dirt chunks can fall out. *Check out "The keyboard."*

4 **B.** The monitor glass carries quite a charge of static electricity, and cleaning it when it is on, especially with a wet solution or cloth, can light up your life. *Look at "The monitor."*

5 **C.** Before you do anything to a hard drive, back it up. Then you can scan it for surface defects and optimize it by defragging it. *Review "The hard drive."*

6 **C.** Many viruses, like the infamous MELISSA.VBX virus, are transmitted as attachments to e-mail messages. *See "Viruses and how they spread."*

7 **B.** A rather nasty danger lurks inside the monitor in the form of a very large capacitor that is just looking for a way to discharge its thousands of volts of stored electricity to the first grounded entity that it can find. Don't let it be you! *Check out "The monitor."*

8 **A & C.** Both an incremental backup and a differential backup copy files that have been updated (meaning written to and saved) since the last backup was created. *Take a look at "Creating a data backup."*

9 **D.** Each virus program has a digital signature that uniquely identifies it. *See "Playing hide-and-seek with viruses."*

10 **C.** The contacts of memory modules and expansion cards should be cleaned periodically with contact cleaner to remove any oxidation that may have accumulated. *Review "Using the right cleaning supplies."*

Chapter 17

Troubleshooting PC Problems

Exam Objectives

▶ Defining basic troubleshooting procedures and good practices

▶ Troubleshooting and isolating problems on a PC

▶ Identifying common symptoms and problems associated with FRMs

• •

*F*ortunately, the job of a PC repairperson isn't just the drudgery of building new customer PCs and upgrading the hard drive or video system.
It also includes the part of the job that attracts and holds the very best PC
technicians — troubleshooting and diagnosing a problem on a PC.

If you've looked under the hood of a car lately, you'll agree that the days
when you could work on your car at home in the garage with just your trusty
toolbox are long gone. Well, if you've looked inside the system unit of a PC
lately, and I know you have, you know that like the car, the PC has become
very complicated and nearly as hard to work on. This is a good news/bad
news situation. The good news is that the PC user is less able to work on the
PC, meaning that more work is available for you, the trained and skilled professional PC repairperson. The bad news is that troubleshooting and isolating
a problem on the PC has become much more difficult. Oh sure, you still have
the occasional data cable missing and keyboard errors, but now you must
also deal with resolving DMA channel conflicts and chipset problems.

It is safe to say that the overriding focus of the A+ exams is troubleshooting.
More than half of the material on the exams involves troubleshooting, diagnostics, and problem-solving in one form or another. Officially, diagnosing
and troubleshooting is 25 percent of the A+ Hardware Technology exam, but
questions on how to deal with common FRM problems can be found in every
domain of the exams.

Quick Assessment

Defining basic trouble-shooting procedures and good practices

1 The best source for information on a PC's problem is _____.

2 Before troubleshooting a hard drive, it is a good practice to create a _____.

Trouble-shooting and isolating problems on a PC

3 Windows 2000 requires the BIOS to be _____ or _____-compliant.

4 The POST signals errors with _____ and _____.

5 Floppy disk drive POST error codes are in the _____ series.

6 Expansion slot covers are technically part of the _____ system.

7 The highest value that can be represented on a three-pole jumper is _____.

Identifying common symptoms and problems associated with FRMs

8 _____ and _____ are applied to the CPU to solve overheating problems.

9 IDE hard drives are configured as either a _____ or a _____.

10 The AT command that is used to reset a modem to its default settings is _____.

Answers

1 *The user.* See "Arriving on the scene."

2 *Full backup.* Review "Backing up before you move forward."

3 *ACPI, APM.* Check out "Matching up the OS and the BIOS."

4 *Beeps, error codes.* Look over "Decoding the beeps" and "Numbering the error messages."

5 *600.* Study "Numbering the error messages."

6 *Cooling.* See "Cooling problems and the CPU."

7 *7 (seven).* Review "Troubleshooting SCSI hard drives."

8 *Heatsinks, fans.* Take a look at "Cooling problems and the CPU."

9 *Master, slave.* Check out "Troubleshooting IDE hard drives."

10 *ATZ.* Study "Troubleshooting modems."

Troubleshooting Can Be Fun

For the A+ Hardware Technology exam, you must know the processes that are used in troubleshooting, diagnosing, and isolating a problem on a PC. By this, I don't mean all the little tricks and shortcuts that you and I have devised over the years. I mean the straightforward, by-the-book way of identifying the source of a problem on a PC. So even if you are a well-seasoned veteran and can tell a PC's problem by the sound it is making, you should at least skim through this chapter — especially this first section — to familiarize yourself with the terminology and processes that the test assumes you know and use.

Getting ready to start

What may be the most valuable tools for troubleshooting a PC hardware problem are paper and a pen. You have a lot to write down as you begin troubleshooting the PC, including the user's comments, the current BIOS settings, the location and arrangement of expansion cards and their cables, and the devices to which the expansion cards are attached. They may even come in handy for writing down the customer's address and the directions to their location.

Always be sure that you have ESD protection with you. Your ESD wrist strap should be like the famous credit card that you should never leave the shop without. Remember that when you don't use proper ESD precautions at a customer site, you're risking not only the customer's systems but also your reputation — or worse, your job.

Arriving on the scene

Observe the customer's environment as carefully as you can, especially the electrical setup that's used for the PC in question. Is the PC attached to a wall socket, plug strip, surge suppressor, or UPS? How many devices are sharing the electrical supply? Is the environment dust-free and otherwise clean? Is it humid or overly dry? All of these conditions tell you about the stresses and strains to which the PC is subjected.

However, do not jump to any conclusions based on what you see. Ask the user how long the PC has been in its current location and electrical situation. Also, don't jump to conclusions about what the apparent problem may be without first speaking with the user. Okay, if the PC is not plugged in, you can go ahead and see if that may be the problem, but for any other problem, ask first, listen to the response, and then begin troubleshooting.

You should ask the following questions to learn more about the problem:

- ✔ When did the problem first happen?
- ✔ Did you add hardware or software to the PC right before the problem appeared?
- ✔ Can you re-create the problem?
- ✔ Did smoke come out of the PC or monitor?

When dealing with a user directly, always use the five *C*s (courtesy, concern, consideration, conscientiousness, and cooperation) and the three *L*s (listen, listen, and listen) of customer care.

Troubleshooting FRMs

Expect to see questions on the A+ Hardware Technology exam about identifying common symptoms, troubleshooting, and isolating problems on the following field-replaceable modules (FRMs):

- ✔ BIOS and CMOS
- ✔ CPU
- ✔ Floppy drive
- ✔ Hard drives
- ✔ Memory
- ✔ Modems
- ✔ Monitor and video cards
- ✔ Power supply
- ✔ Sound card and speakers
- ✔ USB ports

I wouldn't worry about anything that's not in this list.

Be sure that you know all about expansion-slot covers. You don't have much to diagnose, but you should at least know what kind of problems they prevent and their purpose.

Troubleshooting the BIOS

Unless a power failure occurred halfway through a flashing operation on the BIOS, not much can go wrong with the BIOS itself. So most of the trouble-shooting questions on the A+ Hardware Technology exam relate to boot sequence problems. However, you should know about a couple of situations that directly affect the BIOS. For more information about the PC BIOS, see Chapter 4.

Upgrading the BIOS

If a PC has an apparent compatibility problem with an FRM, don't leap to the conclusion that a BIOS upgrade is automatically needed. The BIOS comes under the heading of "If it ain't broke, don't fix it." The BIOS should not be upgraded, except to solve an isolated specific (and documented) compatibility or performance issue. Use only the BIOS or motherboard manufacturer's flashing software, and apply only the BIOS versions (obtained only from the manufacturer) that are listed as compatible with the PCs motherboard, processor, and chipset.

Troubleshooting after a BIOS update

If you have flashed your BIOS (close the raincoat, please), but the system will not boot because it can't see the hard drive (and perhaps other devices as well), one or more CMOS settings may need to be adjusted. Using the written record of the CMOS settings that you made before you flashed the BIOS, enter the Setup program and verify that all the BIOS configuration settings are correct. The BIOS CMOS has default settings, and any settings that were changed in the past must be changed again.

Matching up the OS and the BIOS

If you are installing a Windows 2000 or Windows XP operating system, the type and compliance of the PC's BIOS are very important. Windows 2000 requires the BIOS to be compliant to the Advanced Configuration and Power Interface (ACPI) or the Advanced Power Management (APM) standards. Windows XP requires only ACPI. APM is a legacy power management standard.

If the BIOS is not ACPI-compliant, expect Windows 2000 and XP to have boot errors and to crash frequently. ACPI includes the OnNow standard, which can start the PC from a single keystroke. Without this compatibility, the Windows 2000 Setup program may not be able to communicate with the PC's hardware devices.

To verify that the BIOS is ACPI-compliant, check the BIOS's or motherboard's documentation and the Windows 2000 Hardware Compatibility List (HCL), or contact the PC's manufacturer.

Dealing with BIOS errors

If the PC has the most current and compatible BIOS version, any problems that are generated by the BIOS will most likely be during the Power-On Self-Test (POST) and boot processes. See Chapter 4 for information on the details of the boot sequence.

BIOS systems use the following two means of notifying you of a problem during the boot sequence:

- ✔ **Beep codes:** The system speaker (the small one that's built into the system case) emits a series of short and long tones to indicate a problem in an essential system component during the hardware phase of the boot sequence.

- ✔ **Error messages:** The BIOS displays error messages on the monitor that indicate a problem has occurred in the final stages of the boot cycle.

Unfortunately, each BIOS manufacturer has a unique set of beep codes that it uses to signal boot errors. Fortunately, the A+ folks see the difficulty in testing on beep codes and don't expect you to memorize all the beep codes in the standard IBM, Award, and AMI BIOSs. The error messages that are issued from each different BIOS are fairly standard and generally describe the problem well enough.

Decoding the beeps

Every BIOS has one beep code in common, which is a single beep tone to indicate the end of the POST. However, a single beep tone can also mean a memory problem on the AMI (American Megatrends, Inc.) BIOS (a very popular BIOS).

Don't worry about memorizing BIOS error codes for the exam. Just remember that if an error occurs during the POST, it is identified by the BIOS program's beep codes.

General guidelines on some of the more common POST beep codes are as follows:

- ✔ **0 beeps:** If no beeps are sounded, most likely nothing is displayed on the monitor. The problem is most likely power related. Make sure that the PC is plugged into an AC power source. If it is, check to see whether the motherboard is getting power. Use the motherboard's documentation to locate the Power LED connector and plug the LED wire on this connector. If the Power LED lights up, you know that the motherboard is getting power. Otherwise, a problem exists with the power supply.

✔ **1, 2, or 3 beeps:** Reseat any newly added memory, or replace the memory with known good chips. One beep is also used to indicate a successful POST. If you hear one beep and the boot does not continue, you have a memory problem.

The term *known good* is used frequently on the exam to describe FRMs, components, and software configurations that you know to be good, working parts.

✔ **4, 5, 7, or 10 beeps:** The motherboard has a serious problem. It may need to be replaced or sent to the manufacturer for repairs.

✔ **6 beeps:** If the motherboard has a separate keyboard controller chip, try reseating the chip. If the motherboard doesn't have a separate keyboard controller chip, check the keyboard connection and the keyboard itself. It is unlikely that the Super I/O chip in the chipset is bad, so the problem must be with the physical components of the keyboard.

✔ **8 beeps:** Reseat the video card and check its memory to ensure that the memory is seated properly on the card. If the problem persists, replace the video card.

✔ **9 beeps:** This indicates a faulty BIOS chip, which cannot be corrected by reseating the chips. Check with the motherboard supplier or the BIOS manufacturer. The BIOS may need to be updated.

Deciphering BIOS error messages

Depending on the BIOS in use, the on-screen BIOS error messages all indicate one thing — a serious system problem. The following are examples of boot-cycle error messages for topics that you are likely to find on the A+ Hardware Technology exam:

✔ `BIOS ROM checksum error - System halted`: The American Heart Association has recognized this message as a major cause of minor heart attacks. In a nutshell, the BIOS is hosed, and you need to contact the motherboard or BIOS manufacturer for recovery procedures, if any exist. This error could be caused by an incomplete or faulty flash upgrade, and recovery procedures may be available.

✔ `CMOS battery failed`: The CMOS battery is dead and needs to be replaced. Of course, you will need to reenter the system configuration as well.

✔ `CMOS checksum error - Defaults loaded`: This message indicates that the CMOS has become corrupt. The cause is likely to be a weak battery that needs to be replaced.

If the system clock is losing time, the cause is likely a dying CMOS battery. Like the batteries in your home smoke detectors, the CMOS battery should be checked regularly and replaced when weak.

✔ Display switch is set incorrectly: Some motherboards have a jumper that sets the type of video display that is being supported. This error indicates that the jumper and the video configuration in the CMOS are different.

✔ Floppy disk fail: The BIOS cannot find the floppy disk controller (FDC). If the PC does not have a floppy disk drive, set the CMOS Disk Drive value to None (or Auto). If the FDC is included in the chipset, make sure that the drive's cables are all seated properly.

✔ Hard disk install failure: This is a similar error to the Floppy disk fail error message. The POST cannot find or initialize the hard drive controller (HDC). Make sure that the adapter card — if there is one — is seated snuggly and that the drive cables are connected properly.

✔ I/O card failure: This error indicates that an expansion card has failed or has a parity error at a certain address.

✔ Keyboard error or no keyboard present: Make sure that the keyboard is attached correctly and that no keys are pressed during the POST. Make sure that nothing is lying on the keyboard, such as a book.

✔ Memory test fail: This message indicates that an error was detected during memory testing. The message should also include information about the type and location of the memory error, such as a memory parity error at *xxxx*, where *xxxx* is the location of the memory error.

✔ Primary/Secondary master/slave hard disk fail: The POST process has detected an error in either the primary or secondary master or slave IDE hard drive. Check the cabling and the master/slave jumpers.

Numbering the error messages

Most system BIOSs display a 3- or 4-digit error code along with the error message to help you pinpoint the apparent source of the problem. The documentation for the BIOS system or the motherboard should list the codes that are used on a particular PC.

PC error codes are grouped by device or service types in even hundreds. For example, a 600-series error indicates a problem with the floppy disk drive or the floppy disk drive controller. The error code that's displayed is a number between 600 and 699, with each number identifying a specific problem.

Table 17-1 lists the PC error codes that you should know for the A+ Hardware Technology exam.

Table 17-1	PC Error Codes
Series	*Category*
100	Motherboard errors
200	RAM errors
300	Keyboard errors
600	Floppy disk drive errors
1100	COM1 errors
1700	Hard drive errors
3000	NIC errors

Troubleshooting other boot problems

A boot failure is typically a loose or missing component, including, but not limited to, the CPU, BIOS ROM, chipset, memory, expansion card, or cable. If you are unable to pinpoint the component that is causing the boot to fail, begin removing expansion cards one at a time until the system boots. Eventually, you should find the culprit, and you can then focus on why it is causing the problem.

Many boot and operational problems on a PC are miraculously fixed by merely rebooting the PC. Therefore, rebooting should always be a standard first step in your troubleshooting procedure.

Troubleshooting CPU problems

The first thing that you must know about the CPU is that if it is broken, it must be replaced. However, problems relating to the CPU are usually not a problem with the CPU itself. A problem with the CPU is more likely to be the result of cooling (or the lack of it), power (or the lack of it), or compatibility issues with the motherboard and chipset.

The symptoms of a CPU that is beginning to fail are as follows:

- ✔ The PC will not boot.
- ✔ The PC boots but does not start the operating system.
- ✔ The PC crashes during startup and when running applications.
- ✔ The PC has sudden POST parity error problems in many devices.
- ✔ The PC locks up after a few minutes of operation.

Chapter 6 provides more information on processors and CPUs and their environments.

Cooling problems and the CPU

If a PC boots without problems, but consistently halts or freezes after a few minutes, the CPU is probably overheating. One way to verify this is to shut down the PC, wait a few minutes to let the CPU cool, and then boot the PC. If the same problem happens after the PC operates for a while, the CPU probably has a cooling problem.

Processors are designed to run within a certain temperature range. The operating temperature range varies among processors and their packaging types. On average, processors operate in the range of 40 degrees Celsius (about 100 degrees Fahrenheit) to 90 degrees Celsius (about 200 degrees Fahrenheit). For example, a Pentium III CPU in an SECC (Single Edge Connector Container or Slot 1) package should run at 75 degrees Celsius (167 Fahrenheit), but in its FC-PGA (Flip Chip – Plastic Grid Array) package, the CPU runs at 85 degrees Celsius (185 degrees Fahrenheit). These are *die temperatures,* which indicate the temperature at the core of the processor packaging, not the temperature at which the processor dies.

If the CPU is not fitted with a heatsink or a cooling fan and it is a Pentium-class or higher processor, you have found the problem. A heatsink and fan (they usually come as a single unit) should be attached using liberal amounts of thermal paste.

Some troubleshooting steps that you can use to check out the CPU, heatsink, and fan are as follows:

- ✔ Examine the heatsink and fan to determine whether they are in place or are cracked or broken.

- ✔ Carefully grasp the heatsink (lightly touch it first — it can be very hot!), and try to move it slightly back and forth. If it is loose, you may not have a proper seal between the heatsink and fan.

- ✔ Remove the heatsink and fan, and verify that the CPU is properly secured in its socket or slot. If the CPU is inserted in a ZIF (zero insertion force) socket, make sure that the ZIF socket arm is locked and anchored. Reattach the heatsink and fan, making sure that they are attached securely.

Expansion-slot covers (you know, those narrow metal plates that are used to cover empty expansion card slots on the back of the case) are a hot topic on the A+ Hardware Technology exam. A part of the cooling system, they are primarily used to close holes in the case to preserve the engineered airflow.

Timing is everything

If the PC displays the same symptoms as an overheating problem, but the system is not overheating, the problem may be that the system clock jumpers on the motherboard or the BIOS settings for the system timers are incorrectly set. If the CPU and the motherboard are using different clock timings, it may take a while for them to get so far out of sync that the system halts. Refer to the documentation for the motherboard and CPU to get the proper clock setting, and adjust the clock accordingly.

Remember to shut down and unplug the PC before removing the CPU and to observe all standard antistatic procedures when handling the CPU. Be careful not to bend any of the pins, because you may want to reinstall the CPU later. Use care when installing the new CPU, because bent pins almost always ruin the PC. If a new CPU fails to correct the problem, replace the motherboard.

Power problems and the CPU

If the PC is sounding a POST beep code that indicates a CPU fault, the CPU is probably not getting power. Using a multimeter, check the power outputs to the motherboard. If any of the leads are low or dead, replace the power supply. If the power is as it should be, you may have a dead CPU, and it should be replaced. If the new CPU fails to solve the problem, you have isolated the problem to the motherboard itself.

Checking out the CPU

If the system boots okay but freezes consistently when running a certain application or group of applications, the situation is too weird for normal diagnostics. Try running repetitive tests on the CPU using a third-party diagnostics package, such as Pc-Check from Eurosoft (www.eurosoft-us.com) or AMIDiag from AMI (www.ami.com). If the diagnostics indicate a CPU problem, replace the CPU and test again. If the same problem appears, expand the testing to the motherboard and chipset. You may end up testing the system completely, only to find that the problem is a corrupted file in the application software.

Troubleshooting the floppy disk drive

For a device that was supposed to disappear, floppy disk drives are still found on a large number of systems. Virtually every PC sold today includes a 1.44MB 3½-inch floppy disk drive. In fact, floppy disk drives are so commonplace that they have become disposable technology. If a PC has a problem with its floppy disk drive, it is often less expensive to replace it than to fix it.

Troubleshooting a floppy disk drive boils down to determining whether the drive is the source of a problem. If it is the problem, it should be replaced. If the drive is not the problem, the focus then shifts to other devices.

Booting from the A: drive

Several problems can cause a PC not to boot from the floppy disk drive. You should be familiar with the following potential problems for the A+ Hardware Technology exam:

- ✔ **CMOS settings:** The boot device setting in the CMOS may not have the A: floppy disk drive listed as the first boot drive, or the floppy disk drive may not be listed as a boot device.

- ✔ **Media issues:** The floppy disk may not be a bootable disk, which means that it does not contain the system files that are needed to boot the system, or the floppy disk is unformatted or otherwise no good.

- ✔ **Drive problems:** The floppy disk drive's power supply connector or data cable may be partially disconnected. Look for this problem particularly if you recently worked inside the case. This problem could result in intermittent operational errors. However, this type of error is typically caught during the POST.

Dealing with a floppy failure

If the POST indicates that the floppy disk drive is bad or missing through its beep codes or by displaying an error message in the 600 series (see Table 17-1, earlier in this chapter), the problem may be a general failure of the floppy disk drive, which is a rare event. However, to diagnose the problem, check the following items:

- ✔ **Power connector:** Check the power supply connector for a snug connection, and make sure that the cable is not crimped or loose in the connector. You may want to try a different power supply connector if one is available or check the voltage with a multimeter. The problem could be the power supply.

- ✔ **Cabling:** Make sure that the data cable is connected properly and is not on backward or shifted one pin over. The location of pin 1 can vary by manufacturer and by model, so verify pin 1's location and check that the cable is installed correctly. One clear indicator that the floppy drive's data cable is on backward is that the drive's LED comes on with the boot and stays on while the PC is powered on.

- ✔ **Connecting two drives:** Many older systems had two floppy disk drives, typically one 5¼-inch and one 3½-inch drive. Floppy disk drives have jumpers to indicate which drive is installed without the twist in the cable and which is installed with the twist in the cable. Check the cable and the drives against the drives' documentation. In most cases, the A: drive (the first floppy disk drive) gets the twist.

- ✔ **CMOS:** The floppy disk controller can be disabled in the CMOS setup. Verify that the controller is enabled. Also, verify that the CMOS has the correct drive types indicated for the A: and B: drives.

- ✔ **Resource conflicts:** Floppy disk resource conflicts are rare, because virtually every PC system reserves IRQ 6 and DMA channel 2 for the floppy disk controller, and peripheral device manufacturers avoid these resources. However, devices that work on the floppy drive interface and with the floppy controller, such as a tape drive adapter, may try to use these resources.

- ✔ **Motherboard issues:** If the floppy disk controller is built into the motherboard or its chipset, the problem could be in the motherboard.

Troubleshooting hard drives

Hard drive problems cause more frustration than most other PC problems. The PC won't boot, and the user's data, programs, and treasured MP3 files may be lost. Because of this, the A+ Hardware Technology exam places an emphasis on hard drives, and the majority of the questions that deal with troubleshooting relate to hard drives.

A hard drive problem can result from a number of issues, including some on the drive itself, the hard drive controller, a SCSI host adapter, and the associated cabling. The hard drive types that you need to know for the exam are IDE (Integrated Drive Electronics) and SCSI (Small Computer System Interface).

Backing up before you move forward

Troubleshooting a hard drive always poses the risk of destroying any data that's stored on it. Always make a full backup of the drive and test the backup by restoring a few random files before you begin working on the hard drive. Of course, this assumes that you can access the hard drive. If you are unable to access the drive, ask the user to have the latest backup handy for restoring the drive when you are finished.

Troubleshooting IDE hard drives

As discussed in Chapter 8, most PCs support either one or two IDE channels. Each IDE channel supports up to two hard drives, which are designated as a master and a slave. *Master* actually means disk 0 and *slave* means disk 1 — and neither is the boss of the other. The BIOS assigns a logical device name to the master of the primary channel first, then to the primary channel slave, and then to any drives that are on the secondary channel, if any are installed.

For example, the master drive on the primary IDE channel (assuming that the drive has only one partition) is assigned the logical name of C:. The slave on the primary channel is assigned D:, and the secondary channel drives are E: and F:. The master drive on the primary channel is the boot drive.

Each IDE drive has a jumper that must be set to indicate that the drive is either a master or a slave. You cannot have two masters or two slaves; it just doesn't work that way. Two IDE drives (a master and a slave) on the same channel connect to a common data cable in series. It doesn't matter which of two drives is designated as the slave or the master. If two drives don't work with each other in any configuration as master and slave, something is wrong with the drive(s).

To begin troubleshooting any hard drive problem, you should boot the system from a floppy disk drive that has minimal, if any, AUTOEXEC.BAT and CONFIG.SYS files. This is called a *clean boot* and may indicate that a conflict exists in these system files.

IDE hard drive problems are caused by a variety of issues. You need to be familiar with the following issues for the A+ Hardware Technology exam:

- ✔ **The CMOS hard drive configuration is incorrect.** Check the CMOS configuration for each hard drive. The information that you need should be in the documentation for each drive.

- ✔ **Newly added hardware is conflicting with hard drive.** Check the system resource settings in Windows Device Manager to verify that a resource conflict has not been created by installing a new piece of hardware.

- ✔ **The boot partition on the hard drive may be corrupted.** If the system files on the boot partition are corrupt, the system cannot boot properly. Use the SYS command (from an MS-DOS or command prompt) to transfer the system files back to the hard drive. You may have to format the partition and reinstall the operating system, should this fail to solve the problem. Also, verify that the boot partition has not been accidentally removed.

- ✔ **The hard drive may be infected with a virus.** Many viruses can corrupt the master boot record on the hard drive and cause errors that show up as hard drive errors. If an antivirus program is not installed on the PC, install one and scan the hard drive.

- ✔ **The hard drive cable may be defective or improperly connected.** If the front panel drive LED lights up and stays on constantly, the hard drive data cable is probably not properly connected. This condition should also cause a POST error message indicating that no boot device is available. Check both ends of the cable, at the device and on the motherboard or adapter card. Also check the power supply connectors.

✔ **The hard drive may be defective.** Every drive makes some noise, and users get accustomed to it. However, that louder-than-usual noise that the drive has been making for over a month may have been a sign that the bearings were seizing.

Some of the common PC system error messages for hard drive problems are as follows:

✔ Hard disk configuration error: An incorrect CMOS configuration or a loose data cable causes this message.

✔ Hard disk 0 failure: Disk 0 is the master drive on the primary IDE channel. This message is caused by an incorrect CMOS configuration or a bad connection to the power supply.

✔ Hard disk controller failure: Check the connection of the data cable on the drive and the power connectors.

Troubleshooting SCSI hard drives

You can expect to find several questions on the A+ Hardware Technology exam about SCSI systems and hard drives, although most of this information has been moved to the Server+ exam. Look for my book, *Server+ Certification For Dummies* (published by Wiley Publishing, Inc.) at your local booksellers. I have no shame, obviously.

For the exam, you should know the following facts about SCSI drives for troubleshooting situations:

✔ **CMOS setup:** The hard drive settings in the CMOS should be set to None or Auto-detect.

✔ **SCSI device drivers:** SCSI devices require device drivers. Make sure that the latest drivers are installed.

✔ **Host adapter and hard drive IDs:** The SCSI host adapter is always device 7 on the SCSI chain, and the first SCSI hard drive on the channel should be assigned as SCSI ID 0. If you have two or more SCSI hard drives, or any other SCSI devices, on the same SCSI cable, each device must have a unique SCSI ID number. The ID is set through a three-pole jumper.

✔ **Termination:** If the SCSI hard drive is the only internal device or the last device on the internal SCSI channel, the hard drive must be terminated.

Tempting fate: Mixing hard drive types

If a PC has both SCSI and IDE (ATA) hard drives, you must choose which one is the boot disk. Because the SCSI drive is usually a higher-performance drive, the user may want it to be the boot drive. If the BIOS on the user's PC doesn't allow a SCSI drive to be designated in the boot disk hierarchy, this is not an option.

Before giving up on assigning the SCSI hard drive as the boot drive, check with the motherboard or BIOS manufacturer for an upgrade that supports SCSI boot disks. The only other option is to remove the IDE drives and go with only a SCSI drive, which should boot without a problem with the IDE drives gone.

Troubleshooting memory

After the hard drive, memory is the next largest block of troubleshooting questions on the A+ Hardware Technology exam. Memory problems on a PC typically fall in one of the following general areas:

- **Configuration:** The amount of memory that is installed is more than the PC or operating system supports, or the BIOS CMOS settings are incorrect.
- **Hardware:** At least one memory module is defective, or the memory modules that are installed are not compatible.
- **Installation:** The memory chips or modules are not properly seated in their sockets, or a socket is defective or needs cleaning.

One problem with diagnosing memory problems is that other PC components, such as software or the motherboard, can cause what may appear to be a memory problem.

Identifying memory problems

Knowing when a memory problem happened is often the best clue to the problem's source. Memory problems typically occur in one of the following instances:

- **The first time that a new PC is started up:** The problem is most likely that the memory chips need to be reseated (in the best case) or are missing (in the worst case). If the problem does not appear to be memory related, it may be a bad motherboard. Check with the manufacturer or the vendor.
- **Immediately after new memory is installed:** Check the part numbers and speed of the memory that was installed. Also, verify that the memory was properly installed or configured in memory banks, and ensure that if DIP (Dual In-line Packaging) or SIMM (Single In-line

Memory Module) memory is in use, each bank was filled before memory was placed in another bank. You may also want to verify that the memory is appropriate for the motherboard, chipset, and processor. For example, the memory bus on a Pentium III PC is either PC100- or PC133-compliant, and so must be the memory modules.

Different memory standards are available for a PC, but you must match the memory to the system. The part number of the memory holds a clue as to what it is. For the most part, if the memory's part number ends with a dash and a number, such as -60, it is industry-standard EDO (Extended Data Output) or FPM (Fast Page Mode) memory. If the part number ends with a slash and a number, such as /32, it is industry-standard SDRAM (Synchronous DRAM). SDRAM part numbers also indicate the standard to which they conform. For example, a Kingston Technology memory with the part number KTM66X64/128 is compliant with the Intel 66-MHz standard and is a 128MB Dual In-line Memory Module (DIMM). For more information on memory modules, see Chapter 7.

✔ **Immediately after new software or operating system is installed:** More recent versions of software and operating systems typically require more memory than older versions. New software, especially beta versions, is notoriously buggy and can produce memory errors. The first step to correcting these errors, other than uninstalling the beta software, is to check for a BIOS upgrade or a service patch for the software.

✔ **Immediately after hardware is installed or removed:** New hardware that is installed incorrectly or a connector or cable that is dislodged while removing a device can cause what appear to be memory errors accompanied by memory error messages. After checking the cables and connectors, check with the new hardware's manufacturer for newer device drivers or BIOS updates.

✔ **For no apparent reason:** If a PC has been running okay and suddenly begins having memory problems, check for corrosion on the contacts of the memory modules. Another likely cause is heat. The PC could have been running too hot and has finally damaged the motherboard, memory, or processor to the point of causing errors. Another suspect should be the power supply.

Dealing with memory errors

Typically, a PC will inform you of a problem in predictable ways. You should know the following problems and appropriate solutions:

✔ **The PC fails to boot and sounds a beep code:** Check the memory to ensure that it is properly installed and configured to the BIOS.

✔ **The PC boots, but the display is blank:** A dislodged card, a memory module that's not fully seated, or a memory module that the system doesn't support commonly cause a blank screen. Confirm that all expansion cards and memory modules are seated in their sockets, and verify that the installed memory is compatible with the system by checking memory part numbers. Installing nonparity RAM in a PC that has Error-Checking Code (ECC) memory, or placing SDRAM in a PC that supports only EDO (Extended Data Output) memory can cause the screen to be blank at boot up, because the boot sequence cannot complete.

✓ **The PC boots, but the memory count is wrong:** The POST does a memory count that is displayed on the monitor. If the displayed number is not correct (it will always be less than it should be if it is wrong), the PC didn't recognize all of the installed memory. This could be caused by a wrong memory type being installed, such as dual-bank memory added to single-bank memory, in which case the POST sees only half of the memory added. Also, certain systems only accept specific memory modules and cannot see more than a certain amount of RAM.

✓ **The PC displays a memory error message**, such as the following:

```
Memory mismatch error

Memory parity interrupt at nnnnn

Memory address error at nnnnn

Memory failure at nnnnn, read nnnnn, expecting nnnnn

Memory verify error at nnnnn
```

(where *nnnnn* is the physical address of the faulty memory).

These errors typically indicate problems between old memory and new memory or show a failing memory module. If removing a newly installed memory module eliminates the error, you should replace the old memory module with the new memory module. If the error shows up again, the new memory is either defective or is not compatible with the system. However, these error messages can also show up due to a motherboard problem.

✓ **Other memory problems:** The dreaded nemesis of any PC repairperson is the intermittent memory problem, which shows up sporadically as an error message, system crash, or spontaneous reboot. Hundreds of possible causes exist, including ESD (electrostatic discharge), overheating, corrosion, or a faulty power supply.

✓ **Software-related memory problems:** The problems in this category include Registry errors, general-protection and page faults, and exception errors. Registry errors happen when the Windows operating system writes parts of the Registry to a defective portion of RAM. Software bugs cause faults and exception errors. For example, an application may not release its memory when completed or may try to occupy the same memory address as another application. Rebooting the PC usually solves these problems.

Troubleshooting modems

After it is installed and configured properly, a modem rarely causes problems. Software device drivers, changed connection settings, or another device causing resource conflicts are the causes of most modem problems. Upgrading or replacing the device driver can usually fix software problems. If another device is causing a resource conflict, and it will most likely be contention for a particular COM port, change to a different COM port using the Modems icon in the Windows Control Panel.

However, if the problem is apparently with the modem, two levels of problems should be checked: You have a bad modem card or external unit, or the modem needs to be reset using the AT command set. To reset the modem to its default values using the AT command set, use the command ATZ.

Troubleshooting the video system

The two elements that you must deal with when troubleshooting PC video are the monitor and the video card. The video card is perhaps the more complicated of the two, but you can visually see any problems that it causes. However, unless part of the picture is missing, like with a failing television set, the video card rarely causes video problems on a PC.

Clearing up video problems

The most common problems with a video card are refresh rates and resolution and color depth settings. Fortunately, these problems can be fixed through Windows using the Display Properties settings. You can access the Display Properties dialog box by right-clicking an open area on the desktop and choosing Properties from the menu that appears.

If the displayed image is scrambled or distorted or shows multiple layers of the same image, the monitor is unable to handle the output of the video card. Other symptoms of this mismatch are a blank screen or an irritating high-pitched tone coming from the monitor.

Until you can replace the monitor with a better-quality monitor, these problems can be handled by changing the settings for the display and video card. Using the Display Properties dialog box, set the color depth and resolution to lower levels.

If the screen is blank or dark and you've already checked to see if it is plugged into a power source, check the cables that connect the monitor to the PC. Many newer monitors use a double-ended VGA cable that has an HD-15 connector at the monitor end as well as the video card end. If the cables are okay, reseat the video card.

Your monitor and video card documentation should have a recommended refresh rate for the monitor. The tools that you need to change the refresh rate are accessed by clicking the Advanced button in the Display Properties dialog box.

If the monitor image is unreadable after changing the refresh rate, reboot the PC into Windows Safe mode, use the lower refresh rate, and reboot the PC into Normal mode.

Driving the device

It is common for a video device driver to cause video problems. Video cards are mass-produced, and they sit on store and warehouse shelves before being installed in PCs. Because of this, the device driver that is included with a particular device is often obsolete by the time the device is installed. The device drivers in the Windows device library also suffer from a time lag. Always download the latest device drivers that are available from the manufacturer's Web site whenever you suspect a driver problem. Another source for updated, and usually digitally signed, device drivers is the Windows Update Web site.

Troubleshooting the power supply

A weak or faulty power supply can cause a number of problems to the devices that are attached to it, including the motherboard and disk drives. If unexplained and intermittent memory or hard drive errors cannot be isolated, the problem could well be the power supply.

A faulty power supply can make a good hard drive or motherboard appear to be bad. Extended periods of low voltage can damage the hard drive just as excessive voltages can burn out the motherboard and memory. Troubleshoot the power supply by testing each of its power connectors for the proper voltages. Test the +12VDC and +5VDC supplies with a multimeter. Most power supplies have adjustment screws for setting the voltages. Turning the screw clockwise increases the voltage, and turning it counterclockwise decreases the voltage.

Troubleshooting the sound system

If the PC's sound system is having problems, it is usually easy to hear the problem, but it can be difficult to isolate the source of the problem. However, take the following troubleshooting steps to find the problem:

✓ **Resource conflicts:** Use the Windows System Information window (shown in Figure 17-1), which is accessed from the Accessories⇨Systems Tools menu, to determine if resource conflicts (IRQ, DMA, or I/O address) exist between the sound card and other devices. If a conflict exists, reassign the conflicting device or the sound card. The most common conflict is an IRQ conflict.

✔ **Speakers:** Troubleshooting the speakers is a straightforward process, as follows:

- Make sure that the sound card is connected to the speakers and that the correct cable is plugged into the correct jack on the sound card. Match the color-coded plugs to the jacks, or look carefully at the icons on the jacks.

- Make sure that the volume is turned up on the sound card and the speakers. The sound card's volume can be set either with an adjustment knob or dial on the card or by clicking the Speaker icon in the system tray of the taskbar to open the Play Control panel. Make sure that the volume on the speakers is turned up.

- Make sure that the speaker wires are not crimped or broken and that all the jacks are seated in the appropriate plugs.

✔ **Device drivers:** Sound cards are dependent on their software device drivers. Verify that the latest version of the sound card's driver software is installed by checking the manufacturer's Web site.

✔ **EMF emissions:** Sound cards are susceptible to EMF (electromagnetic field) emissions from other devices and cards. If it is placed too close to a disk drive or the power supply, the sound card may have problems. Place the sound card in an open expansion slot as far away from other components as possible.

Figure 17-1:
Use the Windows System Information window to display the hardware configuration of a PC.

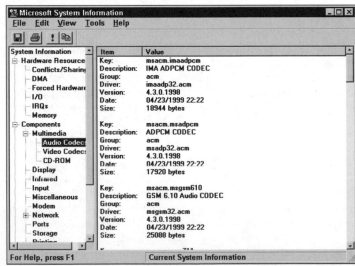

Prep Test

1 **When you arrive at a customer's site, what is the first thing that you should do?**

A ○ Go straight to the problem PC, and begin to work.

B ○ Ask the user about the problem, and actively listen.

C ○ Ask the user about the problem, and passively listen.

D ○ Explain your qualifications and experience to the user to put him or her at ease.

2 **The POST uses which of the following to signal a problem with essential hardware? (Choose two.)**

A ❑ Beep codes that are sounded through the system speaker

B ❑ Error messages and codes that are displayed on the monitor

C ❑ An ASCII display that illustrates the problem device

D ❑ Verbal messages that are played through the sound system

3 **Before troubleshooting a hard drive, what is the first thing that you should do?**

A ○ Disconnect the power supply connector

B ○ Shut down the PC

C ○ Back up the hard drive

D ○ Re-create the problem

4 **A PC's clock is consistently losing time, and recently the PC has failed to boot on occasion. What is likely to be the problem?**

A ○ The time setting in the CMOS needs to be corrected.

B ○ The time should be adjusted on the Windows desktop.

C ○ The BIOS needs to be updated.

D ○ The CMOS battery needs to be replaced.

5 **A POST error message with an error code in the 600 series indicates a problem with which FRM?**

A ○ Hard drive

B ○ CPU

C ○ Floppy disk drive

D ○ Motherboard

E ○ Keyboard

6 Which of the following ensure that a PC's cooling system can work as designed? (Choose two.)

A ❑ All case parts are attached and secured.

B ❑ An oversize fan has been installed.

C ❑ All empty expansion slots have slot covers in place.

D ❑ Extra venting holes have been added to the sides of the case.

7 Which of the following could be the problem if a PC will not boot from a floppy disk drive? (Choose three.)

A ❑ The floppy disk drive may not be first in the CMOS boot device setting sequence.

B ❑ The floppy disk in the drive may not be boot disk.

C ❑ The floppy disk drive does not have power.

D ❑ The system has a CD-ROM drive installed.

8 How is an IDE/ATA hard drive designated as either a master or a slave?

A ○ By a DIP switch on the drive

B ○ Where it is connected to the drive's data cable

C ○ By the drive's installation software

D ○ By jumpers on the drive

9 What is the highest numerical value that a three-pole jumper can have?

A ○ 8

B ○ 7

C ○ 6

D ○ 4

10 A customer has purchased new memory with a part number that ends with -70. He wants you to install the memory in his Celeron PC100 system. What should you do?

A ○ Proceed with the installation, putting the new memory in a different memory bank.

B ○ Explain to the user that this is the wrong memory and that he should return it.

C ○ Remove all existing RAM, and install the new memory.

D ○ Proceed with the installation, changing the PC's CMOS settings.

Answers

1 **B.** One of the best sources of information about a problem is the person who is having the problem. Actively listen to the user to gain all the information that you need, but avoid chitchat if you can. *Check out "Arriving on the scene."*

2 **A & B.** When the video system is not available, the POST uses the system speaker. After the video's BIOS is loaded, error messages can be displayed. *See "Dealing with BIOS errors."*

3 **C.** It is an excellent practice to completely back up a hard drive before troubleshooting it. *Look over "Backing up before you move forward."*

4 **D.** Another clue is that the CMOS begins losing its contents and gives intermittent `Device not found` errors. *Review "Deciphering BIOS error messages."*

5 **C.** Don't worry about memorizing all the BIOS error code numbers and what they represent. But, you should know the first five or six series just to be safe. *Take a look at "Numbering the error messages."*

6 **A & C.** Trust the engineering of the case, keep all its parts in place, and close all empty expansion slots with slot covers. *See "Cooling problems and the CPU."*

7 **A, B & C.** If a tape drive is installed, you may also want to check out the system resource assignments for conflicts. *Review "Booting from the A: drive."*

8 **D.** The jumper positions are usually marked as MS, SL, or something similar. *Check out "Troubleshooting IDE hard drives."*

9 **B.** Think of the poles of the jumper as bits. A 7 is the highest value that can be represented by 3 bits in binary format. *Take a look at "Troubleshooting SCSI hard drives."*

10 **B.** Expect to see a question like this one on the exam, using different memory part numbers and processors. You should know what the part number represents and with which processors or motherboard standards each is compatible. *Study "Identifying memory problems."*

Chapter 18

The Hardware Side of Networking

● ●

Exam Objectives

▶ Networking Windows

▶ Connecting to the network

▶ Swapping and configuring network interface cards

▶ Understanding networking concepts

▶ Identifying Internet concepts

▶ Accessing the Internet

● ●

*E*ven if you may know the Father of the Ethernet and truly understand the basic concepts of networking and how the common network topologies are used, you should still review this chapter. Although I may understand how something works generally, my knowledge or experience may not be sufficient to provide answers to some of the situations that are posed on A+ exams. I recommend that you review the networking fundamentals in this chapter as a part of your test preparation. Also, give this info a quick review before you take the test, just in case.

About 15 percent of what the A+ Hardware Technology and OS Technologies exams require comprises the following topics:

✔ Basic networking terms and concepts, including protocols and cabling, and the different ways that you can connect a PC to a network

✔ How to tell whether a PC is networked

✔ The process that is used to swap and configure network interface cards (NICs) or network adapters

✔ The ramifications of improperly repairing a networked computer

Even though this chapter is in the part of the book that deals with hardware and the A+ Hardware Technology exam, its contents cover the information that you need to know for both A+ exams.

Quick Assessment

Networking Windows

1 A logical group of computers with centralized security and administration is a(n) _____.

Connecting to the network

2 A(n) _____ is the networking device that is used to reduce broadcast storms on a network.

3 Before working on a PC, determine whether it is a(n) _____ PC.

4 The two most commonly used connectors for network hardware are the _____ and the _____.

Swapping and configuring network interface cards

Understanding networking concepts

5 A(n) _____ address is the 48-bit address that is assigned to a NIC by its manufacturer.

6 192.168.1.100 is an example of a(n) _____ address.

7 The command that is used to reset a modem to its default settings is _____.

8 _____ is the most widely used network protocol.

Identifying Internet concepts

Accessing the Internet

9 The software facility that is used to resolve the domain name to its associated IP address is _____.

10 The protocol that is used to transfer files across a network is the _____.

Answers

1   *Domain.* See "The network's domains."

2   *Router.* Review "Passing around the signals."

3   *Networked.* Look up "Working on a Networked PC."

4   *RJ-45* and *BNC.* Check out "Just call me NIC."

5   *MAC (Media Access Control).* Take a look at "Addressing the network."

6   *IP (Internet Protocol).* Study "Addressing the network."

7   *ATZ.* See "AT commands."

8   *TCP/IP.* Connect to "Protocols and other niceties."

9   *DNS (Domain Name System).* Review "Addressing protocols and services."

10 *FTP (File Transfer Protocol).* Check out "Protocols and other niceties."

The Hardware Side of Networking

A *network* is two or more computers that have been connected for the purposes of exchanging data and sharing resources. Networked shared resources range from printers, CD-ROMs, and modems to files and hard drives. Networks vary in size and scope.

Many types of computer networks exist, but you need to be concerned only with the following:

- **Peer-to-peer network:** This type of network includes two or more PCs that are connected to share data files, a printer, or other resources.

- **Local-area network (LAN):** A small business or corporate department may install a LAN that interconnects from two to hundreds of PCs, using permanently installed cabling or perhaps a wireless technology.

- **Wide-area network (WAN):** A corporation may maintain a WAN using dialup, leased, or other dedicated communication means.

You should also be familiar with the following network terminology and characteristics:

- **Topology:** The geometric arrangement of any network is its topology. The most common topologies are the bus, star, and ring topologies.

- **Protocol:** To operate efficiently, any communications-based system must have an established set of rules — its *protocol* — to govern its operation. Popular protocols for LANs are TCP/IP and IPX/SPX.

- **Data packets:** Data, messages, and tokens that are transmitted on any network must conform to the size and format prescribed under the network's protocol. Data packets also vary between network operating systems (NOSs) on the same protocol.

- **Architecture:** A network can be classified as being either a peer-to-peer or a client/server architecture. When all nodes on a network are equal and resources are shared equally, the network is a true peer-to-peer network. When one computer is designated to host programs or files for the rest of the network, it is a server, and the other nodes are clients.

- **Media:** Nodes on a network are connected by twisted-pair copper wire, coaxial cable, fiber-optic cable, or wireless radio wave connections.

- **Server:** This is a network computer from which workstations (clients) access and share files, printers, communications, and other services. Servers can be dedicated to a single service, such as file servers, print servers, application servers, Web servers, and so on. Servers can also be the software that performs, controls, or coordinates a service or resource.

✔ **Node:** This is any addressable network point, including workstations, peripherals, or other network devices. The term *node* is commonly used interchangeably with *workstation*.

✔ **Workstation:** This is a personal computer that runs application or utility software and uses data that is stored locally or provided by a network server to which it is connected by a cable or media. Workstations are also known as *clients*.

The network's domains

A domain has several different uses. The three common uses of domains in networking are the following:

✔ **Windows NT/2000/XP domain:** A logical group of computers with centralized security and administration.

✔ **Internet domain:** An element of the Domain Name Server (DNS) naming hierarchy.

✔ **NetWare domain:** The memory segment within NetWare that is used to separate NetWare Loadable Modules (NLMs) from the operating system.

Internet domains

The highest level of generalized domains defined by DNS is standardized to group domain names by their organization type or geographical location. The generic top-level domains (TLDs) that are used on the Internet are listed in Table 18-1.

Table 18-1	Generic Top-Level Domains (TLDs)
TLD	*Purpose*
.aero	Air-transport industry
.biz	Businesses
.com	Unrestricted, but intended for commercial entities
.coop	Cooperatives
.edu	U.S. educational institutions
.gov	U.S. government agencies
.info	Unrestricted use

(continued)

Table 18-1 *(continued)*

TLD	Purpose
.int	Organizations created through international treaties
.mil	U.S. military
.museum	Well, museums
.name	Individuals (people)
.net	Unrestricted use, but intended for network access providers
.org	Unrestricted use, but intended for nonprofit organizations and organizations that don't fit elsewhere
.pro	Professional service providers, such as accountants, lawyers, and physicians

Network domains

Servers and workstations are classified into domains by the role that they play on the network. Network domains and their controllers and the names of the resources in a domain are important things to know for the exam.

Domain controller

In the context of a Windows NT Server, Windows 2000 Server, or a Windows Server 2003 network, a domain is a collection of hardware and software resources and the user accounts that have access to them. The resources may include multiple servers, printers, CD-ROM drives, RAIDs, and other devices that are attached to the network.

Hello, I'll be your server

Several types of servers can exist on a network, each one performing a different task for the network and its workstations. A server is usually thought of as a computer, but a server is actually the software that performs, controls, or coordinates a service or resource. One computer can physically house many different software servers. To network clients, each server can appear to be a completely separate device, when that is not usually the case. Table 18-2 lists the most common types of servers that are implemented on a network.

Table 18-2	Server Types
Type	*Description*
File server	Stores network users' data files
Print server	Manages the printers that are connected to the network and the printing of user documents on the network printers
Communications server	Handles many common communications functions for the network, such as e-mail, fax, or Internet services
Application server	Shares network-enabled versions of common application software and eliminates the need for software to be installed on each workstation
Database server	Manages a common database for the network, handling all data storage, database management, and requests for data

A network devices primer

The A+ Hardware Technology exam focuses on the hardware that is used to connect a PC to a network, which boils down to the network interface card (NIC) and the cabling to which it attaches. Other hardware devices are used on a network to improve the network's performance or to provide an interface between different types of networks, and you should at least review these for background.

Cabling the network

For one computer to carry on a conversation with another computer, both computers must be able to transmit and receive electrical impulses that represent commands or data. The computers and peripherals of a network are interconnected with a transmission medium to enable data exchange and resource sharing. Cable media has laid the foundation on which networks grew — literally.

Although near and dear to my heart, wireless networks are not included on the A+ exams.

The following types of cabling are used on most networks:

- **Coaxial (coax):** This is similar to the cable that is used to connect your TV set to the cable television service. Two types of coaxial cable are used on networks: thick coaxial cable (commonly called 10Base5, ThickWire, or ThickNet) and thin coaxial cable (10Base2, ThinWire, or ThinNet).

- **Twisted-pair (no, not the upstairs neighbors):** This cable is available in two types: unshielded twisted-pair (UTP) and shielded twisted-pair (STP). UTP, which is the most commonly used network cabling, is similar to the wiring that is used to connect your telephone.

  For networks, UTP cable is the most commonly used. UTP is referred to in many different ways: 10BaseT or 100BaseT, Cat 3 or Cat 5, or simply Ethernet wire. These all translate loosely to "The moon is made of green iMacs," but they all refer to copper twisted-pair wiring.

  You may encounter some terminology that relates to twisted-pair copper wiring on the exams. Don't worry about the really technical issues that surround each term.

- **Fiber-optic:** With this cable, glass or polymer fibers carry modulated pulses of light to represent digital data signals. Although a few different types of polymer cables exist, you care about only one specific kind: fiber-optic. Fiber-optic cable is also known as 10BaseF or 100BaseF cable.

Passing around the signals

You may encounter the following networking terms on the A+ exams. These devices play a key role in the performance of the network. You don't need to memorize them, but you should understand how they're used:

- **Repeater:** This electronic echo machine has no function other than to retransmit whatever it hears, literally in one ear and out the other. A repeater is used to extend the signal distance of the cable by regenerating the signal.

- **Hub:** This device is used to connect workstations and peripheral devices to the network. Each workstation or device is plugged in to one of the hub's ports. A hub receives a signal from one port and passes the signal on to all of its other ports and therefore to the device or workstation that's attached to the port. For example, if an 8-port hub receives a signal on port 4, the hub immediately passes the signal to ports 1, 2, 3, 5, 6, 7, and 8. Hubs are common to Ethernet networks.

- **Bridge:** Bridges are used to connect two different LANs or two similar network segments, to make them operate as though they were one network. The bridge builds a bridging table of physical device addresses that is used to determine the correct bridging or MAC (Media Access Control) destination for a message. Because a bridge sends messages only to the part of the network on which the destination node exists, the overall effect of a bridge on a network is reduced network traffic and fewer message bottlenecks.

✔ **Router:** This device sends data across networks using the logical or network address of a message to determine the path that the data should take to arrive at its destination.

✔ **Switch:** A switch is a device that segments a network. The primary difference between a hub and a switch is that a switch does not broadcast an incoming message to all ports, but instead sends the message out only to the port on which the addressee workstation exists based on a MAC table that is created by listening to the nodes on the network.

✔ **Gateway:** This is a combination of hardware and software that enables two networks with different protocols to communicate with one another. A gateway is usually a dedicated server on a network, because it typically requires large amounts of system resources. The following types of gateways exist:

- **Address gateway:** Connects networks with different directory structures and file-management techniques.

- **Protocol gateway:** Connects networks that use different protocols. This is the most common type of gateway.

- **Format gateway:** Connects networks that use different data format schemes, for example, one that uses the American Standard Code for Information Interchange (ASCII) and another that uses Extended Binary-Coded Decimal Interchange Code (EBCDIC).

Just call me NIC

The network interface card (NIC), also known as a network adapter, is central to the concepts of networking that are covered on the A+ exams.

The NIC is a physical and logical link for a PC to a network. It is installed inside the computer in an open expansion slot. NICs are available for most of the expansion bus architectures, so getting a card for an available slot is easy. However, the most commonly used bus for NICs is the PCI (Peripheral Component Interconnect) bus, but many legacy ISA (Industry Standard Architecture) cards are still in use.

When choosing a NIC for a system, try to get one that is Plug and Play (PnP) compatible to make setup easier. Even with PnP, a network card can be a pain to set up. Some NICs use DIP switches or jumpers, and some use software to configure their identity to and compatibility with the network.

The setup that is needed for the NIC is controlled by two factors: the PC itself and the NOS (network operating system, such as Windows NT/2000 or Novell NetWare). If you have the choice, do yourself a big favor and use the same brand and model of NIC in every PC on the network. Mixing NICs on a network can be a pain, and you know where.

The NIC is a translator that works between the network and the PC. Networks transmit data in a serial data format (1 bit at a time), and the data bus of the PC moves data in a parallel format (8 bits at a time). The NIC acts as a go-between to convert the signal from serial to parallel format or from parallel to serial format, depending on its direction. The NIC also formats the data as required by the network architecture.

The NIC attaches a PC or other networked device to the network cabling and the network system. The primary purposes of the NIC are to serve as a transceiver — a device that transmits and receives data to and from other NICs (installed in the other networked nodes and devices) — and to connect to the network cabling. You should know the following NIC characteristics:

- **MAC (Media Access Control) address:** Each NIC is physically encoded with a unique identifying address that is used to locate it on the network. This address is 48 bits (6 bytes) long.

- **System resources:** A NIC is configured to the computer with an IRQ, an I/O address, and a DMA channel. A NIC commonly uses IRQ3, IRQ5, or IRQ10, and an I/O address of 300h.

- **Data bus compatibility:** NICs are designed with compatibility to a particular data bus architecture. ISA (Industry Standard Architecture) and PCI (Peripheral Component Interconnect) cards are the most common.

- **Data speed:** The NIC must be compatible with the data speed of the network. The data transfer speeds of a network are determined by several factors, including the cable media, the network topology, and the network connectivity devices that are in use. For example, a Token Ring network uses STP cable — the workstations attach to the network through MAUs (Multistation Access Units) — and typically runs at either 4 Mbps or 16 Mbps. An Ethernet network uses UTP cable (or coax), attaches its workstations through hubs or switches, and most commonly runs at either 10 Mbps or 100 Mbps. Many NICs have the ability to sense the data speed in use. A NIC designated as a 10/100 NIC has the ability to autosense between a 10-Mbps and a 100-Mbps network. Newer systems now support data speeds of 1,000 Mbps (or 1 Gbps), and newer NICs now support an autosensing 10/100/1000 port.

- **Connectors:** Several different connectors are used to join NICs to network cabling. The type of connector that is used depends mostly on the type of cable in use. Coax cabling primarily uses a BNC (for which there are several alleged meanings, none of which you need to know for the A+ exams) connector. Fiber-optic cabling is rarely used for cabling to workstations because of its cost. The most commonly used connector for networking is the RJ-45 connector, which is similar to the connector on your telephone, only a little bigger.

Working with NICs

An objective in the Networking domain of the A+ Hardware Technology exam is that you must be able to determine that a PC is networked before working on it. This requires special considerations and actions on your part. Not recognizing that the PC is on a network can result in damage to the PC and possibly to the network, including the following:

- Reduced bandwidth (the data transmission capacity and capability of the network) on the network caused by a faulty NIC signal or improperly set NIC

- A loss of data caused by an interruption in the network structure

- A slowdown in the general operation of the network

Some of the ways that you can determine whether a PC is networked are as follows:

- Look at the back of the PC for a network port with a cable attached to it. If you find one, you have a winner — a networked PC.

- If a network cable is not attached to the back of the PC, this doesn't mean that the PC is not a networked PC; the customer may have already disconnected the PC from the network. Question the customer to determine whether you are working on a networked PC.

- If no network cable exists, check to see whether a NIC is installed. No NIC — no network. However, if a NIC is in the PC, you can make other checks to determine whether the PC is networked.

- If you have access to the hard drive, search it for the telltale signs that the PC has been networked: folders or directories with names like NWCLIENT. Or look in the AUTOEXEC.BAT or CONFIG.SYS files for entries that start networking clients. (This is especially true for Novell software, which places entries in these files.)

- If you have access to Windows 9x or 2000, use Windows Explorer to look for network drives. They usually have drive designators of E:, F:, or higher.

If you determine that the PC is a part of network, follow the steps in Lab 18-1, in the section, "Getting Ready for Work," later in this chapter. You should follow the steps that are described in Lab 18-1 before and after repairing or replacing hardware on the PC.

Please Accept My Topologies

Imagine an aerial view of a network. Picture the network's general shape. The pattern of connections that ties the workstations to the network is its *topology*. You may encounter the following topologies on the A+ exams:

✔ **Ethernet:** Sometimes referred to as *bus topology,* Ethernet uses a full range of network media (using copper or fiber optics) and operates at 10 Mbps, 100 Mbps, or 1000 Mbps (1 Gbps). The 100-Mbps Ethernet is called Fast Ethernet and 1000 Mbps Ethernet is called Gigabit Ethernet. An Ethernet network (LAN) can support about 500 nodes. This is the most commonly installed type of network, probably because it is the cheapest and simplest. Ethernet devices connect to either a hub or a switch that is in turn connected to the network backbone.

✔ **FDDI:** (I've heard this pronounced as *fiddy,* but it's usually just spelled out.) FDDI stands for Fiber Distributed Data Interface. An FDDI NIC contains a laser or diode transceiver that converts its digital data into light to be transmitted on a fiber-optic network or back to a digital signal from incoming light impulses for use by the PC. FDDI is a standard of ANSI and the International Standards Organization (ISO) for data networks that use ring topology with dual and redundant rings and data speeds of 100 Mbps.

✔ **Token Ring:** Sometimes referred to as *ring topology,* Token Ring also uses copper and fiber-optic cabling, operates at 4 Mbps to 16 Mbps, and supports about 260 nodes. A Token Ring network operates reliably but can be difficult to troubleshoot. Because IBM is involved with the exams now, look for at least one Token Ring question.

Connecting a workstation to the network

Each network topology is associated with a network technology or protocol. Ethernet networking is the most common on a bus topology, and Token Ring is the most common on a ring structure.

The network technology in use is important because when you connect a PC to the network for the first time, you need to know the network identity requirements for a new workstation.

Addressing the network

The three addressing elements that are used on a network are as follows:

✔ **MAC (Media Access Control) address:** Every NIC or network adapter is assigned a unique ID (called the MAC address) by its manufacturer when it is made. This address is burned into the NIC's firmware and cannot be changed. The MAC address is the basis for all network addressing, and all other address types are cross-referenced to it. A MAC address is a 48-bit address that is expressed as 12 hexadecimal digits (a hex digit is comprised of 4 bits). To display the MAC address (adapter address) of the NIC or NICs installed in a PC, you can use either the WINIPCFG command on Windows 9*x* and Me systems or the IPCONFIG command on Windows NT, 2000, and XP systems.

✔ **IP (Internet Protocol) address:** Many internal and all external networks use IP addresses to identify nodes on both LANs and WANs. An IP address for a network workstation combines the address of the network and the node into a 32-bit address that is expressed in four 8-bit octets (which means sets of eight). Figure 18-1 shows the results of the `IPCONFIG` command, which displays the IP addressing information for a workstation. To run this command, open a command prompt and enter `IPCONFIG` on the command line.

The `IPCONFIG` command displays the IP address that is assigned to the workstation (in this case, 192.168.1.100), the workstation's subnet mask (which is used to differentiate between the network and host portion of an IP address), and the default gateway of the node.

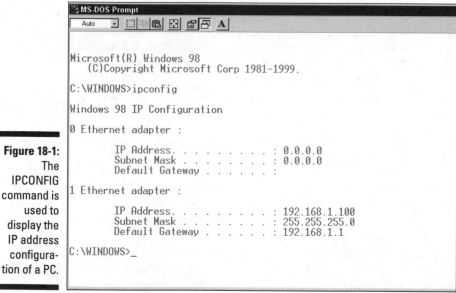

Figure 18-1:
The IPCONFIG command is used to display the IP address configuration of a PC.

✔ **Network names:** The most common form of a network name are computer names, which are also called network names. A network name is the name assigned to a workstation or other networked device and used to identify that node by other network users. For example, it is much easier to find a printer with a network name or MAIN_LASER than trying to remember the printer's MAC or IP address.

Commonly, network names are NetBIOS (Network Basis Input/Output System) names. NetBIOS uses unique 15-character names that are periodically broadcast over the network so the names can be cataloged by the Network Neighborhood function. NetBIOS names are the names that show up in Windows Network Neighborhood.

Addressing protocols and services

Many protocols and services can be used on a network to aid in the correlation and translation of one address form to another. The ones that you need to know for the A+ exams are as follows:

- **DHCP (Dynamic Host Configuration Protocol):** This protocol is used to automatically configure a network workstation with its IP address data. Each time that the workstation is logged on to the network, the DHCP server software, running on a network server or router, assigns or renews the IP configuration of the workstation. Typically, the address that is assigned is from blocks of IP addresses that have been set aside for use by internal networks. Depending on the network operating system, the IPCONFIG or WINIPCFG command can be used to view, renew, or release DHCP data.

- **DNS (Domain Name System):** DNS is used to resolve (translate) Internet names to their IP address equivalents. For example, when you request www.wiley.com from your browser's location line, a nearby DNS server (typically at your ISP) converts it to an IP address, such as 12.168.1.100, which is then used to request the data across the Internet.

- **WINS (Windows Internet Naming Service):** WINS is Microsoft's network name resolution software that converts NetBIOS names to IP addresses. Windows machines are assigned NetBIOS names (see the section, "Addressing the network," earlier in this chapter), which are converted into IP addresses for use on a network using TCP/IP (Transmission Control Protocol/Internet Protocol), the foundation protocol suite of the Internet. The use of a WINS server allows nodes on one LAN segment to find nodes on other LAN segments by name.

Connecting to an Ethernet network

When a new workstation is added to an Ethernet network, the workstation identifies itself using its MAC address and computer name to the rest of the network. Those devices that need to hold this addressing information, such as a switch or bridge, store the information in their MAC address tables. When requests come in for a particular IP address, the MAC address of the node is looked up and the message is sent to that workstation. Before you bury me in e-mails, please understand that this description is highly simplified, but it represents the essence of what happens.

Connecting to a Token Ring network

When you add a new node to a Token Ring network, the node must first establish that its address is unique. The workstation sends out test frames with its ID address, and the system responds with its own test frames that are sent to that address. If no other node responds (oops), the new ID address is accepted and established for the new ring node. If a duplication exists (it can happen), jumpers or DIP switches on the NIC can be used to alter the address.

Protocols and other niceties

In addition to the three network protocols (Ethernet, Token Ring, and FDDI) described earlier in this chapter, other protocols can be used to interconnect PCs to other PCs or networks. For the test, you need to know the names of these protocols, their acronyms, and the scope of what they interconnect. Table 18-3 lists other protocols that you may encounter on the A+ exams.

Table 18-3	Networking and Communications Protocols	
Protocol/Layer	*Acronym*	*What It Does*
Point-to-Point Protocol	PPP	Used to connect and manage network communications over a modem
Transmission Control Protocol/Internet Protocol	TCP/IP	The backbone protocol of the Internet
Internetwork Packet	IPX/SPX	The standard protocol of the Exchange/ Sequenced Novell network operating system's Packet Exchange
NetBIOS Extended User Interface	NetBEUI	A Microsoft protocol that is used only by Windows systems for LANs with no external connections; does not support routing (addressing through a router to other networks)
File Transfer Protocol	FTP	Used to send and receive files in client/ server mode to or from a remote host
Hypertext Transfer Protocol	HTTP	Used to send World Wide Web (WWW) documents, which are usually encoded in HTML, across a network
Network File Services	NFS	Allows the network node to access network drives as if they were local drives, files, and data; also performs the file-access and data-retrieval tasks that are requested of the network
Simple Mail Transfer Protocol	SMTP	Used to send electronic mail (e-mail) across a network
Telnet	Telnet	Used to connect and log in and manage a remote host

Discussing modems

Modems don't hold the vaulted position on the A+ Hardware Technology exam that they have in the past, but expect to see questions on the exam about installing, configuring, and troubleshooting both internal and external modems.

Modem facts that you should know

A modem (which is an acronym for modulator/demodulator) converts the digital data signal of the PC into the analog data signal that is used on the plain old telephone system (POTS) — which is also called the public telephone switched network (PTSN). Modems can be installed inside the PC in an expansion slot, or they can be attached to the PC externally through a serial or USB port.

You may have heard of modems for other types of communications besides dialing into a network, such as an ISDN (Integrated Services Digital Network) modem or a DSL (Digital Subscriber Line) modem. You don't need to know about these modem types for the A+ exams — and they're not really modems.

Internal versus external modems

An internal modem is installed like any other expansion card — into a compatible expansion slot. Modern modems do not require physical configuration, but some modems have DIP switches or jumpers that need to be set. Fortunately, most of a modem's configuration is performed automatically by the operating system.

AT commands

One modem topic that continues to be included on the A+ exams — although I'm not sure why in today's world of software configuration tools and Plug and Play modems — is the AT command set. AT does not mean Advanced Technology, as it would with a motherboard or power supply. On a modem, AT refers to *attention,* which is used to precede each command that's given to the modem from the AT command set.

The AT command set, which is officially known as the Hayes Standard AT Command Set, is used to drive and configure Hayes-compatible modems. For the A+ Hardware Technology exam, you should know the AT commands that are listed in Table 18-4.

Table 18-4	AT Modem Commands
Command	*Action*
ATDT *xxx-xxxx*	Dial the telephone number (indicated by the letters *x*) using touch-tone dialing
ATH	On hook (hang up)
ATL	Speaker loudness (volume)
ATZ	Reset the modem to default settings

Other commands can be used to control the modem during the dialing process. For example, if you are in an office or hotel where it is necessary to dial 9 to get an outside line, that digit can be entered into the string, along with appropriate pauses to wait for a second dial tone. For example, to dial out of an office, you could use the following command string:

```
ATDT 9,,15095551212
```

This string issues the following command sequence to the modem:

1. Prepare to dial a phone number.
2. Dial 9 to get an outside line, and pause 2 seconds (as indicated by the two commas) to wait for the outside dial tone.
3. Dial the number 1-509-555-1212.

Troubleshooting a modem connection

If the internal modem will not begin the dialup process, the problem is probably either a resource conflict or a device driver problem. Modems do not have a default IRQ assignment and must use an unassigned IRQ or share one with another device, such as a USB controller. An updated, newer version of a device driver can often solve a modem/operating system conflict.

An external modem uses the resources that are assigned to the COM port that it uses. Conflicts can arise when both an external modem and an internal device have both been assigned the same IRQ. To remedy this situation, move the external modem's connector to a different COM port or reassign the internal device.

To check the resources and drivers that are assigned to a modem, use the System Information applet. Access this applet by choosing Start⇨Programs⇨ Accessories⇨System Tools⇨System Information.

If the system has not detected the modem on startup after installing an internal modem, use the Add New Hardware icon in the Control Panel to start the Add New Hardware Wizard. Should that fail, open the system case, reseat the modem, or move the modem to another open slot and reboot the PC.

Connecting to a server

Windows NT, Windows 2000, and Windows Server 2003 versions support Remote Access Services (RAS), which is the service that is used to manage and control incoming dialup connections. Not all dialup access is made to Internet providers. A remote user may need to dial up the RAS of a corporate server and log on to the corporate LAN and gain access to its WAN.

Getting Ready for Work

In this section, the two labs demonstrate important processes that you should know and use when working on a PC that is connected to a network. In fact, you may even encounter a question on the A+ Hardware Technology exam regarding these processes.

Determining if a PC is a networked PC

As explained earlier in this chapter (see the section "Working with NICs"), it is important to know whether a PC on which you are about to work is connected to a network. Use the steps that are listed in Lab 18-1 to make this determination, and check them again, after you've finished your work, to make sure that the PC is once again connected to its network.

Lab 18-1   Working on a Networked PC

1. **Check to see whether the PC is logged on to the network.**

   Open a drive or folder on a network device. If you can open a file, the PC is logged on. If the drive is not available, the PC may be a node, but it is not logged into the network.

2. **If you are working on the hard drive, make a backup of all the files.**

   Especially important is backing up any networking information that's on the hard drive.

3. **Log off the PC as necessary.**

4. **Disconnect the network cable from the NIC, and proceed with the repair of the PC.**

5. **After the repair is complete, reconnect the network cable, verify that the network files are on the hard drive, and restore them if needed.**

6. **Ask the customer to log on to the network to verify that all is well.**

Installing and configuring a NIC

Although many manufacturers now include a NIC as a standard device in newer PC configurations, not every PC comes with a NIC installed. This is why the A+ Hardware Technology exam expects you to be able to install and configure a NIC in a PC.

A NIC is installed in a PC to connect it to the network, or when a PC's NIC has gone bad. Lab 18-2 details the steps that are used to install a NIC in a PC.

Lab 18-2   Installing a NIC in a PC

1. **If the PC already has a NIC installed — even if it is the same manufacturer and model as the new NIC that you are installing — uninstall the NIC from the operating system.**

   See Book II, Chapter 7 for instructions on uninstalling a NIC. If the PC doesn't have a NIC installed, you must determine the type of slot that's available for the NIC. On most new PCs, expansion slots are usually available.

   If a PCI slot is open, obtain a PCI card. Otherwise, you must use an ISA or EISA (Enhanced ISA) card, depending on the expansion slots that are available (see Figure 18-2). You need to identify these expansion slots by sight on the exam, so take a good look at this figure.

2. **Before inserting the card in a slot, study the card's documentation to determine whether any physical configuration steps are necessary.**

   Most PCI cards are Plug and Play compatible but may still require a DIP switch or a jumper to be set. You must do this before installing the card. Be sure to handle the card only by its nonconnecting edges.

3. **Open the case and install the NIC in the appropriate expansion slot.**

   Of course, I am assuming that you are wearing your ESD protection and that you used the steps that I listed in Lab 18-1 to disconnect the PC from the network.

   The remainder of the installation, aside from replacing the case, is performed on the operating system (see Book II, Chapter 7).

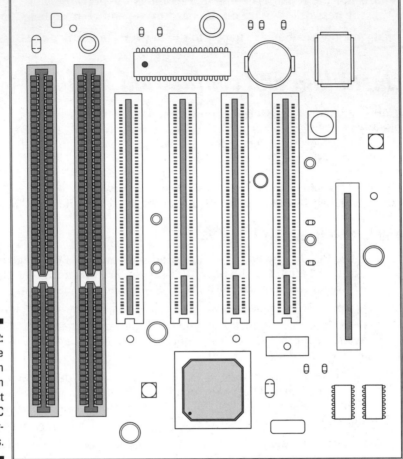

Figure 18-2:
The expansion slots on most newer PC mother-boards.

Prep Test

1 Which of the following protocols is used to transmit data over a dialup connection?

  A ○ ICMP

  B ○ PPP

  C ○ TCP/IP

  D ○ NetBEUI

2 Which of the following FRMs is responsible for converting the signal between the PC and the network media?

  A ○ Router

  B ○ Bridge

  C ○ NIC

  D ○ Hub

3 If a PC doesn't detect a modem on startup immediately after an internal modem is installed, what Windows tool should you use to add the modem to the system?

  A ○ Add New Hardware Wizard

  B ○ Automatic Skip Driver

  C ○ Modem Wizard

  D ○ Network Neighborhood

4 The address 44-45-53-54-00-00 is an example of which of the following?

  A ○ NetBIOS name

  B ○ IP address

  C ○ IPX address

  D ○ MAC address

5 A new PC is added to a Token Ring network. What will the network establish first?

  A ○ Unique ID of the new node

  B ○ MAC address

  C ○ IP address

  D ○ NetBIOS name

6 Also very popular on intranets, which of the following is the foundation protocol suite of the Internet?

A ○ TCP/IP

B ○ NetBEUI

C ○ IPX/SPX

D ○ NetBIOS

7 Which of the following is the protocol that automatically sets up the IP addressing configuration of network PCs?

A ○ TCP/IP

B ○ WINS

C ○ DHCP

D ○ DNS

8 UTP network cable typically has what type of connectors at each end?

A ○ RJ-45

B ○ RJ-11

C ○ AUI

D ○ BNC

9 Which of the following is the software service that resolves (translates) a domain name on the Internet, such as www.wiley.com, to its IP address?

A ○ WINS

B ○ PING

C ○ DNS

D ○ DHCP

10 Which of the following Windows NT/2000 services allows remote PCs to dial in?

A ○ PPP

B ○ IPX/SPX

C ○ RAS

D ○ MAU

Answers

1 **B.** PPP is used to transmit data from the sending to the receiving computer. PPP is used to encapsulate packets for transmission over the telephone line. *Review "Protocols and other niceties."*

2 **C.** The NIC serves as an interface between the PC and the network. The NIC is connected to both the PC and the network, and it translates the PC's data for transmission over the network and translates data from the network for transmission over the PC's bus. *Take a look at "Just call me NIC."*

3 **A.** The Add New Hardware Wizard is started from the Add New Hardware icon on the Windows Control Panel. Using this tool, you are able to pick the modem manufacturer and model and use any proprietary drivers that were supplied with the modem. *Check out "Troubleshooting a modem connection."*

4 **D.** This is a MAC (Media Access Control) address, also known as a Layer 2 address (after the Data-Link Layer of the OSI Reference Model). *Study "Addressing the network."*

5 **A.** The Token Ring network requires each node to have a unique identity. Before the node is allowed to join the network, it must establish that its ID is unique. *See "Please Accept My Topologies."*

6 **A.** TCP/IP (Transmission Control Protocol/Internet Protocol) is actually a suite of protocols and services that form the foundation services of the Internet as well as most intranets. *Review "Getting down to specifics."*

7 **C.** DHCP (Dynamic Host Configuration Protocol) is used to configure network workstations with their IP addressing data. *Link up with "Addressing protocols and services."*

8 **A.** Looking like a big telephone connector, the RJ-45 connector is easy to work with and adapts well to use in buildings. *Review "Just call me NIC."*

9 **C.** Domain Name Service (DNS) is used to translate a domain name to its IP address or back again. *Take a look at "Addressing protocols and services."*

10 **C.** Remote Access Services (RAS) supports dialup access to a Windows NT system. *Connect with "Connecting to a server."*

Book II

Operating System Technologies Exam

Part I
Operating Systems

The 5th Wave   By Rich Tennant

"A centralized security management system sounds fine, but then what would we do with the dogs?"

In this part . . .

*O*kay, calm down! Yes, there does seem to be more material in this book about the Core Hardware exam than for the OS Technologies exam. However, this is actually an optical illusion. There is a good deal of overlap between the two exams in the area of networking and memory management. A significant amount of what you need to know for the OS Technologies exam is embedded in the Core Hardware mini-book, which you assumed to be purely dedicated to helping you pass the Core Hardware exam. Au contraire, some of that stuff really helps for the OS Technologies exam as well.

The A+ exams expect you to be conversant with Windows 9*x*, Windows NT Workstation, Windows 2000 Pro, Windows Me, and Windows XP Pro. You must know how they are installed, configured, and networked to do well on the test. And don't forget to look at the Core Hardware book just a bit.

Chapter 1

Windows OS Basics

. . . .

Exam objectives

▶ Identifying the popular operating systems

▶ Detailing the functions of operating systems

▶ Listing commonly used DOS commands

. . . .

The A+ exams assume that you have at least six months of on-the-job experience as a professional PC repairperson. If you have been working as PC repairperson for at least six months, you know how much of the job is installing, configuring, and troubleshooting the Windows operating system. Without this hands-on experience, the A+ OS Technologies exam may be a bit of a struggle for some. Many of the questions on the test assume that you are able to recognize a situation from your experience. For example, a question may begin "The Video Adapter Properties window is displayed on the screen. What is your next action to change . . . ?" Only because you've used this particular window many times on the job are you be able to recognize the situation and intelligently answer the question. At least that's what the test assumes.

To prepare yourself completely for the A+ OS Technologies exam, I highly recommend that you get as much hands-on experience as you can with the Windows operating systems. Concentrate on the processes of installing, configuring, and debugging it on a PC, in both networked and stand-alone modes. Also, take the time to learn the commands that are entered at the command-line prompt in Windows 9*x*, Windows NT Workstation, Windows 2000 Professional, Windows Millennium Edition (Me), and Windows XP Professional.

Even if you have already taken the A+ Core Hardware exam or if you are taking the A+ OS Technologies exam first, there are parts of Book I in this book that provide background information for the topics in Book II. Specifically, you should read Book I, Chapters 4 through 9, 14, and 18 as a part of your preparations for the OS Technologies exam.

Quick Assessment

1 _____ is the most popular operating system.

2 The version of Windows that is designed to operate on palmtop and other portable computing devices is _____.

3 The ability of an OS to support more than one active program at a time is called _____.

4 _____-mode operations limit an application to its own memory space, but that space can include memory above 1MB.

5 _____ mode restricts applications to addressing only the first 1MB of RAM.

6 _____ means that the operating system supports more than one processor.

7 The _____ command can be used to copy whole directories, including subdirectories and files, to and from a fixed disk.

8 The DOS command prompt that is displayed on the C: drive root directory is _____.

9 The command that is used to change the attributes of a file is _____.

Answers

1 *Windows.* See "Meeting the Operating System."

2 *Windows CE.* Check out "Getting down to specifics."

3 *Multitasking.* Review "Multitasking, multiprocessing, and multithreading."

4 *Protective.* Take a look at "Protected versus real mode."

5 *Real.* Review "Protected versus real mode."

6 *Multiprocessing.* Study "Multitasking, multiprocessing, and multi-threading."

7 *XCOPY* or *XCOPY32.* Check out "Some DOS commands that you should know."

8 *C:\>.* See "Interfacing with the DOS and Windows command prompt."

9 *ATTRIB.* Review "Changing file attributes."

The A+ Operating Systems Technologies Exam

The second of the two CompTIA A+ exams is the OS Technologies exam, which is intended to assess your knowledge of the client operating systems that are currently popular (at least at the time that the test is developed) and have a large installed base. Only one client operating system meets these criteria, as far as the OS Technologies exam is concerned, and that OS is Microsoft Windows. So, a detailed knowledge of the structure, features, functions, and tools available in the various Windows versions that are still largely installed around the world is vital to passing this exam.

Table 1-1 lists the four domains (topic areas) of the OS Technologies exam and the major topics that are included in each domain.

Table 1-1	A+ OS Technologies Exam Domains
Domain	**Objectives**
OS Fundamentals	
	1.1 Identify the major desktop components and interfaces and their functions.
	1.2 Identify the names, locations, purposes, and contents of major system files.
	1.3 Demonstrate the ability to use command-line functions and utilities to manage the operating system, including the ability to use the proper syntax and switches.
	1.4 Identify the basic concepts and procedures for creating, viewing, and managing disks, directories, and files.
	1.5 Identify the major operating system utilities and their purpose, location, and available switches.
Installing, Configuring, and Upgrading	
	2.1 Identify the procedures for installing Windows 9x/Me, Windows NT 4.0 Workstation, Windows 2000 Professional, and Windows XP, and for bringing the operating system to a basic operational level.

Domain	Objectives
	2.2 Identify the steps to perform an operating system upgrade from Windows 9x/Me, Windows NT 4.0 Workstation, Windows 2000 Professional, and Windows XP.
	2.3 Identify the basic system boot sequences and boot methods, including the steps to create an emergency boot disk with utilities installed for Windows 9x/Me, Windows NT 4.0 Workstation, Windows 2000 Professional, and Windows XP.
	2.4 Identify the procedures for installing/adding a device, including loading, adding, and configuring device drivers, and for installing the required software.
	2.5 Identify the procedures necessary to optimize the operating system and major operating system subsystems.
Diagnosing and Troubleshooting	
	3.1 Recognize and interpret the meaning of common error codes and startup messages from the boot sequence, and identify the steps to correct the problems.
	3.2 Recognize when to use common diagnostic utilities and tools.
	3.3 Recognize the common operational and usability problems, and determine how to resolve them.
Networks	
	4.1 Identify the networking capabilities of Windows.
	4.2 Identify the basic Internet protocols and terminologies.

Meeting the Operating System

In its most basic form, the operating system provides an interface to the hardware and system software that makes the system and its resources available to the user in a useful way. By far, the most popular operating system in the world is the Microsoft Windows operating system, in all of its various versions. For this reason, the A+ Operating Systems (OS) Technologies exam focuses on the Windows operating system. Windows is the operating system that you are most likely to encounter on the job, which is why it is the operating system that dominates the exam.

Defining a few operating system terms

For the exam (and the sections that follow), I need to explain some operating system terms and concepts that you need to know.

Protected versus real mode

Protected mode operations limit an application to its own memory space, but that space can include memory above 1MB. Protected mode gets its name from the fact that programs in this mode are protected from other programs that desire its memory. *Real mode* restricts applications to addressing only the first 1MB of RAM.

All Windows versions after 3.*x* run in protected mode, which can lead to some problems. For example, when a Windows system is booted into DOS (real) mode, protected-mode device drivers cannot be used, so real-mode drivers must be loaded. The devices that are affected may include the CD-ROM drive, the sound card, and other devices that were not widely implemented before Windows 95. An additional problem is that loading these drivers to real mode can fill memory very quickly, because only the first 1MB can be used.

Multitasking, multiprocessing, and multithreading

Multitasking means that the operating system supports more than one program at a time. Windows 3.*x* supports what is called *cooperative multitasking,* which means that the programs running on the PC are expected to give way when another program requests use of a resource. If a program hogs a certain resource, there is no way of policing it. The other programs have to wait until the program releases the needed resource. Windows 9*x* introduced support for *preemptive multitasking,* which gives the operating system the authority to suspend a program that is monopolizing a needed resource.

Multiprocessing means that a computer has more than one processor. You don't need to worry about this for the OS Technologies exam, but the term does come up in the Hardware Technology exam.

Multithreading means that a single program has the ability to create (*spawn* is the technical term) several activities under its control that all run concurrently. The example that's usually given for this is a word processor that can run a repagination process while it is also running a spell checker and a grammar checker.

Symmetrical multiprocessing

Symmetrical multiprocessing (SMP) is the capability that enables an operating system to utilize more than one microprocessor on a single computer. SMP divides the work and assigns tasks to each of the different processors, which results in each processor getting better utilization. Windows NT Workstation supports two processors on the same PC, and Windows NT Server supports four to eight processors.

The opposite of SMP is *asymmetrical multiprocessing (ASMP),* which assigns a particular program or portion of a program to a particular processor that runs the program to its end.

Getting down to specifics

The operating systems that you should be somewhat familiar with for the A+ Operating System (OS) Technologies exam are as follows:

- ✔ **DOS (Disk Operating System):** What you need to know are the DOS commands that are used to prepare a system to take an operating system or in troubleshooting errors on the system.
- ✔ **Novell NetWare:** You need to know the Windows protocols that are used to connect a Windows client to a NetWare server.
- ✔ **Windows 3.x:** This version of Windows is mentioned once or twice, and you need to know how it relates to DOS and to Windows 95.
- ✔ **Windows 95:** Some questions on the exam reference the OSR2 (OEM) release and the features that it added.
- ✔ **Windows CE:** Windows CE (which allegedly stands for consumer electronics) is implemented on palmtop and other handheld PC and computing devices. All you need to know for the test is that Windows CE is never the right answer.
- ✔ **Windows Millennium Edition (Me):** Windows Me, pronounced "em-ee," is an upgraded version of Windows 98 SE. You don't need to know much about Windows Me beyond what's discussed in Chapter 2.

The operating systems that you should know very well for the OS Technologies exam are as follows:

- ✔ **Windows 98/98 SE:** Believe it or not, this is still the number one network client OS, and you need to know about installing, configuring, and troubleshooting Windows 98.

✔ **Windows NT 4.0 Workstation:** Because Windows 2000 and XP are based on Windows NT, expect to see references to this Windows version. However, because the A+ exam isn't the Server+ exam or an MCSE exam, you don't need to get too concerned with Windows NT.

✔ **Windows 2000 Professional:** For the exam, focus on Windows 2000 Pro for desktop, networking, configuration, and most operational questions. Some questions still refer to Windows 98, but most are about Windows 2000 features.

✔ **Windows XP Professional:** Be sure that you know the differences between Windows 2000 and Windows XP.

Interacting with the operating system

As a PC repairperson, much of your interaction with the operating system, regardless of which one it is, is through its command-line prompt. You need to be able to recognize only two very distinctive command-line formats on the exam: the DOS/Windows command-line prompt and the shell prompt of the UNIX and Linux operating systems.

Interfacing with the DOS and Windows command prompt

For the OS Technologies exam, you should know the following command-line DOS prompt by sight:

```
C:\WINDOWS>_
```

This command prompt is used for all versions of the Windows operating system. In this prompt, `C:` indicates the active disk drive and `\WINDOWS` indicates the active directory (folder). If the active directory is a subdirectory of another directory, the command prompt shows the entire directory pathname of the active directory. For example: `C:\WINDOWS\COMMAND` is the command prompt that is displayed when the `COMMAND` subdirectory of the `WINDOWS` directory is the active directory.

You can customize the command prompt to include a variety of information, but the format shown is the default format in DOS and all versions of Windows. The `PROMPT` command is used to customize the command-line prompt in DOS and Windows.

Interfacing with UNIX/Linux

The command prompt for a UNIX or Linux system can seem even less friendly than the DOS command prompt. In its default form, this command prompt is only a single character, but both the character displayed and the prompt itself can be modified so that this command prompt is as information-packed as the DOS prompt.

The prompt that is displayed by a UNIX or Linux system depends on the shell type that's in use. The two standard defaults that you should know are

- ✔ The Korn shell, which displays a dollar sign ($)
- ✔ The Bourne shell, which displays a percent sign (%), as follows:

    ```
    %_
    ```

It's as easy as that — just a percent sign or a dollar sign.

Identifying the Windows system files

Windows loads a significant number of files to a PC during the installation of the OS. For the most part, it doesn't matter what is inside these files, but on occasion, you need to know the type of these files. If you are missing a DLL or a DRV file, the system may not start up or a peripheral may not work — typically just when you need it the most.

The system files that are found on a Windows system, which are hidden by default, are identified by their file extensions. The extensions that you should know for the exam are as follows:

- ✔ **386:** Virtual device driver
- ✔ **DLL:** Program extension file
- ✔ **DRV:** Device driver
- ✔ **INI:** Program initialization file
- ✔ **SYS:** System file
- ✔ **VXD:** Virtual device driver

Some DOS commands that you should know

The DOS commands that you should know for the OS Technologies exam are as follows:

✔ **COPY:** This command is used to create a copy of a file and place it into another directory or disk drive. Its format is `COPY FILENAME.EXT NEWFILE.EXT`.

✔ **DEFRAG:** As files are created, modified, and removed, the disk can become fragmented. Disk fragmentation can impact system performance, because disk-drive heads must perform multiple seek operations to access a file. The `DEFRAG` command reorganizes the disk to eliminate fragmentation. The `DEFRAG` command can be executed from the command prompt or can be started from the desktop. From the desktop, choose Start➪Programs➪Accessories➪System Tools➪Disk Defragmenter to start the command. The command-line format is `DEFRAG X:` (where *X* is the disk drive to be defragged).

✔ **DIR:** This command lists the file and subdirectories that are in the active directory.

✔ **EDIT:** This command opens a text editor that can be used to make changes to some system and user-defined text-format files, such as `INI` files and the `AUTOEXEC.BAT` and `CONFIG.SYS` files.

✔ **FDISK:** This command is used to partition hard drives prior to formatting them for use with an operating system. This command is discussed in more detail in Chapter 2.

✔ **MEM:** This command displays the current usage of system memory. Commonly used options of this command are as follows:

- View memory usage by classification — MEM /C

- View memory usage by module — MEM /M *module name*

- View the amount of free memory — MEM /F

✔ **SCANDISK:** This command runs automatically at the next startup after a Windows 9*x* system is shut down improperly. The `SCANDISK` command fixes errors on hard drives, floppy disks, RAM drives, and DBLSPACE compressed drives. `SCANDISK` can be started from the desktop with either of these steps:

- Choosing Start➪Programs➪Accessories➪System Tools➪ScanDisk

- Executing it from the command line with the format `SCANDISK X:` (where *X* is the drive letter of the disk to be repaired).

✔ **XCOPY/XCOPY32:** This command is used to copy directories, subdirectories, and files to and from a fixed disk. Using `XCOPY`'s extensive list of options, the files or directories that are copied can be expanded or limited by a variety of options, including choosing only files with an archive attribute. Because `XCOPY` cannot deal with long filenames, `XCOPY32` should be used with later versions of Windows. The format is `XCOPY32 A:\*.* C:*.* /S`, where the /S switch tells the operating system to copy the contents of all subdirectories as well.

Hard drives are a significant topic on both of the A+ exams. Be sure you also review Book I, Chapter 8 for more information on data storage devices in general and hard drives in particular as a part of your OS Technologies exam preparations.

Identifying the components on the desktop

Although the overall look and feel of the Windows desktop has changed from what it was in Windows 1.0 to what it is in Windows XP, a number of elements that are associated with the desktop have not changed. For the A+ OS Technologies exam, you should be familiar with the following desktop elements, and you should know what each element is used for:

✓ **Start menu:** This menu is displayed when the Start button is clicked. The Start menu provides access to the major activities areas of the Windows OS, including the menus for Programs, Settings, Documents, and Favorites, as well as access to the Run box, Help system, and Find/Search function.

✓ **Accessories:** This menu, accessed by choosing Start⇨Programs⇨ Accessories, contains several add-ins and snap-ins that cover a variety of usage areas. Perhaps the more important selections on this menu for the A+ OS Technologies exam are System Tools — which contains access to the Disk Defragmenter, ScanDisk, and other tools — and the Calculator.

✓ **Command-line/DOS prompt:** Several commands that are used to diagnose or troubleshoot a PC problem have not been included on a system menu or in a graphical user interface (GUI) dialog box and must be executed from a command-line prompt.

  To open a command-line prompt in Windows 9*x*, choose Start⇨Programs⇨ MS-DOS Prompt. In Windows NT/2000/XP, choose Start⇨Run, enter **cmd** in the Run box that appears, and click OK.

✓ **Computer Management Console (CMC):** This utility, which is referred to as the Microsoft Management Console (MMC) in Microsoft's literature, shown in Figure 1-1, is used to access the system management and maintenance utilities; Microsoft refers to these utilities as *snap-ins*. To reach this interface on Windows 2000 and XP computers, enter **MMC** in the Run box and click OK. You can also right-click the My Computer icon and choose Manage from the pop-up menu that appears.

✓ **Control Panel:** The Control Panel, which should be an old friend by now, contains icons that allow you to configure the user environment, including Add/Remove Programs, Desktop Themes, Network, Internet, and Users. On Windows 2000 systems, you can choose how the Control Panel is displayed.

Figure 1-1:
The
Microsoft
Computer
Management
Console.

✔ **Device Manager:** The Windows Device Manager is used to view, modify, and update the properties of the hardware that is attached to a PC. To access Device Manager, right-click the My Computer icon on the desktop and choose Properties from the pop-up menu that appears. In the Computer Properties dialog box that opens, use the appropriate tab for the operating system:

- On Windows 9*x* and Me systems, choose the Device Manager tab.

- On Windows 2000/XP systems, choose the Hardware Tab and then click the Device Manager button (which is about halfway down in the dialog box).

✔ **My Computer:** This Desktop icon can be used to navigate the Windows file systems, but its primary purpose for a PC repair professional is to provide access to hardware and device-driver maintenance in the Windows Device Manager and other administrative tools.

✔ **Network Neighborhood/My Network Places:** This Desktop icon provides access to network resources to which a PC has been granted sharing permission.

✔ **Taskbar/system tray:** The taskbar and the system tray provide a visual status of what is running on a PC at a given instance. All open documents, applications, and utilities (such as downloading files) are displayed on the taskbar. The system tray (or systray) contains icons for programs that are loaded during startup and are running in the background, such as the Task Scheduler, an antivirus program, or a printer toolbox.

> ✓ **Windows Explorer:** The Windows Explorer has remained a valuable tool for managing the folders and files that are stored on a PC's permanent and removable storage devices. It is also valuable when you want to find, move, rename, or remove a file or a folder.

Starting Up the Operating Systems

The processes that are used to start up a PC running the Windows operating system are basically the same through the completion of the BIOS power-on self-test (POST) operation. At that point, which is when the operating system is started, Windows 9*x* and Windows 2000 systems use different methods to start up.

Booting to the command prompt

Starting the system to only a command prompt requires a boot disk (typically a floppy disk that's placed in the A: drive) that contains, at a minimum, the DOS system files. To make a floppy disk boot disk, you can either

✓ Right-click the drive letter in Windows Explorer and choose Format from the pop-up menu that appears.

✓ Type the following DOS command at a command-line prompt:

```
C:\>FORMAT A: /S
```

Another way to add the system files to a formatted floppy disk or hard drive partition is by using the SYS command, as follows:

```
C:\>SYS A:
```

To create a boot disk that includes other commands and perhaps CD-ROM support, you may need to follow the SYS command with one or more of the following entries:

```
C:\>COPY AUTOEXEC.BAT A:\
C:\>COPY CONFIG.SYS A:\
C:\>COPY \WINDOWS\HIMEM.SYS A:\
C:\>COPY \WINDOWS\COMMAND\FDISK.EXE A:
C:\>COPY \WINDOWS\COMMAND\MSCDEX.EXE A:
```

The MSCDEX.EXE (Microsoft CD Extensions) file is the native DOS/Windows device driver for the CD-ROM drive. To have the CD-ROM drive available after booting the system to the command prompt, add the following line to the CONFIG.SYS file:

```
C:\WINDOWS\COMMAND\MSCDEX.EXE /D:MSCD001 /M:10
```

The following files must be loaded to boot the system to the command prompt: IO.SYS, MSDOS.SYS, and COMMAND.COM.

Understanding Virtual Memory

The software in use today requires more random-access memory (RAM), or system memory, than most PCs have installed or even have room to install. As a result, the PC and its operating system needed another way to supply memory on an as-needed basis.

When a PC has its operating system kernel, a Web browser, an e-mail client, and perhaps a word processor all loaded in RAM at the same time, the typical 32MB, 64MB, or even 128MB of RAM isn't sufficient. This lead to the development of *virtual memory*. This type of memory is hard drive space that is used as a substitute for system memory.

Virtually memory works like this: After the RAM is full and the user asks for a new application, document, or instance of a running program, the only way that the PC can allocate the required RAM to the requested function is to free some of its resources. To free space, the Virtual Memory Manager (a system utility) copies the least-used item in memory (several algorithms are used to choose what gets copied) to a reserved and set-aside space on the hard drive, called page files. *Page files* hold pages of RAM contents until the time that these contents are required again. At that time, the contents of virtual memory are copied back into RAM, presumably after something else has been written to a page file in virtual memory.

In the Windows 9*x* and Me operating systems, virtual memory page files have the extension .SWP. Windows 2000/XP systems use a .SYS extension, and the virtual memory file is specifically named PAGEFILE.SYS.

Virtual memory is configured slightly differently in the various versions of Windows. For information on configuring virtual memory on a Windows 9*x* system, see Chapter 2. For details about configuring a Windows 2000 system, see Chapter 3.

Displaying the Windows Build Number

To display the version number, also called the *build number,* of the Windows version that's installed on a PC, there are two different methods:

✔ Right-click My Computer, choose Properties from the pop-up menu that appears, and select the General tab (see Figure 1-2).

✔ Display the version number from the command prompt by using the DOS command VER.

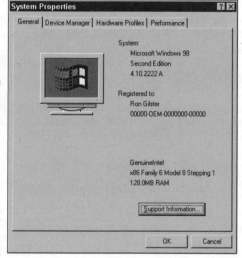

Figure 1-2: The General tab in the System Properties window includes the Windows version number.

As shown in Figure 1-2, the version number has three parts. The first two parts (such as 4.10) are considered to be the *version number* and the third part is the *build number* (the current release of a particular version). Build numbers are used more extensively in beta versions and reflect the evolution of the trial system. When the operating system is released, the build number usually becomes arbitrary.

Some examples of build numbers are as follows:

✔ **Windows 98:** 4.10.1998 and 4.10.2222 (Windows 98 SE)

✔ **Windows 2000 Professional:** 5.00.2195 [Service Pack 1 (SP1)]

✔ **Windows XP:** 5.00.2600

To display the version (and the latest service pack that's installed) on a Windows 2000/XP system, choose Start➪Run, type **winver** in the Run box, and press Enter. A display box appears with the version and service pack information. On a Windows 98 system, entering **winver** only tells you that the OS is a Windows 98 system. Duh!

Getting Ready for Work

The A+ folks are somewhat enamored with the ATTRIB DOS command. As a result, you may encounter one or two questions about how to change the file attributes of a Windows file. The following sections guide you through this process.

Changing file attributes

Another file-related action that you need to know for the exam is how to change file attributes. The following four file attributes can be set for a file (or folder) in Windows:

- ✔ **Archive:** Indicates that a file that is marked to be backed up.

- ✔ **Hidden:** Prevents a file from appearing in directory listings.

- ✔ **Read-only:** Indicates that a file that can be read but cannot be changed or deleted.

- ✔ **System:** Indicates that a file that is used only by the operating system and is not typically displayed in a directory listing.

The ATTRIB command is used to display and modify the file attributes of a file. To view or change the file attributes for one or more files from the command prompt or through Windows Explorer, follow the processes that are described in Labs 1-1 and 1-2.

Lab 1-1	Changing File Attributes from the Command Prompt

1. **To display the current attributes of a file, change to the directory of the file and enter the following command:**

```
ATTRIB MYFILE.DAT
```

The system displays something like this:

```
A SHR   MYFILE.DAT
```

The series of letters at the beginning of this line are the first letters of the current attributes: *A* stands for Archive, *S* is for System, *H* is for Hidden, and *R* is for Read-only.

2. **To remove an attribute from a file, use the minus sign (–).**

   For example, this command example removes the System, Hidden, and Read-only attributes from the file:

   ```
   ATTRIB -S -H -R MYFILE.DAT
   ```

3. **To add an attribute to a file, use the plus sign (+).**

   For example, this command example adds the Hidden attribute to the file:

   ```
   ATTRIB +H MYFILE.DAT
   ```

Lab 1-2   Changing File Attributes in Windows Explorer

1. **In Windows Explorer, right-click the file and select Properties from the pop-up menu that appears.**

   In the Attributes section of the Properties window, the attributes that are enabled have check marks next to them.

2. **To remove or add an attribute to a file, simply check or uncheck the attributes as you desire.**

3. **To change the System attribute, you must use the command prompt (see Lab 1-1).**

Prep Test

1 **Which of the following can be used to display the version and build numbers of a Windows system? (Choose two.)**

A ☑ VER

B ☐ winver

C ☑ My Computer, Properties, General

D ☐ Right-click desktop, Properties, About

2 **Which operating system mode restricts programs to running in the first 1MB of system memory?**

A ○ Restricted

B ○ Protected

C ✓ Real

D ○ Unprotected

3 **Which of the following terms describes the condition where a single program has the ability to spawn several activities under its control and have them run concurrently?**

A ○ Multiprocessing

B ✓ Multitasking

C ✓ Multithreading

D ○ Synchronous multiprocessing

4 **Which of the following is not the extension of a common Windows system file?**

A ○ SYS

B ✓ DAT

C ○ DLL

D ✓ 386

5 **Which of the following attributes are assigned to DOS and Windows files?**

A ✓ System, Archive, Read-only, Hidden

B ○ Archive, Reserved, Read-Write, Hidden

C ○ Hidden, System, Private, Write-only

D ○ System, Archive, Read-only, Reserved

6 Which of the following is the command prompt that is displayed for the COMMAND **subdirectory of the Windows directory on the primary hard drive?**

A ○ A:\COMMAND

B ⊘ C:\WINDOWS\COMMAND>

C ○ D:\WINDOWS\COMMAND>

D ○ A:\WINDOWS\COMMAND>

E ○ C:\COMMAND>

7 Which Windows 2000/XP utility is used to access the system management and maintenance utilities that Microsoft calls *snap-ins*?

A ○ Device Manager

B ⊘ Management Console

C ○ Systray

D ○ Task Manager

8 What Windows feature can be used to view, modify, and update the properties of the hardware that's attached to a PC?

A ○ System Information

B ○ Add Hardware Wizard

C ⊘ Device Manager

D ○ Task Manager

9 Which of the following DOS commands could be used to copy an entire directory, including its subdirectories and files — some with long filenames — from one disk drive to another?

A ○ XCOPY

B ○ DIR

C ⊘ XCOPY32

D ○ COPY

10 Which of the following is the native DOS/Windows device driver for the CD-ROM drive?

A ○ CDROM.EXE

B ○ DOSCD.DRV

C ○ CDDRV.SYS

D ⊘ MSCDEX.EXE

Answers

1 **A & C.** The `winver` command runs on a Windows 9*x* system, but it shows only the operating system, such as Windows 98, not the version and build numbers. *See "Displaying the Windows Build Number."*

2 **C.** Real-mode operation, which, in effect, is DOS emulation mode, does not address memory above 1MB. *Review "Protected versus real mode."*

3 **C.** Multiprocessing refers to a system with more than one processor, and multitasking means that the system can run more than one program. *Check out "Multitasking, multiprocessing, and multithreading."*

4 **B.** The other common file types not listed are DRV, INI, and VXD. *Take a look at "Identifying the Windows system files."*

5 **A.** The Archive, Read-only, and Hidden attributes can be modified through a file's Properties window. However, the System attribute must be managed through the ATTRIB command-line command. *Study "Changing file attributes."*

6 **B.** Yes, I make the assumption that the primary hard drive is the C: drive, because this is always the case. *See "Interfacing with the DOS and Windows command prompt."*

7 **B.** The Microsoft Management Console, or the Computer Management Console, provides access to tools, utilities, and features that can be used to manage and maintain the PC. *Review "Identifying the components on the desktop."*

8 **C.** Device Manager lists all the system and peripheral devices that are attached to the PC and indicates the status for each device. Device Manager can be used to add, remove, or modify PC devices. *Check out "Identifying the components on the desktop."*

9 **C.** If you aren't concerned about long filenames being lost and files perhaps being overwritten as a result, COPY or XCOPY could be used. XCOPY32 handles the long filenames and file systems of Windows 9*x* systems. *Review "Some DOS commands that you should know."*

10 **D.** I'm willing to bet that you will see a question similar to this one on the exam. *Study "Booting to the command prompt."*

Chapter 2

Windows 95, 98, and Me

• •

Exam Objectives

▶ Identifying DOS and Windows files and commands

▶ Installing or upgrading Windows 9*x*/Me

▶ Creating an emergency boot disk

▶ Recognizing common error and startup messages

• •

*T*he A+ OS Technologies exam could easily be called the A+ Windows exam because it focuses heavily on the processes of installing, configuring, and troubleshooting the various versions of Windows. Because not everyone sees the same exact test, you should be ready for questions about the two Windows 98 versions (Windows 98 and Windows 98 SE), some references to earlier versions (Windows 3.*x* and Windows NT Workstation), and the newer Windows versions (Windows Millennium Edition, or Me, Windows 2000 Pro, and Windows XP Home and Windows XP Pro). MS-DOS may be mentioned as well.

The A+ exams deal only with the PC itself. In the operating systems area, the focus is on network clients, not the network operating system (NOS) or server versions. What you won't find in the latest edition of the OS Technologies exam is Apple, UNIX, and Linux, so you can relax and not worry about those operating systems. Say what you will about Windows, but it is the most common PC operating system in the world. For this reason, a professional PC repairperson, like you, must have a good working knowledge of the Windows OS and how Windows and the PC hardware affect each other. Today, PC technicians are called on to solve software problems as much as, if not more than, hardware problems. You need to know how to add Windows to a PC, how to configure it properly for either stand-alone or networked operation, and how to fix any problems.

Quick Assessment

Identifying DOS and Windows files and commands

1 The _____ command is used to delete a directory or folder and all its subdirectories or subfolders.

2 The first files to be loaded during the boot process are IO.SYS, _____, and CONFIG.SYS, if present.

3 _____ enables expanded memory and allows the use of upper memory as system memory.

4 The _____ file includes the BootMulti parameter, which controls a system's capability to boot to multiple operating systems.

5 A(n) ____ device can be automatically configured and assigned a device driver by Windows.

Installing or upgrading Windows 9x/Me

6 The files that make up the Windows 9x Registry are _____ and _____.

7 The Windows 9x utility that is used to edit the Registry is _____.

Creating an emergency boot disk

8 The _____ command is used to create an emergency repair disk (ERD).

Recognizing common error and startup messages

9 0E and 0D error messages reflect errors with _____ and _____, respectively.

10 A Windows protection error is associated with a(n) _____.

Answers

1   *DELTREE.* See "First, some DOS facts."

2   *MSDOS.SYS.* Review "First, some DOS facts."

3   *EMM386.EXE.* Check out "First, some DOS facts."

4   *MSDOS.SYS.* Review "Modifying MSDOS.SYS."

5   *Plug and Play (PnP).* Look over "Installing Hardware in Windows 9*x.*"

6   *USER.DAT, SYSTEM.DAT.* Take a look at "The Windows 9*x* System Files."

7   *REGEDIT.* Study "Working with Windows utilities."

8   *RDISK.EXE.* See "Running with the ERD."

9   *Memory, video.* Check out "Friendly Windows 9*x* error messages."

10 *Virtual device driver (VXD).* Take a look at "Dealing with Windows protection errors."

Putting in the Windows

You should understand the steps that are used to install each version of Windows and the procedures that are used to upgrade from one version to the next. Practice installing as many of the Windows versions as you can. However, if you lack all the various versions, concentrate on installing Windows 98 and work on upgrading it to either Windows 2000 Pro or Windows XP Pro.

First, some DOS facts

You'll encounter some DOS commands, files, and features on the exam. Although you may not be asked directly about the DOS operating system itself, you need to know the files and commands that are still in use by Windows and those that come in handy to diagnose certain software-related problems.

You should know something about the following DOS/Windows files, commands, and terms for the OS Technologies exam:

- ✔ CONFIG.SYS is not required for DOS or Windows to start up.
- ✔ COMMAND.COM displays the DOS command prompt, contains the internal DOS commands, and is required for DOS and Windows 3.*x* to boot.
- ✔ EMM386.EXE enables expanded memory and allows the use of upper memory as system memory.

- ✔ The boot sequence for a DOS system is IO.SYS, MSDOS.SYS, CONFIG.SYS, COMMAND.COM, and AUTOEXEC.BAT. To boot to a DOS command prompt, only IO.SYS, MSDOS.SYS, and COMMAND.COM are required to load.
- ✔ DOS memory is divided into three areas:
    - • *Conventional* memory (640K)
    - • *Expanded* or *upper* memory (384K)
    - • *Extended* memory (above 1024K)

According to the A+ OS Technologies exam objectives, you need to know the following MS-DOS commands and terms:

- ✔ **CD:** Change the current directory.
- ✔ **DEL:** The DEL (Delete) command allows you to remove one or more files or folders from permanent storage, such as a disk.

✓ **DELTREE:** The DELTREE command can be used to delete a directory or folder and all its subdirectories or subfolders.

✓ **ECHO:** This command turns the display or commands in a batch file on or off, and it can be used in a batch file to display a message.

✓ **EDIT:** This command opens a text-editor utility that can be used to create new files or modify existing files.

✓ **FDISK:** Together with the FORMAT command, the FDISK command is one of the most important DOS commands that is still in use. FDISK is used to create and manage primary, extended, and logical partitions on a hard drive.

✓ **FORMAT:** When you are getting ready to install an operating system, the disk partition on which you are installing the system must be made ready for use by running the FORMAT command on it. Disk media must be formatted before it can be written to or read by the PC.

✓ **MD:** Create (make) a new directory.

✓ **MEM:** This command displays the amount of memory that is installed and the amount that is available in conventional, extended, expanded, and upper memory areas.

✓ **RD:** Remove an existing directory.

✓ **REN:** This command is used to rename a file or directory. You must conform to the 8.3 naming convention of MS-DOS when using this command. (The 8.3 naming convention refers to a filename in which the prefix does not exceed 8 characters and the suffix does not exceed 3 characters.)

✓ **SET:** This command is used to insert a string value into a command variable that can be accessed later by another program or batch file.

✓ **SETVER:** This command displays the version of the running version of MS-DOS and allows the running version to be set to that needed by real-mode programs.

✓ **TYPE:** This command displays the contents of a file on the display.

✓ **VER:** This command reports the running version of MS-DOS, which may not be the installed version of MS-DOS.

Reviewing Windows 9x

Many of the features in Table 2-1 that are indicated as not available on one or both of the Windows 95 versions could be added through downloads and application software. For example, Windows 95 did not include device drivers for a DVD, and the drivers must be downloaded from the manufacturer. Also, the Active Desktop had to be implemented through Internet Explorer 4.0. The information in Table 2-1 shows the native features of each Windows 9*x* release for comparison purposes. You may see questions on the OS Technologies exam that require you to know which versions had which features.

In Table 2-1, Y (Yes) indicates that a feature is included while N (No) shows that a feature is not included.

Table 2-1	Features of Windows 9*x* Versions			
Feature	*98 SE*	*98*	*95 OSR2 (95b/OEM)*	*95a (Retail)*
ACPI support	Y	Y	N	N
Active Desktop	Y	Y	N	N
Backup utility	Y	Y	N	N
Dial-Up Networking	Y	Y	Y	Y
Disk management	Y	Y	N	N
DVD support	Y	N	N	N
FAT32	Y	Y	Y	N
FAT32 conversion	Y	Y	N	N
Internet Connection Sharing	Y	N	N	N
Multiple monitors	Y	Y	N	N
OnNow support	Y	Y	N	N
Task Scheduler	Y	Y	N	N
USB support	Y	Y	Y	N
Windows Update Utility	Y	Y	N	N

Don't forget about Me

Windows Me is a home-user alternative to Windows 2000 and not the merger of Windows 98 and Windows 2000, as rumored. Windows Me is an updated version of Windows 98 and was intended to serve as an interim solution for home- and small-office users until a personal edition of Windows 2000 could be released. (The updated personal version of Windows was eventually released as Windows XP Home Edition.)

Perhaps the best way to review an operating system for the A+ OS Technologies exam is to practice navigating around the various Properties functions of Windows 98, including those that you access by right-clicking the desktop and the My Computer icon. You should also review

✔ Functions on the Settings menu (choose Start⇨Settings)

✔ System, Printers, Modems, and Network icons of the Control Panel

The exam has questions about how to access each of these functions and what actions are available on each of them.

Installing Windows 9x and Me

Windows 98 and Windows Me offer two choices for file systems: FAT16 and FAT32. (The number listed after the letters indicates the number of bits that are used to address files on the drive.)

✔ FAT16 is supported by all Windows versions (including 3.x, 9x, NT, Me, 2000, and XP) and DOS, as indicated in Table 2-2.

DOS and Windows 3.x users knew FAT16 simply as FAT, which means *File Allocation Table*.

✔ FAT32 is supported by Windows 9x, Me, 2000, and XP. In fact, of the later Windows versions, only Windows NT doesn't support FAT32.

Another FAT derivative that isn't really a file system is VFAT (Virtual FAT), which is a software interface that acts as an intermediary between FAT and applications.

In Table 2-2, Y (Yes) shows that a particular version of FAT is supported by the OS; N (No) indicates no support.

Table 2-2	FAT File System Support	
OS	*FAT/FAT16*	*FAT32*
DOS	Y	N
Windows 3.x	Y	N
Windows 9x	Y	Y
Windows NT	Y	N

(continued)

Table 2-2 *(continued)*

OS	FAT/FAT16	FAT32
Windows 2000	Y	Y
Windows Me	Y	Y
Windows XP	Y	Y

Checking for names

Both FAT16 and FAT32 in Windows 9x and Me allow *long filenames* (LFNs). Some LFN facts that you should know are as follows:

✔ Each LFN has a DOS 8.3 filename alias that consists of the first six characters of the LFN followed by a tilde symbol (~) and a number that increments for multiple occurrences of filenames with the same first six characters.

For example, the first occurrence of the long filename THIS IS MY FILENAME.DOC has an 8.3 alias of THISIS~1.DOC.

✔ An LFN is limited to 255 characters, but an 8.3 filename is limited to its 11 characters (plus the period). An LFN full-directory pathname is limited to 260 characters, and an 8.3 pathname is limited to 80 characters.

Removing all barriers

Before upgrading the Windows version on a PC, halt all running applications, including the antivirus software. Windows upgrades the master boot record on the hard drive, which is usually tenaciously protected by the antivirus software.

Windows cannot load or run if HIMEM.SYS is not loaded to memory.

Meeting the minimums — Windows 9x and Me

Microsoft has two sets of minimum hardware requirements for the Windows 9x and Me systems: a bare minimum on which the system can run (but who knows how well?) and a recommended minimum on which the system can smoothly run (but perhaps not much better). Tables 2-3 and 2-4 list Microsoft's minimum and recommended system requirements for Windows 98 and Windows Me, respectively.

Table 2-3	Minimum and Recommended System Requirements for Windows 98	
Component	*Minimum*	*Recommended*
Processor	486DX/66	Pentium
Memory	16MB	24MB
Hard drive	180MB	295MB
Video card	VGA	SVGA
CD-ROM drive	Required (2X)	Required (2X)
Mouse	Required	Required

Table 2-4	Minimum and Recommended System Requirements for Windows Me	
Component	*Minimum*	*Recommended*
Processor	Pentium/150 MHz	Pentium/150 MHz
Memory	32MB	32MB
Hard drive	480MB	645MB
Video card	VGA	SVGA
CD-ROM drive	Required (2X)	Required (2X)
Mouse	Required	Required

Installing Windows 98

The process that is used to install Windows 98 involves the following five major steps:

- **System check:** SETUP.EXE verifies that the minimum hardware requirements are met and that antivirus software is not running, and it runs SCANDISK to check the integrity of the hard drive.

- **Information collection:** Windows 98 collects the information that it needs to complete the installation. The information may come from the user, a script, or an existing Windows 9*x* version that is being updated. This information includes the type of installation (Typical, Compact, Portable, or Custom), the user's name, the PC's name, and more.

 ✔ **Copying files:** The Windows 98 files are copied to the hard drive.

 ✔ **System restart:** The PC is restarted into Windows 98. The OS then makes its modifications to the system files (`WIN.INI`, `SYSTEM.INI`, and the Registry) and adjusts the `CONFIG.SYS` and `AUTOEXEC.BAT` files, if present.

 ✔ **Hardware setup:** Windows 98 searches for any Plug and Play and legacy devices on the system and configures them. The system is restarted once again after this step.

All versions of Windows install from the `SETUP.EXE` command, which can be executed from My Computer, Windows Explorer, or a command-line prompt, or by the Autorun feature of the CD-ROM drive. Windows 9*x* and all later versions can be installed from a CD or across a network. However, Windows 2000 does have a floppy disk option that allows you to create four floppy disks that can be used to install that Windows version.

Dealing with installation problems

During the installation process, the Windows 9*x* and Me systems create a variety of log files that can be used to recover from installation crashes. For the most part, the log files are written to the root directory of the *destination disk* (the disk on which Windows is being installed). However, some of the log files are written to the Windows directory on the destination disk. These log files are as follows:

 ✔ `BOOTLOG.TXT`: The results of the initial boot of the Windows system.

 ✔ `DETLOG.TXT`: The results of the hardware-detection steps.

 ✔ `DETCRASH.LOG`: An internal file that is used by Windows 9*x* to recover from a crash during installation.

 ✔ `MODEMDET.TXT`: This file, which is found in the WINDOWS directory, contains the results of autodetecting a modem on the PC.

 ✔ `NETLOG.TXT`: The results of the network software startup.

 ✔ `SETUPLOG.TXT`: A log of the Setup program's actions before and after hardware detection.

Dual-booting Windows 9x

With Windows 9*x* systems, you can create a dual-boot environment on a PC. You should know the following things about creating a dual-boot environment:

 ✔ **Disk space:** Enough disk space must be available to support both operating systems. If the dual boot is with MS-DOS, the DOS version must be able to support disk partitions greater than 32MB.

✔ **Private directory:** Windows 9*x* must be in its own directory with no other version of Windows present.

✔ **Compatibility:** Windows 95 and Windows 98 can be dual-booted with MS-DOS, OS/2, Windows NT, Windows 2000, and Windows XP.

Modifying MSDOS.SYS

Entries in the MSDOS.SYS file tell the system that you want to boot the system from a menu that is displayed before the operating system is loaded each time that the PC starts up. To select which OS should boot, the following command is added to the [OPTIONS] area in the MSDOS.SYS file:

```
BootMulti=1
```

This option causes a boot menu to be displayed that lists the operating systems present on the PC. If the BootMulti option is set to 0, only Windows 9*x* boots. Other system options that are controlled by entries in the MSDOS.SYS file are the Windows splash screen, logo pages, and other displays and a few other system-level attributes and characteristics.

To change the MSDOS.SYS file, you must remove its blocking attributes by using the second command line. After this is done, you can use a text editor to modify the file. Remember to replace the attributes when you are finished editing the file.

If you edit the MSDOS.SYS file, make sure that its total file size remains greater than 1024 bytes.

Installing and running application software

The following processes can be used to install application software on a Windows system:

✔ The application may come with a self-extracting or self-installing application, which is titled SETUP.EXE, INSTALL.EXE, or something similar.

✔ The application is distributed on a CD-ROM that has an autorun applet, which automatically opens an installation window.

✔ The name of the installation applet is entered in the Start menu's Run box.

✔ The application is installed through the Control Panel's Add/Remove Programs icon.

Windows 9x System Files

For the A+ OS Technologies exam, know the part each system file plays in the boot process and its role in establishing the operating environment. You should study the Windows 9*x* files because many of them are still in use in later Windows versions. You should know about the following files:

- ✔ COMMAND.COM: This is the command processor for DOS and Windows 9*x*. It displays the DOS prompt and processes the commands that you type at the command prompt.

- ✔ HIMEM.SYS: This is the device driver for extended and high memory. If it is not loaded during startup, an error message is displayed and the system boots to a command prompt.

- ✔ IO.SYS: This binary executable file is loaded during the boot sequence. This file contains many of the commands and actions that were previously run from the CONFIG.SYS and AUTOEXEC.BAT files in early versions.

- ✔ LOGO.SYS: This is the 320 x 400 bitmapped wallpaper that is displayed during the boot sequence. To replace this file, create a 320 x 400 bitmapped (8-bit) file in MS Paint or another drawing package and save it as LOGO.SYS in the C: drive's root directory. Be sure to back up the original LOGO.SYS file first.

- ✔ MSDOS.SYS: This text file contains a number of startup and configuration variables and settings, including the BootMulti and BootMenu parameters that are used to indicate a system with multiple operating systems.

- ✔ SCANDISK.LOG: This is a log file that records the results of the most recent ScanDisk operation. The file is overwritten each time that this disk utility runs.

- ✔ SETUPLOG.TXT: This is a log file record that is created and updated during the installation process of Windows 9*x* by the Setup program. Should Setup crash, Windows uses this file to help identify the problem.

- ✔ SYSTEM.DAT: Along with USER.DAT, this is one of the two files in the Windows Registry. The Registry is a database of configuration data about a PC's hardware and operating environment.

- ✔ SYSTEM.INI: This system initialization file describes a PC's system environment, including device drivers, DOS application execution, and internal Windows settings.

- ✔ USER.DAT: Along with SYSTEM.DAT, this is one of two files in the Windows Registry.

- ✔ VMM32.VXD: This file is created during the Windows setup. It includes all virtual device drivers (VXDs) that are required by the system. At startup, it is much faster to load this one large VXD file than to load each of the individual drivers.

- ✔ WIN.INI: INI files are initialization files that describe or define the Windows environment. The WIN.INI file contains entries that tell Windows which programs to load and run and defines the screen, keyboard, mouse, display, and fonts. This file is read by the Windows operating system during startup.

Looking into the new IO.SYS

Many of the commands that were included in the CONFIG.SYS file on DOS and Windows 3.x systems are included in the IO.SYS file on a Windows 9x system. The IO.SYS file is not used on Windows NT or Windows 2000 systems. See Chapter 3 for more information on Windows NT and Windows 2000.

The COMMAND.COM files that are included in IO.SYS

The commands that the IO.SYS file loads on Windows 9x systems are as follows:

- ✔ DOS=HIGH: This command indicates that DOS (kernel) should be loaded into the high memory area. A UMB (upper memory block) parameter is included if EMM386.EXE is loaded from the CONFIG.SYS file. IO.SYS does not load EMM386.EXE.

- ✔ DEVICE=HIMEM.SYS: This command enables real-mode memory managers, specifically EMM386.EXE. HIMEM.SYS must be loaded before Windows 9x can start up.

- ✔ DEVICE=IFSHLP.SYS: This command enables file and print sharing and 32-bit disk access.

- ✔ DEVICE=SETVER.EXE: This command allows the operating system to appear to be any operating system version that a legacy application requires, which is typically a DOS version.

- ✔ FCBS=4: This command sets the number of file control blocks (FCBs) that the system can have open at one time.

- ✔ SHELL=COMMAND.COM /P: This command sets the permanent (/P) command interpreter for the system. *Permanent* means that the command interpreter should not be unloaded from memory.

✔ DOS compatibility commands: The following commands, which are used only by DOS and Windows 3.*x* systems, are also included:

- `FILES=60`: This command sets the number of DOS file handles.

- `LASTDRIVE=Z`: This command sets the highest drive letter that can be assigned to a device or a network drive.

- `BUFFERS=30`: This command sets the number of file buffers that the system should create.

- `STACKS=9,256`: This command sets the number and size of stack frames.

To override any setting in the `IO.SYS` file, enter the command into the `CONFIG.SYS` file. This command is loaded after the `IO.SYS` file, and any commands and parameters supersede those that are loaded from the `IO.SYS` file.

AUTOEXEC.BAT commands that are included in IO.SYS

The `IO.SYS` file also loads many of the commands that are loaded from the `AUTOEXEC.BAT` file in earlier versions of Windows, including the following:

✔ `TMP=C:\WINDOWS\TEMP`: This command assigns the folder for temporary files.

✔ `PROMPT=$P$G`: This command establishes the format of the command prompt to `C:\>`.

✔ `PATH=C:\WINDOWS; C:\WINDOWS\COMMAND`: This command and its two parameters add the two pathnames to the DOS search path.

✔ `COMSPEC=C:\WINDOWS\COMMAND\COMMAND.COM`: This command specifies the location of the command interpreter file.

Entries in an `AUTOEXEC.BAT` file in the root directory of the boot disk override or add to those in the `IO.SYS` file.

The command-line prompt

You should recognize the following as the DOS/Windows command-line prompt:

```
C:\>
```

This version of the command-line prompt indicates that the C: drive is the active hard drive and that the active directory (folder) is the root (\) directory. Commands that can be entered in the Run box on the Start menu can also be entered at the command-line prompt and vice versa. To display the command-line prompt (in its own window), choose Start⇨Run and enter **COMMAND** in the Run box.

On a Windows 9*x* system, you can open the command prompt in an MS-DOS command prompt window from the Programs menu (choose Start⇨ Programs⇨MS-DOS Prompt). On Windows NT, 2000, and XP systems, choose Start⇨Run and enter the command **CMD** in the Run box to open a command prompt window.

Starting Windows 9x

The steps used to start up a Windows 9*x* system are as follows:

1. After the BIOS performs the POST, Plug and Play devices are configured if the PC has a Plug and Play BIOS.

2. The partition table is accessed, and the boot record activates IO.SYS.

3. The Windows 9*x* boot sequence starts in real mode and then switches to protected mode. From this point, the boot sequence is in real mode.

4. The MSDOS.SYS file is checked for any user-defined parameters (such as BootMulti or BootMenu).

5. If all is normal, the message Starting Windows 9*x* displays, and the sequence pauses for 2 seconds to wait for a function key. LOGO.SYS is displayed.

6. If file compression is in use, DRVSPACE.BIN loads.

7. The Registry (SYSTEM.DAT) is checked, and if it's valid, it loads.

8. Windows 9*x* performs hardware detection and identifies any new hardware.

9. If the CONFIG.SYS and AUTOEXEC.BAT files exist, IO.SYS processes their commands.

10. The boot sequence switches to protected mode, and WIN.COM is loaded.

11. The VMM32.VXD file and all virtual device drivers that are included in the Registry or the SYSTEM.INI file load.

12. The Windows 9*x* core components — Kernel, GDI, and User — load, along with Windows Explorer and all configured networking components.

13. Any applications that are in the Startup (Run Once) section of the Registry start.

14. The boot sequence ends.

Working with Windows utilities

The A+ OS Technologies blueprint lists a wide variety of Windows system utilities that you should know for the exam. As I recall, most of them are mentioned on the exam, either in a question or as an answer (correct or incorrect). You should know the following commands:

- ✔ ASD.EXE: ASD stands for *Automatic Skip Driver.* Whenever a driver cannot be loaded or when Windows 9*x* simply skips loading a driver, the action is recorded in a log file. ASD.EXE displays the contents of this log file so that you can determine why a particular device driver may not be active. This command is executed from the Start menu's Run box. Most of the time, ASD responds that no current ASD critical operation failures exist on the PC.

- ✔ CHKDSK: This utility can be used to check FAT and directory errors on a drive. The /F option can be added to the CHKDSK command to fix any errors found.

- ✔ EDIT.COM: This is a DOS/Windows utility that can be used to modify or create a text file. This command-line utility can also be used to print the contents of a text file.

- ✔ EXTRACT.EXE: This is a command-line utility, which means that it doesn't have a graphical user interface (GUI) display; it's used to extract and uncompress a file or multiple files from a compressed drive. This command is used to replace a corrupted system file with one that is located in the CAB (cabinet) directory (folder) of a Windows installation floppy disk or CD-ROM.

- ✔ HWINFO.EXE: This command-line utility opens a window that displays about everything that you would ever want to know about the hardware configuration and utilization of your PC. To execute this command, type **HWINFO.EXE /UI** in the Start menu's Run box. Figure 2-1 shows the display from the HWINFO command.

- ✔ MSCONFIG: As shown in Figure 2-2, this Windows 9*x* command, which is executed in the Start menu's Run box, opens a window that contains a variety of tabs. Each tab shows the data and current selections of a number of system files. The General tab of this window controls the process that is used during the operating system startup.

- ✔ REGEDIT.EXE: This command, which is executed from the Start menu's Run box, is the Registry editor for 16-bit Windows systems. Both this and the 32-bit Registry editor (REGEDT32.EXE) are distributed with Windows NT and 2000. See "The Windows Registry," later in this chapter, for more information on the Registry.

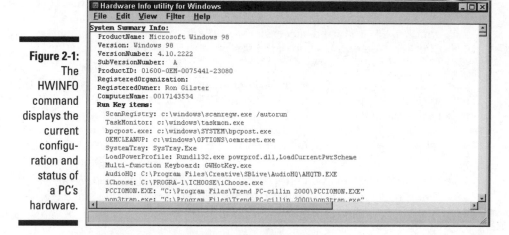

Figure 2-1:
The
HWINFO
command
displays the
current
configu-
ration and
status of
a PC's
hardware.

Figure 2-2:
The
Windows
System
Configu-
ration Utility
is started
with the
MSCONFIG
command.

✔ REGEDT32.EXE: This is the Registry editor for 32-bit Windows systems. Both this and the 16-bit Registry editor (REGEDIT.EXE) are distributed with Windows NT and 2000. REGEDT32.EXE allows for editing values in the Registry that are greater than 256 characters. See the section "The Windows Registry," later in this chapter, for more information on the Registry.

✔ SCANDISK: This utility is used to find and repair errors on the drive, including the file system structure (such as lost clusters and crosslinked files) and to rebuild the file allocation table (FAT) and the directory tree structure. It does not repair fragmented files, which is the job of DEFRAG.

✔ SCANREG: Windows 98 and Me include a very flexible Registry tool that can be used to back up and restore Registry files. Each time that a Windows PC is started successfully, SCANREG, or the Windows Registry Checker, creates a backup of the system and Registry files, including SYSTEM.DAT, USER.DAT, SYSTEM.INI, and WIN.INI.

✔ SYSEDIT: This stands for *system configuration editor*. This utility is used to view or edit system files, including the AUTOEXEC.BAT and CONFIG.SYS files and the WIN.INI, SYSTEM.INI, and PROTOCOL.INI initialization files. Each file is opened in a separate window (that is very much like the Windows Notepad text editor). Figure 2-3 shows the display of the SYSEDIT utility.

✔ WSCRIPT.EXE: This Windows 98 and 2000 utility enables you to run *scripts* (strings of instructions that are written in a scripting language, such as VBScript, Jscript, and PERL) in Windows.

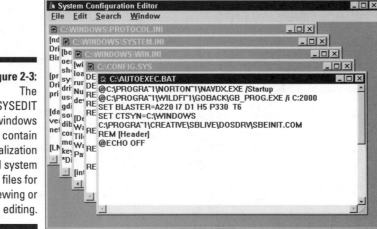

Figure 2-3: The SYSEDIT windows contain initialization and system files for viewing or editing.

Dealing with Windows Startup Errors

Much of the diagnosing and troubleshooting domain of the A+ OS Technologies exam consists of knowing the sequence of events that occurs in the boot sequences of Windows 9*x* systems, and recognizing error messages and their associated corrective actions. Memorize the boot sequences, and familiarize yourself with the error messages in each environment.

If the Windows startup sequence has problems, restart Windows and immediately press and hold down the Ctrl key during the boot process or press F8 after the message `Starting Windows 9x` appears to display the Startup Menu (from which you can start Windows in Safe mode). Safe mode starts Windows with only the essential device drivers being loaded. If the computer can successfully boot in Safe mode, you know that the problem is in a device or its driver.

Another boot menu option that can help you to isolate a boot problem is Step-by-Step Confirmation. This choice forces the system to boot by displaying system file entries one at a time so that you can include or exclude an entry from the boot process with keyboard entries. Answering No to every option is the same as booting in Safe mode.

If Windows won't boot to Safe mode, the system may have any of the following problems:

- ✔ The CMOS settings are incorrect.
- ✔ A hardware conflict exists, such as advanced BIOS settings, IRQ conflicts, duplicated COM ports, or defective memory modules.
- ✔ The `MSDOS.SYS` file contains an erroneous setting.
- ✔ The video drivers are not compatible.

You may also want to examine the contents of the `BOOTLOG.TXT` file, which is located in the root directory. This file contains a log of the results of device driver activation. The last line should list the driver that was attempting to load when the error occurred. If you suspect that the video driver is the problem, set the video drivers to either `VGA.DRV` or `VGA.VXD`; you can find both on the Windows CD-ROM.

Friendly Windows 9x error messages

Because DOS and Windows 3.*x* used up all the really good error messages, Windows 9*x* systems have had to resort to messages that actually make sense on occasion. Some of the very best error messages (or lack thereof) that Windows 9*x* has to offer are as follows:

- ✔ (No error message): The startup stops at a point after the POST but before Windows starts, but no error message is displayed. Run `FDISK` from a command-line prompt with the `/MBR` option to rebuild the MBR (master boot record). You may want to scan the disk with an antivirus program first, because the problem may be a boot virus or some equally scary problem with the MBR.

✔ `General Protection Fault in USER.EXE`: The User core component has run out of file space. Add the line `FILES=100` to the `CONFIG.SYS` file to fix this problem.

✔ `0E or 0D exception`: 0E errors refer to bad memory, and 0D errors are video problems. These errors are usually displayed on the "blue screen of death." Restart the system to clear the error. If the problem persists, check the CMOS for exceptions and verify the device drivers that are in use. To avoid the problem, try switching to standard VGA video mode.

✔ `Out of Memory`: This error is caused by memory leaks — programs that end without releasing their memory allocations. Reboot the system and reduce the activity on the system.

Booting Windows

Typically, when you start up your Windows 9*x* PC, the operating system runs through its normal startup procedure, which ends by displaying the desktop on the screen and showing all the applications that are included in the startup procedure running in the system tray. However, for the A+ OS Technologies exam, you should know how to access the Startup menu and start Windows 9*x* and Windows 2000 from it. You should know what each selection on the Startup menu does.

Changing your boots

To access the Windows Startup menu, you can either

✔ Press and hold down Ctrl while the PC is booting

✔ Press the F8 key right after you hear a beep, after the `Starting Windows` message displays, or when the Windows splash screen appears

The Windows 9*x* Startup menu includes the following entries:

✔ **Normal:** This selection is just what it sounds like: the normal Windows boot. Choosing this option (by entering **1**) continues the standard boot process.

✔ **Logged (**`BOOTLOG.TXT`**):** This selection completes a normal startup, but all startup actions are recorded in the `BOOTLOG.TXT` file in the root directory or on the startup disk.

✔ **Safe mode:** This selection completes the startup but bypasses the system files and loads only the essential system device drivers. You can go straight into Safe mode during the startup by pressing F5 right after the Windows splash screen appears (in Windows 98, Me, 2000, and XP) or by entering **WIN /D:M** at a command-line prompt.

✔ **Safe mode with network support:** This selection starts Windows in Safe mode but also loads the drivers that allow access to a network.

✔ **Step-by-step confirmation:** This selection allows you to confirm each of the actions that are contained in the system files one at a time. For each action, you are required to respond with a Y or an N to start the action or not to start it, respectively.

✔ **Command prompt only:** This selection starts up the operating system and loads the normal system files and the Registry but displays only a command-line prompt in place of the Windows desktop.

✔ **Safe mode command prompt only:** This selection starts Windows in Safe mode but displays only the command-line prompt.

The function-key options that can be used to select the Windows startup options are controlled by the BootKeys variable in the MSDOS.SYS file. If the BootKeys variable is set to 1 (the default), the function keys are available for use during startup. Setting this variable to 0 or setting the BootDelay variable to 0, which removes the delay that allows you to press a function key, removes the ability to use function keys to change the startup process.

When Windows won't boot

If Windows does not start normally, you should try to start it in Safe mode, which bypasses the real-mode drivers and configuration and loads a minimal protected-mode configuration that disables the Windows drivers and provides only a VGA display.

However, if Windows will not start in Safe mode, one of the following conditions is likely the cause:

✔ **The PC is infected with a virus.** Install and run an antivirus program on the PC.

✔ **The CMOS settings are wrong.** If you can access the BIOS setup program and the configuration data, check them for accuracy. Hopefully, you have a paper backup of what the CMOS settings should be. If not, you may need to contact the manufacturer to get the CMOS settings.

✔ **A system resource or hardware conflict exists.** Check for IRQ conflicts, duplicated COM ports, PCI BIOS settings, and possible defective RAM.

✔ **MSDOS.SYS has an incorrect setting.** Verify that no incomplete or invalid settings exist in this file.

✔ **A DriveSpace drive cannot mount a compressed volume file (CVF).** Follow the procedures in the Windows Help files for CVF files and for troubleshooting DriveSpace.

✔ **A Registry error exists.** Boot to the Command prompt only startup option and run SCANREG from the command-line prompt. See the preceding section for information on Windows startup options.

When all else fails, reinstall Windows into a new folder to determine if the problem is something that was left over from the previous operating system or Windows version.

If Windows boots to Safe mode, you should step through the startup process using the Selective Startup option of MSCONFIG (executed from the Start menu's Run box) to try several different startup options.

Using Device Manager to isolate startup problems

If a PC boots to Safe mode but the problem remains unsolved after scanning the Registry and startup process, the problem may be hardware related. Follow these steps to use Device Manager to help isolate the problem:

1. **Open Device Manager from the Control Panel's System icon or by right-clicking the My Computer icon and choosing Properties.**

2. **On the Device Manager tab, disable all the devices that are listed under the following device trees by right-clicking each device, choosing Properties, and checking the Disable in This Hardware Profile box, as shown in Figure 2-4:**

   - Display adapters
   - Floppy disk controllers
   - Hard drive controllers
   - Keyboard
   - Mouse
   - Network adapters (if present)
   - Ports
   - PCMCIA socket (if present)
   - SCSI controllers (if present)
   - Sound, video, and game controllers

3. **If the PC starts without the problem, begin enabling the devices in the following order until the problem repeats:**

   - COM ports
   - Hard drive controllers
   - Floppy disk controllers
   - Other devices

4. **Restart the PC after enabling each device. Also, check the Resources tab for each device to see whether any problems are shown in the Conflicting Device List.**

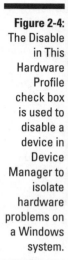

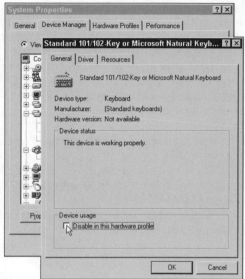

Figure 2-4: The Disable in This Hardware Profile check box is used to disable a device in Device Manager to isolate hardware problems on a Windows system.

Using Automatic Skip Driver

The Automatic Skip Driver (ASD) agent attempts to enable any disabled device that may be causing the startup problem and reports the problem. The ASD tool is located on the Accessories menu. To access the tool, choose Start⇨ Programs⇨Accessories⇨System Tools⇨System Information⇨Tools⇨ Automatic Skip Driver Agent.

Dealing with Common Problems

The A+ OS Technologies exam includes a number of questions about a variety of common Windows errors that a PC repairperson should be familiar with to isolate and solve problems on a user's PC.

When the system crashes

When Windows or one of its applications is seriously malfunctioning, the OS typically halts — this is also known as a crash, hang, freeze, or lockup — and displays an error message. General protection faults (GPFs) and invalid page faults are memory protection errors that are commonly the problem. These errors typically cause the crash of one or more Windows 9*x* programs and perhaps even Windows itself. They can either be the indicators of very serious problems or something very trivial that can be fixed with a restart.

Computer crashes, GPFs, and page faults are caused by Windows trying to store information in a space that's already in use by another program. Yes, Windows should know better and keep better records, but at the speeds that it is swapping data in and out of RAM and with programs starting and stopping, it easily becomes confused. Other error messages that you may see when the system crashes are: `Access Violation`, `Exception Error`, `Illegal Operation`, `Segment Load Failure`, and `Violation of System Integrity`. (I just love the presumption in the last one.)

GPF messages usually indicate where the error is occurring. The message is typically `General Protection Fault in module . . . at address . . .` or `Program name . . . has caused a General Protection Fault in module . . .` and may include an error code as well.

In most cases, restarting the PC clears the problem, but if the problem persists, you need to track it down and stamp it out.

Elementary, Dr. Watson

When you are investigating the mystery of a system crash, if you can imagine that you are Sherlock Holmes, Windows can offer assistance to help you track down the culprit with a software-environment sleuth named Dr. Watson.

Dr. Watson, although a valuable tool, is not included on the Programs menus. It is located in the `Windows` directory, and you can start it in the background by entering **DRWATSON** in the Run box. To isolate software failures, Dr. Watson must be running in the background at all times, which means that you must add it to the Startup folder. An icon is displayed in the taskbar tray when Dr. Watson is running. When you click this icon, Dr. Watson takes a snapshot of the system and displays any errors that it finds or possible problems that it foresees.

Other sources of help

If you isolate which program is causing the system to crash, check the publisher's Web site for troubleshooting help or upgrade information. A good example of a publisher's troubleshooting Web site is Netscape's GPF pages, which are located at the following URL:

```
http://help.netscape.com/kb/consumer/19970702-6.html
```

Dealing with Windows protection errors

A Windows protection error may appear when you start up or shut down a Windows system. During startup, you may see an error message like the following:

```
While initializing device . . . Windows Protection Error
```

The device name is inserted after the word *device*. When you are shutting down Windows, the error message is simply as follows:

```
Windows Protection Error
```

A Microsoft Windows protection error happens when a virtual device driver (VXD) is being loaded or unloaded. Typically, if the error occurs when a driver is being loaded, the message contains the name of the device, which makes it easy to isolate and fix the problem. However, these errors can also occur due to several other problems, including the following:

- A real-mode driver and a protected-mode driver have been loaded for the same device.
- The Registry is corrupted.
- WIN.COM or COMMAND.COM is damaged or infected with a virus.
- A file that is referenced in SYSTEM.INI, WIN.INI, or the Registry is invalid.
- The CMOS settings for peripheral devices that are built into the motherboard (cache, hard drive controller, and others) are incorrect.
- The BIOS program's Plug and Play feature is not working.
- The motherboard, system cache, or memory is not working properly.

Other Windows problems

The A+ OS Technologies exam also references other Windows problems in the context of "If this or that happens, what is your next action?" In most cases, the action to take is a choice between one or two common-sense items. Count on questions that give you scenarios and ask you what your action is. For example, if you encounter a question about an illegal operation error, your response should depend on the cause of the error. The most common cases are as follows:

- **After new hardware or software is installed:** Remove the new item and reboot.
- **In only one software application:** Uninstall the program, delete its folder, and reinstall the program.
- **If the problem appears to be power related:** Move the power supply's cord to a new electrical outlet.
- **Undetermined hardware problem:** Remove all external devices, and add them back one at a time to find the problem device.

See Book I, Chapter 17 for more information on troubleshooting procedures for hardware issues.

A few other Windows errors that you should be familiar with are as follows:

- **Invalid working directory:** This error typically occurs when the user is trying to start a program from a shortcut or icon. This message means that the working directory of the program (the one that is used to store temporary files or initialization data) is not valid or is missing. Either the entry in the icon's properties has a typo or the directory has been inadvertently deleted. Either correct the icon's Start In line in its Properties window or restore the folder.

- **System busy:** This message usually accompanies the blue screen of death and suggests that you wait for the system to become available or reboot. Depending on your patience, you can wait awhile before you reboot.

- **Application will not start or load:** There are a couple of possible problems:

  - Enough system resources may not be available to start the job, or the application's EXE file may be corrupted. If the application should be able to load but won't, uninstall it, reboot, and reinstall it. Another cause for this problem may be that the application requires more memory space than the PC has available. In this case, more memory should be installed, or a different application used.

  - The application may be a DOS application that cannot run in a Windows DOS window. Try running the application after rebooting into MS-DOS mode.

- **Cannot log on to network:** Let me count the ways that you may see this error message: The network configuration has been changed or corrupted, the cable is missing from the network interface card (NIC), the network itself is down, the user has been removed from the network users list, and so on. On a Windows 9x system, check out the Network settings in the Control Panel and, if all is well, check the network end before opening the hardware. Chapter 7 covers networking and networking problems in more detail.

- **Windows printing problems:** The A+ OS Technologies exam's blueprint lists a number of printing errors that you should know about. The good news is that you find virtually no questions about this area on the exam. Book I, Chapter 13 details how a printer is added and set as the default printer on a Windows system; this is what you need to know about printing for the exam.

Installing Hardware in Windows 9x

If Windows recognizes a device as a supported device, hardware installation proceeds with virtually no external input needed. If a device is a supported device (other than PnP), Windows suggests system resource assignments and prompts for confirmation to complete the installation. Intervention from the user is usually needed for legacy cards or unsupported devices to supply a device driver to be loaded.

On a Windows 9x system, hardware belongs to one of the following four groups:

- **Plug and Play (PnP):** Windows 9x systems (including Me) are PnP operating systems that configure PnP devices, even when the PC's BIOS is not PnP-compliant. On some systems, you may need to disable the BIOS program's PnP settings and just let Windows take care of configuring PnP devices.

- **32-bit supported devices:** Windows 9x carries a variety of 32-bit device drivers for peripheral devices that are directly supported. These drivers are included on the Windows CD-ROM and are loaded automatically when the devices are detected during the installation process.

- **Unsupported 32-bit devices:** These devices may be compatible with a user's computer, but Windows may not include drivers for them. The manufacturer usually supplies compatible drivers on a floppy disk, which means that when you are installing the device, you should use the Have Disk option.

- **Legacy cards and adapters:** These 16-bit or 8-bit adapters and interface cards may cause system resource conflicts. They are usually configured through DIP switches and jumpers.

The Windows Registry

While Windows 3.x was a virtual forest of INI files, beginning with Windows 95, the configuration and execution instructions for Windows and its installed applications were consolidated into the Windows Registry. The Windows Registry is a special hierarchical database that contains a complete profile of the system configuration and program settings, eliminating the need for most of the INI files.

The Registry records the overall hardware and software configuration and associations of the Windows system. Expect to see at least three or four test questions about the Windows Registry. The questions do not drill down to a specific Windows version and are very generic, recognizing that a PC repairperson should not necessarily be mucking about in the Registry.

You should know these facts about the Registry:

- ✔ The two Registry files are USER.DAT and SYSTEM.DAT.
- ✔ The file extension for Registry file backups is .DAO.
- ✔ The acronym HKEY stands for Handle for a Key.
- ✔ If you export part of or the entire Registry to back it up, the exported data is placed in a file with an .REG extension.
- ✔ The Registry is organized in a tree hierarchy around six major keys. Each key is a major branch of the Registry database and holds information that relates to the subject of the branch.

The six major keys of the Windows Registry are as follows:

- ✔ HKEY_CLASSES_ROOT: This key holds file associations and OLE (Object Linking and Embedding) data.
- ✔ HKEY_USERS: This key holds user preferences, including desktop setup and network connections.
- ✔ HKEY_CURRENT_USER: On a PC with only a single user, this key is a duplicate of the HKEY_USERS key. However, on a PC with multiple logins, this key contains the preferences of the currently logged-in user.
- ✔ HKEY_LOCAL_MACHINE: This key manages the hardware and software that is installed on the system.
- ✔ HKEY_CURRENT_CONFIG: In addition to duplicating the HKEY_LOCAL_MACHINE key when running, this key also contains any configuration changes that were made in the current session and has information on the printers and fonts that are installed.
- ✔ HKEY_DYN_DATA: This key records system performance information and keeps information on Plug and Play devices.

The Registry is organized into keys, and you need to know the contents of each key. The A+ OS Technologies exam doesn't ask you to match the key to the type of information that it contains, but the exam may include a key name in a question, and you need to know the context that it connotes.

Editing the Registry, if you dare

Use the REGEDIT.EXE program to edit Registry files. Make changes to the Registry only with extreme caution and care. Be sure that you back up both the SYSTEM.DAT and USER.DAT files before making any changes to the Registry. You may want to back up these files before you install new Windows software to the system as well, because each installation modifies the Registry. Figure 2-5 is a screen capture of this program, displaying the contents of a Windows 98 Registry.

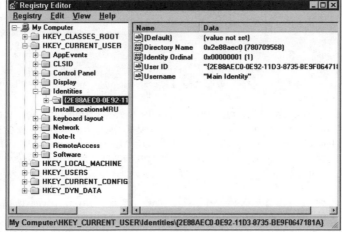

Figure 2-5:
A Windows 98 Registry that is displayed in a REGEDIT window.

Getting Around in Windows without a Mouse

Many different key combinations can be used to manipulate, navigate, and configure Windows straight from the keyboard. You should know the following key combinations for the A+ OS Technologies exam:

 ✔ **Alt (or F10):** Toggles the cursor control between the menu bar of the current application and the application itself.

 ✔ **Alt+Esc:** Cycles through the applications that are running in the taskbar.

 ✔ **Alt+F4:** Closes the current application. If no applications are running, this key combination displays the Shut Down box.

✔ **Alt+Spacebar:** Displays the Control menu of the current application window. Pressing Alt closes the menu.

✔ **Alt+Tab:** Shows a menu and cycles through the icons of the applications that are running in the taskbar.

✔ **Ctrl+Alt+Delete:** Displays the Close Program box when you are not faced with an error screen. From the blue screen of death, this key combination restarts the system.

✔ **Ctrl+Esc:** Shows the Start menu and taskbar.

✔ **Ctrl+Tab and Ctrl+Shift+Tab:** Move you through the tabs in a dialog box.

✔ **Shift:** When inserting a CD-ROM, stops autorun programs that are on or associated with the CD-ROM.

Getting Ready for Work

Windows 9*x* uses a virtual memory manager (VMM) that includes default settings for how much drive space is to be used for virtual memory. For the average user, the default settings should meet your needs. However, for users that have more than one hard disk drive or require speed-tuning their system, some manual configuration of the virtual memory system may be required.

To configure virtual memory on a Windows 9*x* system, follow these steps:

1. **Open the Control Panel and double-click the System icon to open the System Properties window.**

2. **Click the Performance tab, and click the Virtual Memory button.**

3. **In the Virtual Memory settings window, click the Let Me Specify My Own Virtual Memory Settings option (assuming that you want to do this) to activate the configuration options.**

4. **Choose the hard drive that you want to configure, assuming that you have more than one.**

   If you have only one drive, skip to Step 6.

5. **I recommend that you split the virtual memory equally between the physical hard drives that are installed in the PC.**

6. **In the Minimum box, enter the smallest hard drive space that you want virtual memory to allocate on the currently chosen hard drive.**

   The minimum should be 2MB.

7. **In the Maximum box, set the largest space for virtual memory.**

   You can assign as much drive space as you want to virtual memory, up to and including the total space on the hard drive. (This is not recommended if you have only one drive in the PC.) A safe maximum is two times the amount of system RAM. The default is 12MB more than the amount of RAM in the PC.

8. **Close the dialog boxes to return to the Control Panel, and if you are not asked to do so, restart the PC.**

Prep Test

1 **What command displays the version of the running version of MS-DOS and allows the running version to be set to that needed by real-mode programs that are running on a PC?**

A ○ VER

B ○ SETVER

C ○ CHGVER

D ○ MKVER

2 **The ScanDisk utility can fix errors in which of the following? (Choose two.)**

A ❑ Directory tree structure

B ❑ Fragmented files

C ❑ File system structure

D ❑ Media defects

3 **What key combination is used to display the Windows 9*x* Start menu and taskbar?**

A ○ Ctrl+Alt+Delete

B ○ Alt+Tab

C ○ Ctrl+Esc

D ○ Alt+F4

4 **Pressing F5 during system startup allows Windows to start in which mode?**

A ○ Command prompt only

B ○ Safe mode command prompt only

C ○ Safe mode with network support

D ○ Safe mode

5 **Which of the following files is required in a Windows 9*x* CONFIG.SYS file?**

A ○ HIMEM.SYS

B ○ FILES=

C ○ UMB-

D ○ DOS=HIGH

E ○ None of the above

6 **What are the minimum requirements for Windows Me?**

A ○ 100-MHz Pentium processor, 16MB of RAM, 120MB of free hard drive space

B ○ 233-MHz Pentium processor, 8MB of RAM, 200MB of free hard drive space

C ○ 150-MHz Pentium processor, 32MB of RAM, 480MB of free hard drive space

D ○ 133-MHz Pentium processor, 32MB of RAM, 650MB of free hard drive space

7 **To dual-boot a Windows 9x system, the** `BootMulti` **variable must be set in which system file?**

A ○ `IO.SYS`

B ○ `AUTOEXEC.BAT`

C ○ `MSDOS.SYS`

D ○ `CONFIG.SYS`

8 **Which of the following are Windows 98 Registry files? (Choose two.)**

A ❑ `SYSTEM.DAT`

B ❑ `USER.DAT`

C ❑ `SYSTEM.SYS`

D ❑ `REG.DAT`

9 **Which of the following utilities and applications can be used to troubleshoot an application error?**

A ○ `SCANREG`

B ○ `HWINFO.EXE`

C ○ Dr. Watson

D ○ `MSCONFIG`

10 **A Windows 9x system has displayed an error message and booted to a command-line prompt. What is likely to be the problem?**

A ○ `HIMEM.SYS` did not load.

B ○ `VMM32.VXD` is corrupted.

C ○ A file referenced in `SYSTEM.INI` is invalid.

D ○ The Registry is missing.

Answers

1 **B.** The SETVER command creates a real-mode emulation that allows programs that were written for legacy DOS versions to run. *See "First, some DOS facts."*

2 **A & C.** This command is used during installation to verify the integrity of the hard drive and during startup to check the drive when the system has not been shut down properly. *Check out "Working with Windows utilities."*

3 **C.** For some unknown reason, CompTIA has decided that you need to know these keystrokes to pass the A+ exams. *Review "Getting Around in Windows without a Mouse."*

4 **D.** You could also press F8 and choose Safe mode from the Startup menu. *Take a look at "Changing your boots."*

5 **E.** Okay, so this is a trick question, but the lesson here is to examine every available answer choice. Yes, the CONFIG.SYS file is not required for a Windows 9*x* system, which means that no required entries are in it. *See "The Windows 9x boot sequence."*

6 **C.** I wish I knew a shortcut to remembering these numbers, but I don't. You just need to memorize them. *Look over "Meeting the minimums — Windows 9x."*

7 **C.** The MSDOS.SYS file contains many startup variables that are used to set the operating environment for Windows. *Review "Modifying MSDOS.SYS."*

8 **A & B.** These are the primary files in the Registry database on Windows 98 systems. *Check out "The Windows Registry."*

9 **C.** Dr. Watson can be executed to run in the background and monitor all applications, or it can be run periodically, to take a snapshot of the system. *Investigate "Elementary, Dr. Watson."*

10 **A.** If I haven't already told you, HIMEM.SYS must be running for Windows 9*x* to start up. *Take a look at "Windows Files and Commands."*

Chapter 3

Windows 2000 Professional

• •

Exam Objectives

▶ Identifying the components and functions of Windows 2000 Professional

▶ Upgrading to Windows 2000

▶ Explaining the startup and shutdown procedures of Windows 2000

▶ Recognizing Windows 2000 error messages

• •

*T*he A+ OS Technologies exam deals only with personal computer operating systems in the context of the PC repairperson's ability to install, configure, and troubleshoot the entire PC, including its operating system. You need to be aware of the problems that an operating system has so that you can separate software problems from hardware problems.

You don't need to know Windows 2000 Professional (or any other operating system) so thoroughly that you could single-handedly put Microsoft's technical support hotline out of business (not that we haven't all had that thought in more violent tones at one time or another). However, you must be able to set up a Windows 2000 PC and use its features and utilities to configure the PC for a user and be able to troubleshoot and isolate problems.

As the hardware of the PC becomes more mature and sophisticated, software plays an increasing role in the PC repairperson's daily life, not to mention a huge role in his or her certification.

Quick Assessment

1 The _____ is used to verify if a hardware device or computer is compatible with Windows 2000.

2 The _____ contains the device drivers and control software that are used by the kernel to communicate with the hardware on a Windows 2000 system.

3 The editing tool that is used to add or change settings in the Windows 2000 Registry is _____.

4 The _____ utility can be used to check for system resource and file-sharing conflicts.

5 To display the command-line prompt from a Windows 2000 system, enter the command _____ in the Run box.

6 The phases of the Windows 2000 setup are _____, _____, and _____.

7 The command that is used to create a set of Windows 2000 startup disks is _____.

8 _____ is the bootstrap loader program for Windows 2000.

9 The boot mode that starts up Windows 2000 with only essential device drivers and services is _____.

10 Windows 2000 _____ messages are also known as blue screen messages.

Answers

1 *HCL (Hardware Compatibility List).* See "Upgrading to Windows 2000."

2 *HAL (Hardware Abstraction Layer).* Review "Looking into Windows NT."

3 *REGEDT32.EXE.* Check out "Managing a Windows 2000 computer."

4 *MSINFO32EXE.* Take a look at "Managing a Windows 2000 computer."

5 *CMD.* Read over "Displaying the Command Prompt."

6 *Setup loader, text-mode setup, GUI-mode setup.* See "The phases of the Windows 2000 setup."

7 *MAKEBOOT.EXE.* Review "Creating startup disks."

8 *NTLDR.* Look over "Starting Up Windows 2000."

9 *Safe mode.* Check out "Playing it safe."

10 *Stop.* Study "The joy of Windows 2000 stop messages."

Looking into Windows NT

As is proudly advertised on the splash screen of Windows 2000 and Windows XP, both of these Windows versions are based on the technology that was first introduced with the Windows NT system. In many instances, to know something about Windows NT and its core functions is to know how Windows 2000 and XP operate. If you are new to operating systems, especially the latest Windows operating systems, knowing about NT may not be needed — just understand 2000 and XP in detail. However, for those of you who have worked with NT in the past (or use it in the present), your road to understanding 2000 and XP is definitely a lot shorter.

If Windows NT is mentioned on the A+ OS Technologies exam, it is Windows NT Workstation that is being referenced.

Windows NT is a multithreaded, multitasking operating system that runs its applications in protected-mode memory space. This means that an unruly application cannot crash the entire system, and a problem with one application can't cause problems in other applications.

Windows NT requires a logon, which then assigns security and control permissions through the user's profile. Windows NT is designed for use in a networked environment and includes support for Internet protocols such as TCP/IP, IPX, and Dial-Up Networking. It also works well in a stand-alone mode.

Windows NT can run on a wide variety of hardware, because it isolates any unique programming that is needed to support a specific piece of hardware in the *Hardware Abstraction Layer (HAL)*. Windows NT has releases that are compatible with the Intel *x*86 architecture, the MIPS RISC architecture, Digital Alpha, and Motorola PowerPC RISC. In comparison, Windows 2000 runs only on the *x*86 and Digital Alpha platforms, so far.

One area where Windows NT outperforms Windows 9*x* is security. The logon sequence begins by the user pressing Ctrl+Alt+Delete, the key combination that is typically used to warm-start the PC. This prevents a program from spoofing the logon to steal your account name and password. By the way, after you've logged on, pressing Ctrl+Alt+Delete displays the Windows NT Security dialog box.

Windows NT supports *RAID (Redundant Array of Independent Disks)* on SCSI drives. RAID is a high-availability, high-reliability data-redundancy feature that is usually reserved for servers. See Book I, Chapter 8 for more information on RAID systems.

Table 3-1 compares the technical features of Windows NT and Windows 9x. Note the differences in the hardware requirements (RAM, hard drive, and CPU) without memorizing them. However, take a good look at the networking support and file systems.

Table 3-1	Comparison of Windows 9x and Windows NT	
Feature	*Win 98*	*Win NT 4.0*
Min. RAM	16MB	32MB
Min. hard drive	80MB	100MB
Min. CPU	486–66 MHz	Pentium–100 MHz
Networking	NetBIOS	NetBIOS
	IPX	IPX
	TCP/IP	TCP/IP
	DHCP	DHCP
	Dial-Up Networking	Dial-Up Networking
File system	FAT16/FAT32	FAT16/FAT32/NTFS

Know the system files that are used in Windows 2000, and understand how they replace or compare to the files that are used in Windows 9x and Windows NT. Remember that you are getting certified as PC repairperson, so don't get sidetracked studying the functions of Windows NT Server or Windows 2000 Server. That part of operating system technology has been reserved for the Server+ exam, for which you'll surely need a copy of my *Server+ Certification For Dummies* (Wiley Publishing, Inc.), available at book stores everywhere.

Getting to Know Windows 2000

Some people say that Windows 2000 is just the next version of Windows NT 4.0, and Windows 2000 was unofficially known for a short while as Windows NT 5.0. Windows 2000 comes in four distinct versions, but only Windows 2000 Professional (the name Professional replaces the name Workstation for business desktop systems) and Windows 2000 Server are mentioned on the A+ OS Technologies exam. To satisfy your curiosity, the other versions are Windows 2000 Advanced Server and Windows 2000 Datacenter Server.

You can upgrade a PC to Windows 2000 Professional from either Windows 98 or Windows NT Workstation. Windows 2000 has a Windows 98/NT–like desktop and interface, and it reads and supports FAT32 files — which incidentally is something that Windows NT 4.0 wouldn't do.

Table 3-2 lists the minimum system requirements for Windows 2000. Understand that when referring to minimums, Microsoft means "bare minimums," and more or bigger everything is always better.

Table 3-2	Windows 2000 Minimum System Requirements
Component	*Minimum Requirement*
Processor	133-MHz Pentium-compatible
Memory (RAM)	64MB
Hard drive capacity	2GB
Hard drive free space	650MB
Required drive	CD-ROM or DVD
Display resolution	VGA or higher
Input device required	Keyboard (mouse recommended)

Windows 2000 requires a CD-ROM drive because a CD-ROM is the standard distribution media. Although a mouse isn't a requirement and is only recommended for Windows 2000, believe me, you definitely need a mouse or some kind of pointing device on any Windows version.

Installing Windows 2000

For the A+ OS Technologies exam, you need to know what steps are used to prepare for and install Windows 2000 on a PC and how to verify compatibility between the operating system and the hardware, software, and file structure of the PC.

When installing Windows 2000, whether it's a clean installation or an upgrade from an earlier Windows version, you must first take a few steps to ensure that installation will be successful and that you won't encounter serious problems during or after the installation.

However, before installing Windows 2000 on any system, check the Windows 2000 Hardware Compatibility List (HCL) for all the field replacement modules (FRMs) that are installed. Check Windows 2000's hardware and software compatibility lists to see if your hardware and software are listed, and then convert your operating system to Windows 2000. Take a few minutes to orient yourself with the HCL by visiting Microsoft's Hardware and Software Compatibility Web site. An HCL is located on the installation CD-ROM, but it is likely to be out of date. Your best bet is to use the online HCL at the following Microsoft Web site:

```
www.microsoft.com/windows2000/professional/howtobuy/upgrading
```

The HCL on the Microsoft Web site includes any recent updates to the compatibility list. You can also check the compatibility of your software applications on this Web site.

If you find that your hardware is not supported, check with the manufacturer for a Windows 2000–compatible device driver or for information on when a Windows 2000 driver will be available.

Upgrading to Windows 2000

Whether you're installing Windows 2000 on a fresh (clean) hard drive or upgrading a previous version of Windows, the process is essentially the same. Of course, you must complete a few preparation steps when upgrading, most of which are required and some that are just highly recommended (which you should interpret as being highly required).

Getting ready to install Windows 2000

When upgrading to Windows 2000, before you even put the Windows 2000 installation CD-ROM in the drive, you must complete the following six actions:

- ✔ **Ensure that the current Windows version is upgradeable.** Table 3-3 lists the Windows versions that can and cannot be upgraded to Windows 2000. Just because a Windows version cannot be upgraded doesn't mean that you can't install Windows 2000 on that PC. However, Windows 2000 must be installed with a clean install, that is, using a freshly partitioned and formatted hard drive. Even when an upgrade is permitted, I recommend that you install Windows 2000 using a clean install.

- ✔ **Verify that the hardware and application software are compatible.** Windows 2000 claims to support a wide selection of PCs, peripheral devices, and application software. However, it doesn't support a significant amount of hardware and software. Before you begin, verify that the PC meets the minimum system requirements (see the section "Meeting the minimums," earlier in the chapter). Check the HCL on either the CD-ROM or on Microsoft's Windows 2000 Web site. (See the section "Installing Windows 2000," earlier in this chapter, for Web site information.)

✔ **Make sure that the device drivers for all active devices are Windows 2000 compatible.** Make sure that you have compatible versions of all device drivers before installing Windows 2000, especially for essential devices, such as the monitor and printer. It's hard to know what is going wrong when Windows does not complete the boot because of an incompatible video driver.

✔ **Ensure that the PC's BIOS is current and compatible with Windows 2000.** If the BIOS isn't the latest version available, the advanced power management and device configuration features of Windows 2000 may not function. See Book I, Chapter 4 for information on updating the system BIOS.

✔ **Have a recovery plan in case Windows 2000 cannot be uninstalled.** You can cancel the installation process at a couple of points during the process, but once Windows 2000 is installed, you must format the hard drive and install another operating system using a clean install to get rid of Windows 2000. Of course, if you installed Windows 2000 in a multi-boot environment, not all is lost. I also recommend making a full backup of your hard drive before beginning a Windows 2000 installation.

✔ **If you plan to install Windows 2000 from a DOS command prompt, determine which installation command you should use.** You have a choice between WINNT.EXE and WINNT32.EXE. Refer to the following hints when making your choice:

- WINNT.EXE: This program is used when the system is booted to DOS (from a DOS partition) or from a DOS boot floppy disk.

- WINNT32.EXE: This program is used when you are performing an upgrade installation from within a 32-bit system, such as Windows 9*x* or Windows NT.

Table 3-3	Is It Upgradeable to Windows 2000?
Windows Version	*Upgradeable?*
Windows 3.*x*	No
Windows 9*x*	Yes
Windows Me	No
Windows NT Workstation 3.51 or 4.0	Yes

Checking out the disk

Along with the installation files, the Windows 2000 CD-ROM also contains tools and utilities that you should know about. You can find the following folders on the CD-ROM:

- BOOTDISK: This folder contains

  - The image files that are used to create the four boot disks for Windows 2000.

  - The MAKEBOOT.EXE and MAKEBT32.EXE command-line programs that are used to create the book disks. MAKEBOOT.EXE is a 16-bit program that is used to make boot disks from a DOS prompt. MAKEBT32.EXE is the 32-bit version and should be used to make boot disks from 32-bit Windows versions, such as Windows 98, 2000, Me, or XP.

- I386: This folder contains a variety of files and folders that make up the Windows 2000 installation set. Included are the command-line programs that can be used to execute the Windows 2000 setup from either a DOS or Windows 9*x* boot disk (WINNT.EXE) or directly from Windows 9*x*, Windows NT, or Windows 2000 (WINNT32.EXE). Of course, you can also let the Autorun feature of the CD-ROM start the installation automatically.

- SETUPTXT: This folder contains two Windows 9*x* Notepad–compatible files that contain the release notes and setup documentation for Windows 2000.

- SUPPORT: This folder contains the TOOLS folder, which has a subset of the full Windows 2000 Resource Kit, a version of the HCL that was issued on a previous date (for example, many are dated December 7, 1999), and the APCOMPAT.EXE utility, which is the Windows 2000 version of the DOS SETVER command. Use the HCL on the CD-ROM first. Then visit the Microsoft Windows 2000 Web site to check compatibility. (See the section "Upgrading to Windows 2000," earlier in this chapter.)

Running the Windows 2000 Setup

Depending on the PC and its operating system, the Windows 2000 setup program can be started in one of the following ways:

- **From a DOS or Windows 9*x* command line:** Execute WINNT.EXE.

- **From a Windows 9*x* or Windows NT Run box:** Execute WINNT32.EXE.

- **From any upgradeable system:** Allow the CD-ROM's Autorun feature to execute the Setup program.

To suppress the Autorun feature on a Windows installation CD-ROM, press Shift when you close the CD-ROM tray.

The phases of the Windows 2000 setup

The three general phases of a Windows 2000 installation are as follows:

- **Setup Loader:** This setup phase is initiated by WINNT.EXE or WINNT32.EXE from a command-line prompt or by the Autorun feature on the CD-ROM. Setup Loader copies the installation files and SETUPLDR to the hard drive and either creates or modifies the BOOT.INI file.

  SETUPLDR is a special version of NTLDR (see the section "Starting Up Windows 2000," later in the chapter) that loads NTDETECT.COM and NTBOOTDD.SYS. These files perform initial hardware detection, load the drivers for the hard drive controller, and pass control to the kernel.

  If setup was started from WINNT32.EXE or the CD-ROM's Autorun feature, the End-User License Agreement (EULA — pronounced "you-la") and the Product ID dialog box are displayed in this phase.

- **Text-mode setup:** This phase is distinctive for its blue screen. Setup performs an inventory and check of the system hardware (CPU, motherboard, and hard drive), creates the Registry, detects the Plug and Play (PnP) devices, partitions and formats the hard drive, and creates the file systems or converts an existing NTFS (NT File System).

- **GUI-mode setup:** The Setup Wizard is displayed on the screen in graphical user interface (GUI) mode, which detects and configures the devices that are found on the computer and creates the Setup log files in the installation directory on the hard drive.

Keeping the logs

During the Windows 2000 setup, a number of log files are created that can be used to help troubleshoot installation problems that may occur. The log files are in a text format and can be opened with Windows Notepad. The log files created by setup are as follows:

- SETUPACT.LOG: Information on the files that are copied to the PC during setup.

- SETUPERR.LOG: Information on any errors that occurred during setup.

- SETUPAPI.LOG: Information on the device driver files that are copied to the PC during setup.

- SETUPLOG.TXT: Additional information on the device driver files that are copied to the PC during setup.

The final part of the setup asks for a logon and password and allows you to customize the system for a variety of options, including accessibility, regional settings, and networking.

Don't worry about memorizing all the features of Windows 2000 for the exam. Concentrate on the features and functions that are included in this chapter.

Starting Up Windows 2000

The Windows 2000 startup process is very different from the process that is used to start up MS-DOS, Windows 95, or Windows 98. In these systems, the IO.SYS file is loaded, followed by the MSDOS.SYS file and the COMMAND.COM program. Windows 2000 does not use these files, and you only find them on PCs that are configured for a multiboot and on PCs with an early version of Windows or MS-DOS.

The general startup sequence that is used to start a Windows 2000 system is as follows:

- **Power-on self-test (POST):** This is the same regardless of the operating system.

- **Initial startup:** After the POST, the system BIOS looks for the drive from which it should start the operating system. The storage devices are checked in the sequence that is prescribed in the BIOS. A number of different error messages can be displayed if the operating system is not found.

- **Bootstrap Loader:** The Bootstrap Loader program NTLDR loads the operating system's files into memory from the boot partition. If the PC is set to multiboot, a multiple-boot menu is displayed, from which you can choose the operating system to be started. NTLDR processes the operating system selection and the hardware detection processes before passing control to the Windows 2000 kernel. NTLDR must be located in the root directory of the boot partition.

- **Operating system selection:** If the PC is configured as multiboot, the system file BOOT.INI contains the list of available operating systems, including the path to the appropriate boot partitions. Windows 2000 can multiboot with multiple Windows 2000 versions, Windows 95, Windows 98, Windows NT 4.0, MS-DOS, and OS/2. An example of the contents in the BOOT.INI file is as follows:

```
[boot loader]
timeout=30
default=multi(0)disk(0)rdisk(0)partition(1)\WINNT
[operating systems]
multi(0)disk(0)rdisk(0)partition(1)\winnt= "Microsoft
        Windows 2000
Professional" /fastdetect
C:\="Windows 98"
```

✔ **Hardware detection:** After the operating system is selected on a multi-boot PC, or when only Windows 2000 is on the PC, `NTDETECT.COM` detects the hardware, creates a list of the installed hardware, and passes the list to `NTLDR`. The information that `NTDETECT.COM` passes includes

- The computer ID and information on the bus

- Installed adapters, keyboard, COM ports, floppy disk controller, mouse, and LPT ports

✔ **Hardware profile selection:** Windows 2000 supports more than one hardware profile to allow multiple non–Plug and Play configurations of the PC. If multiple hardware configurations are defined, `NTDETECT.COM` prompts the user to choose a hardware profile. If only one hardware profile is in use, the default settings are used. One choice that is available on the hardware profile screen is the Last Known Good Configuration option, which overlays all changes in the Registry and control set since the last good boot. After the hardware profile is chosen, control passes back to `NTLDR`.

✔ **Windows 2000 kernel loads:** `NTLDR` loads the Windows 2000 kernel and the Hardware Abstraction Layer (HAL) into memory. (See "Looking into Windows NT," earlier in the chapter.) `NTLDR` then loads the Registry key `HKEY_LOCAL_MACHINE\SYSTEM` from the folder `%SystemRoot%\system32\Config\System` and uses it to create the control set that is used to initialize the PC. This control set is used to start the operating system.

✔ **Startup:** The system kernel initiates the Windows 2000 Professional splash screen, and the Starting Up progress bar is displayed across the bottom of the display. When the status bar completes, `NTOSKRNL` sets up any network information relating to the system.

✔ **Logon:** `WINLOGON.EXE` and the Local Security Administration are started, and the Begin Logon box is displayed. Windows 2000 is still loading drivers and doing other tasks in the background, but you can log on. After the logon is complete, the desktop is displayed and the Last Known Good control set is created.

Solving startup problems

Many PC problems occur at startup. This is when hardware, software, and even operators break down the most frequently. This section covers some things that you should know about problems that occur during a Windows 2000 system startup.

Now where did I put that darn OS?

If the BIOS cannot find a system partition from which to load the operating system, the BIOS displays one of the following messages:

- **Nonsystem disk or disk error:** A floppy disk that is not a boot disk is loaded in the floppy drive. This message appears when the A: drive is designated as the first boot drive.

- **Invalid partition table:** If the BIOS is directed to a hard drive partition (C:, D:, and so on), and the partition is not a system partition, this message or the message `Error loading operating system` or `Missing operating system` is displayed.

Playing it safe

Most startup problems happen immediately after new hardware or software is installed and are typically directly related to that activity. The first step in troubleshooting a startup problem that occurs right after you've installed new stuff in the PC is to remove the new stuff and reboot to see if that really was the problem.

However, if nothing new was added, modified, or reconfigured on the PC, you must start at the beginning and drill down to the facts. If the PC freezes during startup or displays error messages (including those that were discussed in the preceding section), or you lose the function of any peripheral device, your best bet is to boot into Safe mode.

Safe mode loads only a minimal configuration of the operating system and only those device drivers that are essential to starting Windows and allowing you to interface with the OS, such as drivers for the monitor, keyboard, mouse, hard drive, and floppy disk. Other drivers, such as those for serial and parallel ports and network support are not loaded in Safe mode. If the PC will not boot to Safe mode, check for system resource conflicts, a corrupted Registry, or device drivers that are incompatible with Windows 2000.

To enter Safe mode on a Windows 2000 system, press F8 when the prompt `For troubleshooting and advanced startup options for Windows 2000, press F8` appears. Safe mode can be selected from the Advanced Options menu.

If you suspect the problem to be a corrupted Registry, the best course of action is to reboot, press F8 to enter the Advanced Options menu, and select the Last Known Good Configuration option to reset the PC's configuration to what it was the last time that it booted successfully.

Getting the system information

If you are able to boot an ailing PC into Safe mode, use the Windows 2000 System Information utility (MSINFO32.EXE) to check for system resource, device, and file-sharing conflicts.

If you find conflicts, disable the device or devices in question and reboot to see if the problem is solved. Also, check the devices against the HCL to make sure that they are compatible with Windows 2000. You can use the Windows Update feature to search for compatible drivers, but you will probably be more successful in finding drivers at the device manufacturer's Web site.

If no hardware conflicts exist, check the Software Environment of MSINFO32 for a list of the programs that are started when the PC starts. To see if the problem is in one of these programs, disable a program and restart the PC.

If the problem still exists, check the boot log file, NTBTLOG.TXT.

Shutting out shutdown problems

During the shutdown process on a Windows 2000 system, messages are sent to the peripheral devices, system services, and application programs to alert them that the system is shutting down. The system waits for responses from each of these elements, especially the applications, before beginning to shut down the device drivers, services, and applications. If a device driver, system service, antivirus software, or application does not respond, the shutdown process can hang.

The joy of Windows 2000 stop messages

To make sure that you don't get too lonely for your old pal, the blue screen of death, Microsoft included this screen in Windows 2000. When Windows 2000 has an error from which it cannot recover, it displays a stop message — the blue-screen message. The following types of stop messages are generated on a Windows 2000 system:

- ✔ **Stop messages:** This type of message is displayed when the Windows 2000 kernel detects a condition from which it cannot recover. These messages are displayed in full blue-screen glory, and each error type is identified by a hexadecimal error code and a symbolic name for the error. A stop message display looks something like this:

```
Stop 0x0000000A or IRQL_NOT_LESS_OR_EQUAL
```

Stop messages are grouped into the following categories:

- • **Normal operations messages:** Can be from a number of hardware or software sources.

- • **Installation messages:** Are typically HCL problems.

- • **Initialization messages:** Are caused by a device or system component that fails to initialize.

- • **Software trap messages:** Are errors in an application or system service that are detected by Windows 2000.

- ✔ **Hardware malfunction messages:** These messages are displayed when the CPU detects a hardware problem that Windows 2000 cannot recover from. These messages typically take the following form:

```
Hardware malfunction.
Call your hardware vendor for support.
```

Identifying Windows 2000 System Files

Windows 2000, in all its versions, uses a different set of system files than the previous versions of Windows. The Windows 2000 system files are located in the root folder of the system partition, which must be on the first physical drive of the system. The Windows 2000 system files included on the A+ OS Technologies exam are all boot files. You need to know the following Windows 2000 system files:

- ✔ NTLDR: Is the Bootstrap Loader program.

- ✔ BOOT.INI: Contains information on multiple operating systems to which system could boot.

- ✔ BOOTSECT.DOS: Contains information on operating systems other than Windows 2000.

- ✔ NTDETECT.COM: Collects data on the current hardware configuration for use in building the Registry key HKEY_LOCAL_MACHINE\HARDWARE.

- ✔ NTOSKRNL.EXE: Loads the Windows 2000 kernel.

- ✔ HAL.DLL: Contains the Hardware Abstraction Layer (HAL) data libraries.

Tracking NTLDR

As indicated in the section, "Starting Up Windows 2000," earlier in this chapter, NTLDR, which must be located in the root folder of the startup disk, controls the operating system selection and hardware detection phases of the Windows 2000 startup process before passing control to the Windows 2000 kernel.

NTLDR performs or controls the following actions:

- **Switches the processor to run in 32-bit memory mode:** All PCs run in real mode when first started, but because NTLDR and the rest of Windows 2000 are 32-bit programs, the processor must be switched to 32-bit mode.

- **Starts the file system:** NTLDR contains the code to access NTFS (NT File System) or the FAT16 or FAT32 file systems.

- **Reads** BOOT.INI: The operating system choices, if more than one, are displayed on the screen. If an operating system other than Windows 2000 is selected, NTLDR loads the BOOTSECT.DOS file and passes control to it, which starts the selected operating system. If Windows 2000 is chosen or if it is the only operating system listed in BOOT.INI, NTLDR starts NTDETECT.COM, which collects the computer hardware data.

- **Completes the startup:** The computer hardware data is passed to NTOSKRNL.EXE, which completes the startup.

Selecting the OS from BOOT.INI

BOOT.INI contains the list of available operating systems on a computer. Each entry in the BOOT.INI file contains the path of the boot partition for each operating system, the text that is displayed on the Boot Loader screen, and any optional parameters that are used by the operating system when it starts up. In addition to starting multiple versions of Windows 2000, BOOT.INI can start Windows 95, Windows 98, Windows NT 4.0, MS-DOS, and OS/2.

The following is a sample BOOT.INI file:

```
[boot loader]
timeout=30
default=multi(0)disk(0)rdisk(0)partition(1)\WINNT
[operating systems]
multi(0)disk(0)rdisk(0)partition(1)\winnt="Microsoft Windows
          2000 Professional" /fastdetect
C:\="Windows 98"
```

The information of the BOOT.INI file is displayed on the Boot Loader screen and looks something like this:

```
Please select the operating system to start:

Microsoft Windows 2000 Professional
Microsoft Windows 98

Use your arrow keys to move the highlight to your choice.
Please touch Enter to choose.

Seconds until highlighted choice will be started
         automatically: 29

For troubleshooting and advanced startup options for Windows
         2000, press F8.
```

The default operating system is always listed first. If the operating system has not been selected before the countdown timer reaches 0, the default operating system (in this example, Windows 2000 Professional) is started.

Managing a Windows 2000 System

Windows 2000 includes a utility called Computer Management, which helps you manage both local and remote PCs. This tool combines several Windows 2000 administration tools into a single Explorer-like tree arrangement, as illustrated in Figure 3-1. The Computer Management window is opened from the Administrative Tools icon on the Control Panel.

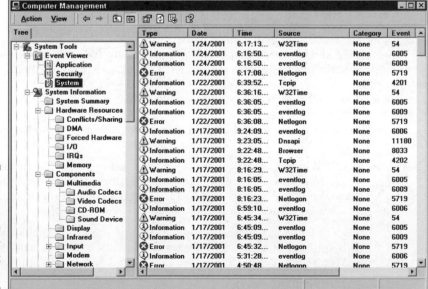

Figure 3-1: The Windows 2000 Computer Management window.

In addition to the Computer Management tools, Windows 2000 also provides a variety of other tools that are used to maintain, troubleshoot, or update the system. Table 3-4 lists the tools that you may encounter on the A+ OS Technologies exam.

Table 3-4	Windows 2000 Maintenance and Update Tools
Tool	*Description*
Disk Defragmenter	A utility that optimizes drive performance by rearranging files, folders, programs, and unused space on the hard drive.
AVBoot	MAKEDISK.BAT can be used to create a boot disk that also scans for and removes MBR (master boot record) and boot sector viruses from RAM and the hard drive.
Windows Update	An online repository of product updates, service packs, device drivers, and operating system updates.
MSINFO32.EXE	The system information utility that collects and displays information about the PC's hardware, system components, and software.
REGEDT32.EXE	The editing tool that is used to add and change settings and create subkeys in the Windows 2000 Registry.

Choosing a file system

Windows 2000 supports a variety of file systems that provide it with good backward and forward compatibility. The primary file systems of Windows 2000 are NTFS (NT File System) and FAT32 (File Allocation Table 32-bit).

Windows 2000 supports the following file systems:

- ✓ **FAT (File Allocation Table):** This is the legacy file system that was first used with MS-DOS and Windows 3.*x* systems.

- ✓ **FAT32:** Windows 2000 allows FAT32 volumes of up to 2TB (terabytes) in size to be used. Larger volumes are supported, but only if they were created under Windows 98. FAT32 is also the file system that is used for dual-boot systems with Windows 98.

- ✓ **NTFS (NT File System):** Windows 2000 fully supports this file system with volumes of up to 16 terabytes (trillions of bytes) in size. Windows 2000 can upgrade NTFS volumes to NTFS 5.0, but only Windows 2000 or

NT 4.0 with Service Pack 4 (SP4) or later can read an NTFS 5.0 volume. NTFS 5.0 includes support for Dynamic Disk features.

- ✔ **CDFS (CD File System):** This is a legacy CD file system that is being replaced by the UDF.

- ✔ **UDF (Universal Disk Format):** This is a newer file system that is supported by newer CD-ROMs, DVDs, and other optical discs.

Encrypting and compressing files

Windows 2000 has the capability to encrypt a file for private use simply by choosing a file property. The encryption method is a standard 56-bit encryption. Microsoft recommends that an NTFS folder be created and that the folder be marked for encryption. Use the following steps to encrypt a file in Windows 2000:

1. **Right-click the file or folder to be encrypted from Windows Explorer or My Computer, and choose Properties from the pop-up menu that appears.**

2. **Under Attributes, click the Advanced button to display the Advanced Attributes dialog box, as shown in Figure 3-2.**

   Your choices are to encrypt your files or folders or to compress your files. (These choices are mutually exclusive — that is, you can't choose them both.) Each choice is described as follows:

   - **To encrypt your files or folders:** Choose Encrypt Contents to Secure Data to encrypt the folder or file, or deselect this check box to decrypt a file or folder.

   - **To compress a file or folder:** Choose Compress Contents to Save Disk Space in the Advanced Attributes dialog box. To decompress the file or folder, deselect this option.

Figure 3-2:
The Advanced Attributes dialog box is used to encrypt and compress a file on a Windows 2000 system.

3. Click OK to close the dialog box.

The file or all the files in the folder are not encrypted (or decrypted). If you encrypted a folder, any new files that are added to the folder are encrypted, and encrypted files cannot be shared.

Encrypted files cannot be compressed, and compressed files cannot be encrypted.

Displaying the Command Prompt

One small but important item that you must know for the A+ OS Technologies exam is how to display a command-line prompt (otherwise known as the DOS prompt) in Windows 2000 or Windows XP.

To display a command-line prompt, choose Start➪Run, enter **CMD** in the Run box, and click OK. That's all there is to it!

Getting Ready for Work

If you expect to install new versions of Windows operating systems (Windows NT, Windows 2000, and Windows XP), you should know how to create an Emergency Repair Disk (ERD). An ERD is unique to the PC on which it was created.

Other valuable disks to have near a Windows 2000 system are the Windows 2000 startup disks. You should know how to create these startup disks, and I've included some practice exercises in doing just that.

Your should create an ERD for each PC immediately after installing the operating system and then store the ERD in a safe place until it is needed. The A+ OS Technologies exam contains at least one question on how to create an ERD. Windows NT and Windows 2000/XP use different methods to create an ERD.

If your new PC doesn't include a floppy disk drive, you can still create an ERD. However, you will need to set the boot sequence in the BIOS to start from the CD-ROM drive (you do have one of those, don't you?). Third-party software, such as ERD Commander from Winternals Software (www.winternals.com) is a better way to go for systems without floppy disks.

Creating an ERD

In the Windows NT world, the utility program RDISK.EXE, found on the installation CD-ROM, copies the critical information about a PC's system software environment, including part of the system Registry, to the ERD floppy disk. This information can help begin the repair process on an unbootable system.

On a Windows 2000/XP system, the ERD is created through the Windows Backup utility and doesn't contain the same files as the Windows NT ERD. For example, the Registry is not copied to the floppy disk, but if you select the Also Back Up the Registry to the Repair Directory check box, the ERD process copies the Registry to the \WINNT\Repair\RegBack folder.

Creating a Windows 2000 ERD

Use the following steps to create a Windows 2000 ERD:

1. **Choose Start➪Run, enter** ntbackup **in the Run box, and click OK to open the Windows 2000 Backup and Recovery Tools window.**

   (I know: If it doesn't work for Windows NT, why is it named *NT* backup?)

2. **Click the Emergency Repair Disk button, which is located on the Welcome to Windows 2000 Backup and Recovery Tools window.**

At this point, the following files get copied to the ERD:

- autoexec.nt
- config.nt
- SETUP.LOG, which contains the Cyclic Redundancy Check (checksum) for the core Windows 2000 files

Recovering a system with an ERD

To use an ERD to begin the recovery or repair process of a Windows 2000 system, use the following steps:

1. **Boot the PC using either the Windows 2000 Setup floppy disks or the installation CD-ROM.**

2. **When asked what action you want to perform, enter** R **to open the Recovery mode.**

3. On the Recovery mode screen, enter R to enter ERD mode.

4. On the ERD mode screen, you can choose either Fast Repair or Manual Repair, depending on what needs to be done. The differences between these two options are as follows:

   • **Fast Repair:** This option tells Windows 2000 to fix anything that it can, including system files, boot sector errors, and the Registry, all without user interaction.

   • **Manual Repair:** This mode provides you with the ability to do exactly what its name implies — to manually go about fixing the system. An assortment of utilities and tools are available to help you, but the assumption is that you know what you're doing.

Creating Windows 2000 startup disks

The Windows 2000 installation CD-ROM contains the MAKEBOOT utility. This utility is used to create system boot and startup disks that can be used to start a PC that is unable to start from the system CD-ROM. Lab 3-1 lists the steps that are used to create a set of startup disks.

Lab 3-1	Creating a Set of Windows 2000 Startup Disks

1. **You need four blank, formatted 3½-inch, 1.44MB floppy disks. Label them as Windows 2000 Startup Disk 1, 2, 3, and 4.**

2. **Insert the Startup Disk 1 in the floppy drive.**

   This procedure can be performed on any PC that is running Windows or MS-DOS and has a floppy disk drive and a CD-ROM drive.

3. **Insert the Windows 2000 CD-ROM into the CD-ROM drive.**

4. **Either choose Start⇨Run and enter the following command or enter the following command at the DOS command-line prompt:**

   ```
   D:\BOOTDISK\MAKEBOOT.EXE A:
   ```

   If necessary, change D: to reflect the drive letter of your CD-ROM drive.

5. **Follow the on-screen prompts to complete the startup disks.**

Before starting a computer using the Windows 2000 operating system CD-ROM or the floppy disks, try starting the computer in Safe mode.

Prep Test

1 Which of the following is not a minimum system requirement of Windows 2000 Professional?

A ○ 133-MHz or higher Pentium processor
B ○ At least 2GB of free hard drive space
C ○ At least 256MB of main memory (RAM)
D ○ A CD-ROM drive

2 Which of the following is used to verify that a PC, peripheral device, or application is Windows 2000 compatible?

A ○ HAL
B ○ MSINFO32
C ○ Computer Management
D ○ HCL

3 Which of the following Windows versions can be upgraded to Windows 2000? (Choose two.)

A ❑ Windows 9*x*
B ❑ Windows Me
C ❑ Windows 3.*x*
D ❑ Windows NT 4.0

4 What is the name of the log file created during the Windows 2000 setup process that contains information on any errors that occurred during the setup?

A ○ SETUPERR.LOG
B ○ ERRSETUP.LOG
C ○ STUPERR.TXT
D ○ W2KERR.LOG

5 During the Windows 2000 startup, a list of the installed hardware is created and passed to NTLDR by which function?

A ○ HAL
B ○ HCL
C ○ NTDETECT
D ○ W2KDETCT

6 **Which of the following actions can be used to enter Safe mode during a Windows 2000 startup?**

A ○ Press F5 during the boot process

B ○ Press F8 during the boot process

C ○ Press F8 when prompted, and select Safe mode from the Advanced Options menu

D ○ Press Delete

7 **A Windows 2000 system will not start up, and you have determined the cause to be a corrupted Registry. What course of action can you take to start the system?**

A ○ Reinstall Windows 2000 to rebuild the Registry

B ○ Access the Advanced Options menu, and choose the Last Known Good Configuration option

C ○ Use `REGEDT32` to rebuild the Registry

D ○ Delete `SYSTEM.DAT`, rename `SYSTEM.DAO` to `SYSTEM.DAT`, and reboot

8 **What utility can be used to download and install product updates, service packs, device drivers, and updates to Windows 2000?**

A ○ `MSINFO32`

B ○ Windows Update

C ○ `MAKEDISK`

D ○ `SETUPAPI`

9 **To configure a Windows 2000 system to multiboot with Windows 98, which Windows 2000 system file must be edited?**

A ○ `MSDOS.SYS`

B ○ `NTLDR.EXE`

C ○ `BOOT.INI`

D ○ `SYSTEM.INI`

10 **Windows 2000 supports which of the following file systems? (Choose three.)**

A ❑ FAT

B ❑ FAT32

C ❑ NFS

D ❑ NTFS

Answers

1 **C.** The minimum RAM requirement of Windows 2000 Professional is only 64MB. Windows 2000 Server requires a minimum of 128MB, but 256MB is recommended. *See "Meeting the minimums."*

2 **D.** The Hardware Compatibility List (HCL) is used to check a device's, PC's, or application's compatibility with Windows 2000. A version of the HCL is included on the distribution CD-ROM, but a more up-to-date version is available online. *Review "Installing Windows 2000."*

3 **A & D.** Windows NT 3.51 (the non-Citrix version) can also be upgraded to Windows 2000. *Study "Upgrading to Windows 2000."*

4 **A.** Log files are text files that can be examined using either Windows Notepad or another text editor or word processor. The `SETUPERR.LOG` file should be empty most of the time, but should errors occur, they are recorded in this file. *Check out "Keeping the logs."*

5 **C.** `NTDETECT.COM` is the full name of this program. All the installed devices on the PC are recorded in the list and passed to `NTLDR`, which compares the list to the hardware profile that was used to configure the system. *Take a look at "Starting Up Windows 2000."*

6 **C.** When the prompt `For troubleshooting and advanced startup options for Windows 2000, press F8` appears, you have about 2 seconds to press F8 and display the Advanced Options menu. Safe mode can be selected from this menu. *See "Playing it safe."*

7 **B.** The Last Known Good Configuration is created each time that the system start ups up completely and trouble-free. *Review "Playing it safe."*

8 **B.** Windows Update is the online extension of the Windows 2000 operating system that can be used to keep the operating system and the services that it supports up to date relatively automatically. *Look over "Managing a Windows 2000 computer."*

9 **C.** `BOOT.INI` lists the multiple operating systems and includes a path statement that directs the system to the boot partition for each operating system. *Check out "Starting Up Windows 2000."*

10 **A, B, & D.** Windows 2000 also supports the EFS (Encryption File System — not on the exam) as well as the CDFS (CD File System) and UDF (Universal Disk Format), which are mentioned on the exam. *Study "Identifying Windows 2000 file systems."*

Chapter 4

Windows XP Professional

. . . .

Exam Objectives

▶ Detailing the installation procedure for Windows XP

▶ Explaining the Windows XP command line and tools

▶ Troubleshooting Windows XP

Windows XP was added to the A+ OS Technologies exam in the fall of 2003, which for the A+ exam is about as close to being current as the test has ever been. Windows XP differs in a few, but noticeable, ways from its predecessor, Windows 2000. The first thing that you'll probably notice is the new desktop GUI and the fact that it may take a few minutes of trial and error to find some of the Windows features that aren't in the same locations or that you don't access in quite the same way. Most of the new bells and whistles that have been added are user features that don't impact the basic operating system functions. New support has been added for CD burning, sound recording and playback, multimedia playback, and so on.

Windows XP has two versions: Windows XP Professional, the one that's on the A+ exam, and Windows XP Home, the alleged successor to Windows Me. If you have Windows XP Home installed on your PC, consider upgrading to Windows XP Professional, if for no other reason than to get ready for the A+ exam.

In this chapter, I focus on the installation process, the startup process, and the tools that are available in Windows XP to troubleshoot application and hardware problems. You are still more likely to encounter Windows 98 or Windows 2000 questions on the exam, but don't be surprised if you run into a few Windows XP questions as well.

This is one of the few chapters in which I haven't included a "Getting Ready for Work" section. After you've read this chapter, you'll understand why. The whole thing is one big on-the-job experience, and I didn't think you needed any additional work.

Quick Assessment

Detailing the installation procedure for Windows XP

1 The minimum RAM requirement for Windows XP Professional is _____ MB, but _____ MB is recommended.

2 Windows XP Professional specifies a _____-MHz processor or better as a minimum requirement.

3 Windows XP provides two tools, _____ and _____, which can be used to check the compatibility of hardware and software on a PC.

4 Windows 95 _____ be upgraded to Windows XP. (Answer *can* or *cannot.*)

5 _____ startups is one feature that differentiates Windows XP from previous Windows versions.

6 Unlike previous Windows versions, the Windows 2000 and XP CD-ROMs are _____.

Explaining the Windows XP command line and tools

7 _____ is the Windows XP command-line tool that is used to display the Boot Loader configuration data.

8 _____ is the Windows XP command-line tool that can be used to display or manage the network configuration of a PC.

Trouble-shooting Windows XP

9 Windows XP stop errors are displayed on _____ or _____ screens.

10 The hexadecimal error number that is associated with a stop error can be used to search the Microsoft _____ for troubleshooting information.

Answers

1   *64, 128.* See "Meeting minimum requirements."

2   *233.* Review "Meeting minimum requirements."

3   *Windows Catalog, Update Advisor.* Check out "Installing Windows XP."

4   *Cannot.* Look over "Checking for eligibility."

5   *Faster.* Study "Getting to Know Windows XP."

6   *Bootable.* Peruse "Checking the preinstallation checklist."

7   *bootcfg.* See "Working at the Windows XP Command Line."

8   *netsh.* Review "Working at the Windows XP Command Line."

9   *Blue, black.* Check out "Troubleshooting Windows XP."

10   *Knowledge Base.* Take a look at "Dealing with general stop errors."

Getting to Know Windows XP

Beyond Windows XP's new fresh-look user interface and a noticeably faster startup, you should be aware of a few new features and requirements for the exam. Beyond that, don't worry about the operational differences between Windows XP and Windows 2000; for the most part, there are none.

One unique feature about Windows XP is that it doesn't have a Server version. The Windows XP versions are Home and Professional. The Home version is for what can be inferred from its name; it is for the home-user market. The Professional version is the business desktop version that is recommended for use in the office and home office and where a PC is a network client.

Table 4-1 lists some of the features that are new in Windows XP and indicates which version supports them. Y (Yes) shows that the version supports a given feature; N (No) indicates no support.

Table 4-1	Windows XP Features	
Feature	*Windows XP Pro*	*Windows XP Home*
Advanced portable PC support	Y	Y
Automatic wireless connection support	Y	Y
Automatic software installation and maintenance	Y	N
Fast startup	Y	Y
Help and support center	Y	Y
Internet Connection Firewall	Y	Y
Network Setup Wizard	Y	Y
Remote desktop access	Y	N
Remote installation service (RIS)	Y	N

Meeting minimum requirements

One startling difference between Windows XP and its predecessors is XP's minimum system requirements, which are more "maximum" than previously needed. Table 4-2 compares the system requirements for Windows XP Professional to those of Windows 2000 Professional.

Table 4-2	Windows XP and 2000 System Requirements	
Component	*Windows XP Pro*	*Windows 2000 Pro*
Processor	233-MHz (300-MHz recommended)	133-MHz Pentium-compatible
Memory (RAM)	64MB (128MB recommended)	64MB
Hard drive capacity	2GB	2GB
Hard drive free space	1.5GB	650MB
Required drive	CD-ROM or DVD	CD-ROM or DVD
Display resolution	SVGA or higher	VGA or higher
Input device required	Keyboard and mouse	Keyboard

Windows XP needs only 64MB of RAM, but in reality, it can't support much in that space. Therefore, 128MB of RAM is typically shown as the minimum requirement.

Perhaps the most startling of the higher minimum system requirements for Windows XP Pro is the processor. Depending on the system and the type of work that the user wants to do, a faster processor may be required.

Windows XP supports both single- and dual-processor systems and no longer requires the Pentium-compatible processor. In fact, in its Windows XP Pro system requirements, Microsoft lists any Pentium/Celeron processor of 233 MHz or higher, the AMD K6/Athlon/Duron processors of 233 MHz or higher, or any compatible processor — which means VIA without saying so. See Book I, Chapter 6 for more information on these processors.

Installing Windows XP

Because the typical installation of Windows XP is an upgrade of a previous Windows version, I'm going to focus on that. Like the installation processes of Windows NT and Windows 2000, Windows XP's installation process requires you to first check the compatibility of the hardware, device drivers, and software before proceeding with the installation. Microsoft provides two options for checking the software and hardware compatibility of a PC: searching the Windows Catalog and using the Upgrade Advisor.

Searching the Windows Catalog

The Windows Catalog is an online tool that allows you to search a catalog of compatible hardware and software using any combination of manufacturer name, product type, or model number. This may sound like the hard way of checking compatibility, but using the Windows Catalog may be appropriate in a few instances, such as the following:

✔ After Windows XP is installed, you may want to check the compatibility of new hardware or software before you attempt to install the hardware or software.

✔ Before installing Windows XP, you may want to check whether key software or hardware is compatible on a particular PC.

Figure 4-1 shows the results of a search for a particular network adapter manufacturer. If a product isn't listed in the Windows Catalog, it may still work with Windows XP but just hasn't been added to the catalog yet. Check the manufacturer's Web site to determine a device's compatibility with Windows XP.

You can find the Windows Catalog at the following URL:

```
www.microsoft.com/windowsxp/pro/howtobuy/upgrading/compat.asp
```

Using the Upgrade Advisor

The Microsoft Upgrade Advisor is a downloadable tool that you can use to verify that a system is ready to be upgraded to Windows XP. Assuming that the current Windows version is eligible to be upgraded to Windows XP Professional, the Upgrade Advisor checks the hardware and software for compatibility, and if you run this tool while connected to the Internet, the tool checks Windows Update for any software updates that need to be applied prior to upgrading to Windows XP.

Because the Upgrade Advisor is about 50MB in size, I recommend that you download it only over a high-speed line, such as a Digital Subscriber Line (DSL) or cable modem service. However, this is the same program that checks the system during installation, so if you are determined to install Windows XP on a PC, you may not need to download the program.

Checking for eligibility

Not every older version of Windows can be upgraded to Windows XP Professional. In fact, the versions of Windows that can be upgraded to Windows XP is a shorter list than those that can't be upgraded. Table 4-3 lists the older Windows versions and indicates whether they can be upgraded to Windows XP.

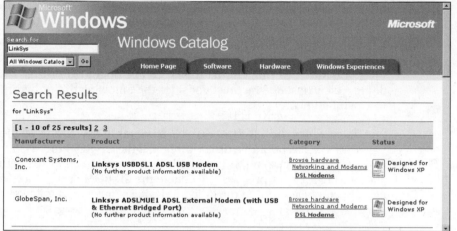

Figure 4-1:
An example
of the
search
results that
were
produced by
the
Windows
Catalog.

Table 4-3	Eligible for Upgrade to Windows XP?	
Version	**Windows XP Pro**	**Windows XP Home**
Windows 3.x	No	No
Any evaluation version	No	No
Any Server version	No	No
Any Windows 95 version	No	No
Windows 98/98 SE	Yes	Yes
Windows Me	Yes	Yes
Windows NT Workstation 3.51	No	No
Windows NT Workstation 4.0	Yes	No
Windows 2000 Professional	Yes	No
Windows XP Home	Yes	N/A
Windows XP Professional	N/A	No

Going the clean route

Perhaps the best reason to install Windows XP using a clean install — in which
the hard drive is freshly partitioned and formatted — is that any remnants
that are left behind by previous Windows versions and application software

are wiped away, freeing valuable hard drive space. Of course, the downside is that you must restore all the data and reinstall all the applications.

Checking the preinstallation checklist

After you have determined that the PC can be upgraded or that you will be doing a clean install, you must consider the following things before you begin the installation process:

- ✔ **Ensure that the CD-ROM drive is a bootable drive.** The Windows XP CD-ROM is a bootable disc. However, if the CD-ROM drive isn't configured as a boot device in the system BIOS, you need to enter the Setup program during the boot process and enable the CD-ROM drive as a boot device. I recommend setting the PC boot device sequence as follows:

    1. CD-ROM drive

    2. Floppy disk drive

    3. First hard drive (if you have multiple drives)

  After you have made these changes, when you boot the system, you are usually prompted to press any key to boot from the CD-ROM drive.

  If you are unable to boot from the CD-ROM drive, all is not lost. Visit the Microsoft Windows XP Web site at the following URL:

  ```
  http://support.microsoft.com/default.
          aspx?scid=kb;en-us;310994
  ```

  Here, you can download an executable file that creates four startup boot floppy disks that can be used to install Windows XP.

- ✔ **Upgrade the BIOS.** Ensure that the PC is running the latest BIOS version for its motherboard, processor, and chipset before installing Windows XP. The feature that you are looking to enable is the Advanced Configuration and Power Interface (ACPI). This feature provides the power management specification and additional startup and shutdown support for Windows XP.

- ✔ **Transfer the previous settings.** On the Windows XP CD-ROM, you can find the File and Settings Transfer (FAST) Wizard, which can be used to back up system and settings files from the previous Windows version for use with Windows XP. To access this tool, start the Windows XP CD-ROM and choose Perform Additional Tasks from the Welcome screen menu. Then choose Transfer Files and Settings from the next screen.

- ✔ **Back up data files.** By all means, back up your data files before installing Windows XP, even if you are planning only an upgrade from a previous version of Windows.

Performing the install

The process that is used to perform a clean installation has only a few more steps than the process that you use to perform an upgrade installation of Windows XP. The steps involved are as follows:

1. **Insert the Windows XP CD-ROM in the CD-ROM drive and close the drive tray.**

   The system should boot from the CD-ROM and begin the installation process.

   After the Setup program has "inspected" the PC, the real-mode portion of the installation begins. This portion of the process is recognized by its blue-and-gray display. Watch the gray bar at the bottom of the screen for data and action requests. The first prompt is to press F6 if you need to install third-party SCSI or RAID device drivers before proceeding with the install. Next, you are presented with the End User Licensing Agreement (EULA).

2. **Read the agreement in its entirety (sure you will), and then press F8 to proceed.**

3. **At this point, you can proceed to set up Windows XP or you can launch the Recovery Console.**

   (See the section "Recovering a Windows XP Setup," later in this chapter.)

4. **The world is a terrible place when we can't trust one another. Microsoft tells you to insert the qualifying media (that is, the install discs for any upgradeable Windows version) if you are installing Windows XP from an upgrade CD-ROM.**

5. **Choose the hard drive partition on which you want to install Windows XP.**

   If you are performing a clean install, this would likely be the C: drive. However, you may want to create two partitions and install XP on one and your data on the other.

   If you are upgrading, Setup displays the disk partition table and asks which partition you want to use.

6. **After you have designated a partition for Windows XP, you must decide what file system you want to use.**

   The only caution here is that if you are upgrading and you decide to convert a FAT file system to NTFS, you must understand that there is no going back to the FAT file system. Choose one of the quick-format options to hurry along with the installation. If you have more time, choose the full-format option. You should use the full-format option if you are upgrading and data has been previously stored in the Windows XP partition.

After the partition is formatted, the Setup program begins copying the system files to the hard drive. When this is completed, the PC will reboot. During this boot, if you see the message Press any key to boot from CD, do nothing and setup will start Windows XP from the hard drive.

The setup program GUI finally displays, signaling the start of the protected-mode portion of the installation. Progress is marked by the changing of the "billboards" that are displayed with Windows XP feature summaries.

Windows XP begins the hardware detection phase and from there begins requesting information about your environment, such as regional and language settings, date and time settings, and so on. Eventually, you are asked to enter the user's name and company name.

7. **Enter the 25-character product key, which is located on the orange sticker that's on the back of the Windows XP CD case.**

If you don't have the product key, too bad — you must have a valid product key to complete the installation.

8. **Assign a computer (NetBIOS) name to the PC, and optionally assign an administrator password for this PC.**

The computer name is the name that is used to locate the PC on the network and the one that shows up in the My Network Places information. Windows can generate a name for the computer, but these names can be weird, so you should assign something sensible, such as Ron's PC. If you assign an administrator password, which I recommend, only someone who knows the password (such as you) will be able to create, modify, or remove certain settings and actions on the PC.

Windows XP next installs the Client for Microsoft Networks, File and Printer Sharing, the Quality of Service (QoS) Packet Scheduler, and TCP/IP protocol on the network adapter that is installed in the PC. If the PC doesn't have a network adapter, this step is skipped. However, if the PC has more than one network adapter, you are asked to choose one to be configured.

9. **Enter the workgroup or domain information.**

Typically, if the PC is a member of a peer-to-peer or small local-area network (LAN), XP requires a workgroup name, which should default to WORKGROUP. If the PC is a part of a large, multiple-segment LAN or connects to a wide-area network (WAN), the PC should be attached to a domain controller and the name of the domain controller should be entered in the text box provided. You should get this information from the network administrator.

The installation is essentially complete. However, after the first boot to Windows XP, you may want to check the display, network, and audio settings to ensure that they are what you need them to be. You should access the Windows Update feature to update the operating system with any service packs and fixes that were published since the CD was manufactured, and you should test all the hardware peripheral devices.

Working at the Windows XP Command Line

Windows XP includes a variety of command-line utilities and programs that can be used to diagnose, maintain, manage, and administer a PC, especially a networked PC. The following command-line tools are available:

- ✔ bootcfg: This utility is used to configure or display the Boot Loader settings, including the default operating system, the selection timeout, and other boot entries and load options.
- ✔ defrag: Performs defragmentation on a drive.
- ✔ diskpart: Manages a PC's disk partitions.
- ✔ driverquery: Displays a list of known device drivers and their properties.
- ✔ fsutil: Displays information about and manages a PC's file systems.
- ✔ getmac: Displays the MAC address of a PC's network adapter.
- ✔ gpresult: Displays the Resultant Set of Policy (RSoP), user settings, and group policy settings.

  RSoP queries are used to identify conflicts in policies that affect the computer/user, site, domain, and unit hierarchy.
- ✔ netsh: Displays or manages network configuration on a PC.
- ✔ openfiles: Is used by an administrator to display and possibly close or disconnect open files on a PC.
- ✔ recover: Recovers information from damaged disks.
- ✔ reg: Displays, copies, restores, and compares elements in the Registry.
- ✔ schtasks: Schedules, starts, modifies, or removes tasks from the local or a remote PC.
- ✔ sfc: Recovers damaged system files.

✔ shutdown: Shuts down or restarts a PC locally or remotely.

✔ systeminfo: Displays system configuration information, including processor type, time zone, virtual memory settings, and more.

✔ taskkill: Ends a running process using its process ID number.

✔ tasklist: Displays a list of the processes that are currently running on a PC.

Troubleshooting Windows XP

The biggest troubleshooting headache on any Windows version is probably stop errors, which are more affectionately known as the blue or black screens of death.

Getting started with stop errors

Stop errors occur when the operating system stops responding. What causes the system to stop responding is some malfunction in application software, a hardware device, a device driver, or even a system utility. It's nice to know that, for once, the user isn't the prime suspect, right?

Dealing with general stop errors

To troubleshoot a general stop error, the kind that shows up as a blue (or black) screen of death, use the following steps:

1. **Restart the PC.**

   If the error reoccurs, you have more work to do. Otherwise, make a note of the problem in the PC's hardware journal (you do have one, don't you?) as something that you should watch.

2. **If any new hardware or software was installed immediately prior to getting this error, check to ensure that it was properly installed.**

   If no new hardware or software was installed in the immediate past, you may want to start removing hardware devices one at a time to determine which one is causing the problem. You may want to go to the manufacturers' Web sites for updated device drivers or other software.

   If no hardware problems exist, you may need to begin uninstalling software, especially the software that was running when the problem occurred, to see if that resolves the conflict.

3. **If you can restart Windows XP, start it in Safe mode and remove or disable any newly updated or added device drivers.**

4. **Use the Event Viewer to scan the System Log file for additional information concerning the error. You should also look for error messages for other processes that may have contributed to the stop error. You can access the Event Viewer and System Log from the Control Panel, the Performance and Maintenance icon, or the Administrative Tools icon.**

5. **Visit the Microsoft Support Web site at** `http://support.microsoft.com/`. **Search the Microsoft Knowledge Base for** Windows XP Professional **and for the 10-character hexadecimal number, such as** `0x0000000A`, **that's displayed with the stop error message.**

6. **If you cannot log on to Windows XP or if it fails to start, reboot and choose the Last Known Good Configuration option from the Advanced Options screen of the Startup menu.**

   Remove any system setting changes that were made since the last time the system was able to boot completely and successfully.

7. **Use the Windows XP Help and Support function to get advice or suggestions from the Windows XP newsgroups or directly from Microsoft. Access the Help and Support function from the Start menu.**

8. **If all the preceding steps have failed to help you find a fix, try entering the BIOS setup program and disabling memory caching or shadowing. If you have memory check or system diagnostic software, use it to try to detect a system problem.**

Solving specific stop errors

Not all stop errors are vague or uninforming. In fact, some are downright finger-pointers. Table 4-4 lists some of the more common stop errors that specify why the system has stopped.

Table 4-4	Windows XP Stop Errors	
Error Type	*Error Number*	*Descriptive Code*
Hardware failure stop errors		
	0x0000000A	IRQL_NOT_LESS_OR_EQUAL
	0x0000001E	KMODE_EXCEPTION_ NOT_HANDLED

(continued)

Table 4-4 *(continued)*

Error Type	Error Number	Descriptive Code
	0x0000007B	INACCESSIBLE_BOOT_DEVICE
	0x0000007F	UNEXPECTED_KERNEL_MODE_TRAP
	0xC0000218	UNKNOWN_HARD_ERROR
File system stop errors		
	0x00000023	FAT_FILE_SYSTEM
	0x00000024	NTFS_FILE_SYSTEM
Software and device driver stop errors		
	0x00000050	PAGE_FAULT_IN_NONPAGE_AREA
	0x0000009F	DRIVER_POWER_STATE_FAILURE
	0x000000EA	THREAD_STUCK_IN_DEVICE_DRIVER

Troubleshooting hardware failure stop errors

When you get a hardware failure stop error for a particular device, the first thing to check is whether the device driver in use is digitally signed by the Windows Hardware Quality Labs (WHQL). Run the SIGVERIF.EXE utility to check for unsigned device drivers. Using an unsigned device driver can result in unpredictable operating problems and intermittent functionality issues with a device.

Beyond that, follow the standard troubleshooting procedure of checking the manufacturer's Web site for updates, updating software that interacts with a particular device driver, uninstalling or reinstalling critical hardware or software, and if all else fails, running the Recovery Console from the Windows XP setup CD-ROM. (See the section "Recovering a Windows XP Setup," later in the chapter.)

Troubleshooting file system stop errors

File system stop errors are typically very specific as to the source of a problem — the hard drives. Different troubleshooting steps are used depending on the type of hard drive(s) that are installed in a PC. Steps to troubleshoot the most common hard drives are as follows:

- ✔ **Integrated Device Electronics/AT Attachment (IDE/ATA) drives:** Try the following steps to isolate the problem:

  - Reconfigure the IDE port on the motherboard as primary-only.

  - Verify the master/slave settings on the hard drives and other IDE devices.

  - Remove all non-hard-drive IDE devices from the system.

  - Remove all software that uses a filter driver to interact with the hard drive. This includes antivirus, defrag, remote control, and backup utilities.

  - Run the `chkdsk /f` utility to determine whether the hard drive is corrupted. If the PC won't run `chkdsk` because of the error, install the device in another computer and run this utility.

- ✔ **Small Computer System Interface (SCSI) drives:** Try the following steps to isolate the problem:

  - Obtain the latest Windows XP–compatible device driver from the hardware manufacturer or vendor.

  - Disable the synchronization negotiation for the SCSI drive.

  - Check the termination on the SCSI chain (both internal and external).

  - Verify the device IDs of the SCSI devices on the SCSI chain.

Troubleshooting software and device driver stop errors

The process that is used to troubleshoot software and device driver stop errors is similar to that used for hardware stop errors in that the cause of the problem is more than likely to be a device driver. To troubleshoot this type of stop error, try the following steps:

- ✔ Run the `SIGVERIF.EXE` utility to verify that the device driver is digitally signed by the WHQL.

- ✔ Disable the device driver using Device Manager.

- ✔ Replace the driver that is identified in the stop error message with either a fresh copy or an updated version from the manufacturer's Web site.

✔ If the driver in question is the video driver, reconfigure to the standard VGA driver or to another compatible driver from the Windows XP installation CD-ROM.

✔ If the error happened immediately after new RAM was added to the system, the memory paging file may be corrupted or the new memory may be faulty or not compatible. Delete the PAGEFILE.SYS file and remove the new memory.

✔ Run the Recovery Console (see the next section).

Recovering a Windows XP Setup

It can happen to anyone. Not every operating system installation goes smoothly, without a hitch. There's no shame in needing to run the Recovery Console, and doing so doesn't mean that you've failed. Running the Recovery Console only means that you are a knowledgeable PC technician who is familiar with all the tools that are readily available to help solve a problem.

The Windows Recovery Console is located on the Windows XP setup CD-ROM and is available to help you identify and solve a variety of system problems.

Using the Windows Recovery Console, you can do the following:

✔ Open or administer operating system files and folders

✔ Enable or disable applications, services, processes, or devices the next time that the PC is booted.

✔ Repair the Master Boot Record (MBR) or a file system boot sector

✔ Add, format, or remove hard drive partitions

After you open the Windows Recovery Console and log on as the system administrator, you can use the command console that's displayed to accomplish the tasks that I've just listed. The Recovery Console's command console has a few limitations: You are only able to access the root folder, the System Root folder (%SYSTEMROOT%) and its subfolders, the cmdcons (command console) folder, and any removable media drives, such as the floppy disk, CD, DVD, or Zip drive.

The Recovery Console supports a variety of commands that you can use to repair a file problem on the system. These commands include attrib, copy, delete, diskpart, enable, fixboot, format, logon, mkdir, and systemroot.

Prep Test

1 What is the minimum system RAM requirement for Windows XP?

A ○ 32MB

B ○ 64MB

C ○ 128MB

D ○ 256MB

2 What is the minimum processor clock rate required by Windows XP?

A ○ 333 MHz

B ○ 233 MHz

C ○ 133 MHz

D ○ 1.2 GHz

3 Which of the following can be used to determine the compatibility of a PC's hardware and software for Windows XP? (Choose two.)

A ❏ Windows Catalog

B ❏ Upgrade Advisor

C ❏ Update Catalog

D ❏ Windows Installation Simulator

4 Windows XP Professional cannot be installed as an upgrade on which of the following systems?

A ○ Windows XP Home

B ○ Windows NT Workstation 4.0

C ○ Windows 98 SE

D ○ Windows 95 OSR2

5 What differentiates the Windows XP setup CD-ROM from the setup CD-ROMs of previous Windows versions?

A ○ It has better label graphics.

B ○ It is bootable.

C ○ It is not bootable.

D ○ It can be multibooted.

6 **Which of the following Windows XP command-line tools can be used to manage a system's disk partitions?**

A ○ `partfix`

B ○ `partdisk`

C ○ `diskpart`

D ○ `openfiles`

7 **What Windows NT/2000/XP startup option removes any system setting changes that were made since the last time the system was able to boot completely and successfully?**

A ○ GoBack

B ○ Recover

C ○ Last Known Good Configuration

D ○ `sigverif`

8 **Who is the authority that provides digital signatures for tested and approved device drivers for Windows operating systems?**

A ○ Microsoft Hardware Testing Labs

B ○ Windows Quality Testing Labs

C ○ Microsoft Hardware Quality Testing Labs

D ○ Windows Hardware Quality Testing Labs

9 **A SCSI hard drive is causing a stop error with an error number of** $0xC0000218$**. Which of the following would you include when troubleshooting this error? (Choose three.)**

A ❑ Disable the sync negotiation for the SCSI disk.

B ❑ Check the termination on the SCSI chain.

C ❑ Call Microsoft technical support because this is a catastrophic error that must be reported.

D ❑ Verify the ID numbers of the devices that are attached to the SCSI chain.

10 **Where is the Windows Recovery Console accessed from?**

A ○ The Microsoft Windows XP Web site

B ○ The Windows XP setup CD-ROM

C ○ A third-party Web site

D ○ The Microsoft Help and Support Web site

Answers

1 **B.** Although Microsoft highly recommends 128MB, 64MB of RAM is the official minimum system requirement for Windows XP. *See "Meeting minimum requirements."*

2 **B.** Just like every minimum system requirement, more is always better. *Review "Meeting minimum requirements."*

3 **A & B.** These two tools, one online (Windows Catalog) and one on the setup CD-ROM can be used to predetermine if a system is compatible with Windows XP. *Check out "Installing Windows XP."*

4 **D.** Windows XP cannot be used to upgrade Windows 95, Windows 3.*x*, Windows NT Workstation 3.51, or any Server version. *Look over "Checking for eligibility."*

5 **B.** The Windows XP setup CD-ROM is a bootable disc. *Study "Getting to Know Windows XP."*

6 **C.** The `diskpart` command-line tool can be used to create, modify, or remove disk partitions. *See "Working at the Windows XP Command Line."*

7 **C.** This option was not introduced with Windows XP but is available with Windows NT and Windows 2000 systems. *Review "Dealing with general stop errors."*

8 **D.** The WHQL test device drivers and those that pass as compatible with Windows XP are digitally signed. Device drivers that are not digitally signed can cause operational problems. *Take a look at "Troubleshooting hardware failure stop errors."*

9 **A, B, & D.** Instead of calling Microsoft technical support, search the Microsoft Knowledge Base using the error number to find additional information. *Study "Troubleshooting file system stop errors."*

10 **B.** This tool is accessed by entering **R** on the first screen that is displayed by the setup program. *Check out "Recovering a Windows XP Setup."*

Part II

Connecting to a Network

In this part . . .

The A+ exams, both the Core Hardware and the OS Technologies exams, have become realistic in the sense that the subject of networking is become a larger and larger part of the exams with each new edition.

In the OS Technologies area, 25 percent of the objectives related to configuring a PC's operating system for connecting the PC to a network, in one form or another. So, bear down on this part, especially if you are new to PCs in general and networking PCs in particular.

Chapter 5

Making the Network Connection

● ●

Exam Objectives

▶ Establishing a network connection

▶ Installing and configuring a browser

▶ Differentiating among the common connectivity technologies

● ●

*1*n today's computing environment, networking is everything. A PC that is a part of a network is also a part of the connected world, with the emphasis on *world,* and all the information and other resources that it can provide. The ability to connect to a network, an essential part of a PC's function, is a system requirement that is sure to increase in importance. Whereas in the past, the power of the computer gave it its identity, in the not too distant future, its networking and communication speed may well be the computer's most important feature.

CompTIA believes that networking is an important topic for today's technicians. This is evidenced by the fact that it has included a domain in each of the A+ exams on networking. In fact, CompTIA believes that networking is important enough that at least 25 percent of the A+ OS Technologies exam relates to networking in some way.

In this chapter, the focus is on connecting the PC to the network, the protocols and services that are involved, the common connectivity technologies, and the process that is used to configure the PC to the network. See Book I, Chapter 18 and Chapters 6 and 7 of this book for more information on networking and the A+ exam.

Quick Assessment

Establishing a network connection

1 A _____ is a set of rules that govern the communication between two entities.

2 The networking term for the software flow that is established between two protocols is _____.

3 The Windows service that creates a Point-to-Point Protocol (PPP) connection between two computers over a telephone line is _____.

4 An IP address is made up of four 8-bit _____ that are separated by periods (dots).

5 A PC that is configured to obtain an IP address automatically receives its IP address configuration from a _____ server.

6 The Windows protocol that allows a DHCP client to self-configure with an IP address between 169.254.0.1 and 169.254.254.254 is _____.

7 A Windows PC that needs to connect with a NetWare server must install the _____ protocol.

Installing and configuring a browser

8 The Windows Scripting Host facilitates the running of _____ files.

9 A _____ temporarily caches downloaded files and provides them to secondary requesters to eliminate the need to forward file requests to the Internet in many cases.

Differentiating among the common connectivity technologies

10 The three most popular alternatives to dialup connectivity for home and office users are _____, _____, and _____.

Answers

1 *Protocol.* See "Configuring the Network dialog box."

2 *Binding.* Review "Configuring a network adapter."

3 *Dial-Up Networking* or *DUN.* Check out "Setting up Dial-Up Networking."

4 *Octets.* Study "Automatically assigning IP addresses."

5 *DHCP.* Study "Using DHCP."

6 *APIPA.* See "Using APIPA."

7 *NWLink.* Review "Speaking Novell."

8 *VBS.* Check out "Disabling script support."

9 *Proxy server.* Take a look at "Configuring proxy settings."

10 *DSL, ISDN, cable.* Look over "Comparing Cable, DSL, and ISDN."

Connecting to a Network

Windows 2000 and Windows XP automatically configure PCs with a typical network setup during installation. Windows 9x and Windows NT PCs don't have that feature and must be configured for a network connection manually. Actually, it is the network interface card (NIC) that is configured to communicate with a network. The PC itself only communicates with the NIC through the operating system and the NIC's device drivers and protocols.

Configuring the Network dialog box

The Network dialog box (see Figure 5-1) is used to configure a PC's network environment. Four network components can be configured from the Network dialog box; each is described as follows:

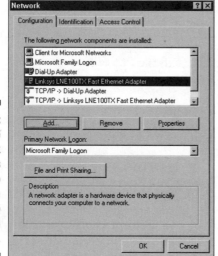

Figure 5-1:
The
Network
dialog box is
used to
configure a
PC to
connect to a
network.

✔ **Adapter:** This choice identifies and loads the device drivers for a NIC. To configure a PC to a network, a NIC or another type of network adapter must be present. Protocols and services are associated to the NIC.

✔ **Protocol:** A *protocol* is a set of rules that govern the communication between two entities. To communicate with a network, the PC must be using the same protocols as the network. In most cases, the protocol stack used is TCP/IP, but verify this with your network administrator before proceeding.

✔ **Client:** Network clients allow a PC to communicate with specific network operating systems, such as the Internet, Windows NT, Windows 2000, Windows 2003, or Novell NetWare.

✔ **Service:** Network services include specialized drivers that facilitate specialized capabilities, such as File and Print Sharing for Microsoft Networks and support for file systems on non-Windows servers.

Configuring a network adapter

Not all network adapters are NICs, but all NICs are network adapters. The two terms are commonly used interchangeably, but this can be misleading. For example, the network adapter for a PC that connects to a thick coaxial cable (ThickNet) network uses an external network adapter and not an expansion card inserted inside the PC. See Book I, Chapter 18 for more information on network media.

The following steps are involved in installing a NIC in a PC:

1. Physically installing the NIC in a Peripheral Component Interconnect (PCI) or, heaven forbid, an Industry Standard Architecture (ISA) slot on the motherboard. (See Book I, Chapter 5 for more information on these and other bus structures.)

2. Configuring the NIC to interact with the PC and the network and to facilitate the interface of these two.

The NIC that you have just installed probably sat in a store or warehouse long enough for its device drivers to become obsolete. So, even though an installation disk is included with the card and Windows has an extensive library of NIC drivers, always check with the manufacturer (online or by phone) to see if later versions of the device drivers are available. Make sure to match the drivers to the operating system, and be sure that the drivers are digitally signed for Windows.

After you have the latest driver, you can perform a software installation of the NIC in one of the following ways:

✔ **Plug and Play (PnP):** If the NIC is a PnP device, it should be automatically configured when the PC is restarted. If Windows cannot identify the adapter, the Hardware Wizard starts and guides you through installing a device driver for the NIC. If a disk came with the card, keep it handy.

✔ **Add New Hardware:** This wizard, which is started from the Control Panel, searches for and detects the new NIC. If new devices are detected, such as a legacy (ISA) NIC, you are prompted to supply a device driver. If a disk came with the NIC, keep it handy.

✔ **Add adapter:** Use the Add button on the Configuration tab of the Network dialog box to add the adapter to the PC. As always, if a disk came with the NIC, keep it handy.

Lab 5-1 details the steps that are used to configure a NIC for network connection. This lab assumes that the NIC has been physically installed in an expansion slot on the motherboard and has been properly configured with the system resources (IRQ, I/O addresses, and so on) and that no conflicts exist, so you are ready to proceed with the software configuration. See Book I, Chapter 18 for information on physically installing a NIC in a PC.

Lab 5-1	Configuring a NIC on a Windows 98 System

1. **Choose Start➪Settings➪Control Panel.**

2. **From the Control Panel, double-click the Network icon to open the Network dialog box (refer to Figure 5-1).**

    An alternative path to the Network dialog box is to right-click the Network Neighborhood or the My Network Places icon and choose Properties from the pop-up menu that appears.

3. **On the Configuration tab of the Network dialog box, highlight the network adapter and click the Properties button.**

    The Adapter Properties dialog box opens with its Driver Type tab displayed. Assuming that the NIC is a PCI card, the Driver Type tab should indicate an enhanced-mode (32-bit and 16-bit) NDIS (Network Device Interface Specification) driver for the NIC. The other choices are for cards without 32-bit NDIS support or for NICs that require ODI (Open Data-Link Interface). Check the NIC's documentation to determine which type you have.

4. **On the Bindings tab, you see a list of the protocols and services for which a binding is established.**

    In most cases, the bindings are preconfigured, but they can be modified. *Binding* is the networking term for the association of two protocols that perform different networking functions and the software flow that is established between them. If you are on an Ethernet network with access to the Internet, the bindings on your PC should reflect a binding of the NIC to TCP/IP. Except for rare instances, the Advanced tab is configured by the system and can be ignored.

5. **Locate the TCP/IP property for the network adapter in the network components list in the Network dialog box.**

    The entry is something like TCP/IP➪*Network Adapter Name*. Highlight this entry, and click the Properties button. The TCP/IP Properties dialog box displays.

6. **When the Network dialog box opens, the IP Address tab is displayed.**

   The user or the network administrator should provide this information. In most cases, you choose the Obtain an IP Address Automatically option to have the IP address of the PC assigned automatically by the network when it boots. (See the section, "Automatically assigning IP addresses," later in the chapter.) If the PC is assigned a static IP address (an address that doesn't change), which you would get from the network administrator, enter the IP address in the Specify an IP Address text box, along with its subnet mask.

7. **On most PCs, you can ignore the DNS Configuration, WINS Configuration, and NetBIOS tabs during NIC configuration.**

   However, if the network administrator has entries for these tabs, enter them as appropriate.

8. **Enter the IP address of the default gateway on the Gateway tab.**

   A *gateway* is a router, proxy server, or other device through which the PCs on a network reach the Internet or a company's wide area network (WAN). This address can be left blank if the network doesn't connect to the Internet or if this information is handled by a cable modem, DSL bridge, in-house router, or similar device.

9. **Review the contents of the Advanced tab.**

   The information displayed on the Advanced tab varies with the NIC and the characteristics of the network to which the PC is connected. The Properties list may reflect the media and connector in use or it may be used to turn on a log file.

10. **Click any Apply or OK buttons that appear.**

    The system updates its information database. Restart the system if you are asked to do so.

The following procedure in Lab 5-2 configures the network adapter/NIC on a Windows 2000 system for a connection to a dedicated broadband service, such as cable, DSL, or ISDN.

Lab 5-2	Configuring a NIC on a Windows 2000 System

1. **Locate the My Network Places icon on the Windows desktop and right-click it.**

   From the shortcut menu, click on Properties to display the Network and Dial-up Connections window.

2. **Right-click the Local Area Connection.**

   Choose Properties from the short cut menu that appears to display the Local Area Connection Properties dialog box.

3. **Locate the network adapter/NIC in the Connect Using panel.**

   If the network adapter is not listed, the network adapter may not be properly installed. You need to stop this process and check out the NIC.

4. **Select Internet Protocol from the components list and click the Properties button.**

   The Internet Protocol (TCP/IP) Properties dialog box displays. On this display, the options for Obtain an IP Address Automatically and Obtain DNS Server Address Automatically should be selected.

5. **On the Internet Protocol (TCP/IP) Properties dialog box, click the Advanced button.**

   The Advanced TCP/IP settings dialog box displays. On this dialog box, select the DNS tab and uncheck the Register the Connection's Address in DNS option. Click OK on the three open dialog boxes to complete this task.

6. **Restart the PC.**

Setting up Dial-Up Networking

A NIC is common in PCs that connect to a local area network (LAN), WAN, or the ultimate WAN — the Internet. However, a NIC isn't the only way to connect to a network, especially the Internet. The most common way to connect to the Internet is still the dialup modem (modulator/demodulator). And a very common service call complaint is a modem problem.

Any Windows PC that uses a modem to connect to a network — whether it is a LAN, WAN, or the Internet — uses Dial-Up Networking (DUN) to make the connection. DUN creates a Point-to-Point Protocol (PPP) connection between two computers over a telephone line. In effect, PPP causes the modem to act like a network interface card. PPP encapsulates the network protocol for transport over transmission lines, which allows the connected and communicating PCs to carry out their network interaction.

DUN automatically installs the Dial-Up Adapter (sorry, no acronym for this one) and the Client for Microsoft Networks (or this one either).

To communicate with a networked device, a PC must speak the other device's language, which means it must use the same protocol.

It seems like virtually all new PCs are shipped with an installed internal modem. However, you may need to upgrade a PC by installing an internal modem or replace a faulty or outdated modem as an FRM (field-replaceable module). After a modem is physically installed inside the PC (in an expansion slot) or externally installed through a serial or USB (Universal Serial Bus) connection (see

Book I, Chapter 10 for information on external ports), the modem should be configured as appropriate for the system. See the section, "Getting Ready for Work," later in this chapter, for Labs 5-3 and 5-4, and for information on how to configure a modem in Windows 9*x* or Windows 2000/XP, respectively.

Connecting to the Internet

Regardless of the process used to connect to the Internet, either by using a dialup or LAN connection, once the connection is made, the communication process and the protocols applied are the same.

Connecting with a dialup connection

Dial-Up Networking uses PPP to send data packets over telephone lines. PPP picks up a packet that has been created by one of the other network protocols and will be received by a remote PC running that same protocol. PPP is merely the intermediary that carries the data packet over the telephone line. If the packet begins the journey as a TCP/IP packet, it arrives at its destination as a TCP/IP packet.

An Internet service provider (ISP) typically assigns an IP address to a PC though its network access services (NASs), or modem banks, and RADIUS (Remote Authentication Dial-In User Service) services after a username and password are verified and the user is authenticated.

If a dialup connection fails, check the following areas:

- ✔ **Phone connection:** Nearly all modems use sound to enable the user to track the connection (handshake) as it is being made. The first of these sounds is the dial tone from the phone line. If the modem is not connecting and you do not hear a dial tone, a problem exists with the wall jack connection or with the phone line itself. You will probably get an error message indicating that you have no dial tone.

- ✔ **Modem problems:** If the modem cannot complete the handshake with the other end of the connection, the modem may be configured incorrectly in terms of its character length, start and stop bits, and speed.

- ✔ **Protocols:** Another common problem, especially for new modems, is that TCP/IP or other protocols have not been properly configured. Dialup connections typically require PPP. Verify that the protocols are enabled and that the proper bindings are set for the protocols.

- ✔ **Remote response:** The NAS that you are attempting to connect to may be down or having problems. Call your ISP to check this.

> ✔ **Telephone company problems:** If sufficient static or crosstalk exists on the telephone line, this noise can cause the modem to disconnect soon after completing the connection or can cause enough data retransmissions that the line appears to be exceptionally slow.

Connecting through a network connection

If a PC connects to the Internet through its LAN, its primary (or default) gateway is the router on the LAN that is used to connect to the WAN (Internet).

The only real difference between establishing a dialup connection and a network connection is that the network connection remains in place and doesn't require a reconnection each time that access is desired. Also, the user doesn't need to be authenticated, except for secure services such as e-mail or a Virtual Private Network (VPN). For more information on networking, read *Networking For Dummies,* 6th Edition, by Doug Lowe, and *Network+ Certification For Dummies,* by Ron Gilster (blush), both published by Wiley Publishing, Inc.

Comparing Cable, DSL, and ISDN

More users are connecting to the Internet and other networks using something other than a LAN or a dialup modem connection. The general availability of high-speed broadband services has allowed many users to move away from dialup connections to an always-on, dedicated connectivity technology. The three most popular alternatives to dialup connectivity are Digital Subscriber Line (DSL), Integrated Services Digital Network (ISDN), and cable.

The common thread among these three services is that they are all transmitted across analog systems. DSL and ISDN transmit digital data across the analog POTS (Plain Old Telephone Service) lines of the telephone company. Cable transmits its digital data across a coaxial cable system, which is primarily used to carry analog (and now some digital) television signals.

The processes that are detailed in Labs 5-1 through 5-4 aren't any different for these other communication services, except for the type of hardware that is used in the connection. All of these services are, in effect, providing a LAN connection as far as the PC is concerned.

The one unique step that is common to each of these connectivity technologies and their hardware is the need to install the proper device driver on the PC to facilitate the communications between the service's interface and the PC. Whether the interface device is a DSL modem, an ISDN terminal adapter, or a cable modem, this device is what the PC's NIC is connected to for its network connection.

Symmetrical versus Asymmetrical DSL

It's not a big deal for the A+ exams, but in case you're wondering, some differences exist between the two primary flavors of DSL.

Symmetrical DSL gets its name from the fact that the same data speed is used to transmit and receive. In other words, the same speed is used to upload and to download, making this service very fast.

Asymmetrical DSL refers to the fact — ah, you guessed it — that this type of DSL uses different data speeds to upload and download. For example, a common service of ADSL is about 128 kilobits per second (Kbps) for upload and 384 to 512 Kbps for download. Anytime that you see DSL referred to generically (such as DSL or xDSL), the reference is typically to ADSL.

Table 5-1 lists the data speeds and types of hardware that are used to interface the carrier lines to a home or office PC.

Table 5-1	DSL/ISDN/Cable Connectivity Technologies
Service	*Hardware Device*
Cable	Modem
Asymmetrical DSL (ADSL)	Modem or bridge
Symmetrical DSL (SDSL)	Bridge or router
Basic-Rate ISDN (BRI)	Network terminators or terminal adapters

Working without a wire

In addition to the connectivity technologies that are shown in Table 5-1 and discussed in the preceding section, you should know about two more connectivity technologies for the A+ OS Technologies exam: wireless networking and satellite Internet access.

Of the two technologies, I would recommend being more knowledgeable about wireless networking, at least for the time being. You don't need to be an expert at either for the current exam version. However, this is likely to change in the future.

Networking wireless

Several standards now exist for a variety of wireless communications technologies, including Bluetooth, General Packet Radio Service (GPRS), Home Radio Frequency (HomeRF), Institute for Electrical and Electronics Engineering (IEEE) 802.11 and 802.15, 3G/Universal Mobile Telecommunications Service (UMTS), and Wireless Fidelity (Wi-Fi).

The most common standards used for networking PCs are IEEE 802.11 and Wi-Fi. In both of these cases, the hardware that interfaces the PC to the network is what is different — not the entries in the PC's network configuration. IEEE 802.11 and Wi-Fi both use expansion card NICs (wireless NICs with a small antenna on the back of the PC) or PC card–type network adapters that interface to wireless hubs and network access points (NAPs).

Beaming it down from above

For those rugged individuals who live miles from the nearest telephone connection or ISP and have some southerly exposure, an alternative to wire-based or short-range wireless services is satellite Internet access.

Companies such as StarBand (`www.starband.com`) and SatCast (`www.direcpc.com`) offer a two-way satellite link to the Internet. This service connects to a PC through a USB port and is configured just like a LAN connection.

Automatically assigning IP addresses

IP addresses are comprised of four sets of numbers, and each set is separated by a period. An IP address is 32 bits long, and each of the 4 numbers is 8 bits long. The highest possible IP address is 255.255.255.255, because the highest value that can be represented in 8 bits is 255.

Each of the four 8-bit numbers is called an *octet,* which means a set of 8. The portions of an IP address are referred to as the first, second, third, and fourth octets. Sounds a like a singing group — the Octets and their new hit "Home, Home on the Domain."

Using DHCP

An IP address can be assigned as a static IP address (a fixed PC location) or as a dynamically assigned IP address (changeable). A static IP address is permanently assigned to a node when it is added to the network. Static IP addresses work as long as the network doesn't move, the NIC is not interchanged with other PCs, and the network is never reconfigured.

Because most networks change (and they change fairly frequently), it's good practice to assign IP addresses dynamically. Each PC that is attached to the network and is configured to obtain an IP address automatically requests and is assigned an IP address to use for a specific length of time by a Dynamic Host Configuration Protocol (DHCP) server. Beginning with Windows 95, all versions of Windows include a DHCP client.

Using APIPA

On occasion, a network PC boots up and finds that the DHCP server is not available. When this happens, the PC continues to poll for a DHCP server using different wait periods.

The Automatic Private IP Addressing (APIPA) service allows the DHCP client to automatically configure itself until the DHCP server is available and the client can be configured to the network. APIPA allows the DHCP client to assign itself an IP address in the range of 169.254.0.1 to 169.254.254.254 and a Class B subnet mask of 255.255.0.0. The address range that is used by APIPA is a Class B address that Microsoft has set aside for this purpose.

Speaking foreign network languages

When configuring a network PC, another consideration is what client interfaces must be installed to allow the PC to communicate with all resources on the network. For example, if Apple Computer or NetWare servers are on the network, the PC must have the applicable clients and linkware to be able to interact with them.

You need to know the following network terms for the exam:

- **AppleTalk:** This is Apple Computer's proprietary network protocol suite.

- **IPX/SPX:** This is a Novell NetWare proprietary protocol suite that is used as the native network operating system prior to Version 5 of NetWare, which uses TCP/IP as its native protocol.

- **NetBEUI/NetBIOS:** The NetBIOS Extended User Interface (NetBEUI — pronounced "net booey") is an enhanced version of the NetBIOS network operating system. NetBEUI is still used by many manufacturers as a network operating system on local networks that don't connect to the Internet.

Speaking Novell

If a PC that is running a Windows operating system wishes to communicate and interact with a Novell NetWare server, the NWLink protocol must be installed and activated in the PC.

To install NWLink on a Windows 2000/XP system, use the following steps:

1. **Choose Start⇨Settings⇨Network⇨Dial-Up Connections.**

2. **Right-click the local area connection on which you need to install NWLink, and click Properties.**

3. **On the General tab of the Properties dialog box, click Install.**

4. **Choose Protocol from the Select Network Component Type area, and click Add.**

5. **In the Select Network Protocol dialog box, click NWLink IPX/SPX/ NetBIOS Compatible Transport Protocol, and click OK to add the protocol.**

Configuring a Wide Window to the Web

The A+ OS Technologies exam objectives include an objective for installing and configuring browsers, but because installing a browser is a no-brainer, I'll skip it. If you need practice installing a Web browser, download Internet Explorer 6.0 and install it a few times.

The rest of this section focuses on the specific configuration items that CompTIA felt strongly enough about to list in the objectives.

Disabling script support

The Windows Scripting Host (WSH) is commonly installed on PCs to facilitate the running of Visual Basic Script (VBS) files. Unfortunately, computer viruses, such as VBS/LoveLet-A, VBS/Anna Kournikova, and others, use the Scripting Host to run and ruin your PC. Because of this, disabling the Scripting Host is a good idea.

The process used to disable the Scripting Host varies depending on the Windows version, but two general procedures are used to disable scripting support on a PC: the Windows 98 way, which also works for Windows 95 and NT, and the Windows 2000 way, which also works for Windows XP and Me.

Disabling script support in Windows 98

The WSH is installed on a Windows 98 system whenever Internet Explorer is installed or upgraded, and in a few other instances. Use the following steps to disable the WSH by removing it from a Windows 98 PC:

1. **Open the Control Panel, and click the Add/Remove Programs icon.**

2. **In the Add/Remove Programs dialog box, click the Windows Setup tab (see Figure 5-2).**

3. **In the Components panel, find and double-click the Accessories folder to open the Accessories options list (see Figure 5-3).**

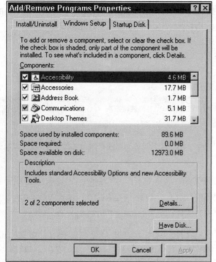

Figure 5-2:
The Windows Setup tab in the Add/Remove Programs dialog box.

Figure 5-3:
The Accessories options of the Windows Setup dialog boxes, showing that the Windows Scripting Host option is installed.

4. **If the Windows Scripting Host entry is selected (checked), deselect this option. Click OK to return to the Add/Remove Programs dialog box.**

5. **Click the Apply button to start removing the Windows Scripting Host, and when you are returned to the Add/Remove Programs dialog box, click OK to return to the Control Panel.**

Disabling scripting support in Windows 2000

The WSH is installed and enabled by default on Windows 2000, XP, and Me systems. To disable this function, the VBS support must be deleted from the system. Use the following steps to disable support for VBScripts by removing the WSH from a Windows 2000 PC:

1. **Log on to the PC as an administrator.**

2. **On the desktop or from Windows Explorer, double-click the My Computer icon to open the My Computer window.**

3. **In the My Computer window, choose Tools⇨Folder Options, and click the File Types tab.**

   In the list of registered file types, look for VBScript Script File. If you can't find this, you have nothing to worry about, and you can click the Cancel button until you return to the desktop.

4. **Highlight the VBScript Script File and click the Delete button to remove it from the system. When asked to confirm the deletion, click Yes.**

5. **Click OK until you return to the desktop.**

Configuring proxy settings

A proxy server saves you time and saves your employer or your school money by reducing the number of times that requests for data are sent to the Internet. A proxy server temporarily caches most downloaded files and later provides these files to users instead of sending each individual request out on the Internet.

This same concept can be used on an individual PC using features built into most of the popular Internet browsers. Microsoft Internet Explorer includes settings that allow the user to retain all, portions, or none of the files downloaded to the PC so that a Web page's data doesn't need to be retrieved from the Internet each time its Web site is visited. The files held in the proxy function by Internet Explorer are stored in a folder named Temporary Internet Files.

This sounds like a good deal, and it can be, but the proxy settings should be configured to support the action the user wishes to use. The following steps can be used to configure the proxy settings in Internet Explorer:

1. **Open Internet Explorer and choose Tools➪Internet Options.**

2. **From the Internet Options dialog box, click the Connections tab and then click the Settings button from the option that corresponds to the way in which the PC connects to the Internet: either the Settings button in the Dial-Up and Virtual Private Network Settings section or the LAN Settings button in the Local Area Network (LAN) settings area as shown in Figure 5-4.**

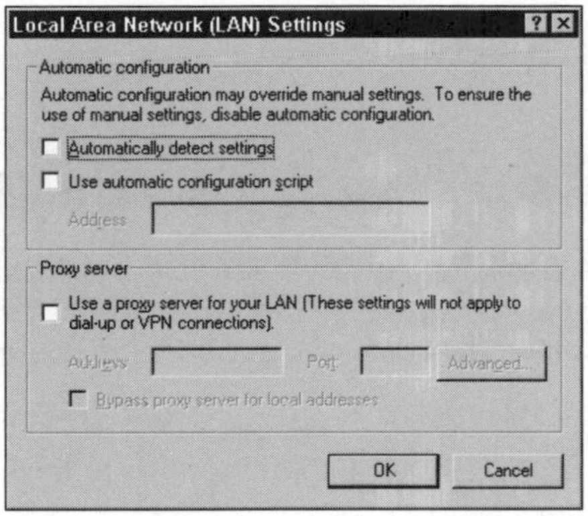

Figure 5-4:
The Local
Area
Network
(LAN)
settings
dialog box
of Internet
Explorer.

Local Area Network (LAN) Settings

Automatic configuration

Automatic configuration may override manual settings. To ensure the use of manual settings, disable automatic configuration.

☐ Automatically detect settings

☐ Use automatic configuration script

Address [   ]

Proxy server

☐ Use a proxy server for your LAN (These settings will not apply to dial-up or VPN connections).

Address [   ] Port [   ] Advanced...

☐ Bypass proxy server for local addresses

[OK] [Cancel]

3. **In the Local Area Network (LAN) Settings dialog box, find the Proxy server area and select the Use a Proxy Server check box.**

   If the Bypass Proxy for Local Addresses check box is not selected, leave it that way or check with your network administrator to determine how it should be set.

4. **Click the Advanced button in the Proxy server area to open the Proxy Settings dialog box (see Figure 5-5).**

   At this point, either an ISP or the local network administrator must provide information for what to insert in the various protocol text boxes. You can check the Use the Same Proxy for All Protocols check box, but you must enter a proxy server URL (Universal Resource Locator) in the HTTP text box (see Figure 5-5) and enter the port that is assigned to the proxy in the Port text box.

5. **Click OK to return to the previous dialog box, and click OK until you are returned to the browser. You should close the browser and restart it before attempting to test these configurations.**

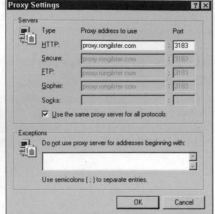

Figure 5-5:
The Proxy
Settings
dialog box in
Internet
Explorer.

Configuring browser security settings

The basis for security in the Internet Explorer Web browser software is its security zones. You can assign any site to any of the four security zones that are defined by Internet Explorer, and you can permit or restrict the assigned site as you set up each zone.

The four security zones defined by Internet Explorer are as follows:

- ✔ **Local intranet:** This zone contains connections that are made on the local network or intranet. These sites are typically identified by computer names or URLs that bypass the proxy server or are located on the host PC. The default security level of this zone is Medium or Low.

- ✔ **Trusted sites:** This zone includes Web sites that you have indicated are safe to trust. By default, no Web site classes are defined in this zone, and its security level is set to Low.

- ✔ **Restricted sites:** This zone is where Web sites that you don't trust end up. You may have reason to believe that these sites will harm your PC and its resources. This is sort of the penitentiary for rogue Web sites. By default, no sites are assigned here, and the security level is High.

- ✔ **Internet:** A Web site that is not included in any of the other zones is assigned to this zone. Security is set to Low, and no sites are assigned here by default.

You have the option of assigning one of three security levels to each of these zones: High security, Medium security, and Low security. You can also define your own security level by combining various aspects of a security level.

Getting Ready for Work

A common user problem is the replacement or new installation of a modem in a PC. Labs 5-3 and 5-4 detail the steps that are used to configure a modem on a Windows 9*x* and a Windows 2000 system, respectively.

Lab 5-3   Configuring a Modem on a Windows 9*x* PC

1. **Open My Computer to determine if DUN is installed.**

   If Dial-Up Networking is already installed, you see a Dial-Up Networking icon in the My Computer window. Otherwise, insert the Windows setup CD-ROM in the CD-ROM drive, open the Control Panel, and choose the Add/Remove Program icon.

   When the Add/Remove Programs dialog box displays, select the Windows Setup tab. Double-click the Communications option, and select the Dial-Up Networking box. Click OK on this and the next dialog box to initiate the loading of the DUN files to your PC. When the installation is complete, click OK to restart the PC.

   When inserting a Windows installation CD-ROM, hold down Shift when you close the CD-ROM tray to prevent the Windows autorun program from starting.

2. **Make a new connection by opening the My Computer window and double-clicking the Dial-Up Networking icon. Assuming that you need to create a new connection, double-click the Make New Connection icon, which starts the Make New Connection Wizard — of all things.**

   If the wizard tells you that the modem that you just installed is not recognized, don't take it personally; just agree to let Windows try to detect the modem again. If Windows can't find the modem after an embarrassing number of retries, cancel the whiz and troubleshoot the modem problem.

3. **Enter the dialing data from the user's ISP, and contact the ISP's technical support for the dialing and configuration information that is needed to set up the connection.**

   This includes the phone number (and backup phone number) to be dialed by the modem.

4. **Create the PC's identification by opening the Control Panel and selecting the Network icon. Click the Identification tab.**

   Ask the user to give the computer a name, a workgroup, and a description. Entering this information updates the device information database and requires you to restart the system.

5. **To configure the network, open the Control Panel, select the Network icon, and click the Configuration tab.**

Click the Add button. In the dialog box that displays, highlight the Protocol selection and click its Add button to display the Select Network Protocol dialog box (see Figure 5-6). Highlight Microsoft, and find TCP/IP in the right pane. Click the OK to return to the Network dialog box, and click OK to exit the dialog box.

Figure 5-6:
The Select
Protocol
dialog box is
used to add
new dialup
or network
protocols to
a Windows
PC.

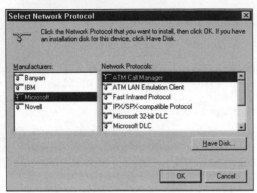

6. Configure the protocol.

Open the My Computer window and double-click the Dial-Up Networking folder. Right-click the icon of the connection that you just created, and choose Properties. Select the Server Types tab, and click the TCP/IP button that's near the lower-right corner to open the TCP/IP Settings dialog box (see Figure 5-7). The settings in this dialog box should be verified with the ISP or the network administrator, depending on how the modem is to be used and the network to which it is connecting. However, except for the IP addresses, which are unique to each ISP, the settings that are shown in Figure 5-7 are fairly typical.

Figure 5-7:
The
Windows
dialog box
opened to
configure
the network
settings
of a dialup
connection.

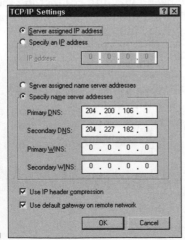

The process that is used to configure a DUN connection in Windows 2000/XP/Me is similar to what's used in Windows 9*x*, but it is a bit less complicated, which is always nice. To configure a DUN connection in Windows 2000, XP, or Me, use the steps of Lab 5-4.

Lab 5-4   Configuring DUN in Windows 2000 and Windows XP

1. **Log on as an administrator.**

   In Windows 2000 and Windows XP, you must log on as an administrator to make any configuration changes, not just changes to DUN. Windows Me doesn't have this requirement.

2. **Right-click My Computer.**

   On the Windows 2000 or Me desktop or from the Windows XP Start menu, right-click the My Computer icon or menu choice and choose Properties from the pop-up menu that appears.

3. **Enter a computer name.**

   Click the Network Identification tab and then the Properties button. In the Computer Name text box, enter a name for the computer to be used on the network and click OK. This is the name that is shown in My Network Places.

4. **Click all the OK buttons that display until you are returned to the desktop.**

5. **Make the new connection.**

   Right-click My Network Places on the desktop or Start menu, and choose Properties from the pop-up menu that appears. In the Properties window, double-click the Make New Connection icon. When the Network Connection Wizard displays, click the Next button to start the wizard.

6. **Configure the connection.**

   Choose the Dial Up to the Internet option, and click Next. On the next screen, choose the I Want to Set Up My Internet Connection Manually and the I Can't Believe It's Not Butter options (you may not find the second option on all Windows systems), and click Next. On the next screen, choose the I Connect through a Phone Line and a Modem option and click Next.

7. **Enter the telephone number and the country/region name and code, and indicate whether you want to use the area code and dialing rules.**

   Use the Windows Help feature to find out more about these entries if you have questions. Click the Next button.

8. **If the ISP has provided DNS addresses, enter them by clicking the Advanced button on the next screen and choosing the Addresses tab.**

   In the text box labeled DNS server, enter the information given and click OK. Otherwise, skip this step.

9. **Enter the username and password for the user.**

   Better yet, have the user enter this information. Click Next, and on the next screen, give the connection a name, such as the name of the ISP.

10. **When the wizard tries to detect Internet Mail clients and asks if you would like to create an Internet Mail account, click No and then click Next.**

    The user can create an Internet Mail account later. On the next screen, deselect the To Connect to the Internet Immediately check box and click Finish.

11. **Test the Dial-Up Networking connection.**

    Open the Network and Dial-Up Connections window from the My Computer window or from the Settings option on the Start menu, and double-click the icon for the connection that you've just created.

Prep Test

1 Which of the following is not a networking component that can be configured through the Control Panel's Network icon?

  A ○ Protocol

  B ○ Service

  C ○ Server

  D ○ Client

2 What is the name of a set of rules that governs the communication between two entities?

  A ○ Protocol

  B ○ Service

  C ○ Server

  D ○ Client

3 What software feature allows a PC to communicate with a specific network operating system, such as Windows NT, Windows 2000, or Novell NetWare?

  A ○ Protocol

  B ○ Service

  C ○ Server

  D ○ Client

4 To configure a PC for DHCP and to enable automatic IP configuration each time that the PC boots, you must establish which Windows configuration setting on the PC?

  A ○ Connect using LAN settings

  B ○ Obtain an IP address automatically

  C ○ Run IPCONFIG /request on boot

  D ○ Obtain client Internet configuration automatically

5 What protocol does Dial-Up Networking use to create a connection between two computers over a telephone line?

  A ○ IP

  B ○ TCP

  C ○ PPP

  D ○ SLIP

6 Which of the following is not an alternative technology to LAN and dialup connectivity?

A ○ DSL

B ○ ISDN

C ○ Cable

D ○ SCS

7 What device is used to interface with an ISDN connection?

A ○ NIC

B ○ Terminal adapter

C ○ Modem

D ○ Bridge

8 Which of the following are wireless communications standards? (Choose three.)

A ❑ Bluetooth

B ❑ 3G

C ❑ IEEE 802.3

D ❑ GPRS

9 What is the APIPA address range from which a PC can self-configure should the DHCP server be unavailable?

A ○ 10.0.0.1 to 10.255.255.254

B ○ 169.254.0.1 to 169.254.255.254

C ○ 192.168.0.1 to 168.168.11.255

D ○ 240.0.0.1 to 240.255.255.254

10 Which of the following is not a security zone supported by Microsoft Internet Explorer?

A ○ Trusted

B ○ Local intranet

C ○ Restricted

D ○ Unrestricted

Answers

1 **C.** The Network window supports the configurations of protocols, services, clients, and network adapters. *See "Configuring the Network dialog box."*

2 **A.** Protocols contain rules about message formatting, data speeds, and other controls regarding the transmission of data. *Review "Configuring the Network dialog box."*

3 **D.** Client software establishes the request/reply relationship between a client workstation and a server. *Check out "Configuring the Network dialog box."*

4 **B.** This option is found on the IP Address tab of the Network dialog box. *Look over "Configuring a network adapter."*

5 **C.** DUN uses the Point-to-Point Protocol (PPP) to establish a direct connection with a remote device. *Study "Setting up Dial-Up Networking."*

6 **D.** I made this one up. (SCS stands for soup can and string.) The others, along with wireless and satellite connectivity technologies, offer a range of alternatives to dialup connectivity. *See "Comparing Cable, DSL, and ISDN" and "Working without a wire."*

7 **B.** ISDN interface devices are also called network terminators. *Review "Comparing Cable, DSL, and ISDN."*

8 **A, B, & D.** The wireless networking standards that were developed by IEEE are 802.11 and 802.15. *Check out "Working without a wire."*

9 **B.** The Automatic Private IP Addressing (APIPA) service allows the DHCP client to automatically configure itself should a DHCP server not be available. *Take a look at "Using APIPA."*

10 **D.** The fourth IE security zone is Internet, which is the catchall zone. *Study "Configuring browser security settings."*

Chapter 6

Working with the Network

Exam Objectives

▶ Creating network shares on a Windows PC

▶ Mapping a network drive

▶ Identifying TCP/IP protocols and their functions

*I*t is becoming increasingly rare that a PC is not connected to a network of some type. Regardless of whether the connection is a simple dialup connection to a local Internet service provider (ISP) or a sophisticated multihomed, totally redundant connection to a LAN, WAN, or VPN, just about every PC connects to some form of a network today. So, requiring you to know a bit about networking isn't all that radical.

The A+ OS Technologies exam has an objective domain that is dedicated to creating a networking environment on a PC. Don't be confused about the fact that a Networking objective domain also exists on the A+ Hardware Technology exam. The A+ OS Technologies exam focuses on the software tools that are available in the Windows operating system to set up and configure a PC to access and be accessed from a local network. You should expect about 8 to 12 questions on the A+ OS Technologies exam that deal with the general and specific networking features and functions of the Windows operating systems.

Don't study only this chapter to get ready for the Networking domain of the A+ OS Technologies exam. You should also equally focus on Chapters 5 and 7. They cover how to connect the PC to a network and how to interface the PC to the Internet, respectively.

Quick Assessment

Creating network shares on a Windows PC

1 The resources on the network or networks to which a PC is attached are displayed on the _____ in Windows 98 and the _____ in Windows 2000 and XP.

2 The service that must be enabled on your PC to allow you to share resources across the network is _____.

3 Placing a _____ at the end of a share name creates a hidden share.

4 Windows XP includes two sharing tools, _____ and _____.

Mapping a network drive

5 When mapping a network drive to your PC, you must enter the full _____ of the remote drive.

6 You must assign a _____ to the remote drive to map it to your PC.

Identifying TCP/IP protocols and their functions

7 The _____ defines the logical addressing scheme that is used to move messages across the Internet.

8 _____ is an extension of HTTP that focuses on the secure transmission of messages.

9 The command-line utility that displays the current configuration for a PC that is connected to a TCP/IP network for Windows NT/2000/XP systems is _____.

10 _____ is the TCP/IP utility that is used to determine whether an IP address is online or reachable.

Answers

1 *Network Neighborhood, My Network Places.* See "Showing off the neighborhood."

2 *File and Printer Sharing for Microsoft Networks.* Review "Getting ready to share."

3 *$ (dollar sign).* Look over "Granting shares to devices.

4 *Simple File Sharing (SFS), Access Control List (ACL).* Check out "Sharing a Windows XP file."

5 *Share name.* Study "Mapping a drive in Windows 98."

6 *Drive letter.* See "Mapping a drive in Windows 2000/XP."

7 *Internet Protocol (IP).* Review "Identifying the TCP/IP protocols."

8 *SHTTP or HTTPS.* Take a look at "Identifying the TCP/IP protocols."

9 *IPCONFIG.* Check out "Checking out the connection."

10 *PING.* Study "Checking out the connection."

Navigating the Neighborhood and a Few New Places

Windows 9*x* and Windows NT Workstation have Network Neighborhood, while Windows 2000, Windows XP, and Windows Me have My Network Places. In all of these cases, the respective icons, which are located on the Windows desktop, are used to access and display information about other PCs and the networked resources that are located on the same network segment as your PC.

Showing off the neighborhood

The Network Neighborhood and My Network Places icons work similarly to the My Computer icon, which is also located on the desktop. However, whereas My Computer displays the resources that are found on your PC, My Network Places or Network Neighborhood shows the resources that are found on the PC's network.

My Network Places (which is meant to refer to both My Network Places and Network Neighborhood for the sake of brevity) displays a tree structure of the resources that are on the local network in a form similar to that used by Windows Explorer to display files and folders. In fact, Windows Explorer can also be used to display the network structure, if you prefer to use that tool. Figure 6-1 shows the network connections for a Windows 98 PC that is connected to a Windows 2000 server.

Figure 6-1: The network resources that are available to a PC are displayed in Windows Explorer.

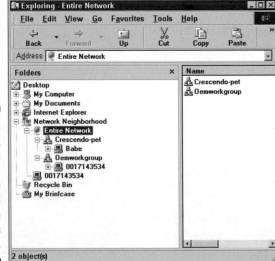

If you click the My Network Places icon and no PCs are shown, check to see whether you have enabled printer and file sharing and whether other PCs on the network have also set up resources to be shared.

Sharing and sharing alike

The My Network Places display or that in Windows Explorer, as shown in Figure 6-1, may include other workgroups and other PCs, but the display may also include public printers, CD-ROM drives, fax machines, and private devices. A *private device* is a peripheral device that is attached to a specific PC and owned by its user. Private devices, such as a printer, a hard drive, or even a DVD-ROM drive, must be shared by their owner before the following things happen:

✔ They show up on your network resources display

✔ You can access them

One of the problems with sharing on a Windows system is that all resources, including those shared and those not shared, are displayed on the My Network Places and Network Neighborhood windows. Those that are shared have a special icon that includes a sharing hand to indicate that a share has been granted.

May we please have your name?

Like the PCs that are shown in Figure 6-1, all resources on the network should have a computer name (used by the network) or a share name (used by users to whom permission has been granted).

Creating a computer name for a PC and assigning it to either a domain or a workgroup is typically done during installation of the Windows operating system. However, you can complete this step later (things can change in a networked environment).

To assign a computer name to a Windows 98 PC, use the following steps:

1. **Choose Start⇨Settings⇨Control Panel⇨Network to access the Network dialog box.**

2. **Choose the Identification tab in the Network dialog box (see Figure 6-2). Complete the text boxes as follows:**

   • Enter the computer name in the Computer Name text box.

   Use only alphabetic characters (a to z and A to Z) and numeric characters (0 to 9) for this name. Avoid the use of punctuation and other special characters.

• Enter the name of the workgroup of which this computer is a member. Most of the time, this name is `Workgroup`, but your network administrator may have customized the name. It does happen! Only PCs in the same workgroup can see each other across the network. So, if a network has more than one workgroup, each workgroup must obviously have a different name. For this and the next entry, check with your network administrator.

• Enter a descriptive phrase in the Computer Description text box. You can enter just about anything you want, but keep it simple.

• Click OK, and continue to click OK until you are returned to the desktop. Reboot your PC if you are asked to do so.

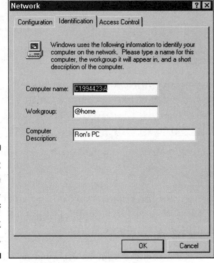

Figure 6-2:
The
Identifica-
tion tab of
the Network
dialog box.

On Windows NT, 2000, XP, and Me systems, these fields were most likely entered during installation. However, if you want to change them, click Change on the Identification tab in the Network dialog box, and make your changes. The guidelines that I recommended for Windows 98 still apply.

Getting ready to share

After a Windows 98 PC has been configured to connect to a network (see Chapter 5), it is configured as a stand-alone network client. To access shared network devices, the File and Printer Sharing for Microsoft Networks service must be installed and enabled on the PC.

On Windows NT, 2000, XP, or Me PCs, the File and Printer Sharing for Microsoft Networks service is automatically enabled during installation. In the event that this didn't happen, use the following steps to install and activate this service:

1. **Open the Network icon on the Control Panel.**

   (See the section, "May we please have your name?" earlier in this chapter, for the required steps.)

2. **Click the File and Print Sharing button on the Configuration tab in the Network dialog box.**

3. **Based on what you are willing to share — your files or your printer — select one or both of the check boxes in the File and Print Sharing dialog box that displays (see Figure 6-3).**

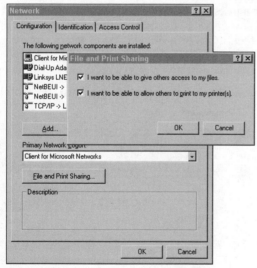

Figure 6-3: File and Printer Sharing for Microsoft Networks allows you to share files, printers, or both.

4. **Click OK, and continue to click OK until you are asked to reboot your PC.**

5. **Reboot the PC.**

Granting shares to devices

Just as you can't access something that you can't see in My Network Places, other network users can't access your resources if they can't see them or don't know that they can see them. To create a network share, which opens access to a device or a folder on a drive to others, use the steps that are listed in Labs 6-1 or 6-2.

Lab 6-1 Creating a Share on a Peripheral Device

1. **Open My Computer from the desktop.**

2. **Right-click the device for which you want to create a share.**

   For example, to share a printer, open the Printers folder and right-click the printer that you want to share, as shown in Figure 6-4.

   To hide a shared device from the My Network Places display, place a $ (dollar sign) at the end of the share name. This indicates to the system that this is a hidden share.

3. **From the pop-up menu that appears, choose Sharing.**

4. **On the Sharing tab or in the dialog box that appears, enter a share name (and a comment, if you want to).**

5. **Enter a password (optional).**

   Whether you enter a password depends on whether you plan to limit access to the device or allow all users to access it. To grant access to the device to only a select group or a single user, create a password that you share with only those to whom you grant access. To allow any network user to access the device, entering a password may be unnecessary.

6. **Click OK, and respond Yes when asked if you want to restart the PC.**

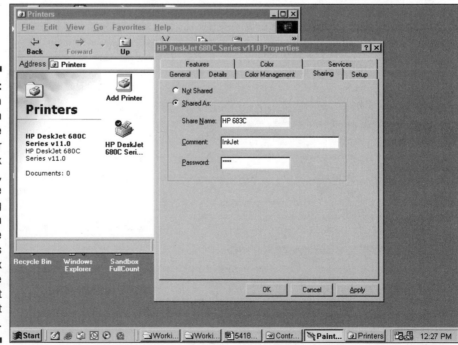

Figure 6-4:
To share a printer with all or some of the other network users, access the Sharing function in the Properties dialog box of the device that you want to share.

One final bit of information about share names is that you can assign as many share names as you want to a single device, and each device can have (or not have) its own password.

Sharing a folder

It is common practice among users on peer-to-peer networks and users that belong to the same workgroup to share folders and files. As with hardware devices, file sharing can be restricted or unrestricted. The procedures that are used to share a file for Windows 98, NT, and 2000 are similar. To set up a share on a folder, use the steps that are shown in Lab 6-2.

The process that you use to create a share on a drive's folder is similar to that used to add a share on a hardware device (see Lab 6-1). Lab 6-2 focuses on the steps that are unique to opening a share on a data folder.

Lab 6-2   Creating a Network Share on a Windows 98 Folder

1. **Access the folder that you want to share by using Windows Explorer or by navigating through the My Computer icons.**

    You could also use the Search or Find function to locate the folder.

2. **Right-click the folder that you want to share, and choose Properties from the pop-up menu that appears.**

3. **In the Properties dialog that opens (see Figure 6-5), select the Sharing tab.**

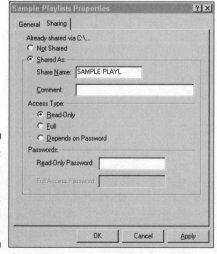

Figure 6-5:
The Sharing tab of a folder's Properties dialog box.

4. **To share the file, choose the Shared As option.**

   If a share has been granted to the C:\ folder (the root folder on the hard drive), the following message displays above the Not Shared/Shared As option buttons: `Already Shared Via C:\`. If you want to grant access to your entire hard drive, the share that is on C:\ has taken care of that. However, to share only certain folders, I recommend removing the share at C:\ (unless you want to place passwords on every folder that you don't want to share).

5. **Choose the level of access that you want to grant: read-only (no changes) or full access (read, write, modify, and remove).**

   You can also choose both and grant access to the folder based on the password entered.

   To grant just read-only permission, enter a password in the Read-only Password text box. To grant full access, enter a password in the Full-Access Password text box. However, to establish read-only access for some users and full access for others, choose Depending on Password, and enter passwords in both text boxes.

6. **Click Apply, and then click OK.**

   I recommend restarting the PC immediately to set the permission that you've just entered.

7. **Verify the share by viewing the shared folder.**

   If the share was successful, the icon for the folder should now look like a folder being held in a hand (see Figure 6-6).

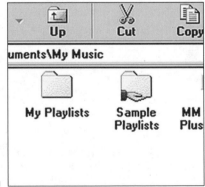

Figure 6-6: The right icon is a shared folder; the left icon is unshared.

Sharing a Windows XP file

Windows XP introduced new methods for sharing a PC's resources with other network users that include protections for a PC's owners when creating shares. For example, Windows XP replaced password-based access, which had inherent problems, with two share security alternatives, Access Control Lists and Simple File Sharing. These are described as follows:

- ✔ **Access Control List (ACL):** This option, also available in Windows 2000, is used to create a list of users and to indicate what permissions they have been granted for each shared resource.

- ✔ **Simple File Sharing (SFS):** SFS is like an on/off type of method to grant access to a resource. A user has the choice of sharing a file or making the document private; the latter is the choice that is shown on the Sharing and Security dialog box for a resource.

Mapping a Network Drive

In addition to giving you the ability to share private local resources with other users on a network, Windows includes a feature that allows you to connect a remote folder to a local PC so that the drive essentially becomes a local drive. This process is called *mapping a drive*. Lab 6-3 details the steps that are used to map a resource in Windows 98/NT, and Lab 6-4 shows how to map a resource in Windows 2000/XP.

Mapping a drive in Windows 98

The process that is used to map a drive is simple in Windows 98 and requires only two entries. Lab 6-3 details how to map a resource (a shared folder or drive from another computer) on a Windows 98 or NT system.

Lab 6-3   Mapping a Shared Resource in Windows 98

1. **Right-click My Computer, My Network Places, or Network Neighborhood and select Map Network Drive.**

2. **In the dialog box that displays, enter the computer name of the host (remote) PC on which the resource is located in the Folder or Path box.**

   The resource must have a share on it before you can map it to your system. The share name should be entered in the following format:

   ```
   \\computername\sharename
   ```

   For example, to map to the My Music folder on my PC, you would enter the following:

   ```
   \\Ron's PC\My Music
   ```

3. **Assign a drive letter to this resource.**

   The drive letter will be linked (mapped) to the device, and it will be shown in the My Computer and Windows Explorer windows.

4. **If you don't want to remap the resource to your system each time that you reboot it, select the Reconnect at Logon check box.**

   The mapping will now be created automatically each time that you log on to the network.

Mapping a drive in Windows 2000 and XP

In Windows 2000 and Windows XP, mapping a network drive is almost as simple as it is in Windows 98, but the additional complexity is well worth the effort. Lab 6-4 details how to map a network drive in Windows 2000. (I explain the primary XP difference where it exists.)

Lab 6-4	Mapping a Network Resource in Windows 2000

1. **On a Windows 2000 system, right-click My Computer and select Map Network Drive from the pop-up menu that appears.**

   On a Windows XP system, select Map Network Drive as follows:

   1. Click Start.

   2. Right-click My Computer.

   3. Select Map Network Drive from the pop-up menu that appears.

2. **In the dialog box that appears, select a drive letter (hopefully, one that is not in use) that you want to assign to the logical device that you are creating.**

3. **In the Folder text box, enter the computer name and share name in the form that is shown in Lab 6-3, Step 2.**

4. **Select the Reconnect at Logon check box.**

   Otherwise, you are indicating that this is just a one-time thing (which it very well could be).

5. **Click Finish.**

   The resource should appear in the My Computer and Windows Explorer lists under the assigned drive letter.

Getting to Know the TCP/IP Suite

The Transmission Control Protocol/Internet Protocol (TCP/IP) suite, also known as just the Internet Protocol suite, has quickly become the standard for network communications at both the global and local levels. TCP/IP was developed with portability and universal support in mind. Its adaptability and open structure have been important reasons for its rapid and widespread growth.

Identifying the TCP/IP protocols

TCP/IP is a suite, or stack, of protocols that interconnect and work together to provide reliable and efficient data communications across an internetwork. The TCP/IP protocols and tools that you should know for the A+ OS Technologies exam are as follows:

- **Domain Name System (DNS):** DNS is the service that is used to translate domain names (such as `wiley.com`) to their associated IP addresses (such as 205.99.254.16).

- **File Transport Protocol (FTP):** FTP is a protocol that is used to copy files from one computer to another over a TCP/IP network. FTP includes functions that allow it to log on to a remote network, navigate the network's directory structure, list the contents of the network's directories, and copy files by downloading them to the local computer.

- **Hypertext Markup Language (HTML):** HTML is the authoring language that is used to structure the documents for transmission across the internetwork and the World Wide Web (WWW) for interpretation and display by browser software.

- **Hypertext Transfer Protocol (HTTP):** HTTP is the foundation protocol of the WWW. It controls how messages are formatted and transmitted in response to the HTML code in a document and the actions of the user.

- **Internet Message Access Protocol (IMAP4):** Used for retrieving e-mail messages, this protocol provides additional message-management services over the POP3 protocol.

- **Internet Protocol (IP):** IP defines the logical addressing that is used across the Internet (which is why an address such as 10.100.100.1 is called an IP address) and defines the formatting of the message units, called packets or datagrams, that are sent across the physical media.

- ✔ **Post Office Protocol (POP3):** This is an e-mail protocol that is used to retrieve messages from an e-mail server. POP3 is the protocol that is used by most e-mail clients.

- ✔ **Secure HTTP (SHTTP or HTTPS):** This is an extension of the HTTP protocol that focuses on the secure transmission of messages.

- ✔ **Secure Sockets Layer (SSL):** This is a protocol service that focuses on establishing a secure connection between transmitted stations. SSL is complementary with SHTTP, which focuses on the secure transmission of the data.

- ✔ **Simple Mail Transport Protocol (SMTP):** This is the most common protocol for sending e-mail between mail servers.

Don't waste time memorizing all the protocols in the TCP/IP suite. (Besides, I haven't listed them all.) Look over the preceding list and note the function that is performed by each protocol. That's what you need to know for the A+ exam.

Checking out the connection

Windows 9x, Windows 2000, and Windows XP include and support a variety of TCP/IP tools and utilities that can be used to monitor or diagnose network problems that affect a single PC.

CompTIA lists the following protocols, utilities, and tools in its objectives, so you should know them for the exams:

- ✔ IPCONFIG **(IP Configuration):** This command-line utility displays the current configuration for a PC that is connected to a TCP/IP network for Windows NT/2000/XP systems. Figure 6-7 shows an example of an IPCONFIG display. This utility can also be used to manage the IP configuration of a networked PC (see Chapter 5 for more information).

- ✔ NSLOOKUP **(Network Lookup Service):** This utility is used to find an IP address or hostname of a particular PC.

- ✔ PING **(Packet Internet Groper):** This Internet utility is used to determine whether an IP address is online or reachable. Either an IP address or a domain name can be pinged over a network.

- ✔ Telnet: This is a terminal emulation protocol that is used on TCP/IP-based networks to remotely log on to a device to run a program or manipulate data.

- ✔ TRACERT **(Trace Route):** This TCP/IP utility is used to display the path between one network point and another, and the routers and timing on those routers along that route.

✔ WINIPCFG **(Windows IP Configuration):** This is the Windows 9*x* (and Windows Me) work-alike for the IPCONFIG utility. This utility can also be used to manage the IP configuration of a networked PC (see Chapter 5 for more information).

```
MS-DOS Prompt                                                    _ 8 X
Auto      ▼  □ 📋 🔁 🔄 🖵 A

        Host Name . . . . . . . . : C1994423-A.attbi.com
        DNS Servers . . . . . . . : 204.127.198.4
                                    63.240.76.4
        Node Type . . . . . . . . : Broadcast
        NetBIOS Scope ID. . . . . :
        IP Routing Enabled. . . . : No
        WINS Proxy Enabled. . . . : No
        NetBIOS Resolution Uses DNS : No

0 Ethernet adapter :

        Description . . . . . . . : Linksys LNE100TX Fast Ethernet Adapter
        Physical Address. . . . . : 00-A0-CC-34-0A-CE
        DHCP Enabled. . . . . . . : Yes
        IP Address. . . . . . . . : 12.207.247.187
        Subnet Mask . . . . . . . : 255.255.248.0
        Default Gateway . . . . . : 12.207.240.1
        DHCP Server . . . . . . . : 12.242.16.34
        Primary WINS Server . . . :
        Secondary WINS Server . . :
        Lease Obtained. . . . . . : 06 14 03 5:59:28 PM
        Lease Expires . . . . . . : 06 18 03 5:59:28 PM

C:\WINDOWS>_
```

Figure 6-7:
The
IPCONFIG
utility
displays
the IP
configura-
tion of a
networked
PC.

Getting Ready for Work

It's one thing to know what the protocols and utilities listed in the previous section are and what they do, but to really get an understanding of their value, you must use them in the heat of battle, er, in the art of helping a distressed customer.

Imagine that you are the technician in the Information Technology (IT) department at Big Deal Corporation's corporate offices. By association, this makes you a Big Deal IT technician, which is what your mother tells everyone you are anyway.

One day, while you are studying for the A+ OS Technologies exam, you get an urgent call from a user who claims that her PC cannot connect to the company's intranet, a local network that is running TCP/IP and is intended solely for employees. You know that her problem can't be valid. Just this morning, you installed that PC, and you're certain that you tested the network adapter's connectivity. (You did, didn't you?)

Well, not to worry. If you follow the steps that are shown in Lab 6-5, you will surely discover the problem. This lab shows how the TCP/IP and Windows utilities can be used to diagnose and isolate a network connectivity problem.

Lab 6-5   Troubleshooting a Network Connection

1. **Let the user explain exactly what she thinks the problem may be.**

   Be courteous and listen intently for clues of things that may have happened. Judging from what the user has told you, your experience with the PCs, and your experience with the network, you should follow a structured diagnostics routine for this problem.

2. **Check the port that's on the external edge of the network adapter, where the network media connects.**

   The connection is most likely an RJ-45 connection, and the media is usually a form of twisted-pair copper wiring. Check that the connection is snugly coupled and that the NIC is showing network activity on its activity lights. No lights, no connection — you've already found the problem.

3. **If the activity lights are on, check the Windows configuration**.

   Using the checklist that you used for installation and the information from the network administrator, recheck the configuration of the PC. If all is well, check the Device Manager for problems with the network adapter and be sure that the correct device driver is installed.

   At this point, if everything appears to be configured and working properly, the problem may not be with the PC. Now it's time to use a few of the utilities that are discussed in this chapter to find the problem.

4. **If the PC is running Windows 9*x*, choose Start⇨Run and enter** WINIPCFG **in the Run box.**

   The display should look like Figure 6-8. The display includes the physical (also called the MAC) address of the adapter (NIC) and the IP address that is assigned to the PC. If the IP address is not valid or begins with 169.254, the PC has not been configured with a usable IP address. To remedy this, check the TCP/IP configuration of the network adapter (see Chapter 5).

Figure 6-8:
The
WINIPCFG
display on a
Windows 98
PC.

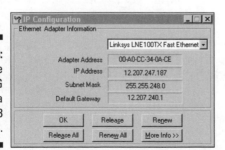

5. **If the PC is running Windows NT, Windows 2000, or Windows XP, choose Start⊃Run and open a command prompt window by entering CMD. At the command prompt, enter** IPCONFIG.

The display should look like that shown in Figure 6-7. Notice that much of the same information is available, including the physical address and the IP address. If the DHCP enabled line has a status of No or if the IP address is invalid or begins with 169.254, go to the TCP/IP configuration for the adapter and make the necessary changes (see Chapter 5).

6. **If none of the previous steps have solved the problem, do the following:**

   • In Windows 98, open an MS-DOS prompt.

   • In later versions of Windows, choose Start⊃Run.

Enter **PING** along with the IP address of the network server or the default gateway that is listed in either the WINIPCFG or the IPCONFIG displays. Figure 6-9 shows the results of the PING command. If the connection was interrupted between the local PC and the remote IP address target, the request would have timed out.

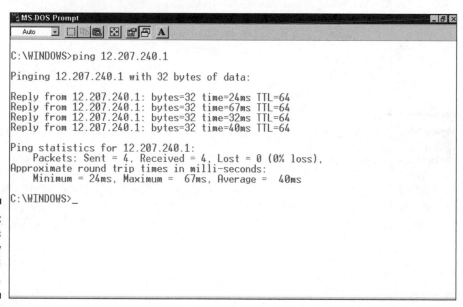

Figure 6-9: The results displayed by the PING command.

7. **If the** PING **command finds the target address, use the** TRACERT **utility.**

   The TRACERT function maps each of the routers that the request moves through as it attempts to move from the local network to the remote address. Figure 6-10 shows the output from the TRACERT command. If any of the hops (routers) is unable to forward the request or times out, the problem may be on the network. Notify the network administrator, and reassure your user.

8. **Determine who is responsible for fixing the problem.**

   On a Windows 98 system, access an NSLOOKUP site on the Internet. On a Windows NT/2000/XP system, you can run the NSLOOKUP command at a command prompt, which you can open by entering **CMD** in the Run box, to achieve the same results. Figure 6-11 shows the results from the NSLOOKUP site at www.infobear.com.

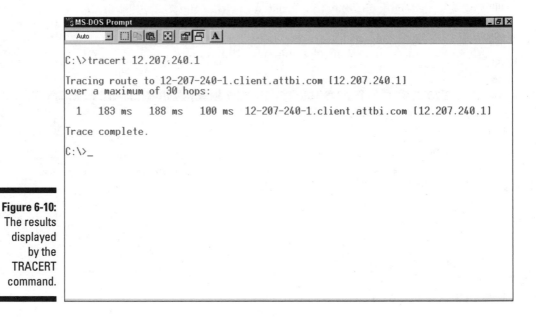

Figure 6-10:
The results displayed by the TRACERT command.

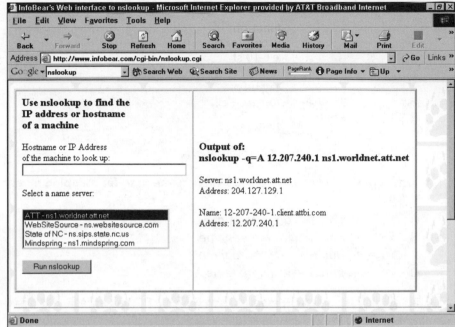

Figure 6-11:
The results
displayed
by the
NSLOOKUP
command.

Prep Test

1 A user on a Windows 98 system cannot grant which of the following share types?

A ○ Read-only access

B ○ Full access

C ○ Write-only access

D ○ Access that depends on password

2 Which of the following is a valid share name path for mapping a network drive?

A ○ //sharename/computername

B ○ \\computername\\sharename

C ○ //computername//sharename

D ○ \\computername\sharename

3 To display the network resources to which a PC has access and on which shares have been granted, which of the following Windows 2000 desktop features is selected?

A ○ My Network Places

B ○ Network Neighborhood

C ○ Network Neighborhood Places

D ○ My Computer

4 Which of the following creates a hidden share?

A ○ $harename

B ○ Sharename$

C ○ Sharename#

D ○ $Sharename$

5 Windows XP provides which of the following sharing mechanisms? (Choose two.)

A ❑ SFS

B ❑ SDS

C ❑ ACL

D ❑ MCL

6 Which of the following commands is used on Windows 2000 and XP PCs to display and manage the IP configuration?

A ○ WINIPCFG

B ○ NSLOOKUP

C ○ IPCONFIG

D ○ TRACERT

7 Which of the following TCP/IP and Windows utilities is used to determine if an IP address or domain name is reachable across the network?

A ○ WINIPCFG

B ○ NSLOOKUP

C ○ IPCONFIG

D ○ TRACERT

E ○ Telnet

F ○ PING

8 Which of the following TCP/IP and Windows utilities is used to display the routing path that is used to transmit a message between a PC and a remote IP address or domain name?

A ○ WINIPCFG

B ○ NSLOOKUP

C ○ IPCONFIG

D ○ TRACERT

E ○ Telnet

F ○ PING

9 Which of the following utilities is used to display and manage the IP configuration of a Windows 98 client?

A ○ WINIPCFG

B ○ NSLOOKUP

C ○ IPCONFIG

D ○ TRACERT

E ○ Telnet

F ○ PING

10 Which of the following TCP/IP utilities can be used to look up the IP address or hostname of a particular networked PC?

A ○ WINIPCFG

B ○ NSLOOKUP

C ○ IPCONFIG

D ○ TRACERT

E ○ Telnet

F ○ PING

Answers

1 **C.** The valid choices are read-only (no changes), full access (read, write, and delete), and either depending on the password entered. *See "Sharing a folder."*

2 **D.** Make sure that you know which way the slashes are leaning and that you place only one slash between the computer name and the share name. *Review "Mapping a drive in Windows 98."*

3 **A.** Windows 2000 and Windows XP replaced the Windows 98 Network Neighborhood with the My Network Places icon. *Check out "Navigating the Neighborhood and a Few New Places."*

4 **B.** Adding a dollar sign ($) at the end of the share name hides the shared device on the My Network Places and Windows Explorer displays. *Look over "Granting shares to devices."*

5 **A & C.** The Simple File Sharing (SFS) and the Access Control List (ACL) features are available in Windows XP. *Study "Sharing a Windows XP file."*

6 **C.** As discussed in Chapter 5, IPCONFIG can also be used to manage the Dynamic Host Configuration Protocol (DHCP) IP address lease. *See "Checking out the connection."*

7 **F.** PING sends out an echo request, which is answered by the addressee. If no answer comes back, the station is either not available or is not connected to the network. *Review "Getting Ready for Work."*

8 **D.** TRACERT traces the routing path between two network points and displays each hop (router) that a message must pass through to reach its destination address. *Take a look at "Checking out the connection."*

9 **A.** WINIPCFG is also available on Windows 95 and Windows Me systems. *Study "Checking out the connection."*

10 **B.** NSLOOKUP, which stands for Network Lookup Service, can help you find the IP address for a station using its computer name (host name) or vice versa. *See "Checking out the connection."*

Chapter 7

Sharing the Internet

• •

Exam Objectives

▶ Understanding browser caching operations

▶ Defining Internet Connection Sharing

▶ Configuring the Internet Connection Firewall

• •

For good reasons, the A+ OS Technologies exam is focusing more on networking and the Internet. Why are PCs connected to a local area network in an office location, if not for surfing the Web, checking stock reports, reviewing sports scores, and getting the latest soap opera plot lines?!

For the A+ OS Technologies exam, you must have an understanding of the basic protocols, terminology, and functions of the Internet and know how it is accessed. Chapters 5 and 6 cover the protocols and terminology, and this chapter deals with Internet access topics, primarily the Internet Connection Sharing feature and the Windows XP firewall feature. Okay, so one shares and the other denies; it's all a part of the smart use of a vital resource.

The Internet browser software in question is Microsoft's Internet Explorer. However, because of legal issues and the fear of the Justice Department, the A+ OS Technologies exam objectives refer to generic Internet browsers. To be politically correct (the other PC), I mention a few of the other browsers, but you should assume that most of my comments refer to Internet Exploder, I mean, Explorer.

Quick Assessment

Understanding browser caching operations

1 Internet Explorer stores its cached files in the _____ folder.

2 The purpose of _____ is to allow a browser to track visited sites.

Defining Internet Connection Sharing

3 The _____ must have a direct link to an Internet connection service.

4 The two primary ways to create Internet Connection Sharing (ICS) are _____ and _____.

5 When configuring ICS, the Home networking connection area displays only if the PC is _____.

6 ICS is intended for use with _____ and _____ networks.

Configuring the Internet Connection Firewall

7 A _____ can protect a network from undesired and unexpected incoming Internet traffic.

8 The Internet Connection Firewall (ICF) is available with Windows _____.

9 The ICF does not filter out packets that are _____.

10 The ICF security log is written to the _____ file in the Windows folder.

Answers

1 *Temporary Internet Files.* See "Caching in Internet Explorer."

2 *History.* Review "Keeping up with history."

3 *Sharing server.* Check out "Creating a sharing server."

4 *Broadband routers, software-based solutions.* Study "Sharing types."

5 *Multihomed.* Look over "Setting up the shared server."

6 *Home, small business.* See "Configuring and Installing ICS."

7 *Firewall.* Review "Configuring the Internet Connection Firewall."

8 *XP.* Check out "Setting Up the ICF."

9 *Outbound.* Take a look at "Setting Up the ICF."

10 *PFIREWALL.LOG.* Study "Setting Up the ICF."

Saving the Past to Service the Present

Today's most popular browsers are largely self-installing and self-configuring, but you or the user may still need to establish a couple of settings to improve or maximize the performance of the browser and the PC. See Chapter 5 for information on security and proxy settings.

The popular Internet browsers are as follows:

- ✔ AOL Netscape Communicator or Navigator (http://home.netscape.com)
- ✔ Microsoft Internet Explorer (www.microsoft.com/windows/ie/)
- ✔ Opera Software ASA's Opera (www.opera.com)

I recommend concentrating your studies on either of the first two of these browsers. You can base your review on the browser that you're using.

Caching in

The caching function of an Internet browser stores images from Internet sites that you have visited. The cache files are stored on the PC's hard drive as a means to increase the performance of the browser when accessing frequently-visited or just-visited Web pages.

For example, if you visit one site frequently, the caching function stores the object files (graphics, sound files, video files, and so on) from the site because these items take the longest to download. On any given site, much of the graphics and other objects rarely change. When you request a site that has been cached, the objects that have not changed are displayed quickly, and the browser spends its time dealing with the text and the graphics or objects that have changed, which are then cached too.

Caching in Internet Explorer

Internet Explorer stores its cache in a folder called Temporary Internet Files. You can set the size or the percentage of your hard drive space that this folder can occupy. Should the space allotted to the cache get full, the space is over-written with newer cache files. To access the cache settings — and most other settings — for Internet Explorer, use the following steps:

1. **From the desktop or taskbar, double-click or click the Internet Explorer icon, respectively.**

   You can also choose Start⇨Programs⇨Internet Explorer.

2. **On the menu bar, choose Tools⇨Internet Options.**

   The Internet Options dialog box displays (see Figure 7-1). This dialog box, with its seven tabs and numerous buttons, controls the configuration and functions of Internet Explorer.

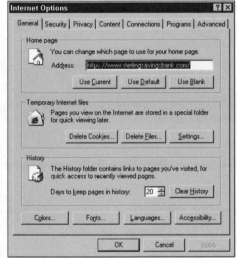

Figure 7-1:
Internet
Explorer's
Internet
Options
dialog box.

Notice the three buttons that are located in the Temporary Internet Files panel: Delete Cookies, Delete Files, and Settings.

3. **Click the Settings button to display the Settings dialog box, shown in Figure 7-2.**

   The Settings dialog box allows you to control three aspects of the caching operation: when cached files are created, where the caching files are stored, and how much of the hard drive space is used for the cached files. You can also view the cached objects and files to see the Web sites that your kids (or Mom and Dad) are surfing.

4. **Click the Cancel button to close the Settings dialog box and return to the Internet Options dialog box.**

5. **Click the Cancel button to close the Internet Options dialog box and return to the browser.**

   You revisit the Internet Options dialog box later in this chapter.

Figure 7-2:
The Settings
dialog box.

Caching in Netscape

Netscape's caching function involves the use of a temporary file caching area. You should periodically delete these temporary files to keep Netscape running smoothly.

To access the caching configuration settings in a Netscape browser, use the following steps:

1. **From the desktop or taskbar, double-click or click the Netscape Communicator icon, respectively.**

   You can also choose Start➪Programs➪Netscape Communicator.

2. **On the menu bar, choose Edit➪Preferences (see Figure 7-3).**

   In the left panel of the Preferences dialog box, click the plus sign (+) next to the Advanced folder to expand the tree (see Figure 7-4). Choose Cache, and set your preferences for how often caching files are refreshed (if ever).

Figure 7-3:
Getting to
Netscape's
Preferences
dialog box.

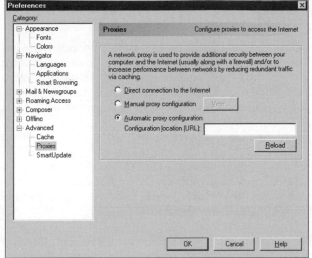

Figure 7-4:
The
Preferences
dialog box,
showing the
Advanced
folder and
its contents.

Keeping up with history

At the bottom of Internet Explorer's Internet Options dialog box is the History panel. The primary purpose of the history files is to allow the browser to keep track of which sites you've already visited. The color of a visited URL is slightly different than that of one you haven't visited. The browser history can also be used to automatically complete a URL as you type its first few characters into the address bar.

Both Internet Explorer and Netscape Navigator allow you to set the number of days of history that you want to keep. In Internet Explorer, in the History panel at the bottom of the Internet Options dialog box, you can enter the number of days to keep pages in history and you can clear the browser's history at any time. The size of the history pages varies depending on the volume of activity and the Web sites visited.

On a Netscape system, access the Options menu, select General Preferences, and choose the Appearance tab. To clear the history file immediately, click the Expire Now option. The Visited Link Expires after *n* Days option is used to set the number of days of history that Netscape will keep.

Don't confuse history with cache. History is a list of the Universal Resource Locators (URLs) or Internet addresses of the Web sites that you have typed into the Address (IE) or Location (Netscape) bar of the browser. The history can come in handy if you forget the URL of a site that you recently visited.

Configuring and Installing ICS

Internet Connection Sharing (ICS), a feature that is included in Windows 98 SE, Windows 2000 Professional, Windows Me, and Windows XP Home and Professional, allows home– and small-office users to share a single Internet connection. The type of connection isn't important; ICS assumes that a network is present and isn't fussy about the type of network or the media used.

ICS builds a type of local area network (LAN), with one PC serving as the network gateway. The other PCs on the network use the gateway PC to connect to the Internet. Each PC must be connected to the gateway via a network connection, and a single modem, proxy server, DSL, ISDN, or other Internet connection line must serve the entire network. Expect to see a question or two on the A+ OS Technologies exam about ICS.

To run ICS properly, the feature needs to be set up on a PC that has two network adapters, one for the Internet connection and another to connect to the other PCs that will share the connection.

Getting ready to share

To share an Internet connection of any kind, you must first have an Internet connection. The connection can be a dialup account at a local Internet service provider (ISP) or a broadband connection (cable, DSL, satellite, and so on) from an ISP, the telephone company, or another provider.

The Windows Internet Connection Sharing function isn't your only option for sharing an Internet connection with multiple workstations. For any of the broadband services, you can purchase a router that allows you to share the connection with two, three, five, or up to ten workstations (and more if you want). Certain modem devices also allow more than one workstation to share the dialup line. But all of these options require the purchase of additional hardware, which can be expensive.

The Windows Internet Connection Sharing feature is a part of the Windows operating system and available at no extra cost, which may be its biggest advantage. However, you will still incur some cost, because you must still network the workstations that are to share the connection. On the other hand, you could get a dedicated phone line for each PC, right? Sure.

Sharing types

Although the focus here is on software connection sharing, other types of Internet sharing methods are available. The two primary ways to create Internet Connection Sharing are as follows:

- ✔ **Broadband routers:** These devices, which are available for cable, DSL, ISDN, and wireless broadband systems, allow multiple PCs to connect directly into the router and gain access to the Internet connection.

- ✔ **Software-based solutions:** Internet Connection Sharing falls in this category, which also includes software proxy server solutions and other software-based connection sharing packages.

Creating a sharing server

Whether the plan is to share dialup or a broadband service, you must have a sharing service in the network to keep your internal network (the internal lines) separate from the ISP's network (the incoming line). To create a sharing server, you must perform the following tasks on the sharing server:

- ✔ Create separate and discrete connections to the internal and the external network.

- ✔ Provide either hardware connection sharing ability (such as a bridge or a router) or software connection sharing ability, such as Internet Connection Sharing (ICS).

You don't need two network adapters on the sharing server if you are using a dialup service; only one adapter is needed to connect to the internal network. However, if you are using a broadband service, you need to install two network adapters in the sharing server: one for the broadband connection and one for the network.

Enabling ICS

Internet Connection Sharing provides you with the ability to connect only one PC to an external Internet link and then share that link with other PCs on a local home– or small-office network. ICS allows each of the sharing PCs to use its full complement of Internet tools, such as Outlook Express and Internet Explorer, as if it were the only PC connected to the Internet service.

ICS should not be used in an environment that is running Windows 2000 Server with existing domain controllers, DNS servers, gateways, DHCP servers, or devices configured with static IP addresses. This means that ICS is essentially intended for use in very small offices and homes.

Setting up the shared server

To enable ICS on a network connection, use the following steps:

1. **Log on to the PC with an owner or administrator account.**

2. **Right-click the Network Neighborhood or My Network Places icon (depending on the Windows version running), and choose Connections or Network Connections (depending on what is displayed) from the pop-up menu that appears.**

3. **From the connections that are listed (typically only one exists), choose the connection that you want to share and click it. From the Network Tasks list, choose Change Settings of This Connection.**

4. **On the Advanced tab, select the Allow Other Network Users to Connect through This Computer's Internet Connection check box.**

   If you are sharing a dialup connection and you want the connection to dial automatically when a sharing PC accesses the connection, select the Establish a Dial-Up Connection Whenever a Computer on My Network Attempts to Access the Internet check box.

   To grant authority to other sharing users to enable or disable the shared connection, select the Allow Other Network Users to Control and Disable the Shared Internet Connection box.

5. **Under Internet Connection Sharing, in the Home Networking Connection panel, choose the adapter through which the sharing computer connects to the other computers on the network.**

   You will only see the Home Networking Connection area in the dialog box if the PC is *multihomed* (has two network adapters installed).

Configuring the Internet Connection Firewall

Although its name is an oxymoron, the Internet Connection Firewall (ICF) can protect a network from undesired and unexpected incoming Internet traffic. As you know, a poor unsuspecting network can be hit with everything from the seriously bored youth to hackers with criminal intentions.

A firewall blocks unknown, unauthorized, and other spurious Internet traffic from entering your network by filtering those entries that don't meet the criteria that are established for permissible traffic.

Setting Up the ICF

The ICF feature, new with Windows XP, is enabled or disabled in the Network Connections folder (which can be accessed through the Control Panel or My Network Places). The ICF must be installed on a PC that has a direct connection to the Internet connection on which it is to be applied. The ICF can be set to activate or deactivate on each type of connection to the Internet. This is good because not every type of connection needs firewall security.

The ICF has its drawbacks as well. For instance, it can't filter outbound traffic, regardless of the source. Spyware, viruses, Trojan horse software, or hacker bots can all transmit out through the ICF unscathed. If you need protection from these sources, consider using a commercial firewall. If you change to a commercial software firewall, be sure to disable the ICF.

Follow these steps to enable ICF on a Windows XP system:

1. **From either My Network Places or the Control Panel, open the Network Connections window.**

2. **Right-click the connection on which you want to apply the ICF, and choose Properties from the pop-up menu that appears.**

3. **In the adapter Properties dialog box, click the Advanced tab. To enable the ICF, select the Protect My Computer and Network by Limiting or Preventing Access to This Computer from the Internet check box. To disable the ICF, deselect this check box.**

   If you choose to disable the ICF, you are asked to confirm your decision with the following warning: `Turning off Internet Connection Firewall could expose your computer to unauthorized access over the Internet. Are you sure you want to turn it off?`

4. **Click Yes to confirm disabling of the ICF. No confirmation is required to turn on ICF.**

5. **Enable security logging by accessing the Advanced tab of the Network Connections Properties dialog box and the Settings tab.**

   To track discarded traffic (the bad stuff), select the Log Dropped Packets option. To track what the firewall is letting through, select the Log Successful Connections option.

   The security log is written to the `PFIREWALL.LOG` file in the Windows folder.

Prep Test

1 Which of the following is not a commonly used Internet browser?

  A ○ Internet Explorer

  B ○ Netscape Communicator

  C ○ ICS

  D ○ Opera

2 Files from frequently accessed Web pages that are stored on a PC's hard drive for the purpose of improving browser responsiveness are a part of which browser service?

  A ○ History

  B ○ Back

  C ○ Firewall

  D ○ Cache

3 Changes to the configuration of an installed version of Internet Explorer are made through which of the following menu functions?

  A ○ Edit⇨Preferences

  B ○ Tools⇨Internet Options

  C ○ Edit⇨Internet Options

  D ○ File⇨Preferences

4 Which of the following is the Windows feature that allows home and small-business offices to share a single Internet connection over a small local area network?

  A ○ ICF

  B ○ ICC

  C ○ ICU

  D ○ ICS

5 Which of the following are types of Internet sharing solutions? (Choose two.)

  A ❑ Multihomed systems

  B ❑ Broadband routers

  C ❑ Software-based solutions

  D ❑ Firewalls

6 What is the minimum number of network adapters that must be installed on a sharing server that connects to the Internet through a dialup modem?

A ○ 0

B ○ 1

C ○ 2

D ○ One for each client PC that shares the connection

7 Which of the following conditions are incompatible with ICS? (Choose all that apply.)

A ❑ Windows 2000 Server with existing domain controllers

B ❑ DHCP servers

C ❑ Multihomed servers

D ❑ Devices with static IP addresses

8 When configuring an ICS client, which of the following options must be disabled? (Choose all that apply.)

A ❑ Automatically detect settings

B ❑ Never dial a connection

C ❑ Use automatic configuration script

D ❑ Use a proxy server

9 Which of the following Windows software features blocks unknown or unauthorized Internet traffic from entering a network?

A ○ ICS

B ○ ICBM

C ○ ICF

D ○ ICX

10 On a Windows XP system, which of the following files is the security log written to?

A ○ \WINDOWS\PFIREWALL.LOG

B ○ \WINDOWS\NTFIRELOG.TXT

C ○ \WINDOWS\LOGS\FIREWALL.LOG

D ○ \PFIREWALL.LOG

Answers

1 **C.** ICS, the Internet Connection Sharing feature, is not a browser. *See "Saving the Past to Service the Present."*

2 **D.** Caching objects and files allows the browser to display items without requesting them each time from the Web server or the Internet, thereby saving response time. *Review "Caching in."*

3 **B.** The Internet Options dialog box includes all configuration settings that affect the performance and functions of Internet Explorer. *Check out "Caching in Internet Explorer."*

4 **D.** ICS stands for Internet Connection Sharing. *Take a look at "Configuring and Installing ICS."*

5 **B & C.** A multihomed system has the potential to share, but some sharing software or hardware is needed. *Study "Sharing types."*

6 **B.** The server needs to have one network adapter for each network connection that it is making. The server can connect to the dialup modem through its COM port. *See "Creating a sharing server."*

7 **A, B, & D.** In addition to these conditions, ICS is also incompatible with DNS servers and gateways. *Review "Enabling ICS."*

8 **A, C, & D.** All of these options must be deselected for a client to activate ICS. *Look over "Setting up a sharing client."*

9 **C.** However, this feature is only available in Windows XP. *Check out "Setting Up the ICF."*

10 **A.** This file can be viewed using a text editor. *Study "Setting Up the ICF."*

Chapter 8

Troubleshooting System Problems

- -

Exam Objectives

▶ Applying standard troubleshooting procedures

▶ Using Windows utilities to manage and diagnose OS problems

▶ Resolving common operational problems

- -

*O*ne of the underlying truths about the PC technical repair profession is that proper installation, configuration, and diligent monitoring of a system is always better than troubleshooting, diagnostics, and repair. In fact, that is my mantra. Whenever I meditate, I repeat this phrase repeatedly as the answer to the meaning of life. I know; I need to get one — a life, that is.

I know that I'm preaching to the choir on this, but doing it right the first time does prevent myriad problems later. However, one slight problem exists with all this global truth — you are not always there to make sure it stays right. Users have a way of doing the very things that nobody thought would ever happen. They have an uncanny way of finding the soft spot in the system within minutes of it being turned over to them. Because users are here to stay (meaning that PC technician jobs are safe for a long while), the task has become isolating, identifying, and resolving problems as fast as possible. Of course, your fastest is never as fast as the user wants, but of course, you try.

This chapter summarizes the conditions, tools, utilities, processes, and procedures that are involved with operating system–related problems and issues that you will encounter on the A+ OS Technologies exam. This means that I haven't included every possible problem and solution that you could ever run into on a PC — just those that are likely to be on the A+ exam.

And remember that without the users — bless them — you wouldn't have a job!

Quick Assessment

1 Many PC problems are the result of recent changes to the _____ or _____.

2 Starting the system in _____ loads only the default device drivers that are needed to start the Windows OS.

3 To reach Safe mode when starting Windows 2000, press _____ when Windows starts up.

4 To restore the last saved version of the Registry and the system configuration, choose the _____ startup option.

5 The startup mode that allows you to manually control which services, protocols, and device drivers are started is the _____ mode.

6 The _____ utility traps application errors from the processor and produces a snapshot of the operating system, attempts to interpret the error, and provides a diagnostic for the cause of the problem.

7 Windows 98, ME, and XP operating systems include the System Configuration Utility, which is executed with the filename _____.

8 A _____ is caused by hard drive or boot disk failures that interrupt the boot process of a system.

9 Windows protection errors are displayed on the _____.

10 Windows 9*x* systems require _____ to load before Windows can start.

Answers

1 *Hardware, software.* See "Asking about changes."

2 *Safe mode.* Review "Booting into Safe mode."

3 *F8.* Check out "Booting into Safe mode."

4 *Last Known Good Configuration.* Look over "Booting into Safe mode."

5 *Step-by-step.* Study "Booting step by step."

6 *Dr. Watson.* See "Using the Windows tools."

7 *MSCONFIG.* Review "Using the Windows tools."

8 *Boot failure.* Take a look at "Boot error messages."

9 *Blue (or black) screen of death (BSOD).* Check out "System startup messages."

10 *HIMEM.SYS.* Study "System startup messages."

Tracking Down System Problems

Windows offers a number of utilities and software tools to help you determine the source of an operating system (OS) problem, including hardware problems that appear to be software problems. Utilities and tools are available to help you start the system in a variety of ways that limit how much of the OS is loaded during startup. And a number of diagnostics and recovery tools are available to help you isolate a problem and resolve it.

Before I get into the utilities and software tools that you need to know about for the exam, I want to talk about the process that is used to (a) identify the problem and (b) isolate the cause, which are two different things.

Eliciting help from the user

Depending on the situation and the procedures of your company, you often have two opportunities to get information about a perceived problem from the user who is reporting the problem. The first opportunity occurs when the customer phones in his computer problem. The second opportunity occurs when you, the technician, arrive at the customer's workplace. Talking on the telephone with an irritated customer seems to intimidate many technicians, but then talking face to face with a customer is a challenge to some technicians as well.

When going into a technical support or service situation, you should understand that the two primary reasons for a service call are as follows:

✔ Operator error, which is typically a user training or nontraining issue

✔ Recent changes that were made to a PC that are causing configuration conflicts or problems

A distant third reason for a service call is that one or more of the PC's components have stopped working.

For the sake of simplicity, and because it is the only situation that's included in the exam objectives, your study should focus on working at the customer's location.

Re-creating the problem

The first thing to do is to have the customer give you her version of what happened. Hopefully, the customer's description can include a re-creation of what happened on the PC and why she thinks that may be a problem.

Of course, some problems are obvious, such as seeing smoke coming from a monitor or system case. In these situations, a re-creation, while perhaps interesting, isn't necessary.

On the other hand, if the customer complains about the operation of the PC, its operating system, or perhaps an application, to make a rational judgment, you need to see what happened to alarm the customer.

Asking about changes

Even if the customer/user is unable to re-create the problem, you should ask about any hardware or software changes that were recently made to the PC. As you know, many PC problems are the result of changes that were made to the hardware or software.

Troubleshooting in the Windows World

You and I both know that most of the problems that PC technicians are sent out to resolve are easily taken care of with user training. However, the A+ exams are measuring your ability to deal with the more serious problems, which is also what your present or future employer is interested in. The A+ OS Technologies exam wants you to demonstrate your knowledge of applying the right procedures, utilities, or tools to the right situations.

If the user's explanation of the problem matches the conditions with which you are familiar, you can start the process of isolation, identification, and resolution.

Booting into Safe mode

If the problem appears to be related to the recent installation of a new or upgraded peripheral device and/or a new or updated device driver, you should restart the system without allowing the device drivers to load — that is, restart the PC and boot it into Safe mode.

Safe mode is one of the startup types that are available for the Windows operating systems. When you start the system in *Safe mode,* the operating system loads, but only the default device drivers, such as the keyboard, mouse, VGA video, and printer drivers, are loaded. The default device drivers are those needed to start up the Windows OS.

See Table 8-1 for information on how to start each Windows version into Safe mode. If you can boot a PC into Safe mode, you at least know that the problem is not with the OS kernel or any of the default device drivers. In Safe mode, you can check the status of a hardware device and its device driver and make adjustments or updates, provided that you have them on a floppy disk or CD-ROM.

Table 8-1		Starting in Safe Mode
OS	*Key*	*Comments*
Windows 95	F8	Press this key as the PC restarts.
Windows 98/Me	Ctrl	Press this key until the Windows Startup menu appears.
Windows 2000/XP	F8	Press this key until the Windows Startup menu appears.

The following types of Safe mode are available in every Windows version, beginning with Windows 98:

- ✔ **Safe mode:** This is the standard Safe mode, in which only the default device drivers are loaded.

- ✔ **Safe mode with command prompt:** This Safe mode option is the same as the standard Safe mode, except that instead of loading the VGA desktop user interface, an MS-DOS command prompt is displayed. The system is *not* booted into MS-DOS; it is running Windows but displaying only a command prompt.

- ✔ **Safe mode with networking:** The name says it all. This is Safe mode with the network connections and the applicable device drivers loaded. This is a good mode to start in if you think that you may need to download something from the Internet or across a network.

In addition to these three Safe mode options, Windows NT/2000/XP make the following additional five Safe mode options available:

- ✔ **Enable boot logging:** This startup mode starts the OS normally but logs the activities of the device drivers and services to a file. In Windows 2000 and XP, this file is NTBTLOG.TXT; in Windows 9x, NT, and Me, the file is BOOTLOG.TXT. If the same background error continues to occur during startup, studying this log file may help you isolate which driver or service is causing the problem. Enabling boot logging allows Safe mode, Safe mode with command prompt, and Safe mode with networking to log the drivers and services that load to the boot log file.

✓ **Enable VGA mode:** Although Safe mode always starts with the default VGA driver, using this option, you can force a normal Windows startup to load the default VGA driver. This option is used when a new video driver or its settings are causing a startup problem.

✓ **Last Known Good Configuration:** Whenever Windows is shut down properly, it saves the active Registry information. The last saved Registry version is overwritten immediately after a successful logon. If newly installed hardware or software seems to have corrupted the configuration or the Registry, choosing the Last Known Good Configuration option restores the last saved Registry information. This option is good for instances caused by incorrect configuration, but it does not solve problems that are caused by missing or corrupted drivers and files. If you apply this option, any configuration changes that were made since the last successful startup and shutdown will be lost.

✓ **Directory service restore mode:** This option is not available for Windows 2000 Professional or Windows XP Professional, so never mind — it's not on the exam.

✓ **Debugging mode:** This option starts the Windows OS and sends debug information to another PC over a serial cable.

Booting step by step

Another Safe mode option that's available in Windows 9*x* (see Figure 8-1) and Me is the Step-by-step confirmation mode, which is also called the single-step mode. This mode allows you to manually control which services, protocols, and device drivers are started during the startup process. You are asked to respond Yes or No to each file that is included in the startup process, that is, those listed in the `IO.SYS`, `MSDOS.SYS`, `CONFIG.SYS`, and `AUTOEXEC.BAT` files.

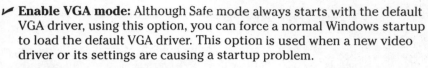

Figure 8-1:
The Windows Startup menu.

```
Microsoft Windows 98 Startup Menu
==============================

1. Normal
2. Logged (\BOOTLOG.TXT)
3. Safe mode
4. Step-by-step confirmation
5. Command prompt only
6. Safe mode command prompt only

Enter a choice: 1

F5=Safe Mode Shift+F5=Command prompt Shift+F8= Step-by-
step confirmation [N]
```

Skipping drivers

Windows 98 and Windows Me include the *Automatic Skip Driver (ASD)* agent, which is used to identify device drivers that may cause Windows to hang during system startup. The ASD agent disables any such drivers so that they are bypassed in future restarts. The identity of any devices that are disabled by the ASD agent is recorded in the ASD.LOG file.

Applying the diagnostic tool kit

You are not defenseless when you are trying to determine a PC's problem. In addition to the hardware tools that are in your tool kit, you also have a number of software tools at your disposal to help you get to the cause of a problem.

Reading the manuals

Contrary to common belief, the manuals that are packed with a PC system are not a part of the protective packaging that is included to keep the PC safe during transit. The user, installation, and component manuals typically have valuable information in them.

Read the manuals and keep them handy for future reference. Also, make it a habit to check the manufacturer's Web site each time that you begin diagnosing a PC problem. Finding information in the frequently asked questions (FAQs) section of a manufacturer's Web site can save you untold hours of agony and help you look like a repair genius to the user.

You should also review any training manuals that you or a coworker may have picked up at a relevant training seminar.

Last, but not least, is the Windows Help system, which could have information about a particular software problem.

Using the Windows tools

Windows has several built-in utilities, programs, and agents that you can apply when diagnosing a PC's problems. You should be aware of the following tools and the general usage of each for the exam:

✔ **Device Manager:** This Windows feature can be used to manage, configure, and update peripheral and system devices and their device drivers. It can also be a quick reference on devices that may be having driver issues.

✔ **Dr. Watson:** This utility traps application errors from the processor and produces a snapshot of the operating system, attempts to interpret the error, and provides a diagnostic for the cause of the problem. All Dr. Watson information is recorded in a log file (with a .WLG extension) in the PC's \Windows\Drwatson folder.

✔ MSCONFIG: The Windows 98, Me, and XP operating systems include the System Configuration Utility (see Figure 8-2). This utility is executed by choosing Start⇨Run and typing **MSCONFIG** in the Run box. Although it is similar to the SYSEDIT utility, MSCONFIG can also be used to selectively enable and disable startup parameters, files, and activities.

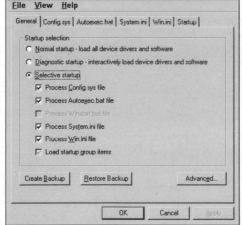

Figure 8-2:
The
MSCONFIG
configura-
tion dialog
box.

✔ MSD/WINMSD: The letters in the name of this utility are alleged to have stood for Microsoft Diagnostics; however, this utility has been known as just MSD for years. The WINMSD utility added a GUI interface, but retained the function of the original package. This can be a great tool for determining the hardware configuration of a PC by using a displayed snapshot of the system. The MSD utility is a Windows 3.*x* and DOS tool, whereas WINMSD is a Windows NT tool that's also found on PCs running Windows 2000 and Windows XP.

✔ **Task Manager:** Many Windows NT administrators learned of the power of the Task Manager utility to provide timely performance, administrative, and monitoring information. This tool is also included on Windows 98, Me, 2000, and XP systems.

Using third-party tools

Literally dozens of commercial software diagnostics programs are on the market. You can use these programs to check out a PC, its hardware, its software, and its configuration for existing problems and for issues that could become problems in the future. For the sake of brevity, I'm only going to mention two of these packages because they are the two for which demo versions are included on the CD with this book. These tools are as follows:

- ✔ **ConfigSafe:** This package, from ImagineLAN, Inc. (www.imaginelan. com), is an independent recovery tool for Windows operating system environments. ConfigSafe protects Windows systems from crashes and configuration issues by tracking changes that are made to a system's configuration and restoring a previous configuration should problems arise.

- ✔ **Pc-Check:** This package, from Eurosoft, Ltd. (www.eurosoft-uk.com), is another independent software tool that provides over 500 hardware and PC configuration tests from a single floppy disk that boots with its own operating system.

Dealing with PC Failures

You will encounter three general types of PC failures: startup errors, operational errors, and shutdown errors. Each type of error has its own troubleshooting and diagnostics approach and procedures. It's knowing which one to use that separates the hobbyists from the professionals in PC repair.

The following sections explain the common errors and problems that occur in each category and show you how to isolate, identify, and resolve each error.

Troubleshooting startup errors

Most startup errors are the result of changes that were made to the hardware or its BIOS configuration. If you are getting some form of hardware error message — either a beep code or an error message (see Book I, Chapter 4 for more details) — the hardware has probably changed, either physically or logically.

Startup errors can be divided into boot errors and system startup errors. Boot errors tend to report missing or corrupted physical resources, while system startup errors deal more with missing or erroneous software or data resources.

Boot error messages

Some of the more common boot errors are as follows:

- ✔ `Bad or missing Command interpreter`: This is a Windows 3.*x* and Windows 95 error message that indicates that the DOS command interpreter (`COMMAND.COM`) is missing. Reinstall this file by booting from a boot disk and running the `SYS C:` command.

- ✔ `Boot failure`: A boot failure error is caused by anything that interrupts the boot process of a system and prevents the process from finishing. These errors are typically associated with hard drive or boot disk failures, but other problems can cause these errors. Windows NT, 2000, and XP boot failures can typically be corrected by booting the system from a boot disk that contains the files `BOOT.INI`, `NTLDR`, and `NTDETECT.COM`.

- ✔ `Inaccessible boot device`: Something is definitely wrong, but in this case, the problem is most likely the hardware, or more specifically the hardware's cables. This error indicates that either the data or power cables aren't connected to the boot device and that the BIOS is unable to find the boot device. If the system has only a single hard drive (that is the boot device), be sure that the drive's jumpers are set to Single.

- ✔ `Invalid boot/system disk`: If you are attempting to start a PC from a boot disk and the boot disk doesn't include the startup elements of the operating system, you see this message. A data disk was probably left in the floppy disk drive when the system was restarted. The problem could also be that the master boot record (MBR) on the hard drive is corrupted or has been damaged by a virus. Try changing the boot disk or running `fdisk /mbr` on the hard drive.

- ✔ `Missing NTLDR`: This self-explanatory message is the Windows NT, 2000, and XP version of the DOS message `Bad or missing Command interpreter`. You should insert the installation media and enter the Recovery Console to fix this problem.

System startup error messages

System startup error messages tend to indicate why the operating system is having trouble getting started. The following error messages are listed in the exam objectives, so you should be familiar with them:

- ✔ `A device referenced in SYSTEM.INI, WIN.INI, or Registry is not found`: This message usually means that the referenced device is no longer installed or that its device driver is missing or corrupted. The first issue is to figure out which device is causing the error message. You should then reinstall this device and its drivers. You can then remove the device properly if you want to delete it from the system.

✔ Device/Service has failed to start: A device or a system software service has failed to start after the operating system attempted to start it. The device or service is identified in the message, so there is no guessing about this error. Reinstall the device and its driver or the software in question. (This may require running the Recovery Console on Windows 2000 or XP systems.)

✔ Error in CONFIG.SYS line *XX*: This error is caused by one of three possible problems: a missing or corrupt device or device driver, missing or corrupt software, or typing errors in the CONFIG.SYS file.

✔ Event log is full: The event log (on Windows NT, 2000, and XP systems) records many of the system-level activities that occur on a PC, during startup as well as during operations. Should the event log get full, it can no longer record new events (including errors), so you may need to adjust how the event log is administered.

To remedy the immediate problem of the full event log, access the Event Viewer by choosing Start⇨Settings⇨Control Panel⇨Administrative Tools⇨ Event Viewer. On the log file tree, click the Event log, and on the Action menu, select Clear All Events to empty the file. If this error happens frequently, try choosing another setting for the Event log — such as Overwrite Events as Needed — or increasing the maximum log file size; both choices are located on the Event log's Properties menu.

✔ Failure to start GUI: This error indicates that the program EXPLORER.EXE is missing or has become corrupted. Reinstall it by running the Recovery Console for Windows 2000/XP or reinstalling Windows 98.

✔ HIMEM.SYS not loaded/Missing or corrupt HIMEM.SYS: Windows 9*x* requires HIMEM.SYS to load before the OS can run. If this file is missing or corrupted, it must be reinstalled. Another cause for this error message is that another startup element has been inserted into the CONFIG.SYS file before the HIMEM.SYS statement.

✔ Registry corruption: There isn't just one message that may lead you to suspect a system has a corrupted Registry. However, if you suspect that a system has a corrupt Registry, use the downloadable (www.download.com) utility RegClean to attempt to resolve the problem. The utility REGEDT32.EXE includes routines to export and restore the Registry's keys. Also the Windows Backup utility allows you to back up the System State, which includes the Registry.

Should you need to recover from a corrupted Registry, search the Microsoft Knowledge Base (http://support.microsoft.com) for help on your particular Windows version.

✔ `Windows protection error`: Several types of protection errors display a system failure on either a blue or a black screen, which is often referred to as the blue/black screen of death (BSOD). These errors are generally caused when a program that's running in RAM attempts to access the RAM that is allocated to another process. Typically, restarting the PC solves the problem, but if this error message occurs frequently when accessing the same application, you should uninstall and reinstall the application. Two of the more common protection errors are as follows:

- `Illegal operation`: Either Windows or an application has requested an operation that is not recognized by the processor or Windows. This error is typically caused by corrupted files, bad disk sectors, memory errors, and possibly an improper device driver.

- `Invalid page fault`: This fault is caused when the operating system or an application references nonexistent data addresses in memory, and the fault can be the result of bad memory, corrupted data, or a bad file.

Invalid page fault errors can also occur when an improper cooling system allows the CPU to overheat along with the memory and other supporting components, or when a power supply is beginning to fail.

Putting out printer fires

If you've worked as a PC technician for a while, you know that no problem brings out more panic in a user than a printer problem. I believe that a PC could be on fire, but if the printer works to the end, the customer would be philosophical about the problem. However, if the user forgets to put the printer online after changing the paper or cartridge, you get a complaint almost instantly.

However, a variety of real printer problems occur on Windows systems. You should be familiar with the following error messages for the A+ exam:

✔ `Incorrect/incompatible driver for print`: This error says only one thing: The person who set up the printer on this PC messed up the installation. You may want to visit the manufacturer's Web site to download the latest driver for the printer and operating system that are in use.

✔ `Incorrect parameter`: This could just mean that the printer's port settings should be reviewed and adjusted, or it could mean that a system resource conflict exists.

✔ `Print spool stalled`: This message is more of an advisory than an emergency or warning. To restart the spool — providing that the resources required for the printer to run are once again available — choose Start➪Settings➪Printers and then select File➪Restart Printing.

Prep Test

1 Which of the following Windows startup modes loads only the operating system and the device drivers that are required by the operating system?

A ○ Normal mode

B ○ Debugging mode

C ○ Troubleshooting mode

D ○ Safe mode

2 Which of the following are Windows startup modes or variations? (Choose all that apply.)

A ❑ Enable boot logging

B ❑ Last Known Good Configuration

C ❑ Registry restore

D ❑ Directory service restore

3 Which of the following keys is used to access the Windows Startup menu on a Windows 2000 system?

A ○ F2

B ○ F5

C ○ F8

D ○ F10

4 On a Windows 98 system, what Windows utility can be used to identify and disable device drivers that could cause Windows to hang during startup?

A ○ MSCONFIG

B ○ ASD

C ○ MSD

D ○ WINMSD

5 Which of the following information sources should be used to gather information about a particular hardware problem and its resolution? (Choose all that apply.)

A ❑ Manufacturer's Web site

B ❑ Warranty documentation

C ❑ Product documentation

D ❑ Product sales Web site

6 Which of the following is the Windows utility that traps and attempts to interpret and diagnose application errors?

A ○ MSCONFIG

B ○ ASD

C ○ Sherlock Holmes

D ○ Dr. Watson

7 What is the name of the third-party software package, listed in the A+ OS Technologies exam objectives, that protects Windows systems from crashes and configuration issues by tracking changes that are made to a system's configuration?

A ○ Pc-Check

B ○ Norton Utilities

C ○ ConfigSafe

D ○ Dr. Watson

8 On a Windows 95 system, you received the message Bad or missing Command interpreter during a system startup. Which of the following actions can you take to remedy this problem?

A ○ Reinstall the COMMAND.COM file using the SYS C: command.

B ○ Copy the WIN.INI file from the Windows directory to C:\.

C ○ No recovery is possible; upgrade to Windows XP.

D ○ Edit the BOOT.INI file for entry errors.

9 The error message Event log is full indicates that no additional system events will be recorded in the log file. Which of the following can be used to allow event entries to once again be recorded to this log file? (Choose all that apply.)

A ❏ Use the Notepad utility to delete existing entries in the event log file.

B ❏ Restart the PC to clear the log files.

C ❏ Increase the maximum size of the event log file.

D ❏ Choose the Clear All Events option for the event log file.

10 Which Windows protection fault occurs when an application references nonexistent data addresses in memory?

A ○ Registry corruption

B ○ Illegal operation

C ○ Invalid page fault

D ○ HIMEM.SYS not loaded

Answers

1 **D.** Safe mode is used to determine which application or hardware device or driver may be causing an operational or startup problem. This is why only the minimum requirements are loaded for the PC to start up. *See "Booting into Safe mode."*

2 **A, B, & D.** The other startup options are Safe mode with command prompt, Safe mode with networking support, Enable VGA mode, and Debugging mode. *Review "Booting into Safe mode."*

3 **C.** Windows NT, 2000, and XP all use F8 to reach the Windows Startup menu during the startup process. Windows 98 and Me use Ctrl. *Check out "Booting into Safe mode."*

4 **B.** The Automatic Skip Driver (ASD) utility also records the drivers that are disabled to a log file for later identification and upgrade. *Take a look at "Skipping drivers."*

5 **A & C.** When all else has failed, perhaps you could use sales or warranty information, but the best sources remain the manufacturer and the documentation that is provided with the system. *Study "Reading the manuals."*

6 **D.** This utility also attempts to identify the reason for the failure so that you can take corrective action. *See "Using the Windows tools."*

7 **C.** ConfigSafe creates a backup of the system configuration files that can be used to restore a system to a good configuration when problems arise. *Review "Using third-party tools."*

8 **A.** Answer A is the best answer given the context of the question. However, Answer C should remain an option as well. *Look over "Boot error messages."*

9 **C & D.** These two actions are available on the Actions menu of the Event Viewer. *Check out "System startup messages."*

10 **C.** The other answer options are valid error messages, and you should know when they are displayed and the meaning of each. *Study "System startup messages."*

Appendix A

About the CD

On the CD-ROM

▶ Practice and self-assessment tests to make sure you're ready for the real thing

▶ Demo versions of A+ exam practice tests

System Requirements

Make sure that your computer meets the minimum system requirements shown in the following list. If your computer doesn't meet most of these requirements, you may have problems using the contents of the CD-ROM.

- ✔ A PC with a 486 or faster processor.
- ✔ Microsoft Windows 95 or later.
- ✔ At least 16MB of total RAM installed on your computer.
- ✔ At least 32MB of available hard drive space to install all the software on this CD-ROM. (You need less space if you don't install every program.)
- ✔ A CD-ROM drive — double-speed (2x) or faster.
- ✔ A sound card for PCs.
- ✔ A monitor capable of displaying at least 256 colors or grayscale.
- ✔ A modem with a speed of at least 28,800 bps.

Using the CD-ROM with Microsoft Windows

To install the items from the CD-ROM to your hard drive, follow these steps:

1. **Insert the CD-ROM into your computer's CD-ROM drive.**
2. **Choose Start⇨Run.**

3. **In the dialog box that appears, type** D:\SETUP.EXE.

   Replace *D:* with the drive letter for your CD-ROM drive, if needed.

4. **Click OK.**

   A License Agreement window appears.

5. **Read through the license agreement, and then click the Accept button if you want to use the CD-ROM. After you click Accept, you are never bothered by the License Agreement window again.**

   The CD-ROM interface Welcome screen appears. The interface is a little program that shows you what's on the CD-ROM and coordinates installing the programs and running the demos. The interface enables you to click a button or two to make things happen.

6. **Click anywhere on the Welcome screen to enter the interface.**

   The next screen lists categories for the software on the CD-ROM.

7. **To view the items within a category, just click the category's name.**

   A list of programs in the category appears.

8. **For more information about a program, click the program's name.**

   Be sure to read the information that appears. Sometimes a program has its own system requirements or requires you to do a few tricks on your computer before you can install or run the program, and this screen tells you what you may need to do, if necessary.

9. **If you don't want to install the program, click the Go Back button to return to the previous screen.**

   You can always return to the previous screen by clicking the Go Back button. This feature enables you to browse the different categories and products and decide what you want to install.

10. **To install a program, click the appropriate Install button.**

    The CD-ROM interface drops to the background while the CD-ROM installs the program you chose.

11. **To install other items, repeat Steps 7 through 10.**

12. **When you finish installing programs, click the Quit button to close the interface.**

    You can eject the CD-ROM now. Carefully place it back in the plastic jacket of the book for safekeeping.

To run some of the programs on the *A+ Certification For Dummies* CD-ROM, you need to leave the CD-ROM in the CD-ROM drive.

What You'll Find on the CD-ROM

The following is a summary of the software included on this CD-ROM.

Dummies test prep tools

This CD-ROM contains questions related to A+ Certification. The questions are similar to those you can expect to find on the exams. I've also included some questions on A+ topics that may or may not be on the current tests or even covered in the book, but they are things that you should know to perform your job.

Practice test

The Practice test is designed to help you get comfortable with the A+ testing situation and pinpoint your strengths and weaknesses on the topic. You can pick the number of questions or you can even decide which objectives you want to focus on.

After you answer the questions, you can find out which questions you got right or wrong. Then you can review all the questions — the ones you missed, the ones you marked, or a combination of the ones you marked and the ones you missed.

Self-Assessment test

The Self-Assessment test is designed to simulate the actual A+ testing situation. The only difference is that this test is not an adaptive test. However, it does try to put a little pressure on you in the same way that the actual test does. You must answer 60 questions in 60 minutes. After you answer all the questions, you find out your score and whether you pass or fail — but that's all the feedback you get. If you can pass the Self-Assessment test fairly easily, you're probably ready to tackle the real thing.

Links page

I've also created a Links page, a handy starting place for accessing the huge amounts of information about the A+ tests on the Internet. You can find the page, Links.htm, at the root of the CD-ROM.

Commercial practice test demos

The following are the eight practice test software demos that have been
included on the CD-ROM. The demos give you a good idea of what the full
practice test from each company is like so that you can find the ones that
fit your style and focus. I recommend that you use at least two practice
tests beyond the ones from this book to prepare for the test.

A+ Certify Exam 8.0 from Super Software

The Super Software (www.aplusexam.com) people produce some of the best
practice exams available. Their reasonably priced CD-ROM contains sample
tests (usually more than one), some specific to each domain of the exam
objectives, and tips and cram notes for the actual test.

A+CoreCert/A+WinCert from Transcender

Transcender is one of the best known names in certification test preparation.
The quality of their MCSE products was carried over into their practice test
products for the previous A+ exams, and I see no reason why they would do
anything different for their products for the new A+ exams. Visit Transcender
at www.transcender.com.

A+ Test Bundle from Self Test Software

Make sure when you go to Self Test's Web site (www.selftest.co.uk) that
you use the co.uk on the end of the URL. The com URL will take you to another
company with a completely different type of self-test. Self Test Software practice tests are very good and the test software simulates the test very well.

Boson A+ from Boson Software

Boson's practice tests (www.boson.com) may be the hardest tests you'll see,
which can be discouraging when just starting out in your test preparation.
If you can pass a Boson test, you are ready for the real thing.

Demo A+ Exam from Vista Net

Check out the demo at www.vista-net.com and if you like it, go get the full
test. Remember that you should use at least two different practice tests
(meaning from two different suppliers) when preparing for the exam.

EasyCert from JRK Software

If you want a practice test that sticks to the test objectives without throwing
in stuff you won't find on the test, you may want to check out the practice
test at www.jrksoftware.com.

Prep! for A+ 2000 from Dali Design

Jeff Thorssell and the Dali Design team have consistently produced the very best practice tests available for the money. Typically, the Prep! tests are the first available and are usually right on target regarding what you need to study for the exams. Check out these tests at `www.dalidesign.com/prepap/`.

Diagnostic software demo

Troubleshooting is a major part of the A+ Core Hardware exam and the exam assumes you can use diagnostic software to diagnose, troubleshoot, and isolate problems quickly. Pc-Check from Eurosoft USA, Ltd., (`www.eurosoft-usa.com`) and the rest of Eurosoft's library of more specialized diagnostic software packages are excellent troubleshooting tools. A demo copy of Pc-Check is included on the CD-ROM for you to use to gain some experience with software diagnostic tools, should you need it.

If You've Got Problems (Of the CD-ROM Kind)

I tried my best to compile programs that work on most computers with the minimum system requirements. Alas, your computer may be somewhat different, and some programs may not work properly for some reason.

The two most likely culprits are that you don't have enough memory (RAM) for the programs you want to use, or that you have other programs running that are affecting installation or running of a program. If you get error messages such as `Not enough memory` or `Setup cannot continue`, try one or more of the following procedures, and then try using the software again:

- ✔ **Turn off any anti-virus software monitors that you may have running on your computer.** Installers sometimes mimic virus activity and may make your computer incorrectly believe that it is being infected by a virus.

- ✔ **Close all running programs.** The more programs you're running, the less memory is available to other programs. Installers also typically update files and programs; if you keep other programs running, installation may not work properly.

✔ **In Windows, close the CD-ROM interface and run demos or installations directly from Windows Explorer.** The interface itself can tie up system memory or even conflict with certain kinds of interactive demos. Use Windows Explorer to browse the files on the CD-ROM and launch installers or demos.

✔ **Add more RAM to your computer.** This is, admittedly, a drastic and somewhat expensive step. However, if you use Windows 95, adding more memory can really help the speed of your computer and enable more programs to run at the same time.

If you still have trouble installing the items from the CD-ROM, please call the very nice and helpful people at Wiley Customer Care phone number: 800-762-2974 (outside the U.S.: 317-596-5430).

Appendix B

Hardware Technology Exam Objectives

● ●

*T*his appendix lists the Hardware Technology exam subjects and the corresponding chapters of the book.

Hardware Technology Topics

Domain/Topic Area	Book I Chapter(s)
1.0 Installation, Configuration, and Upgrading	
Identify the names, purpose, and characteristics of system modules. Recognize these modules by sight or definition.	4–16
Identify basic procedures for adding and removing field-replaceable modules for desktop systems. Given a replacement scenario, choose the appropriate sequences.	16
Identify basic procedures for adding and removing field-replaceable modules for portable systems. Given a replacement scenario, choose the appropriate sequences.	15
Identify the names, purposes, and performance characteristics of standardized/common peripheral ports, associated cabling, and their connectors. Recognize ports, cabling, and connectors by sight.	11
Identify proper procedures for installing and configuring common IDE devices. Choose the appropriate installation or configuration sequences in given scenarios. Recognize the associated cables.	9

(continued)

Domain/Topic Area	Book I Chapter(s)
1.0 Installation, Configuration, and Upgrading *(continued)*	
Identify proper procedures for installing and configuring common SCSI devices. Choose the appropriate installation or configuration sequences in given scenarios. Recognize the associated cables.	9
Identify proper procedures for installing and configuring common peripheral devices. Choose the appropriate installation or configuration sequences in given scenarios.	11–16
Identify procedures to optimize PC operations in specific situations. Predict the effects of specific procedures under given scenarios.	16
Determine the issues that must be considered when upgrading a PC. In a given scenario, determine when and how to upgrade system components.	16 and 18

Domain/Topic Area	Book I Chapter(s)
2.0 Diagnosing and Troubleshooting	
Recognize common problems associated with each module and their symptoms, and identify steps to isolate and troubleshoot the problems. Given a problem situation, interpret the symptoms and infer the most likely cause.	17 and 18
Identify basic troubleshooting procedures and tools, and know how to elicit problem symptoms from customers. Justify asking particular questions in a given scenario.	18

Domain/Topic Area	Book I Chapter(s)
3.0 PC Preventive Maintenance, Safety, and Environmental Issues	
Identify the various types of preventive maintenance measures, products, and procedures, and know when and how to use them.	17
Identify various safety measures and procedures, and know when/ how to use them.	17
Identify environmental protection measures and procedures, and know when/how to use them.	17

Domain/Topic Area	Book I Chapter(s)
4.0 Motherboard/Processors/Memory	
Distinguish among the popular CPU chips in terms of their basic characteristics.	7
Identify the types of RAM (random-access memory), form factors, and operational characteristics. Determine banking and speed requirements under given scenarios.	8
Identify the most popular types of motherboards, their components, and their architecture (bus structures).	4
Identify the purpose of CMOS (Complementary Metal-Oxide Semiconductor) memory, what it contains, and how and when to change its parameters. Given a scenario involving CMOS, choose the appropriate course of action.	5

Domain/Topic Area	Book I Chapter(s)
5.0 Printers	
Identify printer technologies, interfaces, and options/upgrades.	14
Recognize common printer problems, and know the techniques used to resolve them.	14

Domain/Topic Area	Book I Chapter(s)
6.0 Basic Networking	
Identify the common types of network cables and their characteristics and connectors.	19
Identify basic networking concepts, including how a network works.	19
Identify common technologies available for establishing Internet connectivity and their characteristics.	19

Appendix C

Operating System Exam Objectives

· ·

*T*his appendix lists the Operating System exam subjects and the corresponding chapters of the book.

OS Exam Topics

Domain/Topic Area	Book II Chapter(s)
1.0 OS Fundamentals	
Identify the major desktop components and interfaces, and their functions. Differentiate the characteristics of Windows 9*x*/Me, Windows NT 4.0 Workstation, Windows 2000 Professional, and Windows XP.	2, 3, & 4
Identify the names, locations, purposes, and contents of major system files.	2, 3, & 4
Demonstrate the ability to use command-line functions and utilities to manage the operating system, including the proper syntax and switches.	1
Identify basic concepts and procedures for creating, viewing, and managing disks, directories, and files. This includes procedures for changing file attributes and the ramifications of those changes (for example, security issues).	1
Identify the major operating system utilities and their purpose, location, and available switches.	2, 3, & 4
Identify the major desktop components and interfaces, and their functions. Differentiate the characteristics of Windows 9*x*/Me, Windows NT 4.0 Workstation, Windows 2000 Professional, and Windows XP.	2, 3, & 4

Domain/Topic Area	Book II Chapter(s)
2.0 Installation, Configuration, and Upgrading	
Identify the procedures for installing Windows 9*x*/Me, Windows NT 4.0 Workstation, Windows 2000 Professional, and Windows XP, and for bringing the operating system to a basic operational level.	2, 3, & 4
Identify steps to perform an operating system upgrade from Windows 9*x*/Me, Windows NT 4.0 Workstation, Windows 2000 Professional, and Windows XP. Given an upgrade scenario, choose the appropriate next steps.	2, 3, & 4
Identify the basic system boot sequences and boot methods, including the steps to create an emergency boot disk with utilities installed for Windows 9*x*/Me, Windows NT 4.0 Workstation, Windows 2000 Professional, and Windows XP.	2, 3, & 4
Identify procedures for installing/adding a device, including loading, adding, and configuring device drivers, and required software.	1, 2, 3, & 4
Identify procedures necessary to optimize the operating system and major operating system subsystems.	2, 3, 4, & 8

Domain/Topic Area	Book II Chapter(s)
3.0 Diagnosing and Troubleshooting	
Recognize and interpret the meaning of common error codes and startup messages from the boot sequence, and identify steps to correct the problems.	2, 3, 4, & 8
Recognize when to use common diagnostic utilities and tools. Given a diagnostic scenario involving one of these utilities or tools, select the appropriate steps needed to resolve the problem.	2, 3, 4, & 5
Recognize common operational and usability problems and determine how to resolve them.	2, 3, & 4

Domain/Topic Area	*Book II Chapter(s)*
4.0 Basic Networking	
Identify the common types of network cables, their characteristics, and connectors.	6
Identify basic networking concepts, including how a network works.	5 & 6
Identify common technologies available for establishing Internet connectivity and their characteristics.	7 & 8

Index

• F •

• *G* •

Wiley Publishing, Inc.
End-User License Agreement

READ THIS. You should carefully read these terms and conditions before opening the software packet(s) included with this book "Book". This is a license agreement "Agreement" between you and Wiley Publishing, Inc. "WPI". By opening the accompanying software packet(s), you acknowledge that you have read and accept the following terms and conditions. If you do not agree and do not want to be bound by such terms and conditions, promptly return the Book and the unopened software packet(s) to the place you obtained them for a full refund.

1. **License Grant.** WPI grants to you (either an individual or entity) a nonexclusive license to use one copy of the enclosed software program(s) (collectively, the "Software" solely for your own personal or business purposes on a single computer (whether a standard computer or a workstation component of a multi-user network). The Software is in use on a computer when it is loaded into temporary memory (RAM) or installed into permanent memory (hard disk, CD-ROM, or other storage device). WPI reserves all rights not expressly granted herein.

2. **Ownership.** WPI is the owner of all right, title, and interest, including copyright, in and to the compilation of the Software recorded on the disk(s) or CD-ROM "Software Media". Copyright to the individual programs recorded on the Software Media is owned by the author or other authorized copyright owner of each program. Ownership of the Software and all proprietary rights relating thereto remain with WPI and its licensers.

3. **Restrictions On Use and Transfer.**

   (a) You may only (i) make one copy of the Software for backup or archival purposes, or (ii) transfer the Software to a single hard disk, provided that you keep the original for backup or archival purposes. You may not (i) rent or lease the Software, (ii) copy or reproduce the Software through a LAN or other network system or through any computer subscriber system or bulletin-board system, or (iii) modify, adapt, or create derivative works based on the Software.

   (b) You may not reverse engineer, decompile, or disassemble the Software. You may transfer the Software and user documentation on a permanent basis, provided that the transferee agrees to accept the terms and conditions of this Agreement and you retain no copies. If the Software is an update or has been updated, any transfer must include the most recent update and all prior versions.

4. **Restrictions on Use of Individual Programs.** You must follow the individual requirements and restrictions detailed for each individual program in the "What's on the CD" appendix of this Book. These limitations are also contained in the individual license agreements recorded on the Software Media. These limitations may include a requirement that after using the program for a specified period of time, the user must pay a registration fee or discontinue use. By opening the Software packet(s), you will be agreeing to abide by the licenses and restrictions for these individual programs that are detailed in the "What's on the CD" appendix and on the Software Media. None of the material on this Software Media or listed in this Book may ever be redistributed, in original or modified form, for commercial purposes.

FOR DUMMIES®

The easy way to get more done and have more fun

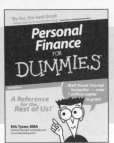

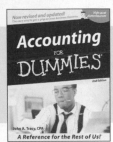
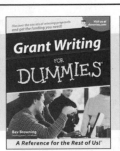

FOR DUMMIES®

A world of resources to help you grow

HOME, GARDEN & HOBBIES

0-7645-5295-3

0-7645-5130-2

0-7645-5106-X

FOOD & WINE

0-7645-5250-3

0-7645-5390-9

0-7645-5114-0

TRAVEL

0-7645-5453-0

0-7645-5438-7

0-7645-5448-4

Available wherever books are sold. Go to www.dummies.com or call 1-877-762-2974 to order direct.

FOR DUMMIES®

Helping you expand your horizons and realize your potential

INTERNET

0-7645-0894-6

0-7645-1659-0

0-7645-1642-6

Also available:

America Online 7.0 For Dummies
(0-7645-1624-8)

Genealogy Online For Dummies
(0-7645-0807-5)

The Internet All-in-One Desk Reference For Dummies
(0-7645-1659-0)

Internet Explorer 6 For Dummies
(0-7645-1344-3)

The Internet For Dummies Quick Reference
(0-7645-1645-0)

Internet Privacy For Dummies
(0-7645-0846-6)

Researching Online For Dummies
(0-7645-0546-7)

Starting an Online Business For Dummies
(0-7645-1655-8)

DIGITAL MEDIA

0-7645-1664-7

0-7645-1675-2

0-7645-0806-7

Also available:

CD and DVD Recording For Dummies
(0-7645-1627-2)

Digital Photography All-in-One Desk Reference For Dummies
(0-7645-1800-3)

Digital Photography For Dummies Quick Reference
(0-7645-0750-8)

Home Recording for Musicians For Dummies
(0-7645-1634-5)

MP3 For Dummies
(0-7645-0858-X)

Paint Shop Pro "X" For Dummies
(0-7645-2440-2)

Photo Retouching & Restoration For Dummies
(0-7645-1662-0)

Scanners For Dummies
(0-7645-0783-4)

GRAPHICS

0-7645-0817-2

0-7645-1651-5

0-7645-0895-4

Also available:

Adobe Acrobat 5 PDF For Dummies
(0-7645-1652-3)

Fireworks 4 For Dummies
(0-7645-0804-0)

Illustrator 10 For Dummies
(0-7645-3636-2)

QuarkXPress 5 For Dummies
(0-7645-0643-9)

Visio 2000 For Dummies
(0-7645-0635-8)

Available wherever books are sold. Go to www.dummies.com or call 1-877-762-2974 to order direct.